A Compendium, Treatise, Compilation and Annotations of over Six Hundred (600) References to Baptism in the Name of Jesus (Acts 2:38) and the Trinitarian formula, Father, Son and Holy Ghost (Matthew 28:19)

Kulwant Singh Boora © 2022

Book 17

FOREWARD BY
BISHOP PAUL D. MOONEY

Copyright © 2022 by Kulwant Singh Boora

All rights reserved, including the right to use or reproduce this book or any portions thereof in any form whatsoever without the written permission of the author, except for provisions noted in the Federal Copyright Act of 1976 regarding fair use. Published by Amazon (USA) 2022.

Bible Version - King James Version (KJV) unless otherwise stated.

"...the formulae 'in the name of Jesus' (Acts 2:38; 19:5)...have explicit grounds in Christian scripture...Meghan Markle's baptism by the Archbishop of Canterbury centered around the possibility that she might have been baptized in a Oneness Pentecostal church that baptized her 'in the name of Jesus' only, not using the formula 'in the name of the Father and of the Son and of the Holy Spirit'...." Note: Meghan Markle is the wife of Prince Harry, Duchess of Sussex or former Prince Harry and former Duchess of Sussex, England [emphasis by author].

Grant, Sharon J. (2019). *Rebaptism Calmly Considered: Christian Initiation and Resistance in The Early A.M.E. Church of Jamaica*. Eugene, Oregon: Pickwick Publications, p. xii, see footnote 3 in Foreword.[1]

---

[1] Sharon J. Grant is Assistant Professor of The History of Christianity at Hood Theological Seminary in Salisbury, North Carolina, the forward is done by Ted. A. Campbell, Albert C Outler Professor of Wesley Studies, Perkins School of Theology, Southern Methodist University. Professor Campbell notes the non-theological publication a secular one, namely, *Vanity Fair*, not renowned for its theological depth notes that the Archbishop of Canterbury, Justin Wells, would not talk about Megan's baptism, see Vanity Fair by Bryant Kenzie, March 16, 2018 "*Archbishop Who Baptized Meghan Markle Speaks.*"

FOREWORD

Mr. Kulwant Singh Boora's publications on baptism in Jesus Christ (Acts 2:38) are authoritative apostolic sources, we have never witnessed any apostolic writer in the apostolic oneness movement worldwide produce such in-depth studies on this subject that has caused the whole oneness apostolic movement worldwide to rethink this subject in greater depth and from different theological and biblical viewpoints. This extensively researched publication gives many principles to guide one to the truth in addition to the supreme authority of the Word of God.

Mr. Boora promotes truth and does not compromise it whatsoever, which is commendable. I too wholeheartedly agree with the apostolic oneness movement that it is very rare and never heard of, to see an apostolic author and writer of this caliber from a Sikh Punjabi American-British Indian background, he is the first ever, which testifies to God's greatness to bring people in from all nations and cultures to apostolic and biblical truth. This work brings out the truth of baptism in the name of Jesus Christ as the only true baptism in the New Testament and throughout the centuries until the present day that can wash away sins.

This work is a must have for preachers, teachers, ministers, pastors, bishops, district leaders, bible colleges and students, bible study groups and layman who are seeking to know truth and gain deeper insight into the subject of baptism in the name of Jesus Christ (Acts 2:38). His work has prompted trinitarian scholars, pastors, leaders, and theologians to revisit and rethink their trinitarian position of baptism and has led hundreds of hundreds worldwide to be baptized and rebaptized in the name of Jesus Christ.

Bishop Paul D. Mooney

Former Assistant General Superintendent United Pentecostal Church, Inc. (UPCi, Eastern Zone), past President of Indiana Bible College (IBC); former Pastor of Calvary Tabernacle and former Michigan and Indiana District Superintendent (UPCi)

"Many thousands have been baptized into the name of Jesus Christ only...."

>Drummond, T. (1809). *To the Editor of The Monthly Repository*, Ipswich, December 14, 1808, in the *Monthly Repository of Theology and General Literature January-December 1808*. Volume III. London: C Stower, Paternoster Row, pp. 715-716.

"Is baptism only in the name of Jesus valid? There are churches which practice 'Jesus' only baptism and follow the formula described in Acts of baptising 'in the name of the Lord Jesus.' It cannot be said that this is wrong or invalid since it is clearly set out in Acts as an effective form of baptism."

> Wright, Nigel G. (2005). *Free Church, Free State The Positive Baptist Vision.* Eugene, Oregon: Wipf & Stock, p. 87.

> Dr. Nigel G. Wright, Principal Emeritus of Spurgeon's College, London, and a former President of the Baptist Union of Great Britain and an ordained Minister.

Journals and Reviews[2]

Baptist Quarterly	*BQ*
Bibliotheca Sacra	*BS*
Bulletin for Biblical Research	*BBR*
BYU Studies Quarterly	*BYUSQ*
Catholic University Bulletin	*CUB*
Calvary Baptist Theological Journal	*CBTJ*
Direction	*DIR*
Early Christianity	*EC*
Evangelical Journal of Theology	*EJT*
Global Journal of Classic Theology	*GJCT*
Harvard Theological Review	*HTR*
HTS Theological Studies	*HTS*
Indian Journal of Theology	*IJT*
Indiana Quarterly	*IQ*
Int. Journal of Systematic Theology	*IJST*
Interpretation	*INT*
Jewish Quarterly Review	*JQR*
Jewish Theological Studies	*JTS*
Journal of Biblical Literature	*JBL*
Journal of Book of Mormon Studies	*JBMS*
Journal of Early Christian Studies	*JECS*
Journal of Ecclesiastical History	*JEH*
Journal of Evangelical Theo. Society	*JETS*
Journal of Liberty Baptist Theo. Seminary	*JLBTS*
Journal of Pentecostal Theology	*JPT*
Journal of Reformed Theology	*JRT*
Journal of Religion	*JR*
Journal for the Study of the New Testament	*JSNT*
Journal for the Scientific Study of Religion	*JSSR*
Journal of Theological Studies	*JTS*

---

[2]This is just a selection of journals and reviews cited in this publication, more may well be cited that are not referenced herein.

Melita Theologica	MT
New Testament Studies	NTS
Oral Roberts University Jour. of Theology	ORJL
Reformed Review	RR
Religions	REL
Review & Expositor	RE
Restoration Quarterly	RQ
Rural Theology	RT
Southwestern Journal of Theology	SJT
Studia Liturgica	SL
The American Journal of Theology	TAJT
The Bible Translator	TBT
The Biblical World	TBW
The Catholic Historical Review	TCHR
The Church of England Quarterly Review	TCEQR
The Churchman	TC
The Ecumenical Review	TER
The Expository Times	TET
The Evangelical Quarterly	TEQ
The Heythrop Journal	THJ
The Irish Monthly	TIM
The International Journal of Ethics	TIJE
The Journal of Theological Studies	TJTS
The Methodist Review	TMR
The Monist	TM
The Muslim World	TMW
The North American Review	TNAR
The Princeton Theological Review	TPTR
The Scottish Review	TSR
The Scottish Journal of Theology	TSJT
Theology	THEO
Theological Studies	TS
Theology Today	TT
Tyndale Bulletin	TB
Vigiliae Christianae	VC
Vox Evangelica	VE
World & World	WW

"There is little mention of baptism. Pistorious, however, was accused of baptizing in the name of Jesus only, and not the three persons of the Trinity."

> Templin, J. Alton (2006). *Pre-Reformation Religious Dissent in The Netherlands, 1518-1530*. Lanham, Maryland: University Press of American, Inc., p. 181.[3]

---

[3] J. Alton Templin is Emeritus Professor of Historical Theology and Church History at the lliff School of Theology.

"IV. The Formula of Baptism.—The Formula of Christian baptism…in Mt 28:19: 'I baptize thee in the name of the Father, of the Son, and of the Holy Ghost.' But it is curious that the words are not give in any description of Christian baptism until the time of Justin Martyr: and there they are not repeated exactly but in a slightly extended and explanatory form…In every account of the performance of the rite in apostolic times a much shorter formula is in use. The 3,000 believers were baptized on the Day of Pentecost 'in the name of Jesus' (Acts 2:38); and the same formula was used at the baptism of Cornelius and those that were with him (Acts 10:48). Indeed, it would appear to have been the usual one, from St. Paul's question to the Corinthians: 'Were ye baptized into the name of Paul?' (I Cor 1:13)…Scholars have exercised a great deal of ingenuity in trying to explain how, with what appear to be the very words of Jesus given in the Gospel of Mt, **another and much shorter formula seems to have been used throughout the apostolic church.** Some have imagined that the shorter formula was that used in baptizing disciples during the lifetime of Our Lord (Jn 4:1-2), and that the apostles having become accustomed to it continued to use it during their lives…Others, again, insist that baptism in the name of one of the persons of the Trinity implies baptism in the name of the Three…**but it is more than likely that the use of the shorter formula did not altogether die out, or, if it did, that it was revived. The historian Socrates informs us** that some of the more extreme Arians 'corrupted' baptism by **using the name of Christ only in the formula**, while injunctions to use the longer formula and punishments, including deposition, threatened to those who presumed to employ **the shorter which meet us in collections of ecclesiastical canons (*Apos. Canons, 43, 50*), prove that the practice of using the shorter formula existed in the 5th and 6th cents at all events in the East**."[4]

Orr, James (General Editor) (1915). *The International Standard Bible Encyclopaedia*. Volume I - A–Clemency. Chicago:
The Howard-Severance Company, pp. 392-393.

---

[4]Socrates of Constantinople, also known as Socrates Scholasticus was a 5th-century Christian church historian, a contemporary of Sozomen and Theodoret. He is the author of a *Historia Ecclesiastica* which covers the history of late ancient Christianity during the years c.305 to c.439. Note how the author makes it clear that well into the 5th and 6th century baptism in the name of Jesus Christ is well noted and in continuous use. See also, The Lutheran Church Review, Thomas E. Schmauk (ed.) (1902), Volume XXI. Philadelphia: Evangelical Lutheran Theological Seminary, p. 210 "…the Eunomieutychians Socrates (H.E.XXIV) says: '*They do not baptize in the name of the Trinity but of the death of Christ.*'" See also "We contend for the Christ, man and God…" page 212.

"Jesus, however, cannot have given his disciples this Trinitarian order of baptism after his resurrection, for the New Testament knows only baptism in the name of Jesus (Acts ii:38l viii, 16; xix, 5; Gal. iii, 27, Rom. Vi, 3; I Cor. I, 13-15), **which still occurs even in the second and third centuries**, while the Trinitarian formula occurs only in Matt. xxviii, 19, and then only again Didache vii, 1 and Justin, *Apol., i,* 61…Judging from I Cor. i, 14-17, Paul did not know Matt. xxviii, 19; otherwise he could not have written that Christ had sent him not to baptize, but to preach the Gospel…Finally, the distinctly liturgical character of the formula Matt. xxviii, 19 is strange; it was not the way of Jesus to make such formulas…But from the very beginning the Christian Church has universally practiced baptism (Acts ii, 38, viii, 36, 38; x, 48; I Cor. xii, 13; Gal. iii, 27; Eph. Iv, 5; John iii, 5), and must therefore have been convinced that it was acting according to the will of the Lord."

Jackson, Samuel M. (editor-in-chief) et. al, (1908). *The New Schaff-Herzog Encyclopedia of Religious Knowledge embracing Biblical, Historical, Doctrinal, and Practical Theology and Biblical, Theological, and Ecclesiastical Biography from The Earliest Times to The Present Day.* Volume I. A Achen–Basilians. New York and London: Funk and Wagnallis Company, pp. 435-436.

"From Shenoute's reassurances about the legitimacy of "Jesus only" baptism, it seems that some people in the fourth-century Egypt must have been baptized only in Jesus' name, and not in the name of the Trinity."[5]

---

[5]McClymond, Michael J. (2018). *The Devil's Redemption A New History and Interpretation of Christian Universalism.* Grand Rapids, Michigan: Baker Academics. Michael J. McClymond is Professor of Modern Christianity at Saint Louis University, St. Louis.

"But on the other hand, it is perhaps the article of Christian belief about which most ordinary Christians are most inarticulate, and which has the least meaning for their lives and their devotions. They mystery of the Trinity has somehow lost its moorings in common Christian experience -so much so that many people will doubt if it ever had such moorings in the first place, and will be tempted to assume that the doctrine is nothing but the product of the over-subtle speculations of theologians in academic ivory towers."

Hill, Edmund (1985). *Introducing Catholic Theology The Mystery of the Trinity*. London: Geoffrey Chapman, p. 3.

"Many people view the theological doctrine of the Trinity as a speculation for theological specialists, which has nothing to do with real life."[6]

---

[6]Wilks, John G. F. (1995). *The Trinitarian Ontology of John Zizioulas*. Vox Evangelica 25, p. 63.

G. T. "Haywood's concluding remarks to his work called *The Birth of the Spirit in the Days of the Apostles* captures the intense concern of these Pentecostals:

If you have never been baptized in the name JESUS CHRIST, you have never been immersed properly. This is the only name under heaven given among men whereby they must be saved. If you repent deeply enough in your heart, and be baptized in the name of Jesus Christ, I will guarantee that you shall receive the baptism of the Holy Ghost as you 'come up out of the water."

Kenneth J. Archer cites G. T. Haywood's comments on baptism in the name of Jesus, see footnote 74 citing Republished in The Life and Writings of Elder G.T. Haywood (Oregon: Apostolic Book Publishers, 4th printing, 1984), p. 40., cited on page 113 of Kenneth J. Archer, *A Pentecostal Hermeneutic Spirit, Scripture and Community* (2009). Cleveland, Tennessee: CPT Press.

"...that biblical evidence of the Trinity were unpersuasive to many theologians and bishops in the first centuries of the Church...Historical-critical scholars generally do not find that the first Christians were Trinitarian in their worship."

Mezei, Balazs M., et. al. (editors) (2021).
The Oxford Handbook of Divine Revelation.
Oxford: Oxford University Press, pp. 124, 136.

"...we may not be able to comprehend logically the various aspects of the Trinity...All attempts to explain the Trinity will fall short, especially when we reflect on the relation of the three persons to the divine essence...all analogies fail us and we become deeply conscious of the fact that the Trinity is a mystery far beyond our comprehension. It is the incomprehensible glory of the Godhead...there are certainly textual and conceptual difficulties with the doctrine of the Trinity...the mystery of the Trinity can never be fully understood by finite man...."

> Pfandl, Gerhard (2003). *The Trinity in Scripture*. Journal of the Adventist Theological Society, 14/2 (Fall 2003): 80–94.
> Biblical Research Institute, pp. 80; 94.[7]

---

[7]Gerhard Pfandl is an Associate Director of the Biblical Research Institute and was former Professor of Religion at Bogenhofen Seminary in Austria a Seventh-Day Adventist Seminary.

ACKNOWLEDGEMENTS

I firstly thank God for all that He has done in my life and for giving me strength from day to day. Without Him I would not be here, He is the source of my strength and life, the only wise God our savior, Titus 2:13, John 20:28, 1 John 5:20.

To my parents whom I dearly love, that have been instrumental in my life, my father and mother who always believed in me, thank you. I also extend appreciation to my brothers and sisters and their families.

To my family all of whom have been very patient while I spent endless hours, hours and months and months in research, study, and preparation of this book, thank you.

"Baptism in the Name of Jesus is common to all…
Through Baptism in the Name of Jesus
was opened a new life…."

W. Vollrath (1927). *The Idea of The Kingdom of God in the Ancient Church and in the Middle Ages*. Theology, Volume 14, Issue 83, p. 267.

"While Trinitarian Pentecostal churches as a norm prohibit baptism in Jesus' name, they seldom formally require that former oneness Pentecostals be rebaptized...the New Testament seemingly portrays the entire Christian life as being done 'in the name of Jesus'...In fact, everything they do in word or deed is to be done 'in the name of the Lord Jesus' (Col. 3:17). What is it about water baptism that causes most Trinitarians to demand a Trinitarian formula for its validity, especially when scripture references even this practice as being done in Jesus' name (Acts 2:38; 8:16; 10:48; 19:5)...."

> Baker, Josiah (2020). *'One Lord, One Faith, One Baptism'? Between Trinitarian Ecumenism and Oneness Pentecostals.* Journal of Pentecostal Theology 29. Leiden: Brill: pp:102-103.

"If Matthew 28:19 is not a formula, then there is no necessary contradiction of the description "in the name of the Lord" in Acts and Paul."

Ferguson, Everett (2009). *Baptism in The Early Church History, Theology and Liturgy in The First Five Centuries*. Grand Rapids, Michigan: William B. Eerdmans Publishing Company, p. 135.

TABLE OF CONTENTS

Acknowledgements	18
Introduction	29
References	37
Conclusion	277
Bibliography	282
About the Author	339

"The recognition that such a belief is still the hallmark of the true Christian is found in the Amsterdam Confession of the World Council of Churches, which stated that the World Council is composed of "Churches which acknowledge Jesus Christ as God and Saviour"…The question that forms the title of this article must be answered in the affirmative. In three clear instances and in five instances that have a certain probability Jesus is called God in the New Testament…"If we date New Testament times from 30 to 100, quite clearly the use of "God" for Jesus belongs to the second half of the period and becomes frequent only toward the end of the period. This judgment is confirmed by the evidence of the earliest extrabiblical Christian works. At the beginning of the second century Ignatius freely speaks of Jesus as God. In Ephesians 18, 2 he says: "Our God, Jesus the Christ, was conceived by Mary"; in 19, 3 he says: "God was manifest as man." In Smyrnaeans 1,1 Ignatius begins by giving glory to "Jesus Christ, the God who has thus given you wisdom." We have already cited Pliny's testimony at the turn of the century that the Christians of Asia Minor sang hymns to Christ as to a God. By mid-second century, the so-called 2 Clement (1,1) can state: "Brethren, we must think of Jesus Christ as of God."…Thus, in the New Testament there is no obvious conflict between the passages that call Jesus God and the passages that seem to picture the incarnate Jesus as less than God or the Father. The problem of how during his lifetime Jesus could be both God and man is presented in the New Testament, not by the use of the title "God," but by some of the later strata of Gospel material which bring Jesus' divinity to the fore even before the Resurrection. Ignatius of Antioch does use the title "God" of Jesus during his human career. This may be the inevitable (and true) development of the New Testament usage of calling the preincarnational and the resurrected Jesus God; but from the evidence we have, it is a post-New Testament development…we have seen that there is a solid biblical precedent for calling Jesus God…."

Brown, Raymond E. (1965). *Does The New Testament Call Jesus God?* Theological Studies, Volume 26, Issue No. 4, pp. 545; 565; 567-568; 571-572, 573.

"Although early Christian theologians speculated in many ways on the Father, Son, and Holy Spirit, no one clearly and fully asserted the doctrine of the Trinity as explained at the top of the main entry until around the end of the so-called Arian Controversy...Many thinkers influential in the development of trinitarian doctrines were steeped in the thought not only of Middle Platonism and Neoplatonism, but also the Stoics, Aristotle, and other currents in Greek philosophy...No trinitarian doctrine is explicitly taught in the Old Testament...The New Testament contains no explicit trinitarian doctrine...In contrast, other Christians admit that their preferred doctrine of the Trinity not only (1) can't be inferred from the Bible alone, but also (2) that there's inadequate or no evidence for it there, and even (3) that what is taught in the Bible is incompatible with the doctrine. These Christians believe the doctrine solely on the authority of later doctrinal pronouncements of the True Christian Church (typically one of: the Catholic Church, the Eastern Orthodox tradition, or the mainstream of the Christian tradition, broadly understood)."[8]

---

[8]Tuggy, Dale, "Trinity", *The Stanford Encyclopedia of Philosophy* (Winter 2020 Edition), Edward N. Zalta (ed.), URL = https://plato.stanford.edu/archives/win2020/entries/trinity/, Winter 2020 (substantive content change) [Accessed 6/19/21].

List of Publications and Books by the Author

The Oneness of God and the Doctrine of the Trinity

Oneness and Monotheism

Apostolic (Acts 2:38) and Post-Apostolic Apostolic Baptism (Matthew 28:19) Volume 1

Apostolic (Acts 2:38) and Post-Apostolic Apostolic Baptism (Matthew 28:19) Volume 2

Baptism in the Name of Jesus (Acts 2:38) From Jerusalem to Great Britain

The Roman Catholic Church And Its Recognition of The Validity of Baptism In The Name of Jesus (Acts 2:38) 100 AD to 500 AD.

Baptism in the Name of Jesus Name (Acts 2:38) and The New Testament Pauline Epistles

British Views on The Oneness of God With Observations on the Doctrine of the Trinity

The Three (3) Roman Catholic Popes on The Validity of Baptism In The Name of Jesus (Acts 2:38) And The Two Catholic Popes (2) On The Oneness Christological View of God

Baptism in the Name of Jesus (Acts 2:38) And The Apostolic Oneness Doctrinal View of God In America From 1600 AD To 1900 AD

New Testament Baptism In The Name of Jesus (Acts 2:38) in Europe, Russia, India, Africa (Egypt), Mexico and Canada 1700 AD to 1900 AD.

Baptism In The Name of Jesus (Acts 2:38) And The Apostolic Oneness

View of God In The Medieval And Middle Ages (Dark Ages) To The Reformation 900 AD to 1600 AD

Genesis 1:26 A Struggle For A Trinitarian Interpretation

Matthew 28:19 Triadic, Jewish or Trinitarian

U.S. Bar Admissions For Foreign Law Graduates and Foreign Lawyers Which Includes State Bar Rules and Case Law

The Acknowledgment, Recognition and Acceptance of Baptism In The Name of Jesus Christ (Acts 2:38) from Biblical and Theological Scholars (Trinitarian & Non-Trinitarian) Including Ecumenical Councils & Committees and Various Religious Organizations and Groups

A Compendium, Treatise, Compilation and Annotations of over Six Hundred (600) References to Baptism in the Name of Jesus (Acts 2:38) and the Trinitarian formula, Father, Son and Holy Ghost (Matthew 28:19)

"...for it might be urged with probability that...baptism in the name of Jesus Christ was for the time valid...."

>Vaughan, Robert editor for The Wycliffe Society, *Tracts and Treatises of John De Wycliffe, D.D., with Selections and Translations from His Manuscript, and Latin Works*. London: Blackburn and Pardon, MDCCCXLV, pp. 161-162.

"First, while Jesus commanded His disciples to baptize in the name of the Trinity (Matt. 28:19), His disciples actually baptized in the name of Jesus Christ in the Acts of the Apostles (Acts 2:38, 8:16, 10:48, 19:5)."

> Ig-Jin Kim (2003). *History and theology of Korean pentecostalism: Sunbogeum (pure gospel) Pentecostalism.* Zoetermeer, Netherlands: Uitgeverij Boekencentrum, p. 106.

INTRODUCTION

It was by extreme popular demand that this work was compiled and published.[9] This publication is a continuation of research and references that speak of baptism in the name of Jesus (Acts 2:38)[10] and Matthew 28:19. Therefore, this publication will contain a body of citations and references that the reader can glean to see how baptism in the name of Jesus has been documented and attested to from various sources, such as, but not limited to: historical literature, religious organizations, biblical and theological scholars, clergyman, laity, trinitarians and non-trinitarians, etc.

The gravity of which baptism in the name of Jesus Christ (Acts 2:38) has been welcomed speaks for itself, since there is no other name given under heaven among men whereby, we must be saved (Acts 4:12). And it is true as John stated while on the isle of Patmos that Jesus "*...love us and washed us from our sins in his own blood*" (Revelation 1:5) and not washed us in the blood of the Father, Son and Holy Ghost (Matthew 28:19).

The vast amount of literature, genre, pericope, narratives, and evidence that exists, supports the long held biblical view that baptisms in the New Testament were conclusively without hesitation and dispute, performed and practiced by invoking the name of Jesus Christ. The need to articulate this view that baptism in the name of Jesus Christ is crucially important that cannot be downplayed or overlooked. And let it be said without confrontation, ill-will, contention or argumentatively that only the blood of Jesus and the name of Jesus in baptism can

---

[9] The author would like to thank all those who from around the world that asked for a publication that would strengthen the apostolic oneness movement nationally and globally.

[10] This publication is primarily a reference of citations in publications, books and articles that talk about baptism in the name of Jesus (Acts 2:38) and Matthew 28:19 (trinitarian form). Whether it is noted directly or indirectly and explicitly or implicitly. There will also be some references to the doctrine of the trinity in this publication, but primarily focusing on baptism.

forgive sins.[11]

The Word of God is clear on this issue of baptism and the secular world in its historical, theological, and biblical context, in which it provides a wealth of information that secures and notably supports the well attested view that baptisms in the New Testament were without question done in the name of Jesus. As you read through the pages of this publication, you too will see that baptism in the name of Jesus Christ is protected and embodied within the world of historical, biblical and theological archives, studies and literature.

The practice of baptism in the name of the Father, Son and Holy Ghost (Matthew 28:19) is without doubt a post-New Testament practice that largely emerged after the time of the apostles, namely, post-New Testament. If baptism in the name of the trinity was crucial to one's salvation and eternal security, we are troubled for the lack of supporting evidence of its practice within the Bible.[12] Notably, as time went on individuals, creeds and councils formulated theories, concepts and ideologies that sought to remove baptism in the name of Jesus from the equation or simply downplay its importance and relevance.

They came up with new ways to articulate Matthew 28:19, while trying to distinguish baptism in the name of Jesus. In other words, they struggled with what they found in the Book of Acts and the Epistles, while trying to find reasoning that would convince, perhaps persuade, and encourage people to baptize in the name of the trinity. As time progressed and as the trinitarian practice emerged, we see the rise of theories after theories of trying to explain away baptism in the name of Jesus (Acts 2:38) in contrast to Matthew 28:19.

From the Didache, Apostles Creed, Apostolic Fathers, the Apologists, Patristic era, Council of Nicea (325 A.D.), Council of Constantinople (381 A.D.), Council of Ephesus (431 A.D.), Council of Chalcedon (451 A.D.) and beyond, numerous individuals, scholars, theologians, Popes and Councils still somewhat reluctantly embraced the

---

[11] For baptism in the name of the Father and of the Son and of Holy Ghost (Matthew 28:19) cannot forgive sins. Similarly, baptism is one important component that gives entrance into the Kingdom of God. One must also repent, receive the gift of the Holy Ghost and live a holy life before God (Hebrews 12:14) and Jesus made it clear in the Gospel of John chapter 3:5 that except a man be born again of the water and spirit *he cannot enter* into the kingdom of God.

[12] The trinitarian form of baptism lacks practical application in the New Testament.

biblical position that the apostles baptized in the name of Jesus,[13] even though some supported the trinitarian form. When one thoroughly investigates the underlying theories, concept and ideologies that emerged, which sought to explain Matthew 28:19, one will see a body of opinions that while seemed convincing fell afoul of the Bible.

Yet what is interesting to this present day, is that theologians, historians, and scholars will agree that with regards to Matthew 28:19 the baptismal formula, when and how it arose they do not know.[14] More importantly, it is practically impossible to place a specific date, time, place and manner of when exactly and specifically of how the first baptisms in the name of the Father, Son and Holy Ghost were ritualistic introduced and ecclesiastically sanctioned, let alone introduced.

In other words, to pinpoint an exact moment in history when the trinitarian form, practice and ritual of baptizing people in the trinitarian formula was solidified by a group of people or introduced into Christendom is silent, let alone sanctioned by a group of people, person or religious or ecclesiastical body. It remains a very difficult issue in the world today to find an exact moment in time when it was practiced in its complete form during the first century church, since the evidence is scant and exiguous.

What is left then, is a piece-by-piece timeline of its development through various mechanisms that would eventually result in its ecclesiastical sanction, such as, but not limited to: a confession of faith, declaration of faith or interrogation or some other secularized Christianized approach or practice.[15] This then paves the way for a more refined explanation of Matthew 28:19 for a triune view of baptism. The trinitarian form in its core developed not from a biblical practice or model–since there is no biblical precedent to supports its practice in contrast to baptism in the name of Jesus–but was birthed out of a sequence of events that coupled together harmonized its Christendom practice.

---

[13]For example, St. Ambrose, St. Basil, St. Thomas Aquinas, Peter Lombard to name a few, in fact, a few Catholic Popes acknowledged that baptism in the name of Jesus was valid i.e., Pope Stephen and Pope Nicholas. There was another Catholic Pope that also acknowledged the validity of baptism in the name of Jesus Christ, the publication is referenced within this book.

[14]For example, one notable scholar makes such comment, which is noted in this study, namely, Arthur Cushman McGiffert who was Washburn Professor of Church History in the Union Theological Seminary, New York.

[15]Since there are several viewpoints of how it emerged.

The trinitarian form naturally made its debut through a variety of forms each contributing to its infrastructure. When one closely exam's how this practice emerged and its quest to become a centralized theme within Christendom, it will enhance a person's understanding and knowledge base. Only then will you clearly see that baptism in the name of the Father, Son and Holy Ghost has its basis and formulation outside of the Bible, yet the skeleton idea of its emergent theory was engrafted and borrowed from the textual passages of the Bible,[16] albeit for anti-apostolic practice.

Put another way, the basis of Matthew 28:19 baptismal ritual was developed and formulated through various bible experiences and passages that were used by writers to develop opinions, ideologies and theories that sought to lay the foundation of a theme that would ultimately introduce a compelling religious story housed within the confines of the Bible. From this, the innovative narrative provided a starting point that would give the trinitarian position the thrust it needed.[17]

These narratives, pericope and genre would then be developed into a story that would convince individuals that it had its root in the Bible experience, irrespective of the biblical practice–i.e. baptism in the name of Jesus. Notwithstanding this, regardless of what has been formulated, and considering the Bible as the supreme authority on the subject of water baptism, the early church baptized individuals in the name of Jesus Christ and no other name. It stands to reasons that if the apostles baptized people in the name of Jesus, they did so with a complete understanding, even in light of Matthew 28:19 a post-New Testament practice.

If one follows the practice of the apostles in baptizing in the name of Jesus, he or she has this assurance that it is written in the Book of Acts and Epistles and practically employed by the apostles. It would seem highly strange for God to allow the Books of Acts to be in the Bible only to find out that what is written in it is completely erroneous and incorrect. Why would God permit such a book to be included in the New Testament only later to find out that is contains substantial

---

[16]Borrowed here means that the ideological framework of water baptism was abstracted from the Bible then reworked into a pro-trinitarian position or remolded into trinitarian theology and ideology.

[17]The rise and development of the trinitarian form of baptism is not the scope of this publication but is probably best reserved for another time and place.

errors on the baptismal ritual, practice, and name, thus plunging the whole world into utter confusion and error, but as we read in the Bible, God is not the author of confusion.

Only when one completely and fully understands when and how Matthew 28:19 came into being as a baptismal ritual, practice and its underlying developmental stages will they see that it is not a formula for use in the ritual of water baptism. The historicity behind Matthew 28:19 and the trinitarian form of baptism brings great insight into its introduction, development, and practice in contrast to Jesus' name baptism. In fact, it will be astonishing at times when you read how and when it emerged and what were the underlying characteristics behind it.

With that said, the author will leave you draw your own conclusions and opinions on what you read. The references and research on this subject of baptism will to a large extent let it be said, enlighten some, and bring some to a greater understanding of this ever-evolving subject of baptism in the New Testament. And as the Word of God says in the Book of Acts that the Lord added to the church daily, without restriction in time, place and manner since the Day of Pentecost to the present.

Kulwant Singh Boora
Author

"The first to bring the Oneness message to Norway was the Norwegian-Canadian Thorsten Severin Austring (1886–1978). His church background was the primarily Canadian denomination Apostolic Church of Pentecost (ACOP), with headquarters in Calgary. Austring was born in Øksnes (Vesterrålen), Norway, but immigrated with his father and one of his brothers to Clifford, North Dakota in 1902. He remained there for only a few years before relocating in 1907 to Swift Current, Saskatchewan, Canada. At some point during 1918–19, Austring became active in a young, small Oneness Pentecostal church. In 1921 he left his secular profession as a farmer and initiated an itinerant ministry as a pioneer evangelist. He succeeded in establishing several ACOP churches within Saskatchewan."

Geir Lie (2020). *Oneness Pentecostalism in Norway*, Journal of the European Pentecostal Theological Association, 40:1, 46-59, page 47.

"It is a predominant feature in Matthew that Jesus is portrayed as the one in whom God is with his people...In its interpretation of the Jesus figure the Gospel of Matthew is a piece of genuine theology. For if 'theology' is defined as a clarification of what we mean when we speak of God, then Matthew is theology. What takes place in this gospel is that all that is said about Jesus is in fact said about God and his will to save sinners...But even though Jesus appears as the one who preaches–and in his teaching reveals–the true meaning of Holy Writ, it is he himself who realizes this meaning in his works and fate. In works and destiny, he becomes one with God's words and acts, indeed, he becomes God such as he is with his people all the days until the close of the age."

Müller, M. (1999). *The Theological Interpretation of the Figure of Jesus in the Gospel of Matthew*.New Testament Studies,
Volume 45, Issue 2, pp. 172-173.

"As God is in Himself Father from all eternity, He begets Himself as the Son from all eternity. As He is the Son from all eternity, He is begotten of Himself as the Father from all eternity. In this eternal begetting of Himself and being begotten of Himself, He posits Himself a third time as the Holy Spirit, that is, as the love which unites Him in Himself. (Barth 1956, 1)"[18]

Karl Barth (1886–1968)

---

[18]Tuggy, Dale, "Trinity", *The Stanford Encyclopedia of Philosophy* (Winter 2020 Edition), Edward N. Zalta (ed.), URL = https://plato.stanford.edu/archives/win2020/entries/trinity/ [Accessed 6/19/2021].

REFERENCES

1. Bennett, W. H. and Adeney, Walter F. (4th ed.) (1907). *A Biblical Introduction With A Concise Bibliography*. New York: Thomas Whittaker, p. 293:[19]

> "16-20, Jesus meeting the eleven in Galilee; His commission to them to evangelise the world. The originality of the Trinitarian baptismal formula (xxviii. 19) is open to question, because (1) it is without parallel in the teachings of Jesus; (2) even St. Paul's most Trinitarian formula (2 Cor. xiii. 14) is less advanced; (3) all other references to Christian baptism in the N.T. give the name of Christ only, not the Three Persons of the Trinity; (4) this clause is omitted in all Eusebius's quotations of the passage earlier than the Council of Nicæa. These facts throw doubt on it...."

2. Mulder, John M. (1991). *Sealed In Christ The Symbolism of The Seal of The Presbyterian Church (U.S.A.)*. Louisville, Kentucky: Geneva Press, p. 49:[20]

> "The evidence about the early practice of baptism is slight, but at least this much is clear. The earliest baptisms were done "in the name of Jesus," and the full use of the trinitarian formula ("in the name of the Father, and of the Son, and of the Holy Spirit") came somewhat later."

3. Macbridge, John David (1853). *Lectures on The Articles of The United Church of England and Ireland*. Oxford: John Henry Press & London:

---

[19] W. H. Bennett, M.A., D.D., Litt. D. Sometime Fellow of St. John's College, Cambridge; Professor of Old Testament Exegesis Hackney and New Colleges, London & Walter F. Adeney, M. A., D.D., Principal of Lancashire College, Manchester. The notation above is speaking on the Gospel of Matthew which starts at page 285 to page 295.

[20] John M. Mulder is President and Professor of Historical Theology, Louisville, Presbyterian Theological Seminary.

Strand, p. 72:[21]

> "...that in the Acts we read of persons baptized only in the name of Jesus...."

4. Conybeare, Fred C. (1898). *The Character of The Heresy of The Early British Church*. The Transactions of the Honourable Society of Cymmrodorion Session 1896-97. London: Issued By The Society, pp. 102, 113:[22]

> "Now in the seventh century synods were not got together in order to condemn imaginary errors, and this decree must have been aimed at a practise which really existed in these islands, especially in the western parts of England, where in the year 600 the Celtic Church was as yet the only form of Christian organisation and the sole evangelising agency. It is clear to demonstration that the Celtic bishops and doctors baptised without using the formula, "In the Name of the Father, and of the Son, and of the Holy Ghost...In the earliest church, as represented in the Acts of the Apostles, baptism in the Name of the Father, and of the Son, and of the Holy Ghost, seems to have been unknown or little used. For converts are baptised in the Name of the Lord Jesus (Acts, viii, 16, and xix, 15), or in the Name of Jesus Christ (Acts, ii, 38). Nor is there any trace of the triple formula in St. Paul's Epistles."

5. Zimmer, Heinrich (1902). *The Celtic Church in Britain and Ireland*. London: David Nutt, pp. 4-6:[23]

> "Mr. F. C. Conybeare has recently adduced some important arguments to show that the British-Welsh Church, even as late as the seventh century, tolerated, if not actual Arianism...And as in A.D. 384 the worldly power of Rome was on the wane, and the political situation during the two subsequent centuries prevented

---

[21]John Henry Macbride (c.1778-c.1868) was Principal of Magdalene Hall, University of Oxford, and Lord Almsner's Professor of Arabic (1813). Macbridge's comments appear in Lecture I who acknowledges that in the New Testament baptisms were done in the name of Jesus only.
[22]Fred C. Conybeare was Professor of Theology at the University of Oxford, England.
[23]Heinrich Zimmer was Professor of Celtic Philology in the University of Berlin.

a strict and complete organisation of the Church, it is conceivable that these views should have lived on, and tradition may possibly still have preserved them as late as the year 600, as Conybeare assumes, in the baptismal formula."

6. _____ (1892). The Scottish Review January and April (1892). Vol. XIX. in Theologisch Tijdschrift. London: Alexander Gardner, p. 228:

> "Paul, it is argued from 1 Cor., chap. i., used…certainly not the threefold formula of Matthew xxviii. The earliest formula was a simpler one, and no special virtue was at first attached to the Name which was invoked…."

7. Douglas, J. D., et. al. (1989). *The Concise Dictionary of The Christian Tradition, Doctrine Liturgy History*. Grand Rapids, Michigan: Zondervan, p. 47:

> "Baptism…some use "in the name of Jesus."

8. Temple, S.T.L., Patrick Joseph (1922). *The Boyhood Consciousness of Christ A Critical Examination of Luke ii. 49*. New York: The Macmillan Company, pp. 6, 8, 10, 15:

> "In support of the first view we have the letter (73rd) of Cyprian, in which we find the following statements: 1. The defenders of heretical baptism uphold the validity of baptism performed by the Marcionites, because they baptise in the name of Jesus Christ. 2. Cyprian's opponents maintain the validity of a baptism performed outside the Church in the name of Jesus Christ. 3. Heretics, in fact, baptise in the name of Christ…We know from Cyprian's 73rd letter (to Jubaianus) that some persons of his time upheld the validity of baptism in the name of Jesus alone…Innocent proclaims the baptisms of the Novatians valid, because they baptised in the name of Christ (ep. 2)…About a hundred years later (ca. 560), we find the first explicit statement concerning heretics who baptise in the name of Jesus alone. It is contained in the letter, Admonemus ut, written by Pope Pelagius I to Gaudentius, Bishop of Volterra in Italy…Consequently, altho John of Ragusa admits that to perform baptism in the name of Jesus alone in his day were invalid, still, he says, it was valid in

the early days of the Church…Trent takes up the question of the baptisms administered by the Apostles in the first century. It says that if the Apostles baptised merely in the name of Jesus, they did it by the inspiration of the Holy Ghost (*Spiritus Sancti afflatu*)…."

9. Scott, Thomas (1879). *The Church of England Catechism*. London: Thomas Scott, p. 24:

"The formula of baptism reminds us of a curious difference in the baptism of the apostles from the baptism in the triune name of God; although Jesus had, according to Matthew, solemnly commanded them to baptize with this formula, we find, from the Acts, that they utterly disregarded his injunction, and baptized "in the name of Jesus Christ," instead of in the name of "Father, Son, and Holy Ghost." (See Acts ii. 38, viii. 16, x. 48, xix. 5, etc.) The obvious conclusion to be drawn from this is, that if the Acts be historical, Jesus never gave the command put into his mouth in Matthew, but that it was inserted later when such a formula became usual in the Church."

10. W. M. Weber (1920). *Manifestation of The Risen Jesus* in The Open Court A Monthly Magazine Volume XXXIV. Chicago: The Open Court Publishing Company, pp. 310-313:

"In such an atmosphere, the words of Matt. xxviii. 19 were bound to be ascribed to Jesus sooner or later. But I doubt very much whether Justin Martyr ever found them in his "Memoirs of the Apostles." He mentions repeatedly that the Gospel was carried to every nation on earth. But in doing so, he rather introduces an accomplished fact. The nearest he comes to ascribing that fact to a direct command of Jesus is that statement (1 Ap., 31): "Some were sent by him to every nation of the human race." But that is very far from being a direct quotation of either our Matthew passage or Acts i. 8f or Luke xxiv. 44ff. Matt. xxviii. 16-20 has, therefore, been written hardly before the death of Justin Martyr. We may assign that section to about the year 150. The second half of Matt. xxviii. 19 contains another clause which, if part of the original text, would bring down the date of the origin of our passage to A. D. 200, or even a later year. I am referring to the words: "Baptizing them into the name of the Father and of the Son and of the Holy Spirit." They are our present-day baptismal formula. But that, while very old, does certainly not go back to the Apostolic Age. The New Testament...mentions baptism and baptizing quite frequently. But wherever the word is modified by a prepositional phrase, it is always baptizing in or into the name of Jesus Christ. On the day of Pentecost St. Peter advised his hearers: "Repent ye and be baptized every one of you in the name of Jesus Christ" (Acts ii .38). People of Samaria, as we learn Acts viii. 14, where baptized "into the name of the Lord Jesus." St. Peter ordered Cornelius and his friends "to be baptized in the name of Jesus Christ" (Acts x. 48). The apostle Paul met at Ephesus certain disciples who had been baptized "into John's baptism" and had them baptized "into the name of the Lord Jesus" (Acts xix. 15). The Epistles of St. Paul give testimony of the same fact. Rom. vi. 3 we find the question: "Are you ignorant that all we who were baptized into Christ Jesus were baptized into his death? " Gal. iii. 27 the apostle states: "As many of you as were baptized into Christ put on Christ." Likewise, the question: "Were you baptized into the name of Paul? " (1 Cor. i. 13), and the clause: "lest any man should say that ye were baptized into my name" (1. Cor. i. 15), imply clearly that the baptism St. Paul knew and practised was performed into the name of Jesus. Here again we encounter a discrepancy between Matt. xxviii. 19 and the whole New Testament which cannot be removed by any explanation. We are thus compelled to regard the words which appear but once as unhistorical. The statement put into the mouth of the risen Jesus must be spurious...The early history of the "Apostles' Creed" is comparatively well known. It is supposed to have originated in Asia Minor after the first quarter of the second century and spread during the second half of that century gradually among the churches of the East and West. It may have been used at Ephesus and Rome as early as A. D. 130. But it was bound to require quite a good while until the trinitarian formula, derived from it, succeeded in replacing the original apostolic formula. That could not happen before the Christians had come to look upon the doctrine of Trinity as the very cornerstone of their religion. The first writer who uses the word "Trinity" and says distinctly "that tri-personality pertains to the one God as He is in Himself" is Tertullian, A. D. 150-230. Consequently, the baptismal formula: " into the name of the Father and of the Son and of the Holy Spirit," has to be assigned to the beginning of the third century. However, the direction: "Baptize into the name of the Father and of the Son and of the Holy Spirit," occurs twice in the seventh chapter of the Didache, which treats of baptism. That little book is assigned by most authorities to the beginning of the second century. Bryennios, the discoverer and editor of the text, places it between 120 and 160. If what was said shortly before is correct, we could not expect to meet the trinitarian formula in such an early writing even though it should belong to the year 160. As a matter of fact, the apostolic formula appears at the end of Chapter IX where we read: "No one shall eat or drink of your Eucharist except those who are baptized into the name of the Lord." How can, under these circumstances, the trinitarian formula be accounted for in Chapter VII? To say: "The shorter form does not necessitate the inference that the larger formula was not in use," means nothing but to refuse to recognize and try to solve the problem, presented by the occurrence of both formulas in one and the same writing…No matter whether one accepts or rejects what has been said about the origin of the trinitarian baptismal formula, the apostolic formula is the older of the two…Nobody can baptize in the name of the Father and of the Son and of the Holy Spirit, for there exists no baptismal commandment given by the three persons of the Trinity. And to baptize into the name of the Trinity is something of which no distinct and adequate idea can be formed."

11. Cooke, R. J. (1900). *History of The Ritual of The Methodist Episcopal Church With A Commentary on Its Offices*. Cincinnati: Jennings & Pye & New York: Eaton & Mains, pp. 189-190:

"The formula as given by the Lord himself, and which must be used in every valid baptism is, "I baptize thee in the name of the Father, and of the Son, and of the Holy Ghost." (Matt. xxviii, 19.) That this form was invariably used by the apostles and the primitive Church seems to have become a matter of doubt among some recent writers. Thus "After the third century," says Allen ("Christian Institutions," p. 403), "the formula of baptism was in the name of the Trinity, and baptism otherwise performed was declared invalid; but in the early Church, as also in the apostolic age, there is evidence that the baptismal formula of the name of Jesus only was not unusual."

12. Smithson, John Henry (1864) [2nd ed] [No. 26]. *On Baptism, and Its Divine Uses In Promoting The Salvation of Man* in *Tracts, Theological, Practical, Controversial and Psychological, etc*, Volume 5. London: Alven; Hodson & Manchester: Bottomley, Son and Tolley, p. 10:

"...from which divine declaration it is reasonable to conclude, that they saw that there is but one personal God, and that the terms Father, Son , and Holy Spirit are the three essentials of His divine nature, and that these three divine essentials, which are the fulness of the Godhead, dwell in the divine person of Jesus Christ, and that when they baptized into the name of Jesus, they virtually fulfilled His divine injunction, because that Holy Name, in their estimation, involved the name of the Father, the Son, and the Holy Spirit. That this was the reason why they baptized into the name of Jesus only, is confirmed by the testimony which St. Augustin gives respecting the opinion of the primitive Christian Church concerning the practice of the apostles in baptizing simply into the name of Jesus, where he says, in reference to Acts ii. 38, "They were ordered to be baptized into the name of Jesus, and yet they were understood to be baptized into the name of the Father, the Son, and the Holy Spirit." The apostles, therefore, were not only strictly correct in baptizing in the name of Jesus only, but were, no doubt, divinely led to do so...."

13. Stevens, George Barker (1905). *The Teachings of Jesus*. New York: The Macmillan Company, p. 159:[24]

"1 The principal objections are: (1) If Jesus had so charged his apostles, how could they have been so slow to adopt the idea of the gospel's universal destination? (2) Jesus elsewhere limits his mission to Israel (Matt. 9:6; 15:24). (3) The apostles actually baptized in the name of Jesus only (Acts 2: 38: 8:16; 10:48; 19:5). They would not have done so if they had been taught to baptize in the name of the Father, Son, and Holy Ghost. Moreover, this trinitarian formula clearly suggests later ecclesiastical usage. I have considered these points in detail in my Theology of the N. T., pp. 146-148."

14. Kresge, Elijah Everett (1922). *The Church and the Ever-Coming Kingdom of God (A discussion on the evolution of a righteous social order with special reference to the mission of the church in the process)*. New York: The Macmillan

---

[24]George Barker Stevens is Dwight Professor of Systematic Theology in Yale University.

Company, p. 188:[25]

"The only Scriptural evidence that Jesus assigned water baptism a place in his program is Matt. 28:19. But it is a debatable question whether this verse as it stands may be attributed to Jesus. The prominence which it gives to an outward form is out of harmony with the spirit of all the previous teachings of Jesus. And, furthermore, there is no trace of the Trinitarian formula of baptism throughout the Apostolic Age. Every one of the Apostles, so far as the New Testament records inform us, baptized in the name of Jesus only, which would be inconceivable if there had been any knowledge of a specific command of the Master to baptize in the name of the Father, and the Son, and the Holy Ghost. On this subject see: Wendt, "Die Lehre Jesu," II, 610; also Gilbert, "The Revelation of Jesus," pp. 127- 129; and Allen, "The International Critical Commentary on Matthew, pp. 305 – 308."

15. Allen, Alexander V. G. (1898). *International Theological Library Christian Institutions*. Edinburgh: T&T Clark, p. 403, 408 (see footnote 1):

"After the third century the formula of baptism was the name of the Trinity, and baptism otherwise performed was declared invalid. But in the early church, as also in the Apostolic age, there is evidence that the baptismal formula of the name of Jesus only was not unusual…Stephen, the bishop of Rome, defended the validity of baptism when performed in the name of Jesus only…In his treatise, *De Spir. Sanc.*, Ambrose († 397) seems aware of the significance of this issue regarding baptism. "He who is blessed in Christ is blessed in the name of the Father and of the Son and of the Holy Spirit, because the name is one and the power is one…So they were baptized in the name of Jesus Christ;…For when it is said, in the name of our Lord Jesus Christ, the mystery is complete through the oneness of the name" (c .

---

[25]Dr. Elijah Everett Kresge, Pastor of Dubbs Memorial Reformed Church, Allentown, Pennsylvania, Chairman of the Committee on Education of the Social Services Commission of the Reformed Church in the United States.

iii.)."[26]

16. Sullivan, William L. (1919). *From The Gospel To The Creeds Studies in the Early History of the Christian Church*. Boston, Massachusetts: The Beacon Press, pp. 121-122:

> "Are there texts in the New Testament which directly express the Trinity by putting the three persons together, Father, Son, and Holy Ghost? If the Trinity is a genuine element in the Christian faith, and if it was taught by Jesus, we should expect to find several such texts. We should further expect that the texts thus pro claiming what is called a fundamental truth should be authentic and sure beyond any likelihood of doubt. What we find, however, is not that at all…The one Trinity-text left is the nineteenth verse of the twenty-eighth chapter of Matthew: "Go ye therefore, and teach all nations, baptizing them in the name of the Father, and of the Son, and of the Holy Ghost." These words are said to have been spoken by Jesus in one of his apparitions after his resurrection. No words of the entire Gospel are more open to doubt…Moreover we know from the Acts of the Apostles that the early method of conferring baptism was not in the name of the Trinity, but in the name of Jesus only. If those early Christians knew that it was an express command of Jesus that they should baptize in the name of the Trinity, how could they directly disobey it by baptizing in a different way? They did not use the Trinity-formula in baptizing because they did not recognize it as imposed by Jesus, and probably for a generation knew nothing of it whatever."

17. Gerfen, Ernst (1897). *Baptizein The Voice of the Scriptures and Church History Concerning Baptism*. Columbus, Ohio: Press of Lutheran Book Concern, pp. 120-121:

> "As far as we know, the above formula was not used by the Apostles. They simply demanded faith in Christ and then administered baptism in the name of Jesus. Acts 2:38; 8:16; 19:5 it is stated that they baptized in the name of Jesus. But the positive words of the institution of baptism are, to baptize in the

---

[26]Alexander V. G. Allen, Professor of Ecclesiastical History in The Episcopal Theological School in Cambridge.

name of the Father and of the Son and of the Holy Ghost. In order to harmonize this commandment with the practice of the Apostles, Cyprian holds, that the Apostles were justified in their practice in baptizing Jewish converts in Jesus' name only, because these were familiar with the law of Moses and the Old Testament, and had simply to acknowledge the Son in addition to the Father. And Irenæus justified the practice of the Apostles by saying: *In nomine Christi tres per sonæ intelliguntur, unctus, unguens et unctio*, i. e. In the name of Christ the three persons are understood, the Anointed One (Christ, or the Son), the Anointer (the Father), and the Ointment (the Holy Ghost)…It is evident that those Antipedobaptists who baptize in the name of Jesus only…."

18. Faulkner, John Alfred (1912). *Crises in The Early Church*. New York & Cincinnati: The Methodist Book Concern, p. 13:[27]

"…that baptism is always given in the name of Christ in the New Testament, not in the name of the Trinity."

19. Milburn, Gordon (1901). *A Study of Modern Anglicanism*. London: Swan Sonnenschein & Co, p. 36:

"There are the Churches of England, Rome, and the East, and there are the various Protestant bodies at home and on the Continent. There are people who have been baptized as infants but who do not more than nominally believe in Christianity, and who do not live according to Christian principles; there are people (chiefly, it seems probable, among the younger members of the Baptist Communion) who have not been baptised but who are living Christian and religious lives. There are the orthodox, the unorthodox, and the heretic who is three-parts non-Christian. There are people who have been baptized in the name of the Father, of the Son, and of the Holy Ghost; others have been baptized in the name of Jesus Christ…."

20. Dods, Marcus, et. al. (ed.) (1907). *An Exposition of the Bible A Series of Expositions Covering All The Books of The Old And New Testament. Vol. V. St. Luke-Galatians*. Hartford, Connecticut: The. S. S. Scranton Co.,

---

[27]John Alfred Faulkner, Professor of Historical Theology in Drew Theological Seminary.

p. 330:

> "The Plymouth Brethren, at least in some of their numerous ramifications, and other sects, have grounded upon the words, "be baptised, every one of you, in the name of Jesus Christ,' a tenet that baptism should not be conferred in the name of the Trinity, but in that of Jesus alone. It Is indeed admitted that while our Lord commanded the use of the historic baptismal formula in the concluding words of St. Matthew's Gospel, the formula itself is never expressly mentioned in the Acts of the Apostles."

21. Symonds, Herbert (1916). *Catholicity*: in *The Constructive Quarterly A Journal of The Faith, Work And Thought of Christendom*. Volume IV March To December 1916. London: Oxford University Press & New York: George H. Doran Company, p. 537:

> "Even in respect of so brief and inarticulated a statement as the Baptismal formula, "The name of the Father and of the Son and of the Holy Ghost," the balance of probability favours those who regard it as a development of an earlier form. In the Acts of the Apostles, the form is baptism in the name of Jesus (See Acts II, 38; viii, 16; xix, 5. Cp. also Romans VI, 3; Gal. III, 27)."

22. Jackson, Samuel Macauley, et. al. (1908). *The New Schaff-Herzog Encyclopedia of Religious Knowledge Embracing Biblical, Historical, Doctrinal, and Practical Theology and Biblical, Theological, and Ecclesiastical Biography From The Earliest Times To The Present Day*. Volume I Aachen-Basilians. London and New York: Funk and Wagnalls Company, p. 435:

> "Jesus, however, cannot have given his disciples this Trinitarian order of baptism after his resurrection; for the New Testament knows only baptism in the of Jesus (Acts ii, 38; viii, 16; xix, 5; Gal. iii, 27; Rom. Vi, 3; I Cor. I, 13-15) which still occurs even in the second and third centuries, while the Trinitarian formula occurs only in Matt. xxvii, 19...Judging from I Cor. I, 14-19, Paul did not know Matt. xxviii, 19; otherwise, he could not have written that Christ had sent him not to baptise, but to preach the gospel...Finally, the distinctly liturgical character of the formula Matt. xxxviii, 19 is strange; it was not the way of Jesus to make such formulae."

23. Carson, Thomas, et. al. (editors) (2003). *New Catholic Encyclopedia* by The Catholic University of America. Michigan: Gale, pp. 61-62:

> "With regard to the formula used for Baptism in the early Church, there is the difficulty that although Matthew (28.19) speaks of the Trinitarian formula, which is now used, the Acts of the Apostles (2.38; 8.16; 10.48; 19.5) and Paul (1 Cor 1.13; 6.11; Gal 3.27; Rom 6.3) speak only of Baptism "in the Name of Jesus...the possibility of its being used thus even as late as the 3rd century cannot be excluded (Stenzel88–93). The validity of Baptism "in the name of Jesus" was still accepted in the age of scholasticism. An explicit reference to the Trinitarian formula of Baptism cannot be found in the first centuries. The Didache, for instance, merely repeats Mt 28.19...Trinitarian formulas, however, also spread at an early time, and they could have appeared as an extension of Christological formulas (see the formula Paul uses for the greeting at the beginnings of his letters). Around the 3rd or 4th century there is evidence that this profession of faith was the baptismal formula...."

24. Schwöbel, Christoph (2009). *The Trinity between Athens and Jerusalem.* Journal of Reformed Theology 3. Leiden: Brill, p. 25:

> "It has been customary to offer as proof texts for trinitarian teaching in the New Testament mainly those texts which offer a triadic enumeration that seems as close as possible to later statements of trinitarian dogma. The *locus classicus* is, of course, the great commission in Matthew 28: 19: "Go therefore and make disciples of all nations, baptizing them in the name of the Father, the Son and the Holy Spirit." While such texts present a relative similarity to trinitarian dogma, their logic can only indirectly be discerned. It is probable that in a pagan environment, baptizing simply in the name of Jesus as the early Christian communities did (cf. Acts 2:38; 8:16)...."[28]

25. Coakley, Sarah (1993). *Why Three? Some Further Reflections on The Origin of The Doctrine of The Trinity* in *The Making and Remaking of Christian*

---

[28]Christoph Schwöbel, Professor of Systematic Theology, Director of the Institute for Hermeneutics, and the Dialog of Cultures Eberhard Karls University, Tübingen.

Doctrine Essays in Honour of Maurice Wiles. Oxford: Clarendon Press, pp. 41-42:

> "It is worth also recalling the testimony of Acts, which refers in its early chapters to a baptism simply 'in the name of Jesus Christ', but promises a specific mark of that baptism the 'gift of the Holy Spirit' (Acts 2:38)…we might suggest that Acts 19:1-6 (the story of Paul at Ephesus) contains some insight into why the more primitive baptismal formula became expanded into the triadic one. Rivalry, with John's baptism (see also Acts 1:5) may have caused the early community to draw attention to the special gits of the 'Holy Spirit' (tongues and prophecy) which marked out baptism in Jesus' name as superior (Acts 19:1-6). If then, despite all the theological overlay, there is a germ of historical truth here in Acts, it was dramatic charismatic gifts—involving the ecstatic capacity—which were the hallmark of some of the earliest Christian baptism."[29]

26. Ferguson, Everett (2009). *Baptism in The Early Church History, Theology and Liturgy in The First Five Centuries*. Grand Rapids, Michigan: William B. Eerdmans Publishing Company, pp. 146-147:

> "One study concluded that Paul took over from the earliest Palestinian Christianity the following aspects of baptism: Baptism presupposes preaching and faith, but preaching and faith do not replace baptism, baptism occurs in the name of Jesus; it mediates the eschatological gift of salvation (forgiveness and the Holy Spirit); baptism is by the leaders of the community and orders the community."[30]

In the same study, a further notation is given with respect to Pope Stephen and Cyprian, Ferguson notes that:

---

[29] Sarah Coakley former Norris Hale Professor of Divinity, Cambridge University, Life Fellow of Oriel College, Oxford University, Honorary Professor St. Andrews University, England. See also the notation on baptism in Jesus' name, Alexander, Kimberly Ervin (2008). *Matters of Conscience, Matters of Unity, Matters of Orthodoxy: Trinity and Water Baptism in Early Pentecostal Theology and Practice*. Journal of Pentecostal Theology, Volume 17, Issue 1, Leiden: Brill, pp. 48-69.

[30] Everett Ferguson, Professor Emeritus and distinguished scholar in residence at Abilene Christian University, Abilene, Texas.

"Stephen may also have made a theological argument from the power of the Name of Jesus, or if not he, some of his supporters did Cyprian comments" Now if they attribute the efficacy of baptism to the power of the Name, so that he was is baptized in the Name of Jesus Christ, not matter where nor in what manner, is judged renewed and sanctified...."[31]

27. Stier, Rudolf (MDCCCLI). *The Words of The Lord Jesus* by Pope, William B. Volume Seventh. Philadelphia: Smith, English, And Co; New York: Sheldon & Co; Boston: Gould & Lincoln, pp. 339; 343:

"...Zinzendorf's...suppose that they baptized merely in the name of Jesus and into Jesus...I baptized thee in the name of Jesus Christ (the form of the Apostles, however, as we read in Acts)...."[32]

28. Harris, Charles (1905). *Pro Fide A Defence of Natural And Revealed Religion.* London: John Murray, p. 384:

"(5) The 'name' of Jesus is used where we should expect to find the name of God. The converts are baptized in the 'name' of Jesus Christ for the remission of sins (ii. 38)."[33]

29. Beard, John R. (1860). *Reason's Why I Am A Unitarian In A Series of Letters To A Friend* (2nd ed.). London: Simpkin, Marshall & Co., p. 92:

"The command to baptize converts in the name of the Father, and of the Son, and of the Holy Ghost, ascribed by Matthew to Jesus, was observed in the days of the Apostles by baptism in the name of "Jesus Christ," (Acts vi. 38, 41.) or in the name of "the Lord Jesus Christ," (Acts viii. 16; xix. 5.)."

30. Smyth, Egbert, et. al., (1889). *The Andover Review A Religious And Theological Monthly. Vol. XI.–January-June.–1889.* Boston: Houghton, Mifflin And Company; Cambridge: The Riverside Press, p. 63:

"The first Christian Church was formed by the baptism of those

---

[31] See page 384.
[32] Rudolf Stier, Doctor of Theology.
[33] Charles Harris, Lecturer in Theology and Parochialia, St. David's College, Lampeter; Examining Chaplain to The Bishop of Llandaff.

who received the Apostle Peter's "word"- a word founded on the fact that the crucified Jesus had been made "both Lord and Christ." This baptism was "in the name of Christ," and in this and many other it is implied that a response to this name was the essential confessional element in the constitution of the church. With this confession were connected the gift of the Spirit, forgiveness, salvation. The progress of the church soon extended beyond Jewish to heathen soil. Baptism "in the name of Jesus" (Acts ii. 38), or "into the name of the Lord Jesus" (Acts viii. 16)...."

31. Johnson, Maxwell E. (2007). *The Rites of Christian Initiation Their Evolution and Interpretation Revised and Expanded Edition.* Minnesota: Liturgical Press, pp. 2, 34:

"Indeed, if Jesus himself actually commanded baptism "in the name of the Father and of the Son and of the Holy Spirit," it would be quite difficult to understand the numerous references throughout the book of Acts to baptism simply "in the name of Jesus" (cf. Acts 2:38) with no indications of such trinitarian language whatsoever...Because of this, it has been natural to view the baptismal command of the risen Lord in Matthew 28:16-20 as indicating that such a "formula" for baptism was already in use in Matthew's community in the late first century. Or, with regard to the phrase "baptism in [or "into"] the name of Jesus" (or "Lord Jesus," or "Lord Jesus Christ"), frequently occurring throughout the book of Acts, it has been natural to assume also that something like "I baptize you in the name of Jesus" functioned as a specific baptismal formula within the communities of Luke-Acts."[34]

32. Draper, Jonathan A. & Jefford, Clayton N. (2015). *The Didache A Missing Piece of The Puzzle in Early Christianity.* Atlanta, Georgia: Society of Biblical Literature, p. 74:

"...one would not be astonished that Did. 9.5 retains the notion that baptism was practiced "in the name of the Lord God." On the other hand, within the "Death Tradition," baptism was

---

[34]Maxwell E. Johnson, Professor of Liturgy at the University of Notre Dame and an ordained Minister of the Evangelical Lutheran Church in America.

performed "in the name of Jesus Christ" (Acts 2:38; 8:16; 10:48; 19:5; 1 Cor 1:13; Gal 3:27)...."

33. Macrae, S.J., George W. (1973). *"Whom Heaven "Must Receive Until The Time"* Reflections on the Christology of Acts. Interpretation 27, No. 2, p. 162:

> "And it is this act of invoking the name which relates the believer to salvation itself: "And there is salvation in no one else, for there is no other name under heaven given among men by which we must be saved" (4:12). In Peter's speech to Cornelius the forgiveness of sins is mediated by the name (10:43). Baptism in Acts, which functions to introduce men into the community of salvation and either to confirm the gift of the Holy Spirit or to induce it, is baptism in the name of Jesus Christ or of the Lord Jesus (2:38; 8:16; 10:48; 19:5)."[35]

34. Wenham, D (1973). *The Resurrection Narratives In Matthew's Gospel*. Tyndale Bulletin 24, pp. 23-24, 38:

> "(3) The story of the guard is regarded as implausible, and so is the final scene in Matthew 28. The command to make disciples of all nations and the command to baptize in the name of the Trinity are both probably read back from the later church situation; for, if Jesus Himself had spoken about the Christian mission in the way Matthew suggests, it is hard to see why the early church should have found the Gentile question such a problem. And if Jesus Himself had commanded the use of the Trinitarian formula in baptism, it is hard to explain the evidence of Acts and of Paul, which both indicate that baptism was simply in the name of Jesus during the earliest days...A much more important question concerns the Trinitarian formula in Matthew, which has no parallel in Luke. Baptism in Luke/Acts and apparently in the Pauline epistles is in the name of Jesus. In the light of this apparent unanimity in the rest of the New Testament and in view of the other parallel, between Matthew and Luke at

---

[35] George W. Macrae, S.J., is Professor of New Testament Weston College, School of Theology. For further reading on Matthew's Gospel, see Christie, Francis A. (1909). *The Composition of Matthews Gospel*. The Biblical World, Volume 34, No. 6 (December). The University of Chicago Press, pp. 380-389.

this point it is tempting to ask for the reading that Eusebius may have known in Matthew 28:19 to be reconsidered…(2) If Jesus instructed the disciples to baptize in the name of the Trinity, why did they, so far as we can tell, baptize only in the name of Jesus?…"

35. Kreitzer, Larry (1991). *Baptism In The Pauline Epistles With Special Reference To The Corinthian Letters.* The Baptist Quarterly 34.2, p. 70:

"The reference to baptism in the name of Paul…probably has as its counterpart an agreed tradition of baptism in the name of Jesus Christ. Both assume baptism 'in the name of' as an expression of discipleship to the one in whose name the baptism occurs…."[36]

36. Burrows, E. W. (1977). *Understanding of Baptism in Baptist Traditions, with Special Reference to Modern Trends.* Indian Journal of Theology 26.1, Jan-Mar., p. 28:

"There are some Pentecostalist groups (e.g. in the U.S.A. and North East India) that insist on the formula 'in the name of the Lord Jesus' (Acts 19: 5) at baptism rather than the Trinitarian formula of Matt. 28: 19. They do not regard baptism in the name of the Trinity as valid, as the Apostles' practice (in Acts) was apparently to baptize in the name of Jesus alone. Probably both the New Testament formulas reflect current liturgical practice, and it is likely that the Trinitarian formula is the later one…Baptists usually use the Trinitarian formula, as do other Churches, but it would not be in the Baptist tradition to insist that any particular form at words makes baptism either valid or invalid…"[37]

37. Neatby, Rev. G. W. (1932). *The Meaning of Baptism And Its Relation To Infant.* The Churchman, The Evangelical Quarterly, Vol 046/1, p. 43:

---

[36] This paper was given at the Biblical Theology and Christian Doctrine Study Group at Tyndale House, Cambridge, on 7th July 1988.

[37] Dr Burrows is on the staff of Serampore College, India. A Paper presented at the Joint Staff Conference of Morning Star College, Bishop's College and Serampore College on Saturday 24th January 1976.

"Once more, in the second chapter of the Acts, verse 38, we have the words of St. Peter to those who, pricked in their hearts, cried out, "Men, brethren, what shall we do?" "Repent and be baptized every one of you in the name of Jesus Christ, with a view to the remission of sins." "And in Acts xxii. 16 are recorded the words of Ananias to the convicted Saul of Tarsus," "And now why tarriest thou? arise, and be baptized, and wash away thy sins. calling on His name" (R.V.). Now, whatever these words may or may not mean, they connect Baptism with something future."[38]

38. Lampe, Geoffrey W. H. (1952). *The Holy Spirt and Baptism.* The Churchman 66.4, pp. 198, 202:

"The first mention of Christian baptism after Pentecost asserts that through this rite the "gift of the Holy Ghost" is conferred on those who repent and are baptized in the name of Jesus Christ (Acts ii. 38)...Nothing suggests that baptism here involved more than the rite as it had become familiar since the time of the Baptist, with the addition that it was in the name of Jesus Christ."[39]

39. Cross, Anthony R. (2008). The Evangelical Sacrament: *baptisma semper rejormandum.* The Evangelical Quarterly 80.3, pp. 201-202:

"In the New Testament it is clear that baptism was a part of the kerygma, the apostolic preaching of the gospel. This is nowhere clearer than in Acts 2.38 when Peter replies to the crowd's question, 'What should we do?', by instructing them, 'Repent and be baptized every one of you in the name of Jesus Christ so that your sins may be forgiven; and you will receive the gift of the Holy Spirit.' Later in Acts it is clear that baptism continued to be a integral part of the early church's proclamation of the gospel for this was the response of hearers, whether it be the first Samaritan

---

[38] G. W. Neatby, Vicar of St. John's, High bury Wale, a paper read at Dean Wace House, E.C., on November 2, 1931, in connection with The Young Churchmen's Movement.

[39] G.W.H. Lampe (1912-1980) was Professor of Theology at the University of Birmingham from 1953-59, Ely Professor of Divinity at the University of Cambridge from 1959-71 and Regius Professor of Divinity at Cambridge from 1971-79.

believers (Acts 8.12-13), the Ethiopian eunuch (Acts 8.36-38), Saul (Acts 9.17 -18), Lydia and her household (Acts 16.14-15), the Philippian jailer and his household (Acts 16.31-33) and so on. The earliest baptism was, therefore, immediate baptism...."[40]

40. Bampton, T. A. (1944). *The Sacramental Significance of Christian Baptism* Baptist Quarterly 11, p. 275:

"After the letters of Paul, it is to the Acts of the Apostles we look for a 'record of the development of the doctrine of Christian; Baptism in the early Church. There is a reference to the Baptism of the Holy Spirit in Acts i.5, but in Acts ii. 38-41 we find Peter, urging upon his auditors the necessity of repentance and: Baptism in the Name of Jesus unto the remission of sins...."

41. Parsons, Martin (1958). *The Theology of Baptism.* The Churchman 72.2, p. 60:

"Every idea expressed is one associated with baptism elsewhere, particularly the name of the Lord Jesus...."

42. Bond, Albert R (1918). *Baptism Into Or Unto.* Review & Expositor 15.2, pp. 203-204:

"Certain Samaritan believers had not been taught fully concerning the Holy Spirit; "only they had been baptized into...the name of the Lord Jesus" (Acts 8 :16). The complete instruction of the disciples of John led them to be baptized in the true sense; "they were baptized into...the name of the Lord Jesus" (Acts 19:5). To be valid the rite must be with reference to Jesus...It is very natural that Christians should everywhere employ in baptizing this phrase, 'unto (into, in) the name of the Father and of the Son and of the Holy Spirit', and we see no reason for departing from it. But it is of doubtful propriety to call this a law, and to insist that baptism would not be 'valid' without the use of this particular phrase. For it must be remembered that baptize is nowhere else in the New Testament associated with this particular expression. In Acts and the Epistles we find only

---

[40]Anthony R. Cross is a Fellow of the Centre for Baptist History and Heritage, Regent's Park College, University of Oxford.

'the Lord Jesus', or 'Jesus Christ', or simply 'Christ.'"

43. Fanning, Don (2014). *"The Great Commission."* Eruditio Ardescens: Vol. 1, Iss. 2, Article 2, in The Journal of Liberty Baptist Theological Seminary, p. 16:

> "The practice of the Early Church suggests that the command to baptize was universally applied to the new converts (Acts 2:38, 41; 8:12, 38; 9:18; 10:47-48; 16:15, 33; 18:8; 19:5). The triadic formula, "in the name of the Father and of the Son and of the Holy Spirit" follows the singular *onoma*, "name," indicating the unity of the three names, i.e., Father, Son and Holy Spirit. As a result of the use of the singular "name," in the Book of Acts the baptismal formula is often shortened to the "name of Jesus" or "the Lord Jesus" (Acts 2:38; 8:16; 10:48; 19:5; Rom 6:3; Gal 3:27). In fact, the triadic formula is never used in the Book of Acts...."[41]

44. Wainwright, Geoffrey (1974). *The Rites and Ceremonies of Christian initiation: Developments in the Past.* Studia Liturgica Vol. 10, pp. 4-5:

> "The Acts of the Apostles state that baptism took place "in the name of (the Lord) Jesus (Christ)" (Acts 2 : 38; 8 : 16; 10 : 48; 19 : 5); Matthew 28 : 19 commands baptism "in the name of the Father and of the Son and of the Holy Spirit" (cf. Didache, 7)...It may be that the early Syrian rite had an indicative formula pronounced by the minister; but it is not until the late fourth century that we find evidence in the East for the passive formula "N. is baptized in the name of (the Trinity)" or in the West for the active formula "I baptize thee in the name of (the Trinity)...There is some New Testament evidence that the initiation rite included an imposition of hands. While Heb. 6:2 remains obscure, Acts 19:5-6 is prima facie a perfectly clear narrative: "On hearing this, they we're baptized in the name of the Lord Jesus..."[42]

---

[41]Don Fanning is Professor of Global Studies at Liberty University Baptist Theological Seminary.

[42]Dr Geoffrey Wainwright is a Methodist minister teaches biblical subjects at The Queen's College, Birmingham, and is a lecturer in the University of Birmingham, England.

45. Kay, James F. (1993). *Critic's Corner In Whose Name? Feminism and the Trinitarian Baptismal Formula.* ThTo 49, pp. 528, 533:

> "Duck reports that (1) Jesus himself never said what he is reported here as saying; (2) Matthew's formula only appears once in the Bible; (3) Matthew's terminology is triadic, not trinitarian; and (4) Matthew 28:19 is not conclusively a liturgical formula. Thus, Duck concludes, "Most historical-critical theories locate the origin of the words 'baptizing them in the name of the Father and of the Son and of the Holy Spirit'…in early Christian communities, and not in Jesus' actual words. Based on this scholarly consensus, Matthew 28:19b need not have privileged status over other New Testament passages that refer to baptism…Duck's call to abandon the one thing ninety-nine percent of us do share in common, namely-baptism "in the name of the Father and of the Son and of the Holy Spirit," deserves all the hermeneutical suspicion it invites."

46. Bratcher, Robert G. (1957). *The Church of Scotland's Report on Baptism.* Review & Expositor 54, pp. 205, 207-208:

> "On May 30, 1955, the General Assembly of the Church of Scotland, meeting in Edinburgh, received the Interim Report of the Special Commission on Baptism, presented by the convener, Prof. T. F. Torrance. This report is now being studied by the Scottish churches, and should be of interest to all who try to keep abreast of current theological trends…Noting the fact that the Trinitarian formula of Matt. 28:19 is not attested by the Acts-which records baptism in the name of Christ only-the Report states that the earliest evidence outside the New Testament, the Didache, Justin Martyr and Hippolytus, shows that the Trinitarian and Unitarian formulas were used indifferently (p. 7)…."

47. Macy, Howard R. (2011). *"Baptism and Quakers"* Faculty Publications, College of Christian Studies. Paper 16, pp. 166-167:

> "Friends generally understand the "Great Commission" in Matthew in this larger context of how the idea of baptism is used in the New Testament as a whole. "Go therefore and make disciples of all nations, baptizing them in the name of the Father,

and of the Son and of the Holy Spirit, and teaching them to obey everything I have commanded you. And remember, I am with you always, to the end of the age" (Matt 28:19–20). More recent study of the textual and literary history of the New Testament text has brought some Friends to wonder (with interpreters from many traditions) about when these words, including a Trinitarian formula, became part of the Gospel of Matthew...It is relevant to note, however, that there are no examples in the New Testament of a Trinitarian formula like that in Matthew 28 being used with baptism."[43]

48. Ascough, Richard S. (1994). *An Analysis of the Baptismal Ritual of the Didache.* Studia Liturgica 24, pp. 206-207, 209-210:

"Almost all scholars agree that there are a number of redactional layers to be found in the Didache...The instructions for baptism in the Didache are far from satisfactory to the modern scholar. Many questions about the nature of baptism are left unanswered. This, in fact, has far reaching implications for the study of the document... Nor does the document make clear whether the trinitarian formula used with the baptism in living water indicates a threefold immersion or not...A second ritual symbol is the trinitarian formula which is to accompany the physical baptism. Again, the text is problematic. In 7.1 the instructions are to "baptize in the name of the Father and of the Son and of the Holy Spirit"...while in 7.3 the formula for baptism does not include the' definite articles...To further complicate matters, 9.5 refers to those who have been baptized "in the Lord's name"...Jonathan Draper is presumably correct in suggesting that "the trinitarian baptismal formula in 7:1 is probably a later redactional retouch, since a slightly different formula is given in 7:3, and the earlier formula...has survived in 9:5." It is unclear whether the trinitarian formula in Didache 7.1 originates from direct dependence upon Matthew's Gospel (Matt 28:16-20), or whether the two redactors simply have access to the same tradition. The use of this phrase in Matthew alone among the gospel writers as well as its association with baptism in both

---

[43]*Howard R. Macy*, Professor of Religion and Biblical Studies at *George Fox University* in Newberg, Oregon.

Matthew and the Didache suggest to some that the redactor of the Didache was directly dependent upon Matthew's Gospel. However, Rordorf points out that dependence cannot be determined...Instead, he suggests that the trinitarian formula may reflect a shift from the Jewish mission to the Gentile mission...Whatever their origin it is obvious that all three means of invoking God in the baptismal ritual still maintained some significant meaning for the redactor and the community. It is probable that there were those among the group whose baptism was "in the name of the Lord" and others who were baptized with the trinitarian formula..."[44]

49. Draper, Jonathan A. (2006). *The Apostolic Fathers: The Didache*. The Expository Times, Volume 117, No. 5, p. 179:

"The Didache presents evidence of the utmost significance for the study of the origins of Christian liturgy and worship, since it offers the earliest picture of baptism...The emphasis in the baptismal instruction is not on repentance and forgiveness of sins, of which there is no mention, but on the ritual purity and therefore the purifying nature of the water (7:2–3). There is no mention of baptism into the death of Christ as this is set out in Paul (Rom 6:1–11), and although baptism is 'in the name of the Father, Son and Holy Spirit' in chapter 7, there is a suspicion that this may have been a later redaction, since 9:5 speaks of baptism 'in the name of the Lord.'"[45]

50. Krentz, Edgar (1996). *Christianity's Boundary-Making Bath: The New Testament Meaning of Baptism, the Sacrament of Unity*. Institute of Liturgical Studies Occasional Papers. 73, p. 113:

"Baptism is related to Jesus in a preeminent manner. Matthew 28:18-20 is the only passage in the New Testament using the trinitarian formula. Baptism in the name of Jesus only) is the norm in the New Testament. Therefore, from a New Testament perspective, the insistence on the trinitarian formula is

---

[44]See also, Meier, John P. (1977). *Two Disputed Questions*. Journal of Biblical Literature, Volume 96, No. 3 (September).
[45]Professor Jonathan A. Draper, School of Religion and Theology, University of Kwazulu-Natal.

overpressing the evidence. Without Jesus, no baptism is Christian."[46]

51. Welch, John W. (1996). *From Presence to Practice: Jesus, the Sacrament Prayers, the Priesthood, and Church Discipline in 3 Nephi 18 and Moroni 2-6.* Journal of Book of Mormon Studies: Vol. 5: No. 1, Article 4., p. 125:

> "From early times, the prophets of the Book of Mormon had taught that things should be done in the name of Christ. The Nephites worshipped GOD in the name of Christ (Jacob 4:5), baptized in his name (Mosiah 18:10), and prayed in the name of Christ (2 Nephi 32:9)."

52. Lupi, Joseph (2000). *God and the Trinity in the Fathers The First Two Centuries.* Melita Theologica, 51(2), p. 154 footnote 1:

> "A study of the earliest history of the Creed reveals two distinct forms: the Christological and the trinitarian formulas. *The most primitive form of the Creed is found in the Acts of the Apostles* (8,37): Philip baptised the eunuch of Ethiopia after the latter had professed his faith thus: "I believe in Jesus Christ the Son of God". Other Christological formulas are found in the letters of St. Paul and in the writings of the Apostolic Fathers, e.g. "His Son, who was made to him of the seed of David according to the flesh, who was predestinated Son of God in power, according to the spirit of sanctification by the resurrection of our Lord Jesus Christ from the dead. (Rom 1,3). See also 1 Cor 15,3;1 Peter 3, 18- 22). Besides the Christological formula there was also a trinitarian formula for the baptismal rite, and we find a reference to this formula in Justin's Apology: candidates of baptism receive the washing with water" in the name of God the Father and Lord of the universe and of our Saviour Jesus Christ, and of the Holy Spirit. The trinitarian formula became the dominant form, and within it we find incorporated a Christological formula which St. Ignatius of Antioch recalls in his letter to the Trallenses: "Jesus Christ who was of the race of David and of Mary, who was truly born...was persecuted under Pontius Pilate, was truly crucified and died...who was also truly raised from the dead...." The earliest

---

[46]Edgar Krentz, Christ Seminary-Seminex Professor Emeritus of New Testament Lutheran School of Theology at Chicago.

form of the ordination formula is found in the Traditio Apostolica...."[47]

53. Schwarz, Hans (2007). *The Christian Church Biblical Origins, Historical Transformation, and Potential for The Future*. Minneapolis: Fortress Press, p. 69:

> "Our consideration of the New Testament church and its worship would be incomplete if we would not at least touch briefly upon baptism, the rite that initiates one into the Christian community. There is no doubt that the first Christian community demanded a baptism "in the name of Jesus Christ" (Acts 2:38) for the forgiveness of sins."

54. Moeller, Wilhelm (1892). *History of The Christian Church A.D. 1-600*. translated from The German by Andrew Rutherfurd. London: Swan Sonnenschein & Co; New York: MacMillan & Co, p. 122:

> "...and shows by 9, 5, that this baptismal formula may also be present where (as in Herm. I.c.) baptism in the name of Jesus only is spoken of, while Hermas I. c. still speaks of baptism in the name of the Lord and therefore seems to presuppose this primitive original Christian form."

55. Otten, Bernard J. (1922). *A Manual of The History of Dogmas Volume I The Development of Dogmas During The Patristic Age 100-869*. (3rd edition). Missouri: B. Herder, p. 351:

> "...Basil and Ambrose seem to have held that baptism in the name of Jesus alone would be sufficient."[48]

56. Bradshaw, Paul F. (2009). *Reconstructing Early Christian Worship*. Minnesota: Liturgical Press, p. 270:

> "...although some scholars have doubts whether these words are

---

[47]Rev. Prof. Joseph Lupi, Professor Emeritus of Patrology at the Faculty of Theology, University of Malta.
https://www.um.edu.mt/library/oar/bitstream/123456789/31906/1/God_and_the_Trinity_in_the_Fathers.pdf [Accessed 12/15/2020] University of Malta library.
[48]Bernard J. Otten, S. J., Professor of Dogmatic Theology and The History of Dogmas in St. Louis University.

intended to refer to an actual liturgical formula as such, while others believe the present text to be a later adaptation of an earlier version that used the name of Jesus alone. It is even possible that the Trinitarian baptismal formula in Matthew 28.19 is also a somewhat later insertion into the Gospel. If these claims are true, it would mean that baptism in the name of Jesus alone might well have continued into the middle of the second century, if not later still, in some parts of the ancient world. The criticism made by Cyprian of Carthage (*Epistulae 74.5; 75.18*) appears to indicate that the church at Rome in the third century was still willing to accept the sufficiency of baptism in the name of Jesus alone, even if its own practice was now Trinitarian."[49]

57. Brownson, James V. (2007). *An Introduction To Baptism in Scripture and The Reformed Tradition*. Grand Rapids, Michigan: William B. Eerdmans Publishing Company, p. 81:

"Finally, a word should be said about the difference between 'in the name of Jesus' and 'in the name of the Father, and of the Son, and of the Holy Spirit.' Baptism 'in the name of Jesus' is the formula we see in the Book of Acts. This may well have been the earliest Christian practice. The wording of the Great Commission, however, with its full trinitarian reference, quickly became the standard wording for baptism in the early church. First, the full trinitarian reference to 'Father, Son, and Holy Spirit' made explicit what baptism 'in the name of Jesus' already implied: that is, that Jesus was being invoked as a manifestation of God."[50]

58. McDonnell & Montague, George T. (1994). *Christian Initiation and Baptism in The Holy Spirit Evidence from The First Eight Centuries*. Minnesota: Liturgical Press, p. 19:

"The only explicit reference to the ecclesial sacrament is in the great commission at the end of the gospel, where the 'trinitarian' formula, 'in the name of the Father and of the Son and of the

---

[49]Professor Paul F. Bradshaw is Professor of Liturgy at the University of Notre Dame and Priest-Vicar of Westminster Abbey and a member of the Church of England Liturgical Commission.
[50]James V. Brownson is James I and Jean Cook Professor of New Testament at Western Theological Seminary, Holland, Michigan.

Holy Spirit' (28:19), reflects a liturgical tradition different from the practice of baptizing in the name of Jesus witnessed extensively in Acts (2:38; 8:12; 16; 10:45; 19:5). It has been generally assumed that Acts tradition is earlier (Cor. 1:13; 15)...."

59. Milavec, Aaron (2003). *The Didache Faith, Hope, & Life of The Earliest Christian Communities, 50-70 C.E.* New Jersey: The Newman Press, p. 271:

"Within the context of the *Didache*, 'Lord' is normally reserved for 'Lord God'...Given the identification of Jesus as 'the servant' of the Father...one would not be astonished that *Did.* 9:5 retains the notion that baptism was, at one time, practiced 'in the name of the Father.' Given the ambiguity surrounding the term 'Lord' however, it is possible that 9:5 makes reference to 'in the name of the Lord Jesus'...In either case, scholars generally agree that 9:5 represents an earlier tradition that was gradually replaced by the trinity of names (Dunn 1977: 155f). This would allow for a transition period when both the single name and the trinity of names were used during the same period...The tradition of acting 'in the name of the Father, the Son, and the Holy Spirit' (7:1, 3) should not be thought of as reflecting early evidence of the doctrine of the Trinity...."[51]

60. Olson, Roger E. & Hall, Christopher A. (2002). *The Trinity*. Grand Rapids, Michigan: William B. Eerdmans Publishing Company, p19:

"...The *Didache* contain no explicit trinitarian reflection...."

61. Sibley, Thomas (2015). *"In Jesus' Name" Is More Than a Closing Phrase of a Christian's Prayer.* Evangelical Journal of Theology, Vol. IX No. 1, p. 81-82; 85:

"In his account of the birth and development of the first generation church, Luke gives witness to what Jesus taught concerning "in my name" within the life and ministry of those who believed "in His name." The apostles gave more than "a cup

---

[51]Dr. Aaron Milavec has been a professor for over 25 years in seminaries and universities and served as the Chair of the new program unit for the Society of Biblical Literature.

of water" in His name. They gave healing in His name (Acts 3:6). They gave the message of salvation, the forgiveness of sins by believing and being baptized "in (or into) His name" (Acts 2:38ff)...The believers at Corinth are part of the church because they were "baptized in the name of Jesus" and no one else (1 Cor 1:10-13)...The reader is reminded that when one is baptized "in (or into) the name of Jesus" he is to live and speak with that responsibility, keeping his words and actions consistent with the teachings, life and commands of Jesus."[52]

62. Chase, F. H. (1905). *The Lord's Command to Baptise (St. Matthew XXVIII 19)*. Journal of Theological Studies 6, No. 24, pp. 508; 512:

"Again, it is often urged that, whereas St Matthew represents our Lord as commanding His disciples to baptize in the name of the Three Persons of the Trinity, the evidence of the Acts and of the Pauline Epistles leads us to the conclusion that as a matter of fact they baptized their converts in the name of the Lord Jesus. So long as we regard the words of St Matthew as laying down the express terms of a baptismal formula, the difference between the alleged command of Christ and the practice of His first followers must give rise to serious difficulties... Again, there is the question, have we here a true saying of Jesus Christ. The Dean of Westminster (*Encyclopaedia Biblica* i 474) suggests, as a possible explanation of the divergence between the Lord's alleged command and the practice of the Apostolic Church, that 'Matthew does not here report the *ipsissima verba* of Jesus, but transfers to Him the familiar language of the Church of the evangelist's own time and locality... Our Lord's words in Matt. xxviii 19 do not prescribe the use of a baptismal formula. They unfold the spiritual meaning of the rite."

63. Taylor, Adam (1818). *The History of The English General Baptists In Two Parts Part First: The English General Baptists of The Seventeeth Century*. London: T. Bore Row, Turnpike, pp. 407-408:

"The right and only way of gathering churches,' in the opinion of

---

[52]Dr. Thomas Sibley, served as head of the Department of Bible and Religion at Columbia Christian College in Portland and now teaches New Testament and Practical Theology at Bible Institute, Zagreb, Croatia.

these professors, 'is, according to Christ's appointment, Matt. xxviii.19, 20, first to teach or preach the gospel to the sons and daughters of men; and then to baptize, (i.e. in English to *dip*) in the name of the Father, Son and Holy Ghost, or in the name of the Lord Jesus Christ…General Baptist…count it indifferent whether they baptize with these words, 'In the name of the Father, and of the Son and of the Holy Spirit,' or with these, 'In the name of the Lord Jesus,'…They (the English General Baptists) consider it as a matter of indifference whether the sacrament is administered in the name of the Father, Son, and Holy Ghost, or in that of Christ alone" *Eccl. Hist. IV*. P. 480"

64. Schnackenburg, Rudolf (2002). *The Gospel of Matthew*. Grand Rapids, Michigan: William B. Eerdmans Publishing Company, p. 299:

"The oldest baptismal formula was the one "in the name" of Jesus Christ (cf. Acts 2:38, 8:16, 19:5; 1 Cor. 1:13, Gal. 3:27)…."[53]

65. Mildert, William Van (MDCCC.LVL). *The Works of The Rev. Daniel Waterland, D.D*. Oxford: At The University Press, p. 172-173:[54]

"There is indeed some ground…arising from the history of the Acts, which nowhere tells us of the Apostles baptizing in the name of the Father, Son, and Holy Ghost; but mentions only their baptizing "in the name of Jesus Christ," or "in the name of the Lord Jesus," or "in the name of the Lord." St. Cyprian, in answer to this difficulty, seems to admit the matter of fact so far, that the Apostles did baptize some in the name of Christ Jesus…."

66. Tixeront, J. (1923). *History of Dogmas*. Translated from the Fifth French Edition by H. L.B. Vol. II. From St. Athanasius to St. Augustine (318-430) (2n ed.). Missouri: St. Louis & London: B. Herder Book Co, p. 309:

"However, in the *De Spiritu Sancto* (I, 42-45), St. Ambrose seems to admit with St. Basil that, absolutely speaking, it suffices for the

---

[53]Rudolf Schnackenburg Professor Emeritus of New Testament Exegesis at the University of Wurzburg, Germany.
[54]Rev. Daniel Waterland, D.D., was formerly Master of Magdalene College, Cambridge, Canon of Windsor and Archdeacon of Middlesex.

validity and efficacy of baptism, to baptize in the name of Jesus...."

67. Smith, William & Cheetham, Samuel (ed.) (1875). *A Dictionary of Christian Antiquities Being A Continuation of The Dictionary of The Bible* In Two Volumes—Vol. I. Boston: Little, Brown And Company, pp. 161-162:

> "The Baptismal Formula...On the other hand we find evidence, even as early as St. Cyprian's (*Epist. lxiii.*) time, that there were some who maintained that it was sufficient to administer "in the name of Jesus Christ." St. Ambrose favours this opinion...*De Spiritus Sancto (lib. i. cap. 111)*...In later times this same opinion was formally maintained by more than on authority. The Council of Frejus, a. 792, and Pope Nicholas I. in his *Responsa ad Bulgaros*, all maintain more or less emphatically the validity of such a formula."

68. Hefele, Charles Joseph (1894). *A History of The Christian Councils From The Original Documents, of The Close of The Council of Nicaea A.D. 325* (2nd ed.). Edinburgh: T&T Clark, p. 109:[55]

> "If then, Cyprian and Firmilian affirm that Pope Stephen held baptism to be valid only when conferred in the name of Christ, we have no need to have recourse to the testimony either of S. Jerome, or of St. Augustine, or of S. Vincent of Lerins, who also affirm it."

69. Burn, A. E (1899). *An Introduction To The Creeds And To The Te Deum*. London: Methuen & Co., pp. 23-24:

> "The early history of the Baptismal Formula is obscure and needs fuller investigation. Some...have dealt with it....asserting that it is not a word of the Lord, and that the primitive formula was Christological rather than Trinitarian—"in the name of Jesus (or the Lord Jesus)"...theologians of unimpeachable repute, from St. Ambrose to Thomas Aquinas, have maintained that the two formulae were equally orthodox...It sems strange that the text of

---

[55] The Right Rev. Charles Joseph Hefele, D. D., Bishop of Rottenburg, formerly Professor of Theology in The University of Tubigen.

St. Matthew does not show any unsettlement of MSS. or Versions if xxviii. 19 did not form part of the primitive oral teaching. It has been suggested that "into the name of the son" stood at first alone and has been added to in the same way as the form of the Lord's prayer given in its shortest form in St. Luke has been enlarged…Archbishop Benson in his book on Cyprian. He writes: "There seem to have been in Africa some who understood baptism 'in the name of Christ,' to be sufficient without the Trinal Invocation…Obviously the Marcionites, Cyprian (Ep.73. 4) says that the epistle sent him by Jubaianus made mention of Marcion, 'saying that not even such as came from him were to be baptized, as appearing to have been already baptized in the name of Jesus Christ"…Neither Cyprian nor the Roman theologians had a better exegesis to offer. They could only point to the common practice of the Church and explain the apostles' divergent practice as due to special circumstances."[56]

70. Britton, Thomas Hopkins (MDCCCLI). *The Sacramental Articles of The Church of England Vindicated From Recent Misrepresentations and Illustrated by The Writings of Their Compliers and Last Editor And by Other Documents Published Under The Sanction of The Church Between The Years 1536 and 1571*. London: Joseph Masters, Aldersgate Street and New Bond Street, p. 168:

"For whereas He commanded them to Baptize in the Name of the Father and of the Son and of the Holy Ghost, they Baptized in the Name of Jesus Christ only…."

71. Wheeler, Edward J (editor) (1905). *Is the Doctrine of the Trinity a Part of Original Christianity?* Index of Current Literature Vol. XXXIX July-December. New York: The Current Literature Publishing Company, p. 407-408:

"The Church historian of Giessen, Prof. Gustav Kruger, has published a special work on the subject, in which he argues as follows: 'The literary history of the baptismal command is by no means settled. The linking together of the words Father, Son and Holy Spirit is found only in the passage in Matthew in the entire

---

[56]A. E. Burn, B. D., Trinity College, Cambridge, Rector of Kynnersley, Wellington, Salop, Examining Chaplain to The Lord Bishop of Lichfield.

literature of Christianity up to the middle of the second century, a single exception in the 'Teaching of the Twelve Apostles' being copied from Matthew. Mark and Luke contain no such command. The present conclusion of Mark, which is not even genuine, contains nothing Trinitarian. Indeed, there are excellent reasons for believing that originally the command in Matthew did not read as it does now. Up to the fourth century there are traces of a simpler form according to which Christians were baptized only in the name of Christ. This would be in perfect agreement with the Apostolic practise of baptizing in the name of Christ only...In the 'Shepherd of Hermes,' which dates from about 100 A.D., mention is repeatedly made of baptism in the one name, but there is not a trace of any baptism in the name of the Trinity...At what time the enlarged formula of baptism in the name of the Father, Son and Holy Spirit, was introduced , it cannot be definitely determined; but probably it was about the period when the doctrine of the Trinity became the subject of debate in the churches. At any rate, it is more than probable that this Trinitarian formula is not a part of original Christianity, but a later development.'"

72. Collins, Raymond F. & Harrington, Daniel J (editors) (1999). *First Corinthians*. Minnesota: Liturgical Press, p. 82:

"Paul's second question implies that the Corinthians were baptized in the name of Jesus Christ...Paul's words make allusion to an early baptismal formula (cf. Acts 8:16, 19:5...It was the baptism of the Corinthian Christians in the name of the same Lord Jesus Christ that entailed their participation in this eschatological situation."

73. Jonge, Marinus de (1988). *Christology in Context: The Earliest Christian Response to Jesus*. Pennsylvania: The Westminster Press, pp. 46, 103:

"...'in the name of the Lord Jesus' is certainly not confined to baptism only...The true baptism is a baptism in the name of Christ (2:21; 10:48), or of the Lord Jesus (8:16; 19:5)."[57]

---

[57]Marinus de Jonge is Professor of New Testament and Early Christian Literature, University of Leiden, The Netherlands.

74. Sandt, Huub Van De & Flusser, David (2002). *The Didache Its Jewish Sources and Its Place in Early Judaism and Christianity*. Minneapolis: Fortress Press, pp. 284, 289:

> "The threefold baptismal phrase is identical with the words found in the Missionary Commission presented at the end of the gospel of Matthew (28:19). In the next section, we will establish that the wording of Matt. 28:19 probably is secondary with respect to the instances of Did 7:1 and 3, which might stand for the oldest attestation. For now, it may suffice to note that we endorse the dominant scholarly view that it is definitely not the three-member formula ("in the name of the Father and of the Son and of the Holy Spirit") but the short clause "in the name of the Lord"…which is the oldest baptismal formula; only later did Christian baptism become connected with the trinitarian phrase…At the beginning of Christianity, baptism took place "in the name of the Lord" or "in the name of (the Lord) Jesus." In the New Testament many instances of baptismal formulas are found consisting of the same or a similar member (Acts 2:38; 8:16; 10:48; 19:5; Rom 6:3; 1 Cor 1:13; Gal 3:27)…When one considers the present form of Matt 28:18-20, it is easy to perceive its asymmetrical structure, since the opening declaration requires not a trinitarian but a Christological statement to follow it. As a matter of fact, the extant passage in Matthew has all the marks of having been modified from a Christological to a trinitarian formula in order to suit to a liturgical tradition current in early days…If the gospel of Matthew does not provide a credible context for the origin of baptism in the name of the Trinity, perhaps Did 7 provides the key. And indeed one cannot completely exclude the possibility that Matt 28:19 was modified into its present form under the influence of Did 7:1 (and 3)."[58]

75. Brandt, Edward J. (1989). *The Book of Mormon: Second Nephi, The Doctrinal Structure*, p. 204:

> "'And they who were baptized in the name of Jesus were called the church of Christ' (3 Nephi 26:21)."

---

[58]Huub Van de Sandt was lecturer in New Testament Studies, Tilburg Faculty of Theology and David Flusser was Professor of Judaism in the Second Temple Period and Early Christianity of Hebrew University, Jerusalem.

76. De Long, Kindalee Pfremmer (2014). *"Look, Here is Water: Baptism in the Book of Acts"* Leaven: Vol. 22: Issue 4, Article 7, p. 201:

> "In this story, baptism in the Holy Spirit guarantees that God has already accepted these Gentiles, welcoming them into the restored community as Gentiles. Because of this acceptance, they also receive water baptism in the name of Jesus Christ."[59]

77. Amanze, James N. (2006). *Ecumenism in Botswana The Story of the Botswana Christian Council 1964-2004.* Gaborne: Paulist Press, p. 37:

> "Baptism is by immersion in a river or dam once…in the name…Jesus alone."[60]

78. Baker, Josiah (2020). *'One Lord, One Faith, One Baptism'? Between Trinitarian Ecumenism and Oneness Pentecostals.* Journal of Pentecostal Theology 29. Leiden: Brill, pp:102-103:

> "While Trinitarian Pentecostal churches as a norm prohibit baptism in Jesus' name, they seldom formally require that former oneness Pentecostals be rebaptized…the New Testament seemingly portrays the entire Christian life as being done 'in the name of Jesus'…In fact, everything they do in word or deed is to be done 'in the name of the Lord Jesus' (Col. 3:17). What is it about water baptism that causes most Trinitarians to demand a Trinitarian formula for its validity, especially when scripture references even this practice as being done in Jesus' name (Acts 2:38; 8:16; 10:48; 19:5)…."

79. Wickham, J. A. (1850). *A Synopsis of The Doctrine of Baptism, Regeneration, Conversion, &.* London: George Bell, p. 580:

> "Ammonites A.D. 251 – 'Not all baptism, but only that into the Lord Jesus, effects the cleansing away of sins.'"

80. Fahey, Michael Andrew (1971). *Cyprian and the Bible A Study in Third-Century Exegesis.* Mohr, p. 573:

---

[59] Kindalee P. De Long, is an Associate Professor of Religion at Pepperdine University teaching New Testament Courses.

[60] James N. Amanze is Professor of Systematic Theology at the University of Botswana in the Department of Theology and Religious Studies.

"...in NT times the baptismal formula 'in the name of Jesus' was permissible...."

81. Jowitt, Robert (1837?). *Thoughts on Water-Baptism.* Darton and Harvey: London, pp. 16-20:

"But, after this negative declaration, Paul goes on to assign a reason for his conduct in so generally omitting to baptize, (with water); "For Christ sent me not to baptize, but to preach the gospel; such is the plain, and (as it appears to me,) unequivocal language of one, who was not a whit behind the chiefest of the apostles. Our Lord after having, in the same interview with his disciples, pointed out the distinction betwixt John's baptism with water, and his own with the Holy Ghost, gave the short, simple command, "Go ye, therefore, teach [or make disciples of] ALL NATIONS, baptizing them in [into] the name of the Father, and of the Son, and of the Holy Ghost," and yet here we find one of the most eminent of his apostles expressly says, "Christ sent me not to baptize," (referring, no doubt, to water -baptism .) If Paul had not received such a commission, who had? It seems to me impossible to reconcile the command of our Saviour with the declaration of his inspired apostle, if water -baptism was enjoined; unless we consider the injunction to baptize as given exclusively to those apostles to whom the words were spoken; which those who differ from me on this subject will not, I presume, be willing to admit. I cannot but regard the injunction of our Lord, as equally obligatory upon his servant Paul, as upon the other apostles; and that in executing his Lord's commission "to preach the gospel," he fulfilled the whole command to go "teach all nations, baptizing them in the name of the Father, and of the Son, and of the Holy Ghost." Through that demonstration of the Spirit and of Power which at tended his preaching, he was doubtless made the instrument of introducing men into the church, even into fellowship with the Father and the Son, through the Holy Spirit, and thus to "teach, baptizing." Some attempt to explain Paul's language, by saying, that he meant, he was not specially sent to baptize; but this plea is, I think, quite inadmissible; for he does not himself say anything of the kind, and it is completely to beg the question. It was, obviously, very important that he should not in any way mislead the Corinthian believers, or give them any reason to doubt his having received a full qualification for the important service to which he had, in so remarkable a manner, been called, which could hardly have failed to be the case, had he told them he had not received a commission to perform one essential part of our Lord's command to his apostles, and that a part which had especial reference to the receiving new converts into the Christian church. Whilst fully prepared to admit that the silence of one of the sacred writers on any particular subject, ought not in any degree to invalidate what another has said on the same subject, it is notwithstanding worthy of remark, that whilst many of the canonical epistles are entirely silent on this subject, others allude to it only in an in direct manner, and none speak of it as a binding ordinance of perpetual obligation. The apostle Paul, in giving special instructions to Timothy and Titus respecting the churches under their care, does not even hint at water baptism, neither does he give any instructions about baptizing, in his epistles to the believers at Rome, Corinth, Galatia, Ephesus, Philippi, Colosse, or Thessalonica. In his epistle to the Hebrews, one great object seems to have been to prove that all ceremonial worship was at an end; that all types were fulfilled in Christ the antitype. If whilst the types of the Mosaic dispensation were done away in Christ, a new outward ordinance had been set up as a part of the religion of Jesus, would not the apostle under such circumstances have not only expressly mentioned it, but been very particular in his instructions respecting it, and yet in his epistle of thirteen chapters we find not one word on the subject, except that in chap. vi. 2, he simply mentions "The doctrine of Baptisms." Adverting to the very precise instructions given by God to Moses, in regard to the numerous typical and ceremonial enactments of the Jewish law, and the fair presumption grounded thereon, that if our Lord had intended to institute an outward rite in his church, his directions as to the mode of administering it, would have been very plain and definite; and more especially when we bear in mind that the gospel dispensation was to do away with one abounding in outward observances, it appears to me, that those who are of opinion that the command in Matt. xxviii. was designed to institute or continue water-baptism, as a Christian ordinance, must admit that so much of particular instruction as our Lord was pleased to give, must be strictly binding-bearing in mind that the rite in itself is inefficacious. We find then the language "baptizing them in the name of the Father and of the Son and of the Holy Ghost" a part of the command of our Lord; was this part of the command duly observed? I am ready to admit, that the advocates for water-baptism might with some reason have assumed that those so likely rightly to understand the language of Christ as his apostles were, would doubtless perform the ceremony in the way prescribed, had no notice been taken by the inspired penman of the manner of its being performed; but this is far from being the case. Have we then Any account of the rite being administered, in which the form of words prescribed was used? None. Have we an account of another form of words being used? So far as we may judge of the form from the narration of the circumstances, we have several - viz. Acts ii. 38, Peter says "Repent and be baptized every one of you in the name of Jesus Christ." Chap. viii. 16, Luke, speaking of the converts of Samaria, says, "Only they were baptized in the name of the Lord Jesus." Chap. x. 48, Peter "commanded them (Cornelius, &c.] to be baptized in the name of the Lord." Chap. xix. 5, (at Ephesus) "when they heard this they were baptized in the name of the Lord Jesus." Thus, so far as we are informed, we see that baptism with water was not performed in the manner prescribed by our Lord, respecting the baptism which He commanded to be used...."

82. Bruce, F. F (1940). *"The End of the First Gospel."* The Evangelical Quarterly 12, pp. 205-206:

"The historicity of this Matthaean appearance has been frequently questioned, chiefly on account of the Trinitarian baptismal formula of verse 19. This, it has been argued, belongs to a later stage of development in the Catholic Church: according to the Acts, believers in the first decades of the Church's history were baptized simply "in the name of Jesus Christ" (Acts ii: 38; x. 48) or "into the name of the Lord Jesus" (viii. 16; xix. 5). The argument is fairly plausible, and the prevailing opinion may be illustrated by the words of A. H. M'Neile who, while admitting that "the threefold Name does not in itself point to a late date for the passage" yet concludes that "the section must probably be regarded as the expression by the evang. of truths which the

Church learnt as a result of the Resurrection, and on which it still rests its faith...In ii. 3 8 and x. 48 the preposition is...which is to be understood instrumentally, as so often in the N.T.: the expression is equivalent to Heb. běshěm, "in the name" or "with the name"; and its exact meaning in these two places is probably to be explained by Acts xxii. 16: arise, and be baptized, and wash away thy sins, calling on His name." So then, to those who were baptized...the Name was an "accompanying circumstance" of their baptism, to use grammatical jargon, either because they themselves confessed or invoked it, as did Paul, or because it was named over them (Acts xv. 17; Jas. ii. 7)."[61]

83. Thistlethwaite, Susan Brooks (1991). *On the Trinity*. Interpretation A Journal on Bible and Theology 45, pp. 162, 164:

"The sum of the Synoptic evidence as authority for a trinitarian formula is sketchy at best. Clearly, the one baptismal formula in Matthew 28:19 is a pericope inserted to further the theology presented in Matthew...The Trinity in its traditional formula as 'Father, Son, and Holy Spirit' owes its doctrinal development to the apologetic efforts of Christians in the Greco-Roman world."[62]

84. Watson, Jonathan D. (2018). *The Ongoing 'Use' of Baptism: A Hole in the Baptist (Systematic) Baptistery?* Southwestern Journal of Theology, Volume 61, Number 1 (Fall), pp. 7-8:

"In Matthew, the apostles, and by extension the church, are commanded to make disciples by "baptizing ...in the name of the Father and the Son and the Holy Spirit" (Matt 28:19)." [but points out in footnote 14 that] "Even baptism administered in Jesus's name only, so long as it is within an orthodox frame of reference, is inherently Trinitarian. Michael Reeves aptly notes, "when you proclaim Jesus, the Spirit-anointed Son of the Father, you proclaim the Triune God." Michael Reeves, Delighting in the Trinity (Downers Grove: IVP Academic, 2012), 37–38... Third,

---

[61] Professor Frederick F. Bruce was a renowned leading British New Testament biblical scholar.
[62] Susan Brooks Thistlethwaite is Professor of Theology, Chicago Theological Seminary.

relating to the doctrine of salvation, baptism is a visible portrayal of conversion (subjective) and union/identification with Christ (objective). As an act of obedience, baptism clearly manifests one's conversion and discipleship unto Christ. Submission to baptism visibly affirms Jesus' declaration, "All authority has been given to Me in heaven and on earth" (Matt 28:18). Commenting on baptism in the name of Jesus as found in Acts, Beasley-Murray notes that when connected to such a formula "submi[ssion] to [baptism] becomes a confession of trust in Him."[63]

85. Farrelly O.S.B., M. John (2005). *The Trinity Rediscovering the Central Christian Mystery*. New York: Sheed & Ward, p. 73:

"In the mid-third century Pope Stephen claimed to know of a form of baptism in the name of Jesus alone and to consider it valid (Cyprian, Ep. 73. 4,1: 16,1,2)."

86. McDonnell, Kilian (2003). *The Other Hand of God The Holy Spirit as the Universal Touch and Goal*. Collegeville, Minnesota: Liturgical Press, pp. 4-5:

"Trinitarian reflection arose in the post-biblical era in response to the quite unsystematic triadic tradition within the New Testament itself...The association of the Spirit with the Father and the Son in the Great Commission of Matthew 28:19-20 raises the question of the Spirit's personality but does not settle it...Exegetes have reach no consensus on the exact number or content of triadic texts...If the doctrine of the Trinity does not come from the New Testament, it came from nowhere. This must be recognized even if a triadic tradition in the New Testament is not yet a conscious trinitarianism."

87. Bratcher, Robert G. (1963). "'*The Name' in Prepositional Phrases in the New Testament*," The Bible Translator 14, p. 73:

"In the baptismal formula it would seem that "the name" represents the one to whom the one being baptized is being dedicated: he "becomes the possession of and comes under the

---

[63] Jonathan D. Watson Assistant Professor of Christian Studies Charleston Southern University Charleston, South Carolina.

protection of the one whose name he bears: he is under the control of the effective power of the name and the One who bears the name"…So against those people in the church in Corinth who would claim "I am of Paul" Paul protests, "Were you baptized *eis* to *onoma* of Paul?…Let no one say he was baptized in my name (*eis* to *emon onoma*)" (1 Cor. 1:13, 15), with Paul, that is, as the object and goal of the rite of baptism, Christ, in whose name, or for whose name, we are baptized, is its only proper object or goal."

88. Stewart, Alistair C. (2011). *The Christological Form of the Earliest Syntaxis: The Evidence of Pliny*. Studia Liturgica 41, pp. 2, 3, 4, 8:

"In his recent work on the Roman creed, Liuwe Westra notes that questions regarding the pre-history of baptismal creeds belong to the realm of speculation, but nonetheless hazards a guess that there was a fusion of christological formulae derived from primitive christological acclamations (such as "Jesus is Lord") and trinitarian formulae at Rome at some time between the middle of the second and the middle of the third centuries…It is on such a basis that the suggestion is made that there has been a fusion of independent christological formulae with trinitarian creedal forms. One may surmise that, in this hypothetical realm, the christological formulae are generated from without the liturgy, for the tendency in scholarship to see a threefold interrogation taking place in the waters as the sole primitive form of baptism, and thus the suggestion that the current creeds are formed from a fusion of christological formulae with an original trinitarian baptismal creed, has to account for the genesis of the christological section. It is hard to see where this assumption comes from, though it is prominent in the literature. However, there is evidence that a single interrogation with christological confession followed by baptism (possibly, thus, generating a formula) might have been an independent and equally ancient form of baptism as there are christological statements of faith within a baptismal context beyond those embedded in trinitarian creeds. In particular we may note the statement of ps-Hippolytus De Theophania 10 that the candidate at baptism, having renounced evil, confesses that "Christ is God" as he joins himself to Christ, and the "Western text" of Acts 8:37 in which the

Ethiopian eunuch makes a confession that "Jesus Christ is the Son of God" and is baptized on that basis...Whereas the suggestion that these statements refer to baptismal rituals is hardly new, what is distinct about the suggestion made here is that full weight is given to the statement that the *carmen secum invicem* is addressed to Christ as God. That is to say, the baptismal interrogation is not made in order to elicit a trinitarian creed but a single, christological, statement of faith, or indeed of commitment, following on directly from the renunciation but before entry into the waters. As such, the worship of these Bithynian Christians is seen as reflecting a pattern known elsewhere."[64]

89. Sim, David C. (2014). *Is Matthew 28:16-20 The Summary of The Gospel.* HTS Theological Studies, 70 (1), pp. 1, 3:

"As to its origin, while some scholars have argued that the Great Commission was completely created by Matthew (so Gundry 1994:593-597; Kingsbury 1974:573-579; Lange 1973:488-491), the majority of scholars contend that Matthew has heavily redacted traditional source material (so Davies & Allison 1997:677-678; Hubbard 1974:101-136; Meier 1977b:407-416; Nolland 2005:1261; Schaberg 1982:313-335). In terms of its genre, the work of Hubbard (1974:1-136), which argues that Matthew based this text on Old Testament commissioning narratives, has won wide support (e.g. Allison 1993:263-265; Davies & Allison 1997:679-680; Nolland 2005:1261)...The triadic formula of baptism in the name of the Father, the Son and the Holy Spirit finds no mention at all in the previous parts of Matthew. In fact, it appears nowhere in the New Testament (Schaberg 1982:9-16). While other early Christian texts know of baptism in the name of Jesus Christ (Ac 2:38; 10:48; Rm 6:3), Christ (Gl 3:27) and the Lord Jesus (Ac 8:16; 19:5), Matthew's baptismal formula is unique in early Christian literature. Whether or not this formula reflects the baptismal practice of the Matthean community is an interesting issue...."[65]

---

[64]The Rev. Dr. Alistair Stewart is priest theologian at Sherborne Abbey in Dorset, England, United Kingdom.
[65]Prof. Dr David C. Sim is a research fellow of Prof. Dr Andries G. van Aarde in the research project 'Biblical Theology and Hermeneutics' located in the

90. Hanson, Anthony T. (1982). *The Image of the Invisible God*. London: SCM Press, p. 87:

> "No responsible New Testament scholar would claim that the doctrine of the Trinity was taught by Jesus, or preached by the earliest Christians, or consciously held by any writer of the New Testament. It was in fact slowly worked out in the course of the first few centuries."[66]

91. Hoff, Marvin D. (1964). *Baptism As A Means of Grace*. Reformed Review, pp. 29-30:

> "The Belgic Confession of Faith holds that there is grace communicated through the sacrament of baptism. The meaning of the rite of baptism is applied to the life of the baptized. This is because "our Lord giveth that which is signified ... "It is through the Lord Jesus Christ that grace is given in the sacrament of baptism. Therefore baptism, to be a means of grace, must be in his name. In the New Testament this fact is taught us especially in connection with the rebaptism of the Ephesian disciples. These men had been baptized with John's baptism, which was only a baptism of repentance. Therefore, they had not received the gift of the Holy Spirit, which accompanied baptism in the name of Jesus Christ. Paul baptized them "in the name of the Lord Jesus Christ." In this baptism they received the gift of the Holy Spirit, and certainly all of the other gifts connected with the sacrament of baptism were given to them. Baptism does not magically convey grace. This grace is given by our Lord Jesus Christ, consequently baptism must be in his name. Only those who have been baptized in his name will receive the gifts of grace which are attached to the sacrament of baptism. For the church today this means that baptism must always be in the name of Jesus Christ. This must not become a mechanical repetition of words. It must always be acknowledged in baptism that the Lord Jesus Christ gives the grace that is communicated. Unless this is the confession of the church it is to be doubted that baptism will be

---

Department of New Testament Studies, Faculty of Theology, University of Pretoria, Pretoria, South Africa.
[66] Dr. Anthony Tyrrell Hanson was Professor of Theology at the University of Hull and former Senior Editor of the Journal for the Study of the New Testament.

a true means of grace in it. It may then have no more meaning than the baptism of John had for the Ephesian disciples. The Heidelberg Catechism also presents a prerequisite for baptism to be a means of grace. Question 72: Is, then, the outward washing of water itself the washing away of sins? No; for only the blood of Jesus Christ and the Holy Spirit cleanse us from all sin. Thus, to the necessity of baptism in the name of Jesus Christ, the Catechism adds the need for the operation of the Holy Spirit. The Catechism takes the position that without the operation of the Holy Spirit there will be no cleansing from sin in baptism. This holds true also in respect to the other elements of grace that baptism represents."

92. Harnack, Adolf Von (1894). *History of Dogma*. Volume 1. Boston: Little, Brown and Company, p.79:

"It cannot be directly proved that Jesus instituted baptism, for Matth. XXVIII. 19, is not a saying of the Lord. The reasons for this assertion are: (1) It is only a later stage of the tradition that represents the risen Christ as delivering speeches and giving commandments. Paul knows nothing of it. (2) The Trinitarian formula is foreign to the mouth of Jesus and has not the authority in the Apostolic age which it must have had if it had descended from Jesus himself."[67]

93. Robson, John (1908). *The Resurrection Gospel A Study of Christ's Great Commission*. Edinburgh and London: Oliphant, Anderson & Ferrier, p. 293-294:

"The first instance we have of the Threefold Name being used is in Justin Martyr, and there it is in the form now used in most of the Churches, in the name of the Father and of the Son and of the Holy Ghost, not into their name—that is, with the authority of the Trinity, not into the faith or Church of the Trinity. There are only few indications of the practice of the primitive Church, but they show that it was always the name of Christ that was used:

---

[67]Professor Adolf Van Harnack, Baltic German Lutheran Theologian and renowned Church Historian. See also the comments that "Dods admits that "*the Trinitarian Formulae in the mouth of Jesus is certainly unexpected*" noted in The Lutheran Church Review (1907) January Volume XXVI...No. I, p. 424."

sometimes, as by Peter, it is baptism in His name; sometimes, as by Paul, it is baptism into His name. Much ingenuity has been expended in trying to reconcile the words of Christ's commission with the apostolic use of only the name of Christ in baptism."[68]

94. _____. (1909). *Twenty-Seventh Annual Session of The Baptist Congress Held in The Madison Avenue Baptist Church New York City. November 9, 10, and 11.* Chicago and New York: The University Press of Chicago Press, p. 145:

"As to Matt. 28:19-20, grave doubt exists among scholars as to its genuineness also. Among the grounds for these questionings is the fact that it contains a clear-cut expression of the Trinitarian formula—a formula not found in any other New Testament book-a formula not connected with any New Testament case of baptism, and nowhere else in the New Testament referred to in speaking of baptism, moreover a formula which in the light of the history of dogma could hardly have come to such perfect expression until long after the death of the apostles, and a formula, be it said, which would tremendously help in the Trinitarian controversy of the early centuries provided it could have been surreptitiously inserted into some New Testament manuscripts."

95. Hultgren, Arland J. (1994). *Baptism in the New Testament: Origins, Formulas and Metaphors.* Word & World 14/1, pp. 8-9:[69]

"II. FORMULAS The baptismal formulas within the New Testament vary, even with the same writer. At the end of the Gospel of Matthew the risen Christ commissions his eleven remaining disciples to i[baptize] into the name of the Father and

---

[68]Rev. Dr. John Robson (1836-1908) was one of the pioneers of the United Presbyterian Church of Scotland (UPS) mission in Rajputana.
[69]Arland Hultgren went to Luther Seminary in 1977 as associate Professor of New Testament and was named professor in 1986. He was chair of the department from 1986 to 1993. He had been on the faculty in religious studies at Wagner College, Staten Island, N.Y., from 1969 to 1977. He was ordained in 1966 and called as assistant Pastor of Trinity Lutheran Church, Tenafly, N.J., where he stayed until 1968. He also took a parish leave from the seminary and served as pastor of St. Andrew's Lutheran Church, Minneapolis, in 1979-80, see faculty Luther Seminary, St. Paul, Minnesota.

of the Son and of the Holy Spirit (28:19). Yet Peter one of the remaining eleven is portrayed right away by Luke on Pentecost as calling upon his hearers, saying: Be baptized...into the name of Jesus Christ (Acts 2:38; cf. 10:48), rather than into the triune name. At other places in Acts there is a slight variation: Paul baptizes into the name of the Lord Jesus (19:5; cf. 8:16). In his own letters Paul speaks of his readers as baptized into Christ Jesus (Rom 6:3) or simply baptized into Christ (Gal 3:27). At one place he says that they are baptized into one body (1 Cor 12:13). Although the trinitarian formula in the Gospel of Matthew appears to be the earliest of all (enunciated by Jesus shortly after his resurrection), in point of fact the letters of Paul are earlier literary productions, and Acts was probably written about the same time as Matthew. These sources give witness to baptismal formulas which are second article (into Christ) only. And since it is difficult to imagine that first-century Christians would dispense with a trinitarian formula in favor of a purely christological one, the latter must be considered earlier, and it appears to have been more widespread. Eventually the trinitarian formula became prominent and then virtually universal...."

96. Morris, Leon L. (1992). *The Gospel According to Matthew*. Grand Rapids, Michigan: William B. Eerdmans Publishing Company:

"We must bear in mind as well that in the early church there are references to baptizing in the name of Jesus (Acts 8:16; 19:5)...For that matter the words about the Trinity are not necessarily meant to be used as a formula...."[70]

97. Bicknell, E. J. & Carpenter, H. J. (ed.) (2007). *A Theological Introduction to The Thirty-Nine Articles of The Church of England* (Third Edition). Eugene, Oregon: Wipf & Stock, p. 370:

"We are not greatly concerned to deny that baptism in the name of Christ may have once been common...."

98. Osborne, Kenan B. (1997). *The Resurrection of Jesus New Considerations for Its Theological Interpretation*. Eugene, Oregon: Wipf & Stock, p. 57:

---

[70]Leon L. Morris was an Australian New Testament scholar and was ordained in the Anglican ministry in 1938.

"The use of the 'trinitarian formula' in connection with baptism in now way connotes that at this early stage of the Jesus community a doctrine of the Trinity had been developed...Nor can one deduce that the trinitarian baptismal formula found in Matthew's gospel was the more original formula for baptism. It would seem, rather, that a baptism in the name of Jesus alone antedated the more mature and developed 'trinitarian formula.' In the history of baptism...one cannot read into Matthew's account a theology of the Trinity that makes its appearance only gradually in the church and finds its major expression in the four great councils of the early church."[71]

99. Ward, Rowland (1996). *Theology The One and Triune God and the life of his People*. The substance of an address as Moderator to the Synod of the Presbyterian Church of Eastern Australia, Armidale, New South Wales, on 27 March 1996. This Synod commemorated the 150th anniversary of the Church's founding. Dr. Rowland Ward is a minister of Know Presbyterian Church of Eastern Australia, Melbourne. This is his address as Moderator of Synod 1996:

"*1. A specific passage: Matthew 28:19-20 (The Great Commission)* Several points may be made in reference to the Great Commission passage:
(1) In response to the argument that this must be a later addition, since elsewhere baptism is administered only in Jesus' name (Acts 2:38; 8:16; 10:48; 19:5; 1 Cor 1:13,15)…(2) In any event, I would argue that Matthew 28:19 in its original intention does not prescribe a formula so much as succinctly sum up the fact that through the work of redemption the character of God has been declared definitively and he is to be recognized accordingly."[72]

100. Forney, C. H. (1883). *The Christian Ordinances Being A Historical Inquiry Into The Practice of Trine Immersion, The Washing of The Saints' Feet And The Love-Feast*. Harrisburg, Pennsylvania: Board of Publication of The General Eldership of The Church of God, pp. 55-56, 83-84:

---

[71]Kenan B. Osborne is a Professor Emeritus of the Graduate Theological Union, Berkeley, he was President of The Catholic Theological Society of America.
[72][Online] https://rowlandward.net/the-one-and-triune-god-and-the-life-of-his-people/[Accessed 7/10/2021].

"Besides, it is generally conceded that during the time of the Apostles, as well as in the earliest post-Apostolic times, baptism was administered in the name of Jesus. Neander, the prince of modern ecclesiastical historians, says that the formula of baptism which is regarded as the older is the "shorter one which refers only to Christ, to which there is allusion in the New Testament." Dr. Hare also says in his Church History: "Baptism as an initiatory rite was performed simply in the name of Jesus" (Apostolic Church). Robinson, in his History of Baptism, says: "There is no mention of baptism in the name of the Father, and of the Son, and of the Holy Ghost in immediately post- Apostolic times. "Dr. William Smith states the same fact in his Dictionary of Christian Antiquities. This testimony, of a negative character, certainly becomes very strong and significant in view of the fact that Peter enjoined baptism "in the name of Jesus Christ " (Acts ii : 38); that when Philip preached in Samaria, to which place Peter and John were sent upon hearing "that Samaria had received the word of God, "those who believed "were baptized in the name of the Lord Jesus" (Acts viii : 5-16); and that under the instructions of Paul those who had been baptized "unto John's baptism" were "baptized in the name of the Lord Jesus" (Acts xix : 3-5). Now, a historical retrospect reveals the following peculiar fact:

1. In the latter part of the fourth century nearly every author who refers to baptism speaks of the triple immersion.

2. At the close of the third century the witnesses are less numerous, though the threefold immersion was evidently widely practiced.

3. At the opening of the third century there are but two witnesses who testify to the practice of trine immersion.

4. In the second century there are various works extant which speak in greater or less detail of baptism, but not one author mentions trine immersion.

5. The Apostolic Fathers, the immediate disciples of the Apostles, though the majority of them speak of immersion, not one of them mentions trine immersion.

6. The inspired historian mentions Peter, Philip and Paul as baptizing in the name of Jesus only, whereas the threefold immersion is never in the name of Jesus alone until after the

fourth century.

7. That there is no claim advanced in favor of trine immersion before the crucifixion of Christ, neither in Christ's baptism, that of John, nor in the Proselyte baptism of the Jews, if there was such baptism.

8. That there is no mention or intimation of a change from single to trine immersion in the Scriptures, but ample reasons in favor of a uniform practice from John the Baptist to John the Apostle. This significant array of adverse facts should be sufficient to produce the most serious doubt touching the divine origin of trine immersion...

And now, let it be remembered that about this time trine immersion was probably first practiced, according to the testimony which we have reviewed, and that it is first mentioned in the very place to which for the first time Pantænus brought the Hebrew Gospel by Matthew. Before this time we have also no record of the use of the baptismal formula in Matthew in the administration of the ordinance. Baptism had been generally administered only in the name of Jesus. Neander, the prince of modern ecclesiastical historiaus, says that the formula of baptism which is regarded as the older is the "shorter one which refers only to Christ, to which there is allusion in the New Testament." Dr. Hare also says in his Church History: "Baptism as an initiatory rite was performed simply in the name of Jesus. "This sentence occurs in his chapter on the " Apostolic Church," in his "History of the Christian Church." Robinson, in his History of Baptism, says: "There is no mention of baptizing in the name of the Father, and of the Son, and of the Holy Ghost," in immediately post-Apostolic times. "This testimony, of a negative character, certainly becomes very strong and significant in view of the fact that Peter enjoined baptism "in the name of Jesus Christ" (Acts ii : 38); that when Philip preached in Samaria, to which place Peter and John were sent upon hearing" that Samaria had received the Word of God," those who believed "were baptized in the name of the Lord Jesus" (Acts viii : 5. 12 , 16); and that under the instructions of Paul those who had been baptized "unto John's baptism were" baptized in the name of the Lord Jesus' (Acts xix: 3,5). But as soon as the doctrine of the Trinity was developed, and the Gospel of Matthew brought from

India to Egypt, trine immersion, with individual exceptions, became gradually the rule."

101. Elazar-DeMota, Yehonatan (2021). *A Comparative Analysis of Berith and the Sacrament of Baptism and How They Contributed to the Inquisition.* Religions 12: 346, p. 5:

> "*2.1. Baptism in the Apostolic Writings.* The Apostolic writings speak of two types of baptisms, namely, the "baptism of John," and the "baptism of Jesus." The former was a physical immersion that demonstrated sincere repentance and the messianic expectation. The latter refers to the physical immersion in the "name of Jesus," for the forgiveness of sins, and the reception of the Holy Spirit.
>
> *2.2. The Baptism of John.* The Gospel of Matthew states, "At that time Jesus came from Galilee to the Jordan River so that John would baptize him" (American Bible Society 1995, Mat. 3:13). Robert Webb argues that John was part of the Essene Jewish sect (Webb 2006, p. 351). He is not alone on this theory. This theory is based on the notion that John's baptism is related to the daily ablution of the Essenes. It is interesting that Jesus comes to be baptized by John, thereby demonstrating the need for repentance of his sins. According to the Book of Acts, those Jews who cherished immediate messianic expectations were baptized by John or by his followers as a sign of repentance (American Bible Society 1995, Acts 13:24). After the resurrection of Jesus, a modified form of baptism was implanted by his followers.
>
> *2.3. Baptism in the Name of Jesus.* In Gospel, according to Matthew, Jesus commands his disciples, "Therefore, go and make disciples of all nations, baptizing them in the name of the Father and of the Son and of the Holy Spirit" (American Bible Society 1995, Mat. 28:19). The Apostle Paul contrasts John's baptism with Jesus', stating, "John baptized with a baptism by which people showed they were changing their hearts and lives. It was a baptism that told people about the one who was coming after him. This is the one in whom they were to believe. This one is Jesus" (American Bible Society 1995, Acts 19:4). It can be inferred from these passages that John prepared the way for

Jesus' messianic movement to spread throughout Judea and the Jewish diaspora. Moreover, Jesus told his apostles, "John baptized with water, but in only a few days you will be baptized with the Holy Spirit" (American Bible Society 1995, Acts 1:5). During the Pentecost, many Jews from various nations were gathered at the Temple in honor of the precept to present their offerings 50 days after the Paschal lamb offering. At that moment, after the apostles began speaking in intelligible languages, in astonishment of the diaspora Jews, Peter proclaimed, "Change your hearts and lives. Each of you must be baptized in the name of Jesus Christ for the forgiveness of your sins. Then you will receive the gift of the Holy Spirit" (American Bible Society 1995, Acts 2:38). Overall, the Apostolic writings portray baptism in Jesus' name, as evidenced by the power of the Holy Spirit."

102. Mueller, Wayne (1975). *The Development of the Baptismal Rite in the Christian Church.* [PT 464–Liturgical and Musical Studies Through the Church Year 1975 WLS Summer Sessions], p. 5:

> "The Trinitarian formula in baptism began in the east, whereas in Rome baptism in the name of Jesus was still used after Nicea."

103. Brink, Gijsbert Van Den & Erp, Stephan Van (2009). *Ignoring God Triune? The Doctrine of the Trinity in Dutch Theology.* International Journal of Systematic Theology Volume 11 Number 1 January, pp. 72-73:

> "The current neglect of the Trinity in Dutch theology, however, is not a new development. Apart from some important historical work, not a single monograph on the doctrine of the Trinity and its ramifications has been published in Dutch Protestant theology during the past century. In Dutch Roman Catholic theology, only Herwi Rikhof has paid explicit attention to the doctrine of the Trinity. This theological neglect signifies that this doctrine is of little influence not only in modern Dutch theology, but also in ecclesial discussions and in the lives and faith practices of most everyday believers in the Netherlands. In this article we will try to establish that this situation can be explained by the fact that leading Dutch theologians either ignored the doctrine, or used it for their own purposes, or uttered critical reservations regarding

its sense and significance."

104. Felton, Gayle Carlton (reprint) (2006). *By Water and the Spirit Making Connections for Identity and Ministry*. This study guide includes the full text of By Water and the Spirit: A United Methodist *Understanding of Baptism*, adopted by the 1996 General Conference of The United Methodist Church. Nashville, Tennessee: Discipleship Resources, p. 17:

> "Jesus commanded the disciples then and commands the church now to baptize in the name of God who was made known to us in the life, death, and resurrection of Christ. Probably the earliest Christian baptisms were administered in the name of Jesus only, but soon, as Christians came to better understand the divine nature, baptisms recognized the triune personality of God traditionally expressed as Father, Son, and Holy Spirit."

105. Marmion, Declan & Nieuivenhove (2011). *An Introduction to The Trinity*. New York: Cambridge University Press, 54:

> "There are also 'triadic' texts, where the Father, Christ and the Spirit appear alongside each other, for example, the baptismal command in Matthew (28:19). The Matthean Church seems to have been familiar with this baptismal formula, which replaced an earlier custom of baptizing solely in the name of Jesus (Acts 2.38; 19.5). This is not a fully worked out trinitarian doctrine...."

106. Brasher, Brenda E. (editor) (2001). *Encyclopedia of Fundamentalism*. Volume 3 of Religion & Society. New York: Routledge, p. 48:

> "...baptism, 'I baptize you in the name of the Father, of the Son, of the Holy Spirit,' is derived from Jesus' Great Commission (Matthew 28:19). Though early apostolic baptism was generally in the name of Jesus Christ...."

107. Due, William J. La (2006). *The Trinity Guide to The Christian Church*. London & New York: Continuum, p. 76:

> "Baptism has been from the outset the rite of entrance into the believing community. Early on, it was conferred in the name of Jesus Christ (Acts 2:38; 8:16)."

108. Heath, Gordon L. & Dvorak, James D. (2011). *Baptism Historical,*

Theological and Pastoral Perspectives. Eugene, Oregon: Wipf & Stock, p. 101:

> "As the Dutch Theologian Herman Bavinck notes, baptism in the name of the triune God 'does not prescribe what the apostles are to say, but what they have to do. The name here indicates that the baptizing person is placed in a relationship with the Father, Son, and the Holy Spirit.'"

109. Evans, Ernest (2016). *Tertullian's Homily on Baptism The Text Edited with an Introduction Translation, and Commentary.* Eugene, Oregon: Wipf & Stock, p. xvii:

> "Twice, at Act 2:38 and 19:5, we read of persons being baptized 'in the name of Jesus the Messiah' or 'into the name of Jesus the Lord' and this may perhaps represent the formula commonly used at the early time."

110. Qualben, Lars P. (2009). *The Lutheran Church In Colonial America.* Eugene, Oregon: Wipf & Stock, p. 27:

> "The baptism was to be in the name of Jesus. In Matthew 28:20 the baptism was to be in the name of the Father, and of the Son, and of the Holy Spirit. Previously in this chapter the apostles had asserted their faith in the Father. The Holy Spirit had just been given. Hence the stress on baptism here in the name of Jesus only indicates that we are dealing with early material."[73]

111. McGrath, Alister E. (1997). *Studies in Doctrine.* Grand Rapids, Michigan: Zondervan Publishing House, p. 44:

> "Matthew 28:19 "Go and make disciples of all nations, baptizing them in the name of the Father, Son and Holy Spirit." Although baptism was initially performed in the name of Jesus (Acts 8:16; 19:5), this passage clearly indicates the implication of practice. To be baptized in the name of Jesus is to be baptized in the name of the "God and Father of our Lord Jesus.""[74]

112. _____ (1917). *The American Journal of Theology* edited by The Divinity Faculty of the University of Chicago and Colleagues in

---

[73] Dr. Lars P. Qualben was Associate Professor of Religion at St. Olaf College and Pastor of Bethel Lutheran Church.
[74] Dr. Alister E. McGrath, Lecturer in Theology, Oxford University, England.

Allied Department, The University of Chicago Press, Chicago, Illinois, Volume XXI, p. 299:

> "The Matthaean formula of baptism is probably only a liturgical expansion of the primitive formula preserved in Acts."

113. Wright, N.T. (1992). *The New Testament And The People of God Christian Origins and The Question of God*. Minneapolis, MN: Fortress Press, p. 447:

> "Our earliest evidence for Christian baptism involves the name of Jesus."[75]

114. France, R. T. (2007). *The Gospel of Matthew*. Grand Rapids, Michigan: William B. Eerdmans Publishing Company, p. 415:

> "Baptism was in fact performed in New Testament times, as far as our records go, in the name of Jesus, which is surprising if Jesus had laid down an explicit trinitarian formula before his ascension. An explanation for this may be found in the argument that these words, which later came to be used as a liturgical formula, were not originally so intended and used. They were rather 'a description of what baptism accomplished."[76]

115. Peerbolte, L.J. Lietaert (2003). *Paul the Missionary, Contributions to Biblical Exegesis & Theology 34*. Peeters Publishing, _____, pp. 133-134:

> "Traces of an older formula, preceding the one under discussion [*Matthew 28:19*], are found in 1 Cor 1, 13; Gal 3, 27, Acts 8, 16; 19, 5; Did. 9, 5; and Herm., Vis. III.7. This older form of the baptismal formula must have been something like 'baptising in the name of (the Lord) Jesus'...." [Emphasis added].

116. McDonnell, Kilian (1996). *The Baptism of Jesus in The Jordan: the Trinitarian and Cosmic Order of Salvation*. Collegeville, Minnesota: The Liturgical Press, p. 181 (noted in footnote 33):

---

[75] N. T. Wright, Fellow, Chaplain and Tutor in Theology at Worcester College, University of Oxford, England.
[76] R. T. France former Principal of Wycliffe Hall, Oxford University, England from 1989-1995 and has taught at London Bible College.

> "We know from Acts 2:38; 8:16; 10:48; 19:5; as well as from Galatians 3:27 and Romans 6:3, that the Trinitarian formulas commanded by Jesus in Matthew 28:19 and Mark 16:16 was not universally part of the liturgical rite."[77]

117. Newman. Carey, C. et. al. (ed.) (1999). *The Jewish Roots of Christological Monotheism Papers from the St. Andrews Conference on the Historical Origins of the Worship of Jesus.* Leiden: Brill, p. 200:

> "By all accounts, the principal rite through which people became members of early Christian groups was a baptism that involved the invocation of Jesus' name (e.g., Acts 2:38; Acts 8:16; Acts 10:48). To make the entrance rite into the elect so directly connected with Jesus is itself notable, for it reflects the belief in Jesus as the living guarantor of the salvation promised to those who trust in him. For this cultic action to involve the invocation of Jesus' name over the baptized...Moreover, as Hartman has noted, the use of the title...in the baptismal formula of this cultic action must mean that Jesus is regarded in ways analogous to God, and the baptismal use of this title for Jesus is itself good evidence that in such uses the title carries the force of a divine title."[78]

118. Fee. Gordon, D. (1987). *The New International Commentary On The New Testament, The First Epistle To The Corinthians.* Grand Rapids, Michigan: William B. Eerdmans Publishing Company, p. 61:

> "It seems altogether likely, especially on the basis of Acts 2:38; 8:16; 10:48 (perhaps see, n. 35 on 6:11); and 19:5 (cf. Rom 6:3), that the early church baptized only in the name of Jesus, rather than in the Trinitarian formula of Matt. 28:19. This text could add to that evidence; however, one needs to be cautious here, since

---

[77]Kilian McDonnell, O.S.B., founder and president of the Institute of Ecumenical and Cultural Research, Collegeville, Minnesota, co-chair of the International Classical Pentecostal/Roman Catholic dialogue, who was also acknowledged by The Catholic Theological Society of America whereby Father McDonnell was awarded John Courtney Murray award for distinguished contribution to theology.
[78]This reference was noted by British scholar, Professor Larry W. Hurtado, *The Binitarian Shape of Early Christian Worship* in *The Jewish Roots of Christological Monotheism Papers from the St. Andrews Conference on the Historical Origins of the Worship of Jesus cited in the publication.*

the concern is so obviously of another kind that one cannot be sure that it adequately reflects the precise formula for Christian baptism. It at least *included* the name of the Lord Jesus."[79]

119. Purves, George T. (1908). *Christianity In The Apostolic Age*. New York: Charles Scribner Sons, pp. 35-36:

"This was in accordance with the express command of Christ (Matt. Xxviii. 19). The administration of it was not always performed by the Apostles (Acts viii. 16, 38)...In Acts and the epistles, baptism is said to have been in or on the name of Christ, or as into (Acts ii. 38; viii. 16; x. 48; xix. 5; Rom. Vi. 8; Gal. iii.27)...On the other hand, it is possible that the words of Christ (Matt. Xxviii. 19) were not at first regarded as a liturgical formula. They are primarily a statement of the threefold faith which summarizes the teachings of Jesus (sect. 16)."[80]

120. Douglas, Finkbeiner (1991). *An Examination of "Make Disciples of AU Nations" in Matthew 28:18-20*. Calvary Baptist Theological Journal 12, Spring, p. 29:

"Based upon the exclusion of the Trinitarian formula in several quotations by Eusebius. and a Jewish-Christian source dating from around the sixth century, some scholars have denied the authenticity of the Trinitarian formula in favor of a shorter reading... Theologically, some have argued that the trinitarian formula is inconsistent with the monadic formula practiced in the early church (Acts 2:38; 8:16; 10:48; 19:5; Gal. 3:27; and Rom. 6:3)...."

121. Bosch, David J. (1983). *The Structure of Mission: An Exposition of Matthew 28:16-20. The Great Commission in Matthew* in *Exploring Church Growth* edited by Wilbert R. Shenk. Eugene, Oregon: Wipf & Stock, pp. 219, 230:

"As a matter of fact, the Great Commission does not function anywhere in the New Testament. It is never referred to or

---

[79]Professor Gordon D. Fee is a New Testament scholar and exegete.
[80]George T. Purves was Professor of New Testament and Exegesis in Princeton Theological Seminary.

appealed to by the early Church...Neither is it necessary to accept that Matthew 28:19 contains the *ipsissima verba* (the very words) of Jesus...And since the Matthean Great Commission could indeed by proved to have been heavily redacted by the evangelist...."

122. Witherington III, Ben (2007). *Troubled Waters The Real New Testament Theology of Baptism*. Waco, Texas: Baylor University Press, p. 83:

"When we are dealing with Paul's theology of water baptism, several facts must be kept in view...
(2) We have no evidence that Paul derives his theology of baptism from some teaching of Jesus, or even the early church. There is this similarity between what we find in Paul and Acts baptism is said to be into Christ in the Pauline corpus and in Acts it is done in the name of Jesus."[81]

123. Stookey, Laurence Hull (1982). *Baptism Christ's Act in The Church*. Nashville, Tennessee: Abington Press, p. 64:

"...we cannot administer baptism in the name of Jesus only, yet we accept it when those so initiated by other groups...."[82]

124. Jenson, Robert W. (2002). *The Triune Identity God According to The Gospel*. Eugene, Oregon: Wipf & Stock, pp. 9-10:

"Baptism is described as 'into Jesus' name...That the biblical God must have some proper name, we have seen in the Hebrew Scriptures. In the life of the primal Church, God is in fact named by the uses that involve the name of Jesus."[83]

125. Penner, Melinda. L. (2001). *The Interaction of Philosophy and Theology in the Development of the Trinity and Christology at Nicaea and Chalcedon*, p. 2:

---

[81]Dr. Ben Witherington, III is Professor of New Testament at Asbury Theological Seminary.
[82]Laurence Hull Stookey, was Professor Emeritus of Preaching and Worship, Wesley Theological Seminary Washington D.C., and Pastor of Ashbury United Method Church, Maryland.
[83]Robert W. Jenson was Senior Scholar for Research at The Center for Theological Inquiry, Princeton, New Jersey and taught at Oxford University.

"The early church believed the doctrine in its general form based on the revelation of Scripture. The foundation of the early doctrine of the Trinity was the baptismal formula and the doxologies in the Epistles along with the Logos doctrine of John. The earliest confessions professed Jesus to be God."

126. Basil Studer edited by Andrew Louth (1993). *Trinity and Incarnation The Faith of the Early Church*. London & New York: T&T Clark, p. 27:

"…it is not certain when this custom of baptism in the name of the Trinity appeared…and…it is hard to distinguish it from 'baptism in the name of Jesus'…."[84]

127. Schaff, Phillip (1854). *History of The Apostolic Church With A General Introduction To Church History*. New York: Charles Scribner, pp. 566-567:

"The full formula of baptism, as prescribed by Christ (Matt. 28: 19), is in the name of the Father, the Son, and the Holy Ghost ; signifying a sinking of the subject into the revealed being of the triune God, a coming into living communion with Him, so as thenceforth to be consecrated to Him, to live to Him and serve Him, and to experience His blessed redeeming and sanctifying power. In practice, however, we find the apostles always using the abbreviated form: "into the name," or "in the name, of Jesus Christ," or "of the Lord Jesus," or simply "into Christ."—And see footnote 4 on page 567—"It is certain that immediately after the time of the apostles the formula given by Christ was in general use (comp. e. g. Justin's *Apol. I. 80*), but also that the abridged form, in the sense above given, was acknowledged valid as far down as the third century (comp. Nean. der: Kirchengesch. I. 535, and especially Höfling: Das Sacrament der Taufe, etc. I. p. 37 aqq)."

128. Schmauk, Theodore & Benze, C. Thedore (1911?). *The Confessional Principle And The Confessions of The Lutheran Church As Embodying The Evangelical Confession of The Christian Church*. Philadelphia: General Council Publication Board MCMXI, pp. 97-98:

---

[84]Basil Studer, O.S.B. is Professor of Early Church History and Patristics at the Pontifical Athenaeum S. Anselmo and at the Patristic Institute, the Augustinianum in Rome, Italy.

"This shorter Baptismal Formula contains in itself all that it to be found in the words which Christ used at the institution of Baptism" and see footnote 4 on page 98 "It has been pointed out that where baptism is mentioned historically in the New Testament, it is into the name of the Lord Jesus (Acts 19:5), etc.), and not into the triune name (Matt. 28:19)."

129. Marsh, Herbert G. (1941). *The Origin and Significance of The New Testament Baptism.* Manchester: Manchester University Press, p. 185:

"Whatever may have been the origin of this formula which mentioned only the name of Jesus, there is no reason for believing that long familiarity with its use caused it to be regarded as a technical expression for Christian baptism...."

130. Wallace, Daniel B. (2003). *Greek Grammar and the Personality of the Holy Spirit.* Bulletin for Biblical Research 13.1, p. 123:

"Further, when we look at Acts we notice that water baptism is apparently never done in the "name of the Father, Son, and Holy Spirit"; it is done in Jesus' name alone (cf. Acts 2:38; 8:16; 10:48; 19:5; 22:16)."[85]

131. Rackham, Richard Belward (1901). *The Acts of The Apostles An Exposition.* London: Methuen & Co., P. 32:

"A (verse 41). The entrance into the society was through Baptism'. Baptism was 'a washing of the body with pure water' which symbolized a simultaneous washing of the soul or forgiveness of sins. Hence there were necessary conditions: (1) previous repentance and confession of sin (Mt iii 6), and (2) as forgiveness was through the blood of Christ, confession of faith in the name of Jesus Christ. From verse 38, x 48, and xix 5?, we should naturally infer that these words were actually the formula used in baptizing. On the other hand the Lord, in Mt xxviii 19, commanded the disciples to baptize "into the name of the Father and of the Son and of the Holy Ghost.' The apparent discrepancy was noticed by the Fathers and various solutions were proposed. A simple explanation is to suppose that "in the name of Jesus

---

[85] Daniel B. Wallace is Professor at Dallas Theological Seminary, Texas.

Christ' had been the original formula, which was afterwards superseded by the name of the Father, Son and Spirit...."

132. Carl, Harold F. *"Relational Language in John 14-16: Implications for the Doctrine of the Trinity"* Global Journal of Classic Theology Issue Volume 2., No. 1 (12/99) see footnote 1:[86]

> "[1] Hendrikus Berkhof writes "As we see it, when we discuss God as the source of everything that arises next in the study of the faith, there is no reason to ascribe to him something like triuneness. As the creator of the world, as the establisher of the covenant, and as the one who reveals himself, we know him as the one God, as a person...can we say then that we have here 'one essence in three persons'? No, there is here one event that happens from God...May we then not call the Spirit a person? No, if thereby we put him separately beside the person of God. Yes, if we understand that this name expresses the personhood in God in its outward actions. The Spirit is precisely God-as-person, God-in-relation." Hendrikus Berkhof, Christian Faith, translated by Sierd Woudstra (Grand Rapids: Eerdmans, 1979), 335-335. I know of one otherwise "evangelical" seminary where Christian Faith was, until recently, the primary textbook for "Introduction to Christian Theology I & II."

133. Parsons, Michael C. (ed.) (2008). *Acts Commentaries on The New Testament*. Grand Rapids, Michigan: Baker Academics, pp. 50-51-266-267:

> "Sometimes baptism precedes reception of the Spirit (8:12–17); sometimes baptism follows reception of the Spirit (10:44–48); sometimes it accompanies baptism in the name of Jesus and the laying on of hands (19:5–6)...With this explanation Luke proceeds to record the remedy of the disciples' deficiencies, first in terms of baptism and then in terms of the Holy Spirit: When they heard (this), they were baptized in the name of the Lord Jesus (19:5). Baptism in the "name of Jesus" is mentioned only three other times in Acts (2:38; 8:16; 10:48). The first occurrence in Peter's Pentecost address is programmatic: "Repent, and be

---

[86] Accessed [Online] at http://www.globaljournalct.com/relational-language-in-john-14-16-implications-for-the-doctrine-of-the-trinity/ [July 25, 2021].

baptized, each of you, in the name of Jesus Christ for the forgiveness of your sins and you will receive the gift of the Holy Spirit." The connection between baptism in Jesus' name and the gift of the Holy Spirit is clear, and the lack of knowledge of and experience with the Holy Spirit on the part of disciples, who know only John's baptism of repentance, is understandable."

134. O'Collins, Gerald (2008). *Catholicism A Very Short Introduction*. New York: Oxford University Press, pp. 2-3, 9:

"Yet the first Christians differed from other devout Jews by administering baptism 'in the name of Jesus' (e.g. Acts 2: 38)… By the 60s, the followers of Jesus had come to be called 'Christians' (Acts 11: 26). Through baptism in the name of Jesus, they knew their sins to be forgiven, received the Holy Spirit, entered the community of the Church…Baptism 'in the name of the Father and of the Son and of the Holy Spirit', reported at the very end of Matthew's Gospel, rapidly became and remained the standard formula for the basic sacrament or rite of Christian initiation."[87]

135. O'Collins, Gerald & Farrugia, Mario (2015). *Catholicism The Story of Catholic Christianity*. New York: Oxford University Press, pp. 4, 6, 16, 145, 251, 317-318:

"But Jesus' followers differed from (other) devout Jews by administering baptism 'in the name of Jesus' (e.g. Acts 2: 38)…By then Jesus' followers had come to be called 'Christians' (Acts 11: 26). Through baptism 'in the name of Jesus Christ' (Acts 2: 38) they knew their sins to be forgiven… Baptism 'in the name of the Father and of the Son and of the Holy Spirit', reported at the end of Matthew's Gospel, rapidly became and remained the standard formula for the basic sacrament of Christian initiation (Matt. 28: 19)…At some point in the first century Christian communities stopped baptizing simply 'in the name of Jesus' (e.g. Acts 2: 38; 10: 48) and began baptizing 'in the name [singular] of the Father and of the Son and of the Holy Spirit' (Matt. 28: 19)…The last NT text to be recalled here, one that provided the threefold structure for the post-NT creeds with their 'articles' dedicated to

---

[87]Dr. Gerald O'Collins is a Catholic scholar and theologian.

the Father, the Son, and the Holy Spirit, is the mandate from the risen Christ at the end of Matthew's Gospel: 'Make disciples of all nations, baptizing them in the name of the Father and of the Son and of the Holy Spirit' (Matt. 28: 19). This baptismal formula in the name of the Trinity, rather than coming from the risen Jesus himself, reflects the practice of Matthew's community in the 70s who experienced the risen Lord present in their midst. At first, Christians seem to have baptized converts in the name of Jesus Christ (e.g. Acts 2: 38)...The first Christians thought of the Church as inseparable from the risen Christ and from the Holy Spirit. He was the heavenly Spouse of the Church (e.g. Eph. 5: 25–7) or 'the head of the body' which is the Church (e.g. Eph. 5: 23). Baptism in the name of Jesus (e.g. Acts 2: 38) or, with what became the normative formula, 'in the name of the Father, and of the Son, and of the Holy Spirit' (Matt. 28: 19)...."[88]

136. Holmen, Tom and Porter, Stanley E. (ed.) (2011). *Handbook for the Study of the Historical Jesus* Volume I. Leiden, The Netherlands: Brill, pp. 25, 149:

"By the same token, this is why we do not regard the baptismal command in Matt 28:18 as authentic. Nowhere else does Jesus speak of ritual baptism or sound like a proto-Trinitarian. The truth is that one could, if so inclined, urge that Matt 28:18 satisfies the criterion of double dissimilarity: Jewish sources certainly nowhere speak of baptism in the name of the Father, the Son, and the Holy Spirit, and (aside from Matthew) first-century Christian sources also here fail us: they rather know of baptism in the name of Jesus. Yet this would be a specious argument for the authenticity of Matt 28:18...Immersion, for John, was no once for all act, as in later Christian baptism. In the practice of the primitive church, after the resurrection, believers felt that they received the Spirit of God when they were immersed in the name of Jesus."

137. Chester, Andrew (2011). *High Christology – Whence, When and Why?* Early Christianity Volume 2, Issue 1, pp. 23, 29, 39, 50:

---

[88]Gerald O'Collins, S.J., A.C., is Professor Emeritus of Gregorian University, Rome and Mario Farrugia, S.J., is Professor of Systematic Theology at Gregorian University, Rome.

"...is that the confession of Christ as divine is not Jewish in origin, nor is it conceivably Jewish. It could come about only when Christianity (or one part of it, at least) had evolved into a Gentile religion, and could be unmistakably identified as such. It took decades (50 or 60 years) for Jesus, the Jewish prophet, to be turned into a Gentile God...that it was possible for Jesus to be proclaimed as God...The early Christians who saw Christ as sitting on God's throne of Glory, and confessed their faith in him as *kurios*, could hardly have failed to understand him as divine to the earliest Judean Jewish Christian circles, as well as the Pauline Christian communities. Thus, there was calling on the name of Jesus, baptism in the name of Jesus, and Jesus' name used in healing and exorcism, along with, in the Pauline communities...It remains, of course, a momentous and astounding phenomenon that Christ could ever be portrayed, and understood as divine, in this way. Yet we at least thus have a clear basis and framework to help us begin to make sense of why and how the early Christians could articulate so high a Christology at so early a stage, in a Jewish context and in language that Jews would reserve for God."[89]

138. Strelan, Rick (1996). *Paul, Artemis, and the Jews in Ephesus* in ll Section Town: Paul in Ephesus, Berlin and New York: Walter de Gruyter, p. 242:[90]

"Repentance together with baptism in the name of Jesus Christ offers forgiveness of sins and the promised gift of the holy Spirit (Acts 2:37-38)."

139. Dunn, G. D. (2004). *Heresy and Schism According to Cyprian of Carthage*. The Journal of Theological Studies, Volume 55, Issue 2, p. 571:

"Burns, 'On Rebaptism', pp. 399–400. S. G. Hall, 'Stephen I of Rome and the One Baptism', in Elizabeth A. Livingstone (ed.), Studia Patristica 17/2 (Oxford: Pergamon Press, 1982), pp. 796–8, thinks that Stephen's use of quacumque is an indication that his policy was first worked out in relationship to Marcionite

---

[89]Dr. Andrew Chester, Faculty of Divinity, Cambridge University, England.
[90]Rick Strelan is retired associate professor in New Testament and early Christianity at the University of Queensland.

baptism (see Cyprian, Ep. 73.4.1 [CCSL 3C, p. 533]; [Cyprian], Ep. 75.18.1 [CCSL 3C, p. 597]), where baptism was administered not with a trinitarian formula but only in the name of Jesus, and then applied to the Novatianist position as well."

140. Peterson, David G. (2012). *Transformed by God New Covenant Life and Ministry*. Downers Grove, Illinois: InterVarsity Press, p. 71:

"Even though Cornelius had a genuine faith in God before he heard Peter's message (10:2–4, 22, 31), his faith became explicitly focused on Jesus as the promised saviour so that he and his companions were baptized 'in the name of Jesus Christ' (10:48)."

141. Bonhoeffer, Dietrich (1963). *The Cost of Discipleship*. New York: MacMillan Publishing Co., Inc., p. 99:

"In fact every command of Jesus is a call to die, with all our affections and lusts. But we do not want to die, and therefore Jesus Christ and his call are necessarily our death as well as our life. The call to discipleship, the baptism in the name of Jesus Christ means both death and life."

142. Bavinck, Herman (2008). *Reformed Dogmatics Holy Spirit, Church, And New Creation* Volume Four. Grand Rapids, Michigan: Baker Academics, p. 531:

"Many expositors regard this last verse as inauthentic, on the ground that in the apostolic era baptism still took place in the name of Jesus, and that the trinitarian formula is of a later date… Now the same thing is meant when Jesus says in Matt. 28:19 that his disciples must be baptized "into the name of the Father and the Son and the Holy Spirit." It is not here prescribing to the apostles what they have to say during the administration of baptism but what they have to do. Christian baptism is and must be an incorporation into fellowship with the God who has revealed himself as Father, Son, and Spirit."[91]

143. Schwarz, Hans (2017). *The Trinity The Central Mystery of Christianity*. Minneapolis: Fortress Press, pp. 28-29, 75-76, 176, 179, 192-193:

---

[91] Herman Bavinck (1854-1921) was a Dutch Calvinist Theologian and churchman.

"...we read in the command of the risen Lord: "Go therefore and make disciples of all nations, baptizing them in the name of the Father and of the Son and of the Holy Spirit" (Matt 28:19)...This contrasts to other New Testament passages in which we read of Baptism "in the name of Jesus Christ" (Acts 2:38; 19:5). Matthew gives no explanation whether or how the Son and the Spirit are coeternal with the Father and therefore would form a Trinity. "The essential point is that the one encountered in Jesus as the Son of God and in the Spirit-led church as the people of God is not some subordinate deity, but the one true God." Yet Baptism administered without at least calling on the name of Jesus is a Baptism without the Spirit... One thing is certain: that Christian Baptism, whether in the name of Father, Son, and Holy Spirit or just in the name of Jesus (Christ) is intimately connected with the Holy Spirit... Augustine ends his work on the Trinity addressing God: "O Lord, our God, we believe in Thee, the Father and the Son and the Holy Spirit. For the Truth would not say, Go, baptize all nations in the name of the Father and of the Son and of the Holy Spirit; unless Thou wast a Trinity." Then he asks to be set free from the multitude of speech, well knowing that his attempt to "describe" the Trinity is futile. We hear nothing here of three persons but of the "one God, God the Trinity." While the errors concerning perception of the Trinity are rejected, the positive elaboration of the doctrine is still not accomplished. Reinhold Seeberg (1859–1935) therefore concludes: "The whole procedure is a freely suspended speculation which moves in the heights of the immanent life of the Godhead bare of any relationship to the reality of divine revelation. It is therefore ultimately just a logical exercise in which persons are vaporized to relations and the threefoldness is in the end nothing but the perception of the one God under various viewpoints... Neither the term Trinity, nor triune, nor any of their variety can be found in the New Testament. Without any emphasis on unity, we only encounter triadic formulas. Even the baptismal formula in Matthew 28:19 ("in the name of the Father and of the Son and of the Holy Spirit") seems to be preceded by an earlier formula that Peter used in his speech in Acts: Baptism "in the name of Jesus Christ" (Acts 2:38)...As the Roman Catholic church historian Norbert Brox (1935–2006) affirms, the faithful perceived the Hellenistic speculations on the Trinity largely as a threat to the faith in the one God, speculations that also jeopardized the unity of the church. They vehemently resisted the Trinity, claiming that with it a doctrine of two or even three gods was promulgated. "The beginnings of a theology of the Trinity by the church were understood as polytheism and rejected as heresy in the name of the biblical God... We have seen that in the New Testament we encounter no doctrine of the Trinity or Trinitarian formulations. At the most, we have triadic formulations, as in the famous commission to the disciples when the resurrected Christ says to them: "All authority in heaven and on earth has been given to me. Go therefore and make disciples of all nations, baptizing them in the name of the Father and of the Son and of the Holy Spirit, and teaching them to obey everything that I have commanded you. And remember, I am with you always, to the end of the age" (Matt 28:18–20). The impetus for transforming such a triadic formulations into a Trinitarian formula arose once Christianity had left Palestine and entered a new religious and philosophical context. As mentioned above, there were triads of gods in many different religions. Often there was one supreme god with whom two other gods were associated, such as in Egypt and Babylonia, and in Rome with Jupiter, Juno, and Minerva. In these other religions there is often the genealogical triad of father, mother, and son. Generally, triads were patterned after the nuclear family, a union of the male and female principles, and a son as the result of that union. The head of that family was often a creator god. We should not forget that in early Christianity some also talked about God the Father, the divine Sophia, and Jesus Christ as the Son of God. The preference for triads is also found in the number three, since this means a totality with beginning, middle, and end. It also denotes the human being, consisting of body, soul, and spirit, as well as the world, with heaven, earth, and the surrounding waters. Yet Christianity went a decisive step further beyond genealogy and numerical considerations. It developed a Trinitarian doctrine, attempting to show the intrinsic and extrinsic relations between the three members of the triad,

Father, Son, and Holy Spirit."[92]

144. Dunn, James D. G. (1996). *The Acts of the Apostles*. Peterborough: Epworth Press, p. 66:

> "(3) Baptism is now Christian baptism ('in the name of Jesus Christ' —similarly 8.16; 10.48; 19.5). That is, the name of Jesus was probably named over the baptisands indicating the one under whose authority they now were being placed (cf. I Cor. 1.12–13)... The first Christians attributed the inspiration for this adoption and transformation of the Baptist's rite to the risen Christ (Matt. 28.19), though the formula used in Acts ('in the name of Jesus Christ') suggests that the three-fold formula of 'the great commission' (Matt. 28.19) also reflects later developments."[93]

145. Grundeken, Mark (1984). *Community Building in the Shepherd of Hermas A Critical Study of Some Key Aspects*. Leiden: Brill, pp. 40-41, 51:

> "In Vis. 3,7,3, "to be baptized in the name of the Lord (βαπτισθῆναι εἰς τὸ ὄνομα τοῦ κυρίου), the name intended may be that of the Son. The idea that "no one can enter into the kingdom of God except through the name of his beloved Son (διὰ τοῦ ὀνόματος τοῦ υἱοῦ αὐτοῦ τοῦ ἠγαπημένου ὑπ' αὐτοῦ)" (Sim. 9,12,5) and that one "carries the name of the Son of God" (τὸ ὄνομα τοῦ υἱοῦ τοῦ θεοῦ φορῇ, 9,13,3) indicates that in Vis. 3,7,3 the name of the Son is meant. God's Son is indeed Lord. He is the lord of the church (the tower) and the one in whose name believers are baptized Hermas does not use traditional Jewish terms like Messiah, or Son of David. Moreover, the triad Father, Son and Spirit is not connected with any Jewish origins...Is baptism in the name of Jesus (or the triune God) an entrance rite to the community?" For Hermas, the entrance rite to the church

---

[92]Hans Schwarz is professor emeritus of systematic theology at the University of Regensburg, Germany. From 1967 to 1981 he was professor at Trinity Lutheran Seminary in Columbus, Ohio.

[93]James D. G. Dunn is Lightfoot Professor Emeritus of Divinity at the University of Durham, England.

is baptism in the name of the Son of God."[94]

146. Regev, Eyal (2004). *Moral Impurity and the Temple in Early Christianity in Light of Ancient Greek Practice and Qumranic Ideology.* The Harvard Theological Review, Vol. 97, No. 4 (October), pp. 394, 404:

> "The alternative means of moral purification available in early Christianity were various types of baptism: John's baptism, the apostles' baptism in the name of Jesus (Acts 2:38), and Paul's theology of baptism in the Holy Spirit… According to Acts, Peter did not screen those who were baptized in the name of Jesus, and he even converted Cornelius, a God-fearing centurion."

147. Dunn, James D. G. (1970). *Baptism in the Holy Spirit A Re-examination of the New Testament Teaching on the Gift of The Spirit in Relation to Pentecostalism today.* Philadelphia, Pennsylvania: The Westminster Press, pp. 4, 50, 55, 93, 99, 118:

> "I hope to show that for the writers of the NT the baptism in or gift of the Spirit was part of the event (or process) of becoming a Christian, together with the effective proclamation of the Gospel, belief in [*eis*] Jesus as Lord, and water-baptism in the name of the Lord Jesus; that it was the chief element in conversion-initiation so that only those who had thus received the Spirit could be called Christians…At all events it is not until Pentecost that this foundational belief of the Church is realized and promulgated, and it is only as a result of Pentecost that the invitation of Acts 2.21 ('whosoever calls on the name of the Lord shall be saved') can be issued in the name of Jesus and the promise of the Spirit be made on condition of repentance and baptism in the name of Jesus Christ (Acts 2.;8)…If they believed and were baptized (v. 12.) in the name of the Lord Jesus (v. 16) they must be called Christians…It has become evident, in fact, that one of Luke's purposes in recording these unusual instances is to show that the one thing which makes a man a Christian is the gift of the Spirit. Men can have been for a long time in Jesus'

---

[94]Mark Grundeken, born 1984, Ph.D. 2013 (KU Leuven), 2013–2014 Wissenschaftlicher Mitarbeiter of Professor Cilliers Breytenbach at the Humboldt-Universität zu Berlin, is Akademischer Rat of Professor Ferdinand R. Prostmeier at the Albert-Ludwigs-Universität Freiburg.

company, can have made profession of faith and been baptized in the name of the Lord Jesus, can be wholly 'clean' and acceptable to God...Although the fulfilment comes at once, because baptism in the name of the Lord Jesus expresses commitment to Jesus as Lord...Paul therefore is challenging the Corinthians to remember that their baptism was performed in the name of Christ."[95]

148. Lloyd-Jones, D. Martyn (1994). *The Baptism and Gifts of The Spirit*. Grand Rapids, Michigan: Baker Book House, pp. 28, 31-32, 46:

"Here they are then, believers, and they are rejoicing in their belief. They have been baptized not with John's baptism but they have been baptized 'in the name of Jesus Christ'...In Acts 19:4 Paul addresses these men and gives them further instruction and then we read: 'When they heard this, they were baptized in the name of the Lord Jesus.' The apostle is perfectly happy that these men are true believers. But they have had John's baptism only, so he says, 'But you must be baptized in the name of the Lord Jesus Christ.' So he baptized them 'in the name of the Lord Jesus Christ'... You remember the story in Acts 19 of the people at Ephesus? The apostle expounded the truth to them, they believed it, and he baptized them in the name of the Lord Jesus Christ..."[96]

149. France, R. T. (2007). *The Gospel of Matthew The New International Commentary on The New Testament*. Grand Rapids, Michigan: William B.

---

[95] At the time this publication was released, James D. G. Dunn was Lecturer in New Testament in the Department of Theology at the University of Nottingham, England.

[96] D. Martyn Lloyd-Jones (1900-1981) gave up his position as physician to England's Royal family to become a missionary to miners and dock workers. He succeeded G. Campbell Morgan to the Westminster Chapel Pulpit. There is another point of interest in his work on page 208-209, he notes that *"In about 1830 the people who had become known as the Plymouth Brethren, including such names as J. N. Darby, B. W. Newton and S. P. Tregelles, and others of the early first leaders of the Brethren movement, began to gather together with Edward... F S.P. Tregelles, a great and famous biblical scholar."* It has been noted that the Plymouth Brethren in the United Kingdom baptized in the name of Jesus only during that time and Lloyd-Jones calls one of them a great and famous biblical scholar during that era citing *F S.P. Tregelles*.

Eerdmans Publishing Company, see 3500, 3501, 1342, 3505:

"Baptisms in Acts are said to be in (or into) 3500 the name of Jesus (Acts 2:38; 8:16; 10:48; 19:5; 22:16; cf. Rom 6:3; Gal 3:27), and there is no other reference in the NT to a trinitarian baptismal formula, though this was well established by the time of Did. 7:1, 3 3501 (cf. Justin, 1 Apol. 61:3, 11, 13). In view of the gradual movement within the NT toward trinitarian (or at least triadic) forms of expression, with the three persons mentioned in a variety of orders, the wording here in Matthew draws attention as more formally corresponding to later patristic formulations than might be expected within the NT period, let alone in the words of Jesus himself. If Jesus had put the matter as explicitly as this, it is surprising that it took his followers so long to catch up with his formulation…What is said here of the exclusive relationship between "the Father" and "the Son" begins to prepare the reader for the climax of the gospel where "the Son" will take his place alongside the Father and the Holy Spirit as the object of the disciples' allegiance (28:19). This is not yet a formulated doctrine of the Trinity, but it is a decisive step toward it…But to say that "the trinitarian formula is established by the period of our first extant Christian documents" is to overstate the evidence. The three persons are indeed mentioned together, sometimes clearly intentionally, but in such a variety of orders and literary forms that to speak of a "formula" is anachronistic."

150. Dunn, James D. G. (1996). *The Acts of the Apostles*. Grand Rapids, Michigan: William B. Eerdmans Publishing Company, p. 32, 33, 38, 110, 115, 155, 256:

"(3) Baptism is now Christian baptism ('in the name of Jesus Christ' -similarly 8.16; 10.48; 19.5). That is, the name of Jesus was probably named over the baptisands indicating the one under whose authority they now were being placed (cf. I Cor. 1.12-13)… The first Christians attributed the inspiration for this adoption and transformation of the Baptist's rite to the risen Christ (Matt. 28.19), though the formula used in Acts ('in the name of Jesus Christ') suggests that the three-fold formula of 'the great commission' (Matt. 28.19) also reflects later developments…What was this new movement which had been launched by the Pentecost event and which had seen such a huge initial success? In boundary-defining terms its most distinctive feature thus far was the requirement of baptism, baptism 'in the name of Jesus Christ' (2.38; cf. 2.21)... Likewise there is no hint that Philip acted wrongly in baptizing the Samarians, that is, baptizing them 'in the name of the Lord Jesus' (8.16)...We are presumably to assume that Philip's exposition included reference to baptism in the name of Jesus (cf. 2.38). The Ethiopian's response (8.36) is consistent with what we read throughout Acts...How these Gentiles who believed, turned to the Lord, and no doubt were baptized in the name of Jesus, were regarded by the Jews who did not so believe is also unknown...that baptism in the name of Jesus would normally be part of a conversion-initiation..."

151. Barrett, C. K. (1994). *A Critical and Exegetical Commentary on The Acts of the Apostles Preliminary Introduction and Commentary on Acts I-XIV* Volume I. Edinburgh: T&T Clark, pp. 79, 226, 489:

"This power is given through the Spirit, and conversely the Spirit in Acts may be defined as the divine agency that gives this power. The Spirit is not defined here as the third of a Trinity of divine Persons, though it is associated with the Father and the Son... Luke had no occasion to theologize about the relation between the Third Person of the Trinity and the Christian life, and probably had no interest in doing so...(44) While Peter was still speaking these things the Holy Spirit fell upon all who were listening to his speech.(45) And the circumcised believers who had accompanied Peter were astonished that the gift of the Spirit had been poured out upon the Gentiles too-(46) for they heard them speaking with tongues and magnifying God. Then Peter spoke up: (47): 'Can anyone forbid the water so as to prevent from being baptized these men who have received the Holy Spirit, just as we did?' (48) And he gave orders for them to be baptized in the name of Jesus Christ. Then they asked him to stay on for some days."[97]

152. Bock, Darrell L. (2011). *A Theology of Luke's Gospel And Acts Biblical*

---

[97]C. K. Barrett was Emeritus Professor of Divinity in Durham University, England.

Theology of The New Testament. Grand Rapids, Michigan: Zondervan, pp. 169-171, 173, 184, 233:

> "Jesus' share of divine power and his role in salvation are seen in his mediation of the Spirit, a fulfillment of the presence of the new era noted in Luke 3:16. Here the key portion of the text is Acts 2:30 –36. These verses affirm that Pss 132:11 and 110:1 are realized in Jesus' receiving the Spirit from the Father and pouring him out onto his followers. The promise of the Spirit is from Joel 3:1–5. Key here is that people are to call "on the name of the Lord" to be saved (Acts 2:21). This looks as if one must call out to the God of Israel, but by the end of the speech, this calling out for salvation is associated with the name and authority of the Lord Messiah Jesus, in whose name baptism takes place (Acts 2:21 with 2:36–39). His authority is active in the distribution of benefits of the divine promise of the divine program...Philip preaches the Christ and the kingdom in the name of Jesus Christ to Samaritans (Acts 8:5, 12). Baptism takes place "in the name of the Lord Jesus" (8:16)...At this point, the Spirit falls on the Gentiles, and they are "baptized in the name of Jesus Christ" (Acts 10:45–48)...In fact, the identity is so strong that one now acts "in the name of Lord Jesus Christ," as we saw so repeatedly in the last chapter's narrative survey. Jesus even bears the title "Lord," the title normally used of Yahweh in the LXX. His exalted position can be seen through a comparison with statements in the Hebrew Scripture about Yahweh. In those texts, such actions had occurred in the name of Yahweh; now they occur in Jesus' name. So the transition to "in the name of Jesus" is significant...to deal with Jesus is to deal with God...When Peter initially makes this remark in his speech, the listener would assume that one calls on the God of Israel for this salvation, but by the time his speech ends, it is clear that it is the name of Jesus Christ, who is Lord as well as Messiah, that is invoked (Acts 2:30–38). Acts 2:38 deserves a closer look on this point. The person who turns toward God calls on the name of the Lord by being baptized "in the name of Jesus Christ..."[98]

---

[98] Darrell L. Bock is Professor of New Testament at Dallas Theological Seminary, Texas.

153. Haenchen, Ernst (1971). *The Acts of The Apostles A Commentary*. Philadelphia, Pennsylvania: The Westminster Press, pp. 92, 554, 556:

> "In his teaching concerning the Holy Spirit, likewise, Luke does not yet show the balance attained by later theology in the doctrine of the Trinity...Hence W. Michaelis 735f. thinks it better to consider Apollos himself a pilgrim to Jordan who had left Palestine before Good Friday. But in that case it still needs to be explained how in the next twenty years he had met no ·perfect Christian' who could have taught him about Easter and Pentecost. Beyer (I14), Schlatter (228) and Lake (Beg. IV 231) think of Apollos as knowing something about the resurrection, but as not yet possessing the correct-or later-understanding of baptism (baptism in the name of Jesus)...Therefore Luke is quite correct in having Paul encounter them not in the Ephesian congregation but in an unidentified place somewhere. It comes to light as their real failing that they were not baptized with the right baptism, the baptism in the name of Jesus."[99]

154. Holmes, Stephen R. (2012). *The Quest for The Trinity The Doctrine of God in Scripture, History and Modernity*. Downers Grove, Illinois: InterVarsity Press, see Chapter 2:

> "I have already mentioned the triadic baptismal formula, to which may be added the witness of Acts that baptism in the name of Jesus alone was also common (Acts 2:38; 8:16; 10:48)."[100]

155. Emery, Giles and Matthew Levering (ed.) (2011). *The Oxford Handbook of The Trinity*. Oxford: Oxford University Press, p. 474:

> "Trinitarian faith has its first attestation in the conclusion of Matthew's Gospel: 'Go, and make disciples of all nations, in the name of the Father, and of the Son, and of the Holy Spirit' (Matt. 28:19). But the dogma of the Trinity was only articulated slowly, under the duress of controversies and through a tremendous work of reflection. Tertullian's Against Praxeas is the first treatise

---

[99] Ernst Haenchen was a German Protestant Theologian, Professor and Biblical Scholar.

[100] Dr. Stephen R. Homes is Senior Lecturer in Systematic Theology at the University of St. Andrews, Scotland.

on the Trinity. It would be followed, in the East, by the writings of Basil of Caesarea, notably in his Against Eunomius (363–4), and of Gregory of Nazianzus (around 380) in his Theological Discourses, and in the West by those of Novatian (c.250), Hilary of Poitiers (356–60), Faustinus (a priest of the Luciferian sect, around 380), and of Augustine of Hippo (399–419)."

156. Freed, Edwin D. (2005). *The Apostle Paul and His Letters*. London & Connecticut: Equinox Publishing Ltd, pp. 29-30:

"(3) Persons are baptized in the name of Jesus without any reference to the Holy Spirit (Acts 8.1-16; see also Acts 8.12; 1 Cor. 1.13-15). (4) Baptism in the name of Jesus brings the Holy Spirit upon believers (Acts 2.38-41). (5) Baptism in the name of Jesus is followed by the apostles laying their hands on the persons baptized in order for them to receive the Spirit (Acts 8.14-18; 19.1-7). We have learned that according to Acts 19.4-6, Paul baptized some disciples of John the Baptist at Ephesus in the name of the Lord Jesus and that when Paul had laid his hands on them, 'the Holy Spirit came upon them... In 1 Cor. 1.13-17 Paul alludes to baptism in the name of Jesus....'"[101]

157. Hare, Douglas R. A. (1967). *The Theme of Jewish Persecutions of Christians in The Gospel According to St. Matthew* Society for New Testament Studies Monograph Series 6. Cambridge: At The University Press, pp. 11, 13:

"The convert was initiated by means of baptism in the name of Jesus, a rite comparable to Jewish proselyte-baptism, but circumcision was not required...Baptism in the name of the Messiah Jesus distinguished those who would survive the eschatological catastrophe from those who would not (Acts 2: 38-40)."[102]

---

[101]Edwin D. Freed is Emeritus Professorj of Religion, Gettysburg College, having taught biblical studies for thirty-six years.
[102]Douglas R. A. Hare, Assistant Professor of New Testament, Pittsburgh Theological Seminary.

158. Levering, Matthew (2012). *Jesus and The Demise of Death Resurrection, Afterlife and the Fate of the Christian*. Waco, Texas: Baylor University Press, p. 65:

> "Wondering whether the kingdom has arrived, the multitude asks Peter what they should do. Peter urges them to repent and be baptized. Now that the Spirit has been poured out, as Joel prophesied would happen prior to the coming of "the day of the Lord" (Acts 2:20, quoting Joel 2:30), repentance and baptism in the name of Jesus brings the gift of the Holy Spirit that will save the people from the coming eschatological judgment."

159. Armstrong, John H. (ed) (2007). *Understanding Four Views on Baptism*. Grand Rapids, Michigan: Zondervan, see Introduction:

> "Baptism in water clearly was universal in the early Christian church. It was accepted and practiced always and everywhere as the self-evident beginning and foundation of the Christian life. By it people were admitted into the visible church. In its form it was a simple action. A person went into or under the water in the name of Jesus (Acts 19:5)....The required response, manifest genuinely by "all whom the Lord our God will call," was repentance and baptism particularly in the name of Jesus Christ. Those who were baptized were the ones "who accepted his message" (2:41)...The baptism "in the name of Jesus Christ" (Acts 2:38) identified their present acceptance of the truth preached about Jesus."

160. Moore, Charles E. (ed.) (2016). *Called to Community The Life Jesus Wants for His People*. Walden, New York: Plough Publishing House, see Chapter 6:

> "On the day of Pentecost, to be saved meant to join the messianic community. On that day, baptism in the name of Jesus Christ was a public act of acknowledging that Jesus was truly the Messiah, the rightful leader of God's people, and a declaration of allegiance to him by throwing in one's lot with the original apostolic band."

161. Peterson, David G. (2013). *Encountering God Together Biblical Patterns for Ministry and Worship*. Nottingham, England: Inter-Varsity Press, pp. 103-104, 144:

"The command to be baptized 'in the name of Jesus Christ' (Acts 2:38) is linked with a call to repent. Baptism in the name of Jesus Christ suggests that the person being baptized actually calls upon Jesus as Lord and Messiah, as a way of confessing faith in him... Baptism 'in the name of the Father and of the Son and of the Holy Spirit' and baptism 'in the name of Jesus Christ' are one and the same. Acknowledging Jesus as Lord and Messiah effectively means confessing that he is the Son of God, sent to be the only Saviour of Israel and the nations. Calling upon him to receive the promised Holy Spirit is another way of acknowledging his divinity and affirming God as Trinity (see Acts 2:33)...Union with Christ in baptism is suggested by its administration 'in the name of Jesus'... The early Christian practice of baptizing three times in response to the confession of God as Trinity is no more valid than a single washing with water. This is an area where custom may vary without hindering our unity in the act of baptism itself. As already noted, calling upon Jesus as Lord for forgiveness and the Holy Spirit in baptism is another way of expressing baptism in the name of the Trinity."

162. Bradshaw, Paul (2010) (2nd ed.). *Early Christian Worship A basic Introduction to Ideas and Practice.* London: SPCK, see Part 1, Christian Initiation:

"Several New Testament passages speak of baptism being 'in the name of Jesus' (see, for example, Acts 2.38), which suggests that his name was invoked in some way during the ceremony. This could have been in the form of a statement made over the candidate (e.g. 'I baptize you in the name of...'), such as we find in later Syrian usage, but it need not necessarily have been restricted to that. It could also have referred to some confession of faith in Jesus made by the candidate at the moment of baptism, such as we find in later Western sources...[see footnote 1] There is also a passage in the apocryphal Acts of Paul where Thecla immerses herself in water, saying, 'In the name of Jesus Christ I baptize myself...', which seems to point to a formula something like 'I baptize you in the name of Jesus Christ' as having been usual in early times. See J. K. Elliott, The Apocryphal New Testament (Clarendon, Oxford 1993), p. 370."

163. Moule, C. F. D. (3rd ed.) (2000). *The Holy Spirit*. London and New York: Continuum, p. 33:

> "Membership in the Christian community is brought to a sacramental focus in Christian baptism. Baptism is in the name of Jesus Christ (Matt. 28.19, Acts 2.38, etc.); it brings one into membership in his body, and so into organic relations with other Christians (1 Cor. 12.13); it means a sharing in the obedience of Christ himself as Son of God, in his death and resurrection (Rom. 6.3 ff.); and it is accompanied by the Holy Spirit (Acts 2.38,1 Cor. 12.13, etc.)."

164. _____. The Nature and Mission of the Church A Stage on the Way to a Common Statement. Faith and Order Paper 198, World Council of Churches, Geneva, Switzerland, p. 21:

> "(e) the difference between the churches which baptise insisting on the Trinitarian formula according to the command of Jesus (Mt 28:19-20), and those which insist that baptism "in the name of Jesus Christ" is more consistent with the practice of the apostles (cf. Acts 2:38)."

165. Voorst, Robert E. Van (1989). *The Ascents of James History and Theology of a Jewish-Christian Community*. SBL Dissertation Series 112. Atlanta, Georgia: Scholar Press, pp. 37, 99, 152, 180:

> "(6) The "three-fold invocation" contradicts the source's uniform use of baptism in the name of Jesus… L has in "by the invocation of his [the prophet's] name" in the statement of forgiveness through baptism. Baptism "in the name of Jesus" is well-attested in the Acts (2:38; 8:16; 19:5) and is the rule elsewhere in the NT where a specific formula is given (Rom 6:3,1 Cor 1:13-15; Gal 3:27). 2 7 Apart from the AJ, the PsCl knows only the triadic formula of baptism, which is found in the NT only in Matt 28:19. Two other second-century witnesses to baptism in the name of Jesus are Did. 7:1 and Justin's Apol. 1.61. For another reference in the AJ to baptism in the name of Jesus, see 1.39.3 (L). Although not a part of the AJ, 1.73.4 refers back to the AJ at 1.69.8 -1.70.1, where baptism in the name of Jesus is implied… Although Rehm and Strecker do not mention it, "observe everything that he

commanded" (L) / "do all those things that he commanded" (S) is drawn from Matt 28:20, "observe all that I have commanded." This verse immediately follows the triadic formula of baptism in 28:19. The AJ must have been familiar with the ending of Matthew to draw on 28:20, yet it can ignore the triadic formula in favor of baptism "in the name of Jesus"...Baptism now conveys in reality what sacrifice formerly was believed to convey: the forgiveness of sins. It is done "in the name of Jesus" because Jesus, the Mosaic Prophet, gave it to complete Moses' work. While this witness to baptism in Jesus' name is preserved only in L, we saw that it likely lies behind S as well...In this study, we have isolated a hypothetical source in R 1.33-71, and identified it as The Ascents of James. The AJ stems from a Greek-speaking Jewish-Christian community living probably in Transjordan and can be dated in the second half of the second century. This community practices baptism in the name of Jesus and observes the law of Moses, of which circumcision is possibly a part."

166. Allen, Ronald J. (2013). *Acts of the Apostles*. Minneapolis: Fortress Press:

"For Luke baptism takes place only in the name of Jesus and not in the name of the Father, Son and Holy Spirit (Matt. 28:16-20)...The focus on the baptism of Jesus invites a sermon on Luke's understanding of baptism, including the fact that Luke sees baptism in the name of Jesus as normative (rather than God, Jesus and the Spirit)...Matthew prescribes baptism in the name of God, Jesus and the Holy Spirit (Matt. 28:16-28), whereas Acts only calls for baptism in the name of Jesus (Acts 10:48; cf. Acts 2:38; 8:16; 19:5)."

167. Swete, Henry Barclay (1912). *The Holy Spirit in The Ancient Church A Study of Christian Teachings in the Ancient Fathers*. London: Macmillan & Co, pp. 120-121, 234:

"Yet the freedom of the Spirit s grace is not to be used as a plea for neglecting the means of grace or the customs of the Church. Baptism in the Name of Jesus Christ by whomsoever given, is to be accepted and supplemented by the invocation of the Holy Spirit, in accordance with the time-honoured practice of our forefathers in the faith...And this reply cannot be set aside by urging that the Apostles baptized in the name of Jesus only."[103]

168. Strange, James Riley (2010). *The Moral World of James Setting the Epistle in its Greco-Roman and Judaic Environments*. Studies in Biblical Literature 136, pp. 35, 47:

> "Within the broader context of New Testament writings, the phrase also resonates with other religious acts done "in the name of Jesus"—primarily baptisms and healings, but also proclamation and gathering together—in the boo k o f Acts and the Pauline literature... Acts 2:38 (baptism "in the name of Jesus Christ"); 3:6 (healing "in the name of Jesus Christ of Nazareth"; cf. 3:16); 10:48 (baptism "in the name of Jesus Christ"); 16:17 (exorcism 'in the name of Jesus Christ"); 19:5 (baptism "in the name of the Lord Jesus"). Incidences of speaking and preaching boldly "in the name of Jesus Christ" (thus mirroring the prophetic discourse of James 5:10) occur in Acts 4:18; 5:40; 9:27. In 1 Cor 1:13 Paul asks, "Were you baptized in the name of Paul?"; he answers his own rhetorical question in 6:11 by asserting, "But you were washed, you were sanctified, you were justified in the name of the Lord Jesus Christ"; and in 5:4 he speaks of the congregation "gathered in the name of our Lord Jesus" (contra NRSV). Cf. Mat 28:19; Col 3:17."[104]

169. Zetterholm, Magnus & Byrskog, Samuel (2012). *The Making of Christianity Conflicts, Contacts, and Construction: Essays in Honor of Bengt Holmberg*. Coniectanea Biblica New Testament Series 47. Winona Lake, Indiana: Eisenbrauns, p. 58:

> "In the book of Acts, John's baptism is consistently spoken of in the singular (1:22; 10:37; 13:24; 18:25; 19:3–4), which suggests that the ritual was not repeated. Josephus also speaks of John's baptism in the singular; seen. 14 below. According to Acts, Apollos, who knew only the baptism of John, was instructed more accurately in the "way of God" by Priscilla and Aquila, but

---

[103]Henry Barclay Swete, Regius Professor of Divinity in the University of Cambridge, Hon. Canon of Ely; Hon. Chaplain to the King.
[104]James Rile Strange, Professor of Biblical and Religious Studies, Samford University.

nothing is said about his being baptized in the name of Jesus (18:24–28). Paul, however, baptizes "in the name of the Lord Jesus" those disciples in Ephesus who knew only the baptism of John and had not received the holy spirit (19:1–7)."

170. Kung, Hans (2007). *Islam Past, Present & Future*. Oxford: Oneworld Publication, pp. 39, 505:

"The background here is made up of Greek-speaking Jewish Christians, probably in Transjordan, in the second half of the second century. They practised baptism in the name of Jesus but at the same time observed the law of Moses (and probably also circumcision)...At the beginning—in the New Testament— threefold formulas appear without emphasis on a unity: simple triadic (not 'trinitarian') confessional statements. The triadic baptismal formula in Matthew's community tradition ('Baptize in the name of the Father, and of the Son, and of the Holy Spirit'1) developed from the simple christological baptismal formula ('Baptize in the name of Jesus Christ'). A trinitarian speculation which was intellectually highly demanding and which emphasized the unity of the three entities came increasingly to be built on this."[105]

171. Thompson, Nicholas (2005). *Eucharistic Sacrifice and Patristic Tradition in the Theology of Martin Baucer 1534-1546*. Leiden: Brill, p. 43:

"In his *Enchiridion* Eck took what Polman describes as the Catholics' 'characteristic pleasure' in arguing that, for the sake of consistency, the Reformers should not accept the perpetual virginity of Mary, the homoousion, or the 'Lord's day,' since none had explicit scriptural warrant. Eck argued that it was clear from references to Baptism in the name of Jesus in the book of Acts, that the apostolic church had seen fit to modify even the trinitarian baptismal formula ordained by Jesus." [Johannes Eck

---

[105]Dr. Hans Kung was a Swiss Catholic Priest, Theologian and was President of the Foundation for a Global Ethic (Weltethos). From 1960 until his retirement in 1996, he was Professor of Ecumenical Theology and Director of the Institute for Ecumenical Research at the University of Tübingen. He is a scholar of theology and philosophy and a prolific writer.

(1486-1543) was a German Scholastic Theologian, Catholic Prelate and Martin Luther's principal Roman Catholic opponent].[106]

172. Pokorny, Petr (2013). *From Gospel to The Gospels History, Theology and Impact of The Biblical Term 'Euangelion.'* Boston & Berlin: Walter de Gruyter, pp. 19-20:

> "Unlike the baptism of John, in Christian baptism (baptism "in the name of Jesus Christ"), the culmination was the moment when the baptised person came up out of the water...Baptism by water in the name of Jesus Christ became the Christian entrance rite in a surprisingly short span of time. In the time of Paul it was already widely practised (see e. g. Gal 3:27). The time in which Christians started to baptise in the name of Jesus and the time in which the gospel was spread through the formula of the death and resurrection of Jesus Christ are almost identical."[107]

173. Hartman, Lars (1997). *'Into The Name of The Lord Jesus'* Studies of the New Testament and Its World. Edinburgh: T&T Clark, pp. 37-38, 48, 164:

> "For some reason the first Christians spoke of their baptism as one 'in the name of Jesus Christ' or 'into the name of the Lord Jesus'...It is entirely possible that, say, in Jewish-Christian circles, baptism was performed 'in the name of Jesus the Messiah'...Be that as it may, we have already touched on the possibility that at an early stage baptism could also be performed 'in the name of Jesus Christ' or 'in the name of Jesus the Messiah'...Thus the formula 'into the name of the Lord Jesus' is older than the earliest of the New Testament texts dealt with above. It seems to suggest that Jesus was very early regarded as being a living, heavenly authority who made the baptismal rite meaningful."[108]

---

[106]Dr. Nicholas Thompson is Lecturer in Church History at the University of Aberdeen.
[107]Petr Pokorny was Professor of New Testament Studies at the Protestant Theological Faculty of Charles University.
[108]Lars Hartman was a Swedish scholar and Professor of New Testament Exegesis at Uppsala University, Sweden.

174. Finn, Thomas M. (1997). *From Death to Rebirth Ritual and Conversion in Antiquity*. Mahwah, New Jersey: Paulist Press, p. 141:

> "To distinguish it from other baptisms, especially John's, earliest Christian baptism was performed "in the name of the Lord Jesus," as one learns from both Paul's letters and Luke's Acts of the Apostles."[109]

175. Bender, Ross T. & Sell, Alan P. I. (ed.) (1991). *Baptism, Peace and the State in the Reformed and Mennonite Traditions*. Waterloo, Ontario: Wilfrid Laurier University Press, pp. 18-19:

> "The inclusion of a reference to baptism in the risen Christ's great commission, "Go therefore and make disciples of all nations, baptizing them in the name of the Father, and of the Son, and of the Holy Spirit" (Matt. 28:19), does not remove this uncertainty. Some commentators see it as a very late insertion, noting that Eusebius and other fourth-century writers quote the great commission text without it…Whether at the end of the first century or in the fourth, it was probably added to reflect the practice of the Church… The rest of the New Testament carries the practice forward with the same subordinate function. Peter commands baptism "in the name of Jesus Christ for the forgiveness of your sins" (Acts 2:38)…that water was used, that the Holy Spirit was received (Acts 19:2-6), and that the act was done in the name of the Lord Jesus, or Jesus Christ."

176. Tuner, S.T.D., Paul (2008). *Catholic Initiation or Christian Initiation of Adults* in Deep Down Things Essays on Catholic Culture. Cirincione, Joseph A. (ed.). Lanham, Maryland: Lexington Books, p. 3:

> "Adults may join the Catholic Church either through the baptismal rites of Christian initiation or through the Rite of Reception into the Full Communion of the Catholic Church. If they have never been baptized, adults celebrate the rites of initiation: baptism, confirmation; and first communion—altogether, normally at the Easter Vigil. If they have already been baptized in another Christian community, the Catholic Church

---

[109]*Thomas M. Finn, Chancellor Professor of Religion, Emeritus, College of William and Mary, Williamsburg, Virginia.*

will probably recognize their baptism. (There are exceptions; for example, baptism in the name of Jesus and not in the name of the Trinity.)"[110]

177. Schweitzer, Albert (2005). *The Quest of The Historical Jesus.* Mineola, New York: Dover Publications, Inc., see II:

> "In the first place the genuineness of the command to baptize in Matt. xxviii. 19 is questionable, not only as a saying ascribed to the risen Jesus, but also because it is universalistic in outlook, and because it implies the doctrine of the Trinity and, consequently, the metaphysical Divine Sonship of Jesus. In this it is inconsistent with the earliest traditions regarding the practice of baptism in the Christian community, for in the earliest times, as we learn from the Acts and from Paul, it was the custom to baptize, not in the name of the Trinity, but in the name of Jesus, the Messiah."[111]

178. Davison, Andrew (2013). *Why Sacraments?* London: SPCK, see section speaking about, *Does the form and matter of sacraments change?*:

> "In the early Church we see a rare example of the Church changing the form of a sacrament, to the extent that a previously valid form came to be considered as invalid, now not a legitimate option. The example relates to baptism 'in the name of Jesus'. Although the Trinitarian form was by far the most common in the early Church, the Jesus-only formula was considered a valid form for the sacrament because it is found in the book of Acts (2.38; 8.16; 10.48; 19.5; 22.16) There was nothing about baptizing in the name of Jesus that contradicted baptism in the Trinitarian name. Once the person of Christ was under heated debate, however, those who denied the Trinity could take refuge in the Jesus-only formula as a way to deny a Trinitarian understanding of God. After Arius—who denied that Jesus was fully divine—the Jesus only form no longer made clear that someone was being

---

[110] Dr. Paul Turner is Pastor of Cathedral of The Immaculate Conception in Kansas City, Missouri, and Director of the Office of Divine Worship for the Catholic Diocese of Kansas City-St. Joseph.

[111] Albert Schweitzer (1875-1965) was a Alsatian-German theologian, philosopher, organist, and mission doctor in equatorial Africa, who received the 1952 Nobel Prize for Peace for his efforts in behalf of "the Brotherhood of Nations."

baptized into the Trinitarian faith of the Church."[112]

179. Mays, James L. (ed.) (1998). *Acts Interpretation A Biblical Commentary for Teaching and Preaching*, Atlanta: John Know Press, p. 38:

"…the early baptismal formula, baptism "in the name of Jesus Christ" (v. 38)…."

180. Walker, Williston (1921). *A History of The Christian Church*. New York: Charles Scribner's Sons, pp. 57-58, 95

"To Christian thought at the beginning of the second century the Holy Spirit was differentiated from Christ, but was classed, like Him, with God. This appears in the Trinitarian baptismal formula,' which was displacing the older baptism in the name of Christ… With the early disciples generally, baptism was "in the name of Jesus Christ," There is no mention of baptism in the name of the Trinity in the New Testament, except in the command attributed to Christ in Matt. 28:19…The Christian leaders of the third century retained the recognition of the earlier form, and, in Rome at least, baptism in the name of Christ was deemed valid, if irregular, certainly from the time of Bishop Stephen (254-257)."[113]

181. Silvoso, Ed (2017). *Ekklesia Rediscovering God's Instrument for Global Transformation*. Bloomington, Minnesota: Chosen Books:

"We see an example of this in Samaria in Acts 8, where such a baptism was done "simply" (only, exclusively) in the name of Jesus… So then, water baptism in the name of Jesus (death of the old), as seen in the New Testament, and baptism in the Holy Spirit (resurrection life and power), as also practiced by the Ekklesia… by baptizing them in water in the name of Jesus and laying his hands on them for the Holy Spirit to come on them… We know that Jesus, through His disciples, baptized in water, as

---

[112]The Revd Dr Andrew Davison is Tutor in Doctrine at Westcott House, Cambridge, where he himself trained, and an affiliated lecturer in the Cambridge University Theological Faculty. He was formerly Tutor in doctrine at St Stephen's House, Oxford and a member of the Oxford Theology Faculty.
[113]Williston Walker was Titus Street Professor of Ecclesiastical History in Yale University.

John did (see John 3:22; 4:1). It was not the baptism with the Holy Spirit, however, as Jesus made clear in John 7:38–39. The baptism His disciples administered in the gospels was a baptism to acknowledge Him as the Messiah, which was also the baptism Philip used when many Samaritans who had believed were "simply baptized in Jesus' name"...the Ekklesia practiced water baptism in the name of Jesus..."

182. O'Collins SJ, Gerald (2014). *The Tripersonal God Understanding and Interpreting The Trinity.* (2nd ed.). Mahwah, New Jersey: Paulist Press:

"What we do not yet find in the Lucan writings is a trinitarian formula for baptism. Acts depicts the first Christians as baptizing in the name of Jesus and the gift of the Holy Spirit being connected with baptism...Luke writes of the gift of the Holy Spirit both as following on baptism in the name of Jesus (Acts 8:14–17; 19:1–7) and as preceding baptism in Jesus' name (Acts 10:44–48)...This is done by Matthew, who puts into the mouth of the risen Jesus the tripartite formula: "Make disciples of all nations, baptizing them in the name of the Father and of the Son and of the Holy Spirit" (Mt 28:19)."

183. Ferguson, Everett (2009). *Baptism in The Early Church History, Theology and Liturgy in The First Five Centuries.* Grand Rapids, Michigan: William B. Eerdmans Publishing Company:

"George Montague writes part one on the New Testament evidence. Although carefully differentiating the viewpoints of different authors, he offers these conclusions on the New Testament evidence (pp. 76-80): the rite of initiation always involves water baptism in the name of Jesus and the gift of the Holy Spirit..." (Matt. 28:18-20)...The historicity of this command is widely rejected in New Testament critical scholarship [see footnote 439 citing] "Jack Dean Kingsbury, "The Composition and Christology of Matt. 28:16- 20," Journal of Biblical Literature 93 (1974):573-584, argues that the whole is a Matthaean composition. B. J. Hubbard, The Matthean Redaction of a Primitive Apostolic Commissioning (Missoula: Scholars Press, 1974), contends that a proto-commission is behind Matthew, Luke, and John (and Ps.-Mark); John P. Meier, "Two

Disputed Questions in Matt. 28:16-20," Journal of Biblical Literature 96 (1977):407-424, concludes that behind this heavily redacted pericope lies a pre-Matthaean tradition. P. Boyd Mather, "Christian Prophecy and Matthew 28:16-20: A Test Exegesis," Society of Biblical Literature Seminar Papers 1977 (Missoula: Scholars Press), pp. 103-115, argues that the words are those of an early Christian prophet speaking for Jesus"... New arguments, however, from context and from the poetry-like structure of other passages in Matthew have been advanced in support of a shorter text as original in Matthew 28:19 [see footnote 443 citing] Hans Kosmala, "The Conclusion of Matthew," Annual of the Swedish Theological Institute, Vol. 4, pp. 132-147, argued for the originality of Eusebius's short text from its poetic structure and the importance of the name of Jesus in Matthew. David Flusser, "The Conclusion of Matthew in a New Jewish Christian Source," in the same journal, Vol. 5, pp. 110-120, supported Kosmala by referring to a Jewish Christian text that rejected Matt. 28:19 among the sayings falsely ascribed to Jesus (because the sect rejected the Trinity); the contention that another saying, "Instruct people in accordance with instructions I have given you, and be for them what I have been for you," shows a dependence on Eusebius's shorter text is tenuous. H. B. Green, "Matthew 28:19, Eusebius, and the lex orandi," in Rowan Williams, ed., The Making of Orthodoxy: Essays in Honour of Henry Chadwick (Cambridge: Cambridge University Press, 1989), pp. 124-141, expanded the literary argument. Eusebius quotes Matthew 28:19 in three forms: (i) a summary form, "Go... nations" (9 times); (ii) the short text, "Go . . . nations in my name" (16 times); and (iii) the canonical text (5 times) (p. 126). Since the short text is Eusebius's preferred way of citing the passage, Green argues that he knew manuscripts with this reading. He sets out Matt. 11:28-30; 5:3-10; and 1:20b-21 as representing a similar structure to this short text (pp. 126ff.)...In the present text (2:38) the baptism is "in the name of Jesus Christ" (a water baptism)...The baptism was an administered act and not self-performed. It was done in the name of Jesus Christ... Cyprian mentions Marcionites "baptized in the name of Jesus Christ" (Letters 73 [72].4.1)...In the same context as the preceding quotation Cyprian speaks of Marcionites being baptized "in the name of Jesus

Christ"…Letters 73 (72).4.1. See chap. 17 and chap. 24, where evidence is given that Marcion did not use a different baptismal formula [see footnote 1194]."[114]

184. Wielenga, Bastiaan (2016). *The Reformed Baptism Form A Commentary*. Jenison, Michigan: Reformed Free Publishing Association, see Chapter Two:

> "Thus we do not need to take more time than necessary regarding whether baptism in the name of Jesus was in vogue in the early Christian church. Where the few expressions in the book of Acts seem to point to such practice."[115]

185. Dunn, James D. G. (1993). *The Theology of Paul's Letter to The Galatians New Testament Theology*. Cambridge: Cambridge University Press:

> "For an analysis of the theology of Galatians itself, however, it is sufficient to note that prior to the Jerusalem consultation Paul had been preaching to Gentiles for some time (as a missionary of the church at Antioch), and that the church at Antioch and its daughter churches accepted Gentiles as members (by baptism in the name of Jesus Christ) without requiring them to be circumcised…We can well imagine, therefore, how important the issue was for the Galatians. By responding in faith to the message of Christ crucified, and by accepting baptism in the name of Jesus."

186. Goll, James W. (2011). *A Radical Faith Essentials For Spirit-Filled Believers*. Bloomington, Minnesota: Chosen Books:

> "What did Jesus tell His disciples to do? He said, "Go therefore and make disciples of all the nations, baptizing them in the name of the Father and of the Son and of the Holy Spirit" (Matthew 28:19). This has become the formulaic wording for baptisms ever since, although the exact wording must be less important than the idea of the Name. After all, the early Church baptized new

---

[114]This work was cited earlier also.
[115]Bastiaan Wielenga (1873-1949) was a prominent minister of the Word in the Reformed Churches in the Netherlands (GKN) in the early to mid-1900s.

converts "in the name of the Lord Jesus" (see Acts 19:5 and elsewhere) without mentioning the Father and the Holy Spirit. Did the Church disobey when those early disciples omitted two members of the Trinity? I don't think so. They meant the same thing. To baptize in the name of Jesus expresses the reality of the fact that in baptism we come into a close unity with God, and that, in fact, we pass into His ownership. Being baptized in the name of the Lord Jesus is the same as being baptized in the name of the Father, the Son Jesus and the Holy Spirit."

187. Johnson, Marshall D. (2002). *Making Sense of the Bible Literary Type as an Approach to Understanding.* Grand Rapids, Michigan: William B. Eerdsman Publishing Company, see section *Christian Hymns and Other Liturgical Texts*:

"Matthew concludes his Gospel with an announcement of the risen Jesus that includes a liturgical baptismal formula: "baptizing them in the name of the Father and of the Son and of the Holy Spirit . . . (28:19). This tripartite formula might well be a development that replaced baptism in the name of Jesus alone (see Acts 19:5; Rom. 6:3; 1 Cor. 1:13)."[116]

188. Streett, R. Alan (2018). *Caesar and the Sacrament Baptism: A Rite of Resistance.* Eugene, Oregon: Cascade Books, see footnote 306:

"Were you baptized into the name of Paul?" supports the premise that baptism "in the name of Jesus" is formulaic. Ferguson, Baptism , 149, rightly concludes, "The force of the argument is that the nature of one's baptism determines one's identity—whose name one wears, with whom one is associated, and to whom one is a disciple."[117]

189. Montague, George T. (2011). *First Corinthians Catholic Commentary on Sacred Scripture.* Grand Rapids, Michigan: Baker Academics, pp. 12-13:

---

[116]Marshall D. Johnson retired Director of Fortress Press and former Fulbright lecturer and researcher at the University of Bergen, Norway.

[117]R. Alan Streett is Senior Research Professor of Biblical Exegesis and the W. A. Criswell Endowed Chair of Expository Preaching at Criswell College, Dallas, Texas.

"...if the simple formula "in the name of Jesus" was used, it would clearly imply everything that Jesus revealed about the Father and the Holy Spirit...The Catholic Church accepts as valid only the Trinitarian formula, as found in Matt 28:19. It is the only place in the New Testament where a baptismal formula is said to be specifically ordered by Jesus. In the Acts of the Apostles, people are said to be baptized "in the name of Jesus" (Acts 2:38; 8:16; 10:48; 19:5)...If at one time the early Church may have baptized "in the name of Jesus," that was not in denial of the Trinity."

190. Thompson, James W. (2020). *Apostle of Persuasion Theology and Rhetoric in the Pauline Letters.* Grand Rapid, Michigan: Baker Academic:

"For the first believers, baptism was "in the name of Jesus"... Baptism in the name of Jesus also reflected an explicit Christology (Acts 2:38; 10:48). Peter's announcement that Jesus has become "Lord and Christ" (Acts 2:36 RSV) indicates the christological reflection at the beginning. Christos, the Greek translation of the Hebrew messiah, was the royal figure of Jewish expectation."

191. Ziesler, J. A. (1979). *The Name of Jesus in the Acts of the Apostles. Journal for the Study of the New Testament.* Volume 2, Issue 4, p. 29:

"1. Baptism 'in the name of' Jesus Christ (Acts 2.38; 8.16; 10.48; 19.5; perhaps 22.16). In 22.16, the conjunction of baptism and forgiveness with 'calling upon his name' justifies us in bearing it in mind when looking at this group of passages. Baptism in the name of Jesus Christ is associated with the coming of the Holy Spirit, which may precede it as in 10.48, or follow it at once as in 2.38 (presumably) and 19.5, or after a considerable interval as in 8.16... It could be that both 10.48 and 2.38 refer to the authority with which the baptism is carried out, 'In the name of Jesus I baptise...it is possible that something like 22.16 is in mind in both 2.38 and 10.48, i.e. the baptisand calls on the name of Jesus."[118]

192. Bevenot SJ, Maurice (1978). *Cyprian's Platform in The Rebaptism Controversy.* The Heythrop Journal. Volume 19, Issue 2 (April), p. 130:

---

[118]J. A. Ziesler was a lecturer in the University of Bristol, England.

"Did Stephen in fact admit that heretical baptism conferred all those blessings which Cyprian rightly held to depend on the presence and activity of the Holy Spirit? We may take it that he attached some importance to 'baptism in the name of Jesus' which, presumably, some of the 'heretics' were using (ep. 743, cf. 73,16)."

193. Soyars, Jonathan E. (2019). *The Shepherd of Hermas and the Pauline Legacy*. Supplement to Novum Testamentum Volume 176. Leiden: Brill, p. 196-197:

"However, most scholars agree that the name of the "Lord" at Vis. 3.7.3 [15.3] into which persons are baptized probably refers instead to the name of Christ.19 The plausibility of this suggestion is confirmed by Hermas's explicitly mentioning the "name of the Son of God" elsewhere in the Shepherd, which he does at least nine times…" see also footnote 19 "Among those scholars who understand "Lord" at Vis. 3.7.3 [15.3] to be a reference to baptism in the name of Jesus are the following: Lake, "Shepherd of Hermas and Christian Life," 35; Dibelius, Hirt, 470; Lampe, Seal of the Spirit, 105; Pernveden, Concept of the Church, 165–66; Brox, Hirt, 138; Leutzsch, Hirt, 419 n. 364; Osiek, Shepherd, 74 n. 49; Sandnes, "Seal and Baptism," 1451 n. 38."

194. Richardson, Canon R. D. (1943). *The Doctrine of the Trinity: Its Development, Difficulties and Value*. Harvard Theological Review, Volume 36, Issue 02, p. 112:

"The grace of our Lord Jesus Christ be with you" 9 was probably the first approach to a formula…" see footnote 9 "Cf. I Thess. v, 28 and I Cor. xvi, 28. Cf. also Baptism in the Name of Jesus only; e.g. Acts xix, 5."

195. Astley, Jeff (2015). *Forming Disciples: Some Educational and Biblical Reflections*. Rural Theology, Volume 13, No. 1 (May), p. 11-12:

"…the practice of baptism 'in the name of Jesus' (Acts 2: 38 etc.), which evidently implied becoming Jesus' follower (1 Corinthians 1: 12 –15), signifies a continuing appropriation of the idea of discipleship beyond Easter."

196. Vorster, Hans (1999). *We Confess One Baptism for the Forgiveness of Sins New Impulses for the Ecumenical Discussion of Baptism.* The Ecumenical Review, Volume 51, Issue 3, The Quarterly of the World Council of Churches, p. 303:

> "In addition, the baptism of John is given predominantly, even if probably not exclusively, to Jews. Bestowal of the Spirit takes place only with the coming of the Messiah. Baptism in the name of Jesus (later in the name of the Father, the Son and the Holy Spirit)...."[119]

197. O'Dea, Paul (1950). *Early Christian Baptism and the Creed by Joseph H. Crehan Review by: Paul O'Dea.* The Irish Monthly, Vol. 78, No. 924 (Jun., 1950), p. 294:

> "Our Lord, in the last chapter of St. Matthew, bade the Apostles baptize" in the name of the Father and of the Son and of the Holy Ghost". Yet, in the Acts of the Apostles we read of people being baptized "in the name of Jesus Christ" (2, 38: 8, 16: 10, 48: 19, 3). The medieval theologians solved the apparent difficulty by supposing that the Apostles used the ' form' "in the name of Jesus Christ" by a special dispensation and only for a short time...But some have held that, while these are the direct meanings of the phrase, yet it implies that the invocation of the Name by the baptizer was an essential part of the rite. Father Crehan's solution is based on the idea that the phrase does not refer to the action of the minister, but to that of the person to be baptized. Baptism "in the name of Jesus" meant baptism in which the candidate invoked that Name."

198. Holladay, Carl R. (2012). *Baptism in the New Testament and Its Cultural Milieu: A Response to Everett Ferguson, Baptism in the Early Church.* Journal of Early Christian Studies, Volume 20, Number 3, Fall 2012, p. 368:

> "For such baptisms to be authentic, they must be predicated on faith in Jesus as the Christ. For this to occur, they must be administered "in the name of the Lord Jesus Christ." This may

---

[119] Hans Vorster served as a Protestant pastor in Stuttgart, then from 1982-1997/98 worked on behalf of the Evangelical Church in Germany at the Okumenische Centrale in Frankfurt am Main.

mean that some confessional formulation appropriating the name of Jesus was uttered in connection with the baptism, either by the baptizer or the one being baptized."

199. Whitaker, E. C. (1965). *The History of The Baptismal Formula.* The Journal of Ecclesiastical History. Volume 16, Issue 1, pp. 5-6:

"Similarly, in the Acts of Paul and Thecla, written the middle of the second century, Thecla is represented as baptising herself and saying, 'In the name of Jesus Christ do I baptise myself for the last day'. If we may assume that we have here a case of a formula in ordinary use adapted to extraordinary circumstances, then it appears that the formula in ordinary use must have been 'I baptise thee in the name of Jesus Christ'. This not only brings our evidence for a baptismal formula of this type to a very early date; it also strengthens the view, suggested in the Acts of the Apostles, that an invocation of Jesus Christ had a place in the baptismal practice of the early Church."[120]

200. Sandnes, Karl Olav (2011). *Seal and Baptism in Early Christianity in Ablution, Initiation, and Baptism, Late Antiquity, Early Judaism, and Early Christianity.* Berlin and New York: Walter de Gruyter, pp. 1451, 1465:

"These are the ones who have heard the word (οὗτοί εἰσιν οἱ τὸν λόγον ἀκούσαντες) and wanted to be baptized in the name of the Lord" (Herm. 15.3 [= Vis. 3.7.3]). This is the only occurrence of βαπτίζειν κτλ. found in the Shepherd of Hermas. Baptism happens "in the name of the Lord," a traditional formula associated with the initiation water rite. The role of the name here has some relevance for Sim. 9, since (see below) the reception of the name and the seal are thus intertwined" see also footnote 38 "I find the arguments that baptism in the name of Jesus is envisioned here convincing; see, e.g. Brox, Der Hirt des Hermas, 138; Osiek, Shepherd of Hermas, 74; L. Hartman, 'Into the Name of the Lord', 37–50. Cf. Acts 2:38; 10:48; 19:5…ATh 34–35 tells how Thecla accepted baptism and thus received the seal. Her request for the seal is now fulfilled, and she is about to suffer martyrdom. She spots a well or a pit with water in the arena,97

---

[120] E. C. Whitaker, Vicar of Kirkby-in-Furness, Lancashire.

"And she threw herself in, saying, 'In the name of Jesus Christ I baptize myself on my last day!'"

201. Martos, Joseph (2015). *Deconstructing Sacramental Theology and Reconstructing Catholic Ritual.* Eugene, Oregon: Resource Publication an imprint of Wipf & Stock, p. 78:

"...immersed in water in the name of Jesus..."[121]

202. Edwards, Mark (2018). *Early Ecclesiology in The West* in *The Oxford Handbook of Ecclesiology* edited by Paul Avis. Oxford: Oxford University Press, pp. 177-178:

"The catholic church in Africa had fallen under the Vandal yoke in 430 but was liberated in 534 by the strategy of Belisarius and the statesmanship of his master Justinian. Determined to return as subjects, not as slaves, the African bishops told Vigilius of Rome, after unctuous flattery of his office, that the royal condemnation of Cyril's antagonists Theodore, Ibas, and Theodoret was unacceptable to them because the dead had no opportunity to recant (Price 2012: 111). Justinian, who had also reconquered Rome through Belisarius, had just enough reverence for the see of Peter to kidnap Vigilius, detain him in Constantinople, and browbeat him into signing the acts of the Fifth Oecumenical Council in 553 (Price 2012: 42–59). Italian bishops outside the sway of Byzantium lost no time in excommunicating Vigilius, since he had forfeited his primacy by anathematizing three men whom the Council of Chalcedon had acquitted or ignored with the approbation of Pope Leo. From this nadir the papacy was rescued by the atrophy of Byzantine power in Italy and by the elevation of Gregory, the second bishop of Rome to be styled 'the Great'. The 'servant of the servants of God', as Gregory preferred to be known, reunited almost the whole of the former Western Empire under Roman primacy in the space of fourteen years (590–604). It was during his pontificate that the Visigoths of Spain, traducing their former selves as Arians, adopted the faith of the subjugated Catholics. It

---

[121] Joseph Martos is a retired Professor of Philosophy and Theology, who has been a visiting professor or guest lecturer at more than two dozen universities and seminaries during his career.

was Gregory who sent Augustine to evangelize the Kentish king who had married a Frankish princess, and thus inaugurated the reconversion of southern Britain. To judge by his Pastoral Rule and his letters, however, nothing was further from his thoughts than ecclesiastical despotism. The first quality required of any ruler, he asseverates in the former work, is humility (1.6); he must covet pre-eminence (Pastoral Rule 1.8), but regard all righteous members of the church as his fellow workers (2.6). His virtues must be fortified by study and maintained by sedulous practice, so that his mind will not be driven to and fro by the fluctuation of worldly affairs (1.2; 1.4). He must learn to temper his preaching to his audience, to be stern with the rich offender while giving solace to the poor, to set the hope of heaven before the sad and the fear of hell before the joyful (3.3). In accordance with his own principles, he weighed the case before he returned an answer when he was consulted (as he desired to be) on questions of ecclesiastical discipline. In Spain he sanctioned the use of baptism in the name of Jesus alone when he learned that immersion in the threefold name had been the usage of the Goths when they were Arians (Letters 1.43)."

203. Witherington III, Ben (2019). *Biblical Theology The Convergence of the Canon*. Cambridge: Cambridge University Press, p. 428:

"First of all, we have to admit that we have no evidence that Paul got his theology of water baptism (not to be confused with Spirit reception) from Jesus or even the early church. There is this similarity between what we find in Acts and in Paul –the latter speaks of being baptized into Christ, the former of being baptized in the name of Jesus (see Acts 2). In regard to the latter, I would suggest that the reason for that formula is that it is Jews being baptized…."

204. Zeitlin, Solomon (1924). *The Halaka in The Gospels and Its Relation to The Jewish Law at The Time of Jesus*. Hebrew Union College Annual, Vol. 1, pp. 357-358:

"In the New Testament we find evidence of the fact that in the time of the Apostles and even of Jesus, baptism was required in the name of Jesus for such as wished to be admitted into the Christ."

205. Imbelli, Robert P (1992). Book Review: Christian Initiation and Baptism in the Holy Spirit: Evidence from the First Eight Centuries. Theological Studies, Volume 53, Issue 2, p. 344:

> "Water baptism in the name of Jesus" and the "gift of the Holy Spirit" together represent constitutive and normative elements of the early Church's understanding and practice of initiation."

206. Barnard, L. W. (1961). *The Epistle of Barnabas: A Paschal Homily?* Vigiliae Christianae, Volume 15, Issue 1 (March), pp. 17-18:

> "The mention of hoping on the Cross and hoping in Jesus, with which may be associated the hoping on the Name of 16. 8, suggests a stereotyped formula. Certainly there is other evidence that baptism in the Name of Jesus or Jesus Christ was not unknown in the early Church and, even in the third and fourth centuries, there were those who held the one name to be sufficient" citing footnote 28 "Cyprian Ep. 73. 4, 75. 5; Ambrose de Spiritu S. 1. 3."[122]

207. Hogsten, James Doug (2008). *The Monadic Formula of Water Baptism: A Quest for Primitivism via a Christocentric and Restoration Impulse.* Journal of Pentecostal Theology 17, pp. 72-74:

> "The theological accentuation of Jesus coupled with premise of primitivism or restorationism, provided fertile ground for the use of the monadic formula of water baptism in the nineteenth-century. 5 Indeed, evidence reveals that many restorationists of this century wrestled with the same issue that would later emerge within the Pentecostal movement as the 'new issue.' For example, Elias Smith, the editor of the first religious newspaper and a key leader of the New England branch of the 'restoration movement', sought to separate himself from all creeds and denominational names; thus, being known as 'Christian' only. In his quest for primitivism, Smith and those who followed him, appear to have embraced the monadic formula of water baptism; indeed, in his account of a baptismal service, Smith testifies that the Grand Master of Masons in Strafford submitted 'to be baptized in the

---

[122]See also, Banard, Leslie W. (1966). *Studies in The Apostolic Fathers and Their Background.* Schocken Books, p. 81, in which Barnard make a similar observation.

name of Jesus with his companion'. Smith reports in the same edition of the Herald that the 300 which attended a communion service in Portsmouth, NH had been baptized in the name of Jesus Christ. It is also interesting to note that Smith also rejected the traditional doctrine of the trinity, although it is unclear whether his understanding of God's nature was unitarian or modalistic...Elias Smith and the restoration movement are not the only ones of the nineteenth century to question the doctrine of the trinity or the triadic baptismal formula. Indeed, the General Baptists adopted a stance on the nature of God 'that explained the deity as one person in three manifestations, rather than three persons in one God'. Likewise, it would seem that one of the key issues that distinguished Freewill and other 'liberal' Baptists from mainline churches was the issue of the baptismal formula: ... in the name of the Father, Son and Holy Ghost, as Christian baptism. But, not one example of using this particular formula occurs in all the practice of the Apostles. They baptized 'in the name of the Lord' Acts 10:48, 'in the name of the Lord Jesus' (8:16 and 19:5); at the Pentecost, even, 'in the name of Jesus Christ' (2:38). Any one of these comprehended the full formula specified by our Lord in His commission. Also, in their work entitled the Okefenokee Album, writers Francis Harper and Delma Presley gave a detailed description of life on Billy's Island which was located in the Okefenokee Swamp. Billy's Island appears to have been settled in 1850 and Daniel and Nancy Lee made their home here in 1884. Dave Lee, one of Daniel and Nancy's fourteen children to reach adulthood, testified that the family embraced the Primitive Baptists, who were so called because 'they retained the old ways of baptism by immersion in Jesus' name'... John Miller, a Presbyterian minister, penned the work ' Is God a Trinity? ' in 1876 which argued for a 'Oneness' view of the Godhead and supported the Jesus' name formula for water baptism. Likewise, in a correspondence with author Thomas Weisser, the American Baptist Historical Society confirmed that 'when triune baptism was discarded in favor of a single immersion, some pastors moved from Matthew's account to Luke's version of Baptism'. Clearly, it would seem that Baptism in the name of Jesus Christ is no new phenomenon in the history of the Church. Martin Luther encountered a dispute over the formula in his day. G.T. Stokes referred to certain Plymouth Brethren and other sects in Great Britain who used the exclusive formula of Acts 2:38...Some had used the formula for years, so its use was no drastic innovation. "[123]

208. Kupp, David D. (1996). *Matthew's Emmanuel Divine Presence and God's People in The First Gospel*. Society for New Testament Studies Monograph Series 90. Cambridge: Cambridge University Press, pp. 213-214:

"The development of the formula is closely bounded temporally on the one side by the initial single-member baptismal formulas well represented in Luke and Paul and on the other by the almost contemporary parallel in Didache 7.1-3... At best we can speculate that Matthew 28.19b is a second-generation development of single-member christological baptismal traditions and of more elementary triadic texts which circulated commonly. From our reading of the Gospel here, however, Matthew appears to have developed and/or incorporated the formula in its current form without fully integrating it theologically into his story...Within Matthew the addition of 'Father' to the simple christological formula for baptism in the name of Jesus is strikingly consistent with the patrocentricity of the First Gospel, and reflects Matthew's explicit concern to establish in his Gospel the identity of the true Israel in continuity with the language and symbols of Judaism."

---

[123]See footnotes cited by Hogsten between page 72-74: "6 Elias Smith, The Herald of Gospel Liberty 1 (Sept. 1, 1808). 7 Smith, Herald (July 7, 1809). 8 Smith, Herald (July 7, 1809). 9 Elias Smith, The Life, Conversion, Preaching, Traveling and Sufferings of Elias Smith (Portsmouth, NH: Beck & Foster, 1816), p. 324. It would seem that true Modalists or Sabellians were often designated as Unitarians by those who misunderstood the doctrine they espoused. Indeed, it is even questionable as to whether the 'father' of the modern Unitarian movement (Servetus) was in truth a Unitarian at all. 10 Robert G. Torbet, A History of the Baptists (Philadelphia, PA: Judson, 1950), p. 86. 11 Oscar E. Baker, The Issues Distinguishing Free and Other Liberal Baptists (Boston, MA: Morning Star, 1889), p. 20. 12 Francis Harper and Delma E. Presley, The Okefenokee Album (Athens, GA: University of Georgia, 1981), p. 29. 13 C.T. Trowell, 'Okefenokee Folk: A kinder, or more hospitable people do not live', The Natural Georgia Series: The Okefenokee Swamp, Online: http://sherpaguides.com/georgia/okefenokee_swamp/okefenokee_folk/."

209. Smith, D. Moody (1974). *Glossolalia and Other Spiritual Gifts in a New Testament Perspective.* Interpretation A Journal of Bible and Theology, Volume 28, Issue 3, p. 313:

> "In the case of the disciples who know the baptism of John only (Acts 19:1-7), baptism in the name of Jesus, presumably also in water, leads directly to their reception of the Spirit...."

210. Mahoney SJ, John (1974). *The Church of The Holy Spirit in Aquinas.* The Heythrop Journal, Volume 15, Issue 1, p. 20:

> "Baptism, for instance, had been conferred in the name of Jesus alone for a time in order, Aquinas suggested, to enhance his glory...."

211. Moehlman, Conrad Henry (1933). *The Origin of The Apostles' Creed.* The Journal of Religion, Volume 13, No. 3 (July), pp. 309-311:

> "The original formula of Christian baptism had been "in," "upon," or "into" the name of Jesus. For the author of the final chapter of Matthew's gospel, it had become "into the name of the Father and the Son and the holy Spirit." In the original form of the Apostles' Creed, it had been expanded to read: "I believe in God, Father Almighty; and in Christ Jesus, his Son, our Lord; and in holy Spirit, holy Church, and resurrection of the flesh"...This appearance of the christological confession at different places in the creed also indicates that the Apostles' Creed was built up out of baptismal confession and christological formula...Hauszleiter holds that the trinitarian baptismal formula and the christological confession underlying the Apostles' Creed existed separately not only at first but also rather late. The christological confession was especially employed at the baptism of Jewish converts to Christianity. The fusion of the nine-member Apostles' Creed and the christological kerygma, Hauszleiter ascribes to Bishop Zephyrinus of Rome, about A.D. 200..."[124]

---

[124] Conrad Henry Moehlman was an American Professor of Church History at Colgate Rochester Divinity School.

212. Moule, C. F. D. (1976). *The New Testament and the Doctrine of the Trinity: a short report on an old theme*. The Expository Times, Volume 88, Issue 1, p. 16:

> "There are several passages of unimpeachable authenticity in the New Testament where God and Christ and the Spirit are named together; but can any of them be properly called trinitarian? Whatever the methods of the patristic writers and the fathers of the councils, we_ cannot to-day be satisfied, if we are inquiring about a New Testament foundation for later credal definitions, with anything less than evidence that the experiences reflected in the New Testament justify such definitions...that the basic Christian baptismal formula probably used simply 'into (the name of) Jesus Christ', and that only subsequently did it need to be spelt out with mention of God and of the Spirit....".[125]

213. Kesich, Veselin (2007). *Formation and Struggles The Birth of the Church AD 33-200*. The Church in History Volume I, Part 1. Crestwood, New York: St. Vladimir's Seminary Press, p. 34:

> "Baptism was performed "in the name of Jesus Christ" (Acts 2:38, 10:48) or "in the name of the Lord Jesus" (Acts 8:16,19:5). This baptismal formula is found only in Act... Like baptism, healings were performed in the church "in the name of Jesus Christ of Nazareth" (Acts 3:6,16; 4:10) The "name" represents Jesus and his power. Only those who are his disciples, utterly committed to him, and incorporated into his community could invoke his name."[126]

214. Blevins, William L. (1974). *The Early Church: Acts 1-5*. Review and Expositor, Volume 71, Issue 4 (December), p. 467:

> "The significance which Jesus had for the early church is disclosed in the "name" motif which is woven throughout the fabric of Acts 1-5. The church baptized in the name of Jesus (Acts 2:38); they healed in the name of Jesus (Acts 3: 6, 16; 4: 10); they spoke in his name (Acts 4: 17-18); they taught in his name (Acts

---

[125] Professor C. F. D. Moule, F.B.A., Cambridge.
[126] Dr. Veselin Kesich, Professor of New Testament emeritus, St. Vladimir's Orthodox Theological Seminary.

4: 17-18;5: 28); and they performed signs and wonders in his name (Acts 4: 30). Indeed, it was because the church carried on its activity in Jesus' name that the Jewish establishment persecuted it (Acts 5: 28)."

215. Jung, C. G. (1969). *A Psychological Approach to The Dogma of The Trinity II* in Collected Works of C. G. Jung, Volume II. Psychology and Religion: West and East. Princeton, New Jersey: Princeton University Press, pp. 129, 136, 138-139:

"I have dwelt at some length on the views of the Babylonians and Egyptians, and on Platonist philosophy, in order to give the reader some conception of the trinitarian and unitarian ideas that were in existence many centuries before the birth of Christianity... Nevertheless, they neither paused in their labours nor rested until they had finally reconstructed the ancient Egyptian archetype... Much the same sort of thing happened when, in A.D. 431, at the Council of Ephesus, whose streets had once rung with hymns of praise to many-breasted Diana, the Virgin Mary was declared the θιοτόκοτ, 'birth-giver of the god.'... The trinitarian conception of a life-process within the Deity, which I have outlined here, was, as we have seen, already in existence in pre-Christian times, its essential features being a continuation and differentiation of the primitive rites of renewal and the cult-legends associated with them. Just as the gods of these mysteries become extinct, so, too, do the mysteries themselves, only to take on new forms in the course of history...there is not a single passage in the New Testament where the Trinity is formulated in an intellectually comprehensible manner..." see footnote 2 "The baptismal formula "In the name of the Father and the Son and the Holy Ghost" comes into this category, though its authenticity is doubted. It seems that originally people were baptized only in the name of Jesus Christ."

216. Hurtado, Larry W. (1998). *The Origin of The Nomina Sacra: A Proposal.* Journal of Biblical Literature, Volume 117, No. 4 (Winter), p. 670:

"The hypothesis that the name "Jesus" was the first of the Christian nomina sacra is also consistent with the rich evidence of the enormous religious significance attached to Jesus' name, and the ritual use of it in early Christian circles. New Testament references to Christian baptism as "in/into the name of Jesus" (e.g., Acts 2:38; 19:5) indicate that the rite included the cultic pronunciation/invocation of Jesus' name."[127]

217. Longenecker, Richard N. (1968). *Some Distinctive Early Christological Motifs*. New Testament Studies, Volume 14, Issue 4 (July), pp. 534-535:

"Extrapolating into the New Testament, instances of the use of' the Name' take on greater significance. And interestingly, it is the Jewish Christian writings of the New Testament which evidence both a greater interest in the name of Jesus generally and an almost exclusive use of 'the Name' as a Christological designation...Acts speaks of Jewish exorcists who wanted to profit by the power of the name of Jesus, and of the Jewish Christian Ananias telling Saul to call 'on his name'. And the Apocalypse evidences an interest in ' a new name' and ' the name of my God' given to Christians. Of course Paul also refers to the name of Jesus: in appeal to the Corinthians' by...the name of our Lord Jesus Christ', in alluding to his converts' baptism in Jesus' name..."[128]

218. Lake, Kirsopp (1924). *The Apostle's Creed*. Harvard Theological Review, Volume 17, Issue 2 (April), pp. 181-182:

"One of the most certain and at the same time puzzling facts is that in the early church there were two formulas. One is represented by the canonical text of Mt. xxviii. 19, "In the name of the Father, and of the Son, and of the Holy Spirit," the other in the Acts of the Apostles, "In the name of the Lord Jesus " (Acts ii. 38, viii. 16, x. 48, xix. 5)... Ultimately the former triumphed everywhere, but the latter is perhaps implied by the Shepherd of Hennas, and that it was once found in copies of Matthew known to Eusebius (were they of Antiochian provenance?)...My guess would be that the custom of baptism "in the name of the Lord Jesus" lasted longer than we think...It

---

[127]Larry W. Hurtado was Professor of New Testament Language, Literature and Theology at Edinburgh University.
[128]Dr. Richard N. Longenecker was a prominent New Testament scholar.

would be tempting to suggest that baptism in the name of the Lord Jesus was preserved by the Adoptionist party in Rome...."[129]

219. Tilborg, Sjef Van (2001). *Acts 17:27—"that they might feel after him and find..."* HTS Theological Studies, Volume 57, Issue 1/2, p. 98:

"The Name of Jesus is a power that leads to salvation. The Name of Jesus is pronounced at baptism over those who are prepared to follow the Way. It is said several times that people are baptized "in the Name of Jesus": in Jerusalem (2:38), in Samaria (8: 16); at the house of Cornelius and his family as the first non-Jews (10:43, 48); as prophecy for the nations (15: 17); and among the followers of Apollos in Ephesus, twelve in number (19:5). The story of the conversion of Paul is paradigmatic. He persecutes the people who invoke the Name (9: 14,21; 26:9) but on his way to propagate the Name among the nations he himself will suffer a lot (9: 16). He has to let himself be baptized in the Name of Jesus (22: 16); he does this, too (9:8), and then acts openly in the Name of Jesus, even immediately in Damascus (9:27), but also in Jerusalem (9:28), in Antioch (11 :26) and afterwards in all the places he sought out."[130]

220. Dix O.S.B., Gregory (1948). *"The Seal" in the Second Century.* Theology, Volume 51, Issue 331, p. 8:

"I submit that when we find in Syria and in Asia Minor a second century Christian rite of initiation, consisting of (a) "the Seal of the Spirit," (b) "Baptism" in water "in the Name of" Jesus...."[131]

221. Wilburn, Ralph G. (1965). *The One Baptism and The Many Baptisms.* Theology Today, Volume 22, Issue 1 (April), pp. 62-63:

---

[129] Dr. Kirsopp Lake was an English New Testament scholar, Church Historian and Winn Professor of Ecclesiastical History at Harvard Divinity School.
[130] Sjef Van Tilborg is Professor of Biblical Exegesis in the Department of Literary-Historical Theology at University of Nijmegen (Netherlands).
[131] Gregory Dix, OS B., was a British monk and priest of Nashdom Abbey, U.K., an Anglican Benedictine community. He was a noted liturgical scholar whose work had particular influence on the reform of Anglican liturgy in the mid-20th century.

"First, in regard to the baptismal formula. According to the book of Acts, the original formula was simply "in the name of Jesus Christ," a formula which is reflected also in the Pauline writings. The great commission, however, provides the trinitarian formula. There are those who feel that the trinitarian formula was the original and that the shorter formula represents "an abbreviation which picks out the determinative name." It is more plausible to hold that the simpler formula was the original and that the trinitarian version represents a development of the latter part of the first century and the early part of the second... Furthermore, the liturgical character of the longer formula, together with its explicit trinitarianism, would seem to cohere better with later ecclesiastical developments. It is significant that in the Didache (c. 120 AD) when specific instructions are laid down regarding baptism, the trinitarian formula is used; 16 yet the validity of baptism "in the Lord's name" is also recognized... According to Cyprian, single immersion (after the analogy of Jewish proselyte baptism) in the name of Jesus Christ was the rule among the early Jewish Christians."[132]

222. Howard, George (1988). *A Note on The Short Ending of Matthew*. The Harvard Theological Review, Volume 81, No. 1 (January), pp. 117, 120:

"In 1965 Hans Kosmala argued in favor of the originality of the short form of the ending of Matthew, suggesting that Matthew's susceptibility to liturgical modification allowed the trinitarian baptismal formula to be added to the text. By the time this formula was added, no other baptismal formula, such as one "in the name of Jesus," was any longer in use...To conclude, it may be said that the Hebrew Matthew preserved in *Shem-Tob's* Even Bohan supports the short Eusebian ending to Matthew by omitting the trinitarian baptismal formula."

223. _____ (1893). *The Great Text Commentary The Great Texts of St. Matthew Matt. xxviii. 18–20*. The Expository Times, Volume 4, Issue 12, p. 558:

"In the instances of baptism recorded in the Acts (ii. 38, viii. 16,

---

[132]Ralph G. Wilburn was a Theologian and Dean of Lexington Theological Seminary.

x. 48, xix. 5), the name of Jesus Christ (or the Lord Jesus) alone occurs in the baptismal formula."

224. Bruce, F. F. (1963). *The Books and the Parchments Some Chapters on The Transmission of The Bible* (revised edition). Westwood, New Jersey: Fleming H. Revel Company, p. 66:

"...baptism 'in the name of Jesus Christ' (Acts 2. 38; 10. 48) probably refers to the pronouncing of His name by the baptizer (cf. Jas. 2. 7; Acts 1 5. 17) or the invoking of His name by the baptized person (Acts 22. 16)."

225. Fee, Gordon D. (1996). *Paul, the Spirit And The People of God*. Grand Rapids, Michigan: Baker Academic:

"1. The image of "washing" as a work of the Spirit first occurs in 1 Corinthians 6:11. Many see here a reference to baptism, especially because it is followed by the phrase "in the name of the Lord Jesus Christ," which is considered a baptismal formula."

226. Hurtado, Larry W. (2000). *At the Origins of Christian Worship The Context and Character of Earliest Christian Devotion*. Grand Rapids, Michigan: William B. Eerdmans Publishing Company, p. 81:

"It is commonly accepted that the 'trinitarian' baptismal formula of Matt. 28:19 and Did. 7:1 (but cf. 9:5!) is probably a somewhat later expression and that earliest practice is the 'in/into the name of Jesus' formula."

227. Meeks, Wayne A. (2002). *In Search of The Early Christians*. New Haven and London: Yale University Press, pp. 24-25, 53:

"...in Ephesians...the passage also contains a clear reference to baptism in verse 26..." see footnote 162 "Moreover, Schlier is very likely correct in seeing in a reference to the *baptismal formula* or the proclamation of the *name* of *Jesus* over the baptizand...."

228. Holmes, Stephen R. (2012). *The Holy Trinity Understanding God's Life*. Crownhill, Milton Keynes: Paternoster:

"I have already mentioned the triadic baptismal formula, to which may be added the witness of Acts that baptism in the name of Jesus alone was also common (Acts 2:38; 8:16; 10:48)"

229. Anderson, K. C. (1915). *Christianity Old and New.* The Monist, Volume 25, Issue 4, p. 607:

"The Old Roman Symbol and the Apostles' Creed were evidently an expansion of an early baptismal formula which was simply "Into the name of the Lord Jesus," or "Into Jesus Christ." This was sufficient for the Jews as their God was the God of the Christians as well, which is evidence that the name "Jesus" was a name for a divine being, and not of a human historical person."

230. Erickson, Millard J. (2000). *Making Sense of the Trinity: Three Crucial Questions.* Grand Rapids, Michigan: Baker Academics, p. 34:

"One of the most important is the baptismal formula in Matthew 28:19, which links the three persons in such an intimate fashion as to imply equality: "Therefore go and make disciples of all nations, baptizing them in the name of the Father and of the Son and of the Holy Spirit." Coming from Jesus himself and given as the formula to be used in the administration of the important rite of baptism, this is a weighty fact. It is especially notable that while three persons are designated here, the word "name" is in the singular. There is an apparent conflict with the baptism into the name of Jesus, in Acts 8:16."

231. Hurtado, Larry W. (2016). *Destroyer of gods Early Christian Distinctiveness in The Roman World.* Waco, Texas: Baylor University Press:

"In earliest references to the rite, the name of Jesus was invoked over the person being baptized. It is also plausible that the person being baptized invoked Jesus by name. This use of Jesus' name seems to be what is referred to as being baptized "in/into the name of Jesus" (e.g., Acts 2:38; 19:5)."

232. Wedderburn, Alexander J. M. (2005) (reprint). *A History of The First Christians.* New York & London: T&T Clark International A Continuum Imprint, p. 35:

"It is, correspondingly, for them a baptism 'in/into the name of

Jesus' and placed the baptized in a special relation to their Lord, whose name and power they invoked at their baptism."

233. Viviano, Benedict Thomas (2010). *God in The Gospel According to Matthew*. Interpretation A Journal of Bible and Theology (October), p. 354:

"6. The Triad. Earlier, I asked the question of whether Matthew had anything distinctive to say about God. In addition to what I have already mentioned, especially Matthew's way of handling the Emmanuel theme, there is also the triadic baptismal formula in the second to the last verse: "Make disciples of all nations, baptizing them in the name of the Father, and of the Son, and of the Holy Spirit." This formula is called triadic, because it does not yet express a full-blown Trinitarian theology. Elsewhere in the NT, one is baptized into the name of Jesus. Matthew has contributed this distinctive formula. How did he arrive at it? In brief, the early Christians after Easter needed a rite of initiation that would be the same for men and women (unlike circumcision). The rite of baptism practiced by John the Baptist lay ready to hand. Matthew most probably shaped this formula on the basis of pre-existing apocalyptic patterns such as that in Dan 7, where you have the Ancient of Days (which Matthew christianized as the Father), the Son of man, and the Saints of the Most High, which Matthew condensed into the Holy Spirit. (The Spirit of God is present in the Bible from the first page of Genesis till the last chapter of Revelation.) In Ezek 1 and 1 En. 14, we find the Elect One and the Angel instead of Son and Spirit."[133]

234. Comfort, Phillip W. (general. editor) (2009). *1 and 2 Corinthians*. Tyndale Cornerstone Bible Commentary Volume 15. Carol Stream, Illinois: Tyndale House Publishers, Inc., p. 32:

"In 1:13, Paul formulates three rhetorical questions, the second and third clearly assuming a no answer. Certainly, none of the Corinthians were baptized into "Paul." At this very early stage of the Christian church, every convert was baptized quite literally into the name of "Jesus," which is why he makes this part of his

---

[133] Benedict Thomas Viviano, Professor Emeritus of New Testament, University of Fribourg, Switzerland.

argument. The common Trinitarian formula reflected in Matthew 28:19 was yet to become universal."

235. McKnight, Scot (2018). *It Takes A Church to Baptize What The Bible Says About Infant Baptism.* Grand Rapids, Michigan: Brazos Press:

> "Notice how the next four verses, all from the book of Acts, understand baptism as being in the name of Jesus… (The book of Acts and the letters of Paul emphasize baptism as baptism into the name of Jesus Christ, so the trinitarian formula of Matthew 28—Father, Son, Spirit—is something the church eventually saw as expressing the fullness of baptism.)"[134]

236. Wernle, Paul (1904). *The Beginnings of Christianity.* Volume II. The Development of The Church. London: Williams & Norgate, New York: G. P. Putnam's Sons, p. 129:

> "At the beginning of the second century baptism into the name of Jesus began to give way to baptism into the name of the Trinity, the latter practice being founded on the passage in Matthew's Gospel which traced the formula back to Jesus Himself. But it was an innovation, for we see from the Acts that the apostles and Paul only baptized into the name of Jesus. How and where the phrase arose we cannot tell, but we are acquainted with a transition stage."[135]

237. Miller, Leo F. (1925). *The Formula of Baptism in the Early Church.* The Catholic Historical Review, Volume 10, No. 4 (January), pp. 516, 528-529, 533:

> "…the trinitarian formula of baptism in our sense was unknown (fremd) to the ancient Church." Though it is impossible to offer an apodictic historical proof of the existence of the present formula of baptism in the first three centuries of the Church on the basis of the evidence which has been preserved to us from this period…The Trinitarian formula is the only one which has

---

[134]Scot McKnight is a scholar, writer, and speaker and is professor of New Testament at Northern Seminary in Lisle, Illinois.
[135]Paul Wernle, Professor Extraordinary of Modern Church History at the University of Basel.

ever been sanctioned by the Church. It is found in all rituals and official documents which mention a formula. The *Responsio ad Consulta Bulgarorum* of Pope Nicholas I is only an apparent exception. The case put before the pope was the question as to the validity of baptism administered by a Jew of whom it was not known whether he was a Christian or a pagan. The pope's reply that the baptism was valid if conferred in the name of the Trinity, or only in the name of Christ, has been construed as acknowledging the validity of a formula in which only the name of Christ is pronounced...This is clear from the authorities he cites for his decision: Acts 2, 38 and 19, 5; St. Ambrose, *De Spiritu Sancto;* and St. Augustine, *De Baptismo* 6, 25...In conclusion it is natural to raise the question why there is so little evidence in the literature of the first three centuries to prove the existence of the formula of baptism. It may be said in reply that an important part of this literature is lost to us we have none of the earliest rituals."[136]

238. Boora, Kulwant Singh (2021) (revised edition). *The Three Roman Catholic Popes on The Validity of Baptism in The Name of Jesus (Acts 2:38) and The Two Catholic Popes on the Oneness Christological view of God.* Published by Amazon, pp. 25-29:

"...in 866, Pope Nicholas I seems to have indicated that the Christological formula was valid."[137]

239. Rosa, Peter de (1988). *Vicars of Christ Darkside of The Papacy* _____, Chapter XII – Papal Heretics, p. 7:

"valid baptism. Nicholas I (858-67) said that calling on the name of Christ is enough."[138]

240. Rogers, Elizabeth Frances (1917). *Peter Lombard And The Sacramental System.* New York, pp. 89, 91:

---

[136] Citing Dr. Leo F. Miller, who was a Catholic theologian and scholar.
[137] This reference is citing the work of Dr. P. Haffner, who also noted that during the patristic era and in the Middle Ages the Christological formula was often recognized as valid.
[138] Peter de Rosa, former Catholic Priest and Jesuit and Dean of Roman Catholic Theology at Corpus Christi College, London.

"Nevertheless we read in the Acts of the Apostles, that the Apostles baptized in the name of Christ, as Ambrose explains, the whole Trinity is understood...They certainly have been baptized, if they were baptized...in the name of Christ, as we read in the Acts of the Apostles; for it is one and the same thing, as Saint Ambrose explains...From the above you have understood clearly that baptism can be administered in the name of Christ...Whoever therefore baptizes in the name of Christ, baptizes in the name of the Trinity, which is thereby understood."

241. Wightman, J. Clover (1874). *Papal Infallibility*. The Baptist Quarterly Volume VIII. Philadelphia: American Baptist Publication Society, p. 39:

"...Pope Nicholas I (858-67) assured the Bulgarians that baptism in the name of Christ alone was quite sufficient."

242. Peoples, William (1904). *Roman Claims in The Light of History*. London: Paternoster Row, New York: E. S. Gorham, p. 81:

"Pope Nicholas I told the Bulgarians that Baptism administered in the Name of Christ only was valid."

243. Prescott, W. W. (1914). *Why We Are Protestants*. The Protestant Magazine Volume VI, No. 2 (February), pp. 71-72:

"...another Pope, Nicholas, assured the Bulgarians that baptism in the name of Christ alone was sufficient."

244. Simpson, W. J. Sparrow (1915). *The Resurrection And Modern Thought*. London: Longman's, Green and Co., pp. 272, 274, 275:[139]

"Cyprian's theory appears to be that Baptism could be validly administered to Jews with the formula "in the name of the Lord Jesus," because they were already in possession of the Father... This is the sense in which Ambrose was understood by the Venerable Bede-"Since it is the rule of the Church," wrote Bede,[140] "that believers should be baptised in the name of the Holy Trinity, it may be wondered why S. Luke throughout this

---

[139]Dr. W. J. Sparrow Simpson was Chaplain of St. Mary's Hospital, Ilford.
[140]Footnote 1 citing Ven. Bede, *'Expositio in Acta Apost. ch. x. Giles' Edition*, vol. xii. pp. 54, 55.

book witnesses that Baptism was not otherwise given than in the name of Jesus Christ. The blessed Ambrose solves this problem by the principle that the mystery is fulfilled by the unity of the name…Thus the sole invocation of Christ includes the Trinity…Pope Nicholas the First, when consulted in 866 by the Bulgarians, what was to be done in the case of a number of persons baptised by a Jew, replied: "if they have been…in the name of Christ, as we read in the Acts of the Apostles, they are baptised; for it is one and the same thing, as Ambrose testifies. This view of the validity of Baptism when conferred with exclusive mention of our Lord evidently prevailed widely through the scholastic period: for it is maintained without hesitation by no less a person than Peter Lombard"[141]

245. Dix, Dom Gregory (2005). *The Shape of The Liturgy*. London & New York: Bloomsbury T&T Clark, p. 275:

"Similarly baptism 'in the Name of the Father and of the Son and of the Holy Ghost' eventually prevailed, though the at least equally primitive formula 'in the Name of Jesus' was accepted as valid by the especially conservative Church of Rome apparently right down to the Council of Trent" see footnote 3 "Pope Nicholas I consulted by the Bulgarians bishops in the ninth century decided in favour of the validity of this form, as had Pope Stephen I in the third century and S. Ambrose in the fourth, in which they were followed…by St. Thomas Aquinas (*S. Th., iii. 66, 6 ad Imum*)."[142]

246. Rosemann, Phillip W. (2004). *Peter Lombard Great Medieval Thinkers*. London & New York: Oxford University Press, p. 147:

"It is true that the apostles used to baptism in the name of Christ alone, as Acts reports happened on several occasions (see Acts 2:38; 8:12; and 19:5); however, Peter decides that the entire

---

[141] Footnotes 2 and 1 citing Nicholas I., *Respons. ad consult. Bulgar.*' c. 104 and Sentent. Lit. iv. Dist. iii. § 2, 3, 4, 5.
[142] It has already stated in that Dom Gregory Dix was an Anglican Benedictine Monk of Nashdom and a renowned scholar.

Trinity is implicitly understood in the name of Jesus."[143]

247. Vos, Geerhardus (2016). *Reformed Dogmatics*. Volume 5: Ecclesiology The Means of Grace, Eschatology. Bellingham, WA: Lexham Press:

> "Zwingli denied that Matthew 28:19 is intended for use as a formula."[144]

248. Otten, Bernard J. (1918). *A Manual of The History of Dogmas*. Volume II The Development of Dogmas During The Middles Ages and After 869-1907. London & Missouri: B. Herder Book Co., p. 300:[145]

> "Regarding the form of baptism...Hugh of St. Victor 8 and Peter Lombard ° were of opinion that baptism administered in the name of Jesus might still be considered valid...To this conclusion they argued from what they found in the Acts of the Apostles, from a statement of St. Ambrose, and from a decision given by Pope Nicholas 1.[146] ...it was ordained that for some time it alone should be used in the administration of the baptismal rite."[147]

249. Tixeront, J. (1923). *History of Dogmas*. Translated from the Fifth French Edition by H. L.B. Vol. II. From St. Athanasius to St. Augustine (318-430) (2n ed.). Missouri: St. Louis & London: B. Herder Book Co., pp. 309, 358:[148]

> "However, in the *De Spiritu Sancto (I, 42-45)*, St. Ambrose seems to admit with St. Basil that absolutely speaking, it suffices for the validity and efficacy of baptism, to baptize in the name of Jesus...the author of the *De Trinitate*, probably Vigilius of Tapsus, admits the validity of the baptism in the name of Jesus because

---

[143]Phillip W. Rosemann, Associate Professor of Philosophy at the University of Dallas.
[144]Geerhardus Vos (1862-1949) was a Dutch American Theologian and is considered by many to be the father of modern Reformed biblical theology.
[145]Bernard J. Otten, S.J., Professor of Dogmatic Theology and The History of Dogmas in St. Louis University.
[146]See footnote 11 and 12 citing *De Spirit. Sanct. c. 3.*; *Ad Bulgaros, DB. 335*.
[147]See footnote 13 citing *Thomas, Sum. Theol. III, q. 66, a. 6 ad im; Bonavent*. In *Sent. loc. cit. a. 2, 1, 2 ad 3*.
[148]J. Tixeront was a Professor of Patristics and a well-known Catholic Historian of Dogma, his work was cited earlier in reference 66.

the names of the Father and the Holy Ghost are included in that of Jesus."[149]

250. Hey, John (1822). *Lectures in Divinity Delivered in The University of Cambridge by John Hey, D.D, As Norrisian Professor, From 1780 to 1795* (2nd ed.). Cambridge: J. Smith, p. 273:

> "In the time of St. Ambrose, Baptism was sometimes administered only in the name of Christ…he urges, that baptizing in the name of Christ only is, in effect, baptizing in the name of the Father, Son, and Holy Ghost, because they are one…."

251. Riddle, J. E. (M.DCCC.XXXIX). *A Manual of Christian Antiquities: or, An Account of The Constitution, Ministers, Worship, Discipline, and Customs of The Ancient Church Particularly During The Third, Fourth and Fifth Centuries to Which is Prefixed An Analysis of The Writings of The Ante-Nicene Fathers.* London: John W. Parker, pp. 465-467:

> "But while baptism in the usual form was invariably prescribed in the liturgies of different churches, baptism administered simply 'in the name of Christ' was explained as sufficient by Cyprian, Hilary, Ambrose, and Fulgentius, and was declared valid by decrees of several councils…Among the writings of the ancients…Gennadius (*De Soriptor Eccles. c. 27*) mentions one Ursinus, an African Monk, who, he says, wrote a book…wherein he asserted…"that it was not lawful to rebaptize those who were baptized…simply in the name of Christ…in the name of Christ alone…which he makes to be lawful…St. Ambrose, I confess, seems to have been of the same opinion: for he takes all those expressions of Scripture, which speak of being baptized in the name of Christ, to mean the using such a form as this, 'I baptize thee in the name of Christ,' without any express mention of the three persons, though the whole Trinity was implied in it…He says further, he that names but one person, designs thereby the whole Trinity; he that names Christ only intends both the Father by whom the Son is anointed, and the Son himself who is

---

[149]See footnote 276 citing *De Trinitate, XII, col. 324.*, this work was cited earlier. Vigilius of Tapsus or Thapsus (c. 484) Bishop of Thapsus who took part in talks between Catholics and Arians at Carthage in 484 A.D.

anointed, and the Spirit with which he is anointed...."[150]

252. Cunningham O.P, James J. (2006). St. *Thomas Aquinas Summa Theologiae Baptism and Confirmation* Volume 57 (3a. 66-72). New York: Cambridge University Press, pp. 27-29:

> "It would seem that baptism can be given in the name of Christ for there's one faith and one baptism. But we find in Acts that they were baptized in the name of Jesus Christ. Thus, even now one could be baptized in the name of Christ...Moreover, Ambrose says baptism...can be conferred in the name of Christ as well...Moreover, Pope Nicholas, in response to questions from the Bulgars wrote those who have been baptized...only in the name of Christ, as we read in Acts of the Apostles, one and the same thing, as St. Ambrose said, out not be rebaptized...Therefore baptism can be conferred in the name of Christ with the form, I baptize you in the name of Christ...it was by reason of a special revelation of Christ that in the primitive Church the Apostles baptized in the name of Christ...Here Ambrose gives the reason why such a dispensation could be fittingly given in the primitive Church; that in the name of Christ the whole Trinity is implied and therefore the form which Christ handed down in the gospel would at least be preserved with implicit integrity."[151]

253. Hastings, James et. al. (1908). *A Dictionary of Christ and the Gospels. Volume II Labour-Zion with Appendix and Indexes*. New York: Charles Scribner's Sons & Edinburgh: T&T Clark, p. 218:

> "...Christian baptism, as we meet with it in the Apostolic Church, is performed in (or into) the name of Christ (Acts 2:38; 8:16; 10:48, 19:5, Rom. 6:3, Gal. 3:27)...But if we accept the triple formula as coming from the lips of Jesus, the fact that we have no direct evidence of its use in the Apostolic Church certainly

---

[150]Rev. J. E. Riddle, M.A. of St. Edmund Hall, Oxford.
[151]St. Thomas Aquinas was a highly regarded and renowned Philosopher and Italian Dominican Theologian of the Middle Ages. His work, Summa Theologiae remains among the greatest documents of the Catholic Christian Church and is a landmark of medieval western thought. It is evidence that in the Middles Ages that baptism in the name of Jesus is clearly acknowledged as valid.

creates a difficulty. The suggestion that the shorter formula is simply a designation of the fact that baptism was administered on confession of Jesus as Christ and Lord, and that the Trinitarian formula would invariably be employed in the actual administration of the sacrament, does not meet the case, for we know that in the 3rd cent, a baptism in the name of Christ was still common, and that in the time of Cyprian the controversy about re-baptism gathered round this very point."

254. Feingold, Lawrence (2021). *Touched by Christ The Sacramental Economy*. Steubenville, Ohio: Emmaus Academic, see section on The Form of Baptism:

"It is not impossible that valid baptism was administered by the Apostles in the first decades of the Church simply 'in the name of Jesus.' The *Catechism of the Council of Trent* has an interesting commentary on this question. It concedes the possibility that the Apostles, through the inspiration of the Holy Spirit, initially did not use the Trinitarian formula but baptized in the name of Jesus alone to highlight the greatness of His name, in whom the other persons of the Trinity are implied."[152]

255. Stone, Darwell (1905). *Holy Baptism* (4th ed.). London: Longmans, Green and Co., p. 138:

"In the time of S. Cyprian there were some who thought that a Baptism administered 'in the name of Jesus Christ' would be valid…that a valid Baptism might be administered 'in the name of Jesus Christ'.…It may perhaps be impossible expressly to deny the validity of such a formula."[153]

256. Armitage, Thomas (1890). *A History of The Baptists; Traced by Their Vital Principles and Practices From The Time of Our Lord and Saviour Jesus Christ to The Year 1889*. New York: Bryan, Taylor, & Co. & Cincinnati: Jones Brothers Publishing Co., p. 247:

"Pope Pelagius complains of The Eumonians: 'That they baptize

---

[152]Dr. Lawrence Feingold is Associate Professor of Theology (and Philosophy) at Kenrick-Glennon Seminary in St. Louis.
[153]Darwell Stone (1859-1941) was an Anglo-Catholic Theologian and Church of England Priest.

in the name of Christ alone and by a single immersion."[154]

257. Wilburn, Ralph G. (1965). *The One Baptism and The Many Baptisms.* Theology Today, Volume 22, Issue 1 (April), p. 66:

"Earlier, however, (c. 560 AD) Pope Pelagius I had objected to the boast of "many" in his day "who assert that they are baptized in the name of Christ alone with only one immersion."[155]

258. Guericke, H. E. F. (M.DCCC.LL.). *Manual of The Antiquities of The Church.* London: John W. Parker and Son, p. 232:

"Baptism merely in the name of Chris occurs only occasionally in the ancient Church."[156]

259. Wace, Henry & Buchheim, C. A. (1883). *First Principles of The Reformation of The Ninety-Five Theses and The Three Primary Works of Dr. Martin Luther Translated into English.* London: John Murray, p. 188:

"I baptize thee in the name of Jesus Christ"–though it is certain that the Apostles baptized in this form, as we read in the Acts of the Apostles."

260. Norris, Frederick (2002). *Christianity A Short Global History.* Oxford: One World Publications, pp. 60-61:

"Fifth century church historians notice that in some Arian congregations baptism had become a single immersion in the name of Jesus Christ."

261. Smedley, Edward et al. (1845). *Encyclopaedia Metropolitana; or Universal Dictionary of Knowledge on an Original Plan: Comprising of Twofold Advantage of a Philosophical and An Alphabetical Arrangement, with*

---

[154]Pope Pelagius I was the bishop of Rome from 556 to his death. A former apocrisiarius to Constantinople, Pelagius I was elected pope as the candidate of Emperor Justinian I. This testifies to the long-held view that baptism in the name of Jesus survived and continued, since Pope Pelaguis (c.556 to c.661) as Bishop of Rome seems to acknowledge its practice during this time around c.556-c.661, this then is in reality direct testimonial evidence of the existence of Jesus name baptism during that time period.
[155]This reference was cited earlier.
[156]H. E. F. Guericke, Professor of Theology at Halle.

Appropriate Engravings. Volume XV. London: B. Fellowes, et al., p. 250:

> "In St. Basil's time there were some who contended on the authority of passages in the Acts of the Apostles…that baptism ought to be administered in the name of Christ alone."[157]

262. _____ (1910). *The Encyclopaedia Britannica* (11th ed.) Volume III. Cambridge: At The University Press, pp. 365-366:

> "In the 3rd century baptism in the name of Christ was still so widespread that Pope Stephen, in opposition to Cyprian of Carthage, declared it to be valid. From Pope Zachariah (Ep. x.) we learn that the Celtic missionaries in baptizing omitted one or more persons of the Trinity, and this was one of the reasons why the church of Rome anathematized them; Pope Nicholas, however (858-867), in the Responsa ad consults Bulgarorum, allowed baptism to be valid tantum in *nomine Christi*, as in the Acts. Ursinus, an African monk (in Gennad. *de Scr. Eccl. xxvii.*), Hilary (*de Synodis, lxxxv.*), the synod of Nemours (a.d. 1284), also asserted that baptism into the name of Christ alone was valid."

263. Edmunds, Albert J. (1917). *Studies In The Christian Religion*. Philadelphia: Innes & Sons, p. 6(?):

> "Second Century—Justin Martyr. alludes to the simpler form (Trypho 39).
> Third Century—Pope Stephen maintains against Cyprian the validity of baptism in the name of Christ alone.
> Fourth Century—The Pneumatomachoi maintain that Father, Son and Holy Ghost are nowhere co-ordinated in the New Testament.
> Seventh Century- The entire Celtic Church is excommunicated for adhering to the older rite.
> A. D. 1284—The Synod of Nemours affirms the validity of the form: I baptise thee in the name of Christ.
> A. D. 1433—John of Ragusa tells the Council of Basle that the

---

[157]Basil of Caesarea (c.330-c.379) also called Saint Basil the Great, was an East Roman bishop of Caesarea Mazaca in Cappadocia, Asia Minor (modern-day Turkey). He was an influential theologian who supported the Nicene Creed and opposed the heresies of the early Christian church.

Apostles and the Church, in spite of the Trinitarian formula, baptized for a long time in the name of Christ."[158]

264. Pohle, Joseph (1917). *The Sacraments A Dogmatic Treatise*. Volume I. St. Louis & London: B Herder (2nd revised ed.), see Section 2 Matter and Form:[159]

> "...Peter Lombard says: "He who baptizes in the name of Christ, baptizes in the name of the Trinity, which is thereby understood.... St. Thomas says: "It was by a special revelation from Christ that in the primitive Church the Apostles baptized in the name of Christ, in order that the name of Christ, which was hateful to Jews and Gentiles, might become an object of veneration, in that the Holy Ghost was given in Baptism at the invocation of that name...Though the Roman Catechism[160] attempts to justify the view that "there was a time when, by the inspiration of the Holy Ghost, the Apostles baptized in the name of our Lord Jesus Christ only...."[161]

265. Temple, S.T.L., Patrick Joseph (1922). *The Boyhood Consciousness of Christ A Critical Examination of Luke ii. 49*. New York: The Macmillan Company, p. 20:[162]

> "...that baptism in the name of Christ was always valid... maintained as late as the 15th and the 16th centuries by Adrianus (d. 1458), Cajetan (d. 1534), and Toletus (d. 1596)...the first, that the Apostles baptised in the name of Jesus alone in virtue of a special dispensation...The first view was the more prevalent one

---

[158] Albert J. Edwards, M.A., Fellow in the University of Pennsylvania 1914.

[159] The Rt. Rev. Joseph Pohle, formerly Professor of Apologetics at the Catholic University of America, now Professor of Dogma in the University of Breslau.

[160] Citing: '*P. 11, c. 2, n. 15 sq*.' He also cites Cardinal Orsi (p.224), who in 1733 wrote a treatise supporting the validity of baptism in the name of Jesus Christ, *4to Milan 1733*.

[161] Citing footnote 49 "P. II, c. 2, n. 15 sq" see also footnote 45 "Summa Theol., 3a, qu. 66, art. 6: "*Dicendum quod ex speciali Christi revelatione Apostoli in primitiva Ecclesia in nomine Christi baptizabant, ut nomen Christi, quod erat odiosum Iudaeis et gentibus, honorabile redderetur per hoc, quod ad eius invocationem Spiritus Sanctus dabatur in baptismo.*" This opinion is shared by St. Bede, Albertus Magnus, St. Bonaventure, Scotus, Cajetan, Toletus, Orsi, et al."

[162] This work was cited earlier.

in the years preceding the Council of Trent. It was held among others by Alexander of Hales, Albertus Magnus, St. Bonaventure, St. Thomas, Duns Scotus, and by the thomistic and scotistic schools generally...."[163]

266. Draper, Jonathan A. (2010). *The Didache* in *The Apostolic Fathers An Introduction*. Waco, Texas: Baylor University Press, p. 18:

"Of course, the Spirit is found also in the Trinitarian baptismal formula, which is probably a later redaction...."

267. Case, Shirley Jackson (1910). *The Missionary Idea in Early Christianity*. The Biblical World, Volume 36, No. 2 (August), p. 124:

"...the trinitarian baptismal formula of Matthew does not appear in the early references to baptism in Paul's letters and in the Book of Acts...."

268. Conybeare, F. C. (1897). *Christian Demonology. IV*. Jewish Quarterly Review, Volume 9, Issue 4 (July), p. 592:

"And though in other parts of the New Testament we hear of baptism in the name of Jesus Christ alone... The only question at issue is this. Was the formula enjoined in Matthew (or the simpler one referred to) expanded... may have worked to expand the brief formula into one more comprehensive...."

269. Conybeare, F. C. (1901). *The Eusebian form of the Text Matt. 28, 19*. Zeitschrift für die Neutestamentliche Wissenschaft, Volume 2, Issue 1, pp. 286-287:

"The official church of Rome however ignored his arguments and adopted the position that baptism in the name of Christ alone was quite valid. As the canon of the Synod of Nemours (1284) expressed it: *Dicimus, infantem baptizatum esse, si baptizans dicit: Baptizo te in nomine Christi*. It in some measure explains this decision of the Popes that the text of Mt 28, 19 was not yet

---

[163]Citing footnote 70 "Cf. Ferraris, Prompta Bibliotheca, tom. 1, s. v. Bapt. art. 3, n. 32. For St. Thomas see the Summa 3, q. 66, art. 6 ad primum; also: Exposit. in Sanct. J. C. Evang. sec. Mt. ad loc. For Scotus see: Lib. IV Sent., dist. 3, 4. 2; also Reportata Parisiensia, lib. 4, dist. 3, q. 2, n. 8."

authoritatively fixed by the church. That the Pneumatomachi of the fourth Century retained the Eusebian reading can be inferred from the arguments used by and against them...Canon Armitage Robinson inclines to the view (Art. Baptism in Encyclopedia Biblica) that Mattliew "does not here report the *ipsissi- verba* of Jesus" but transfers to him the familiar language of the "church of the Evangelist's own time and locality". The German scholar Teller in Exe. 2 of his edition of Burnet: De Fide et officiis christianorum, Halae, 1786, p. 262, disputed the genuineness of the text. So did Evanson, vicar of Tewkesbury in his letter to Hurd Bp of Worcester, 2nd Ed. London 1792. Harnack remarks (Dogmengeschichte, 68): *Dass Jesus die Taufe eingesetzt habe, lässt sich nicht direct erweisen; denn Mt 28, 19 ist kein Herrnwort*. Martineau in his "Seat of Authority" Bk. IV, eh. IV, p. 515 writes thus: "The very account which teils us that at last, after his resurrection, he commissioned his apostles to go and baptize among all nations, "betrayed itself by speaking in the Trinitarian language of the next "century, and compels us to see in it the ecclesiastical editor, and not "the evangelist, much less the founder himself"...Socinus (opera Irenopoli 1656 vol. I, 712 and II, 438) accepted the usual text as genuine, but sought to explain away its obvious meaning by means of tortuous and special pleading. J. H. Schölten in his work: Die Taufformel (übersetzt von Max Gubalke, Gotha, 1885) wrote: *Die gegenseitige Vergleichung der Texte unserer drei ersten Evangelien und die'kritische Untersuchung über ihr Alter führen somit zu dem Schlüsse, dass dem Bericht über die Einsetzung der Taufe durch Jesus in dem nach Matthäus benannten kanonischen Evangelium ein relativ spätes Datum zuerkannt werden muss*. H.'Holtzmann in an article on Baptism in the N. T. in the Zeitschrift f. wissenschaftliche Theol. 1879, p. 401, arrives at a similar conclusion."[164]

270. Beveridge, J. (1901). *Recent Foreign Theology*. The Expository Times, Volume 12, Issue 8 (January), pp. 357-358:

"The question of Baptism is evidently fermenting in Norway just now. Of the ten articles in the three issues of the *Norslz Theologisk Tidsskrzft* already published, no fewer than three deal with that

---

[164]Dr. F. C. Conybeare was a Theologian and Professor of Theology at Oxford University, England.

subject, namely, 'The Rule of Faith of the Ancient Church in its Relation to the Baptismal Confession and Holy Writ,' by Professor Lyder Brun; 'Swiss Anabaptism,' by Rev. Christen Brun; and Baptism in the New Testament,' by Professor Odland, D.D... Dr. Odland... does not see how it can well be doubted that in the apostolic age Baptism was into the name of Christ alone...On the other hand, several pertinent passages in Paul's writings definitely assume that Baptism was exclusively administered in the name of Christ. In I Cor:13-15 for example, the apostle indirectly contrasts a Baptism into his own name with the Baptism which the Corinthians had actually received. Dr. Odland's view is that It 28:19 cannot be proved to be a prescribed formula...It is only a resume of what Jesus on that occasion said, a summing up of a fuller teaching about Baptism, its significance and requirements. And he maintains that although the Didache and Justin in a later age regarded these words as a formula prescribed by Jesus, that does not prove that they were originally meant to be such...."

271. Gilbert, George Holley (1912). *Jesus.* New York: The Macmillan Company, p. 35:

"For that practice, as described in Acts and Paul's epistles was to baptize into the name of Jesus only."

272. Cross, Terry L. (1993). *Toward A Theology of The Word And The Spirit: A Review of J. Rodman William's Renewal Theology.* Journal of Pentecostal Theology, Volume 1, Issue 3, pp. 114-115:

"Williams is currently Professor of Theology at Regent University in Virginia.' He describes his writing as coming from classroom teaching; the text often has the flavor of a lecture. He has been teaching since 1959, and his writing reflects the wealth of information (especially scriptural) that he has gleaned over the years... Following his rigid adherence to biblical theology, Williams supports the possibility of baptizing in the name of Jesus only, since that is the preferred formula of Acts (not of Mt. 28)."[165]

---

[165] Citing footnote 41 "Renewal Theology, III, p. 139."

273. Ramshaw, Gail (2002). *In The Name Towards Alternative Baptismal Idioms*. The Ecumenical Review, Volume 54, Issue 3, p. 344:

> "...many theological conservatives maintain the primitive Christian practice of baptizing "in the name of Jesus."

274. Lemcio, Eugene E. (1991). *The Past of Jesus in The Gospels*. Society for New Testament Studies Monograph Series. New York: Cambridge University Press, pp. 53-55:

> "Baptizing them..." In spite of the prominence given to baptism here, during the course of Jesus' career nothing is mentioned about baptizing anyone, much less Gentiles, and certainly not in the name of the "Trinity"...'Into the name of the Father ..." As the task of baptizing finds no earlier mention, so we should not expect its mode or point of reference to appear prior to this statement. And while the names per se of each member of the Trinity do occur, the expressions "name of the Son" and "name of the Holy Spirit" are entirely absent..."And of the Son..."..."And of the Holy Spirit..." There has heretofore been no reference to "the name of the Spirit" or to baptizing in his name...."[166]

275. Bacon, Benjamin Wisner (1929). *New and Old in Jesus's Relation to John*. Journal of Biblical Literature, Volume 48, No. 1/2, Primitive Christianity and Judaism: A Symposium, p. 45:

> "...that the first Christians immediately after Calvary began to baptize into the name of Jesus...."[167]

In fact, in another work, the Yale University Professor, Professor Bacon, speaking about the Shepherd of Hermas[168] notes he is not trinitarian at all, thus:

---

[166]Eugene E. Lemcio, Professor of New Testament, Seattle Pacific University, Seattle, Washington.
[167]Benjamin W. Bacon, American Theologian and in 1897 was Professor of New Testament Criticism and Exegesis at Yale Divinity School.
[168]The early Christian document *Hermas* or *Shepherd of Hermas*, was known to the early Church Fathers. The Muratorian canon, a list of canonical books from around the 2nd century indicates that *Hermas* was written by the brother of Pius, Bishop of Rome about 140-154 A.D.

"Hermas is not in reality a trinitarian at all for all that logic requires, he might be a unitarian...."[169]

276. _____ (1917). *The American Journal of Theology* edited by The Divinity Faculty of the University of Chicago and Colleagues in Allied Department, Volume XXI. Chicago, Illinois: The University of Chicago Press, Volume XXI, p. 299:

"The Matthaean formula of baptism is probably only a liturgical expansion of the primitive formula preserved in Acts."

277. Barton, John (2002). *The Biblical World*. Volume II. London: Routledge, pp. 166, 269:[170]

"Baptism, from the outset, was accompanied by a regular form of words in which the believer was described as baptized into Jesus' 'name' (Acts 2:38; 10:48), 'in the name of the Lord Jesus...somewhat later, 'in the name of the Father, and of the Son, and of the Holy Spirit' (Mt. 28:19; Didache 7:I)...."

278. Brown, Raymond E. (2008). *Christ in the Gospels of the Liturgical Year*. Expanded Edition. Liturgical Press, p. 282:[171]

"From the very beginning the identity of Jesus' followers was established by what they believed and professed about Jesus. (Our later creeds are an enlarged expression of the faith expressed at baptism). In footnote 8 "As I explained in *A Risen Christ at Eastertime*, the use of the triadic formula in Matthew 28:19 would have been a later development...."

279. Hurtado, Larry W. (2005). *Lord Jesus Christ*. Grand Rapids,

---

[169]Bacon, Benjamin W. (1913). *Two Forgotten Creeds*. The Harvard Theological Review. Volume 6, No. 3 (July), p. 313.

[170]John Barton, Oriel and Laing Professor of the Interpretation of Holy Scripture at Oxford University.

[171]Raymond E. Brown, S.S., (1928-1998), a distinguished Auburn Professor of Biblical Studies at Union Theological Seminary in New York, an author of some forty books on the Bible and past president of three of the most important biblical societies in the world, and by appointment of two Popes (Paul VI 1972, John Paul II 1996) was a member of the Roman Pontifical Biblical Commission and heralded by *Time Magazine* as "*probably the premier Catholic Scripture scholar of the U.S.*" admits the Trinitarian formula was a later development.

Michigan: William. B. Eerdmans Publishing Company, pp. 200-201:

> "Scholars have tended to focus on the use of Jesus' name in baptism (perhaps because they were more comfortable with this more familiar rite, and also perhaps because baptism acquired/retained a more central theological significance in Christian tradition)."

280. Koester, Helmut (2000). *Introduction to the New Testament: History and Literature of Early Christianity*. Volume 2. Berlin: Walter de Gruyter & Co., Berlin, p. 69.[172]

> "Once the older baptismal formula "in the name of Jesus" was replaced by the Trinitarian formula (Matt 28:19. Did. 7.1.), Creedal formulations were expanded accordingly...."

281. Moberly, R.W.L (2000). *The Bible, Theology, and Faith*. Cambridge: Cambridge University Press, p. 197:[173]

> "On the basis of Jesus' unlimited authority and power, the command to make disciples, baptize and teach is given. The baptismal formula (v.19) is important for our discussion because of its christological language. The baptismal formula is perhaps the most striking in that it does not say 'baptizing them in my name' (*elsto onoma mou*). For that would seem to be the obvious corollary of verse 18: if all authority is given to Jesus, then people should be baptized in his name. It is presumably this interest logic of the focal position of Jesus within Christian faith (whether or not expressed in v.18) that led to the early Christian practice of baptism solely in the name of Jesus as attested in Acts (AC. 2:38; 8:16; 10:48; 19:5) and implied by Paul (1 Cor. 1:13, 15)."

282. Mosheim, John L. V (1832). *Institutes of Ecclesiastical History; Ancient And Modern in Four Books, Much Corrected, Enlarged and Improved from the Primary Authorities. Vol. III.* Hew Haven: A. H. Maltby, thus, the late Professor John Lawrence Von Mosheim, Chancellor of the University of Gottingen, notes in his study that in the year 1574, when the first

---

[172]Helmut Koester, Professor Emeritus of Ecclesiastical History at Harvard University.
[173]Professor R.W.L. Moberly was an Anglican Priest since 1982 and was a lecturer in Theology at Durham University, England.

Catechism and Confession of the Unitarians was printed at Crascow presumably Poland (?) notes the following with respect to baptism as cited in this publication, p. 264-266:

> "Baptism, say they, is the immersion in water, in the name of the Father and Son and Holy Spirit, or in the name of Jesus Christ...."

283. Campbell, R. A (1996). *Jesus and His Baptism.* Tyndale Bulletin 47.2 (November), p. 213:[174]

> "Christian baptism, though now performed in the name of Jesus or of the Trinity...."

284. Beyschlag, Willibald (1895). *New Testament Theology or Historical Account of the Teaching of Jesus And Primitive Christianity According to the New Testament Sources.* In Two Volumes. Edinburgh: T & T Clark, p. 319:[175]

> "Baptism was originally, of course, in the name of Jesus (ii. 38, viii. 16, x. 48, xix. 5)...."

285. Bultmann, Rudolf K (2007). *Theology of The New Testament. Trans.* Kendrick Grobel. First Published (1951), 2 volumes. Waco, Texas: Baylor University Press, p.133:

> "The one baptizing names over the one being baptized the name of "the Lord Jesus Christ" later expanded to the name of the Father, the Son, and the Holy Spirit...."[176]

286. Schreiner, Thomas R. and Wright, Shawn (2000). *Believer's Baptism, Sign of the New Testament Covenant in Christ.* B&H Publishing, p. 23:[177]

---

[174]Dr. Ronald A. Campbell, lecturer in Biblical Studies at the United Theological College of the West Indies, Jamaica, former tutor at Spurgeon's College, London, a Baptist Minister.

[175]Dr. Willibald Beyschlag, Professor of Theology at Halle.

[176]*Rudolf* Karl *Bultmann* was a German Lutheran theologian and professor of the New Testament at the University of Marburg, see also page 13 that speaks of Acts 4:12 as being the name of Jesus in baptism.

[177]Professor Thomas R. Schreiner, James Buchanan Harrison New Testament Professor at Southern Baptist Theological Seminary and Assistant Professor Shawn Wright, Professor of Church History also at the Southern Baptist Theological Seminary.

> "...Baptism is to be administered in (*eis*, Lit. *"into"*) the name (singular) of the Father, Son, and the Holy Spirit, one of the most explicit Trinitarian formulas in the entire NT. In light of the fact that the early church is shown to have baptized in the name of Jesus Christ (*Jesou Christou*; Acts 2:38; 10:48) or "Lord Jesus" (*kuriou Iesou*; Acts 8:16; 19:5) and Paul refers merely to baptism in the name of Christ (*Christon* [*Iesoun*]; Gal. 3:27; Rom 6:3), the question arises whether this formulation reflects later baptismal practice. If Matthew was written prior to AD 70; however, there is hardly enough time for a Trinitarian practice of baptism to evolve if this was not already taught by Jesus himself as Matthew's Gospel indicates. It appears more likely that the early church felt no contradiction between Jesus' command to baptize in the name of the Father, the Son, and the Holy Spirit and its practice of baptizing in the name of Jesus, since the latter implied for the former."

287. Williams, Rodman J (1996). *Renewal Theology: Systematic Theology from a Charismatic Perspective (Three Volumes in one)*. Grand Rapids, Michigan: Zondervan Publishing House, p. 286:[178]

> "Another matter that calls for some discussion relates to the difference in formulas for water baptism as set for in Matthew 28:19 and in the books of Acts. We earlier observed that water baptism in invariably depicted in Acts as being the name of Jesus only, but we did not actually deal with the fact that in Matthew the formula is a triune one: "Go therefore and make disciples of all nations, baptizing them in the name of the Father, Son and of the Holy Spirit....Although there is no simple solution to the difference, a few comments relevant to our concerns may be made. First, the longer Matthean statement suggests that water baptism represents entrance into a new relationship to God as Father, Son and Holy Spirit. Second, the shorter Lukan formula (in Acts) specifies that at the heart of this relationship is the forgiveness of sins that comes in the

---

[178] J. Rodman Williams, Professor of Theology at Regent University. Despite Professor Williams' assertion in the foregoing statement, he suggests in a footnote on page 286 (footnote 48) that: *"Hence either formula is suitable for use in water baptism."*

name of Jesus Christ (the Son). Third, since Jesus is "the fullness of the Godhead," baptism in relation to the fullness of the divine reality: it is also, by implication, in the name of the Father, Son and Holy Spirit. Thus there is no essential difference between the Matthean and Lukean formulas: the former highlight's the fullness of the relationship into which one enters at baptism, the latter specifies the purpose of baptism...."

288. Thompson, John (1994). *Modern Trinitarian Prospective*. New York: Oxford University Press, p. 98:

"...In the New Testament the Church began to baptize in the name of Jesus for the forgiveness of sins on the basis of His work on the Cross...since the early baptismal formulae was 'in the name of Jesus'...."[179]

289. Sabatier, Auguste (1904). *The Religions of Authority And The Religion of The Spirit*. London: Williams & Norgate and New York: McClure, Phillips & Co., p. 52:

"Was the institution of baptism the act of Jesus himself? In the present condition of the text it is impossible to prove it. The command of Matthew xxvii, 19, which seems to attribute it to him, is not only posthumous, but even appears late in the tradition of the Apostolic Church. No other Gospel contains it."[180]

290. Drown, Edward S (1917). *The Apostles Creed To-Day*. New York: The MacMillan Company, p. 31-32, 36:

"The most probable explanation, and the one now generally accepted by New Testament scholars, is that originally Baptism was given in the name of Jesus or of Christ, and that the Trinitarian form is a later, even although a perfectly legitimate, development of the original formula. He who was baptized into the name of the Lord Jesus was baptized into the name of the

---

[179]John Thompson, Professor of Systematic Theology at Union Theological College, Belfast.

[180]Dr. Auguste Sabatier, Professor in The University of Paris, Dean of The Protestant Theological Faculty.

Father whom He revealed, and into the name of the Spirit whom He brought. The Trinitarian form became established, and the earlier form gradually disappeared from use...Thus, Baptism into the name of Jesus became baptism into the name of the Father, and of the Son and of the Holy Ghost."[181]

291. Lockett, H. D. (1905). *Inaugural Lectures Delivered by Members of the Faculty During if First Session, 1904-05*. Publication of the University of Manchester Theological Series No.1. London & Manchester: Sheratt & Hughes Publishers, p. 241:

"...further that we never read in the New Testament of the use of the Trinitarian formula, but of baptism into the name of Jesus Christ or the Lord Jesus, and that this simpler form lasted on with the other into the third century..."[182]

292. Dale, James W. (1874). *An Inquiry into the Usage of Baptize and the nature of Christic and Patristic Baptism as Exhibited in the Holy Scriptures and Patristic Writings* by James W. Dale, D.D. (Pastor of Wayne Presbyterian Church, Delaware County, PA). Pennsylvania: WM. Rutter & Co, pp. 415-416:

"Prof. Godwin, *Christian Baptism, 151, London*: "It has been supposed that in Matt. 28:19 we have the institution of the ordinance of Christian baptism, and also the form of words to be used in administration of the rite. John 3:22, 4:1, clearly show that the rite of Christian baptism existed long before. There is nothing in this commission to make it more probable that they had not before baptized Jews, than that they had not before taught Jews. Had this been a form of words for the administration of baptism, the expression would rather have been–Baptizing them, saying, I baptize thee, etc. There is no indication of the use of this form in the Acts of the Apostles. The great object of baptism is denoted by the terms, 'For the Father, and the Son, and the Holy Ghost.' The name of a person, by a Hebrew idiom indicates that person

---

[181]Dr. Edward S. Drown, Professor in the Episcopal Theological School in Cambridge.
[182]Reverent H. D. Lockett, M.A., Lecturer on the History of Doctrine; Principal of Ordsall Hall, in the inaugural lectures delivered by members of the faculty in the University of Manchester, England during session 1904-05.

himself."

293. Schaberg, Jane (1982). *The Father, The Son And The Holy Spirit The Triadic Phrase in Matthew 28:19b*. SBL Dis. Series 61. CA: Published by Scholar Press, pp. 335-336:

"The most important conclusion of this study is that the triadic phrase in Matt 28:19b, naming Father, the Son and the Holy Spirit, is a development of the triad found in Daniel 7; Ancient of Days, one like the son of man and angels. It is not to be traced to the triad found in the similitude, although evidence has been found of the use of the common Dainelic traditions. The NT development is more than the adjustment and alteration of titles; it is the process of 'organic growth' alive by adaptation. The Matthean triad and Matthew's understanding of it are integral parts of an interpretation of Daniel which emphasizes the wisdom and apocalyptic elements of that work, highlighting the theme of transcendence of death on the part of authentic Israel and highlighting the importance for all nations of Israel's exaltation. In Christian belief in the exaltation of the historical Jesus of Nazareth, the mythological and semi-mythological elements of the book of Daniel and of its interpretative tradition come to a new distinctive focus. The vision of the eschatological theophany is not left "in the world of myth." Joined to the commission to make disciples, it is presented as inspiration and impetus for the renewal of history by means of the formation of a new community of the Son of Man. I conclude also that behind Matt 28:16-20 a traditional midrash, containing the triadic phrase, can be isolated. This midrash may have functioned as a liturgical tradition associated with the rite of baptism, possibly seen by some as the fulfillment and extension of the rite of John the Baptist. Matthew has redacted this midrash in line with his emphasis on the essential importance of obedience to Jesus as ultimate *Maskil*, whose life and teaching offer a hermeneutical key to the interpretation of Torah for the present age. The Matthean pericope is a statement of the Evangelist's ideal of balance between enthusiasm and righteousness. I conclude further that there is not sufficient evidence to indicate that the triadic phrase, either at the midrashic or at the Matthean redactional state, is trinitarian."[183]

294. Clemen, Carl (1912). *Primitive Christianity And Its Non-Jewish Sources.* Edinburgh: T&T Clark, p. 214:

> "...but even at a previous time Jesus cannot, I think, have instituted a form of baptism in the name of the Father, Son, and Holy Spirit; for such a triadic formula of baptism—and that is surely what is wanted to correspond with the baptismal command—is not found elsewhere before the second century." See also footnote 1 in which Clemen states that "The formula..., or the like, still occurs in the second century; but that does not prove that a triadic formula of baptism was in existence even at an earlier time, when we always hear only of a baptism in the name of Christ...."[184]

295. McFayden, John. E (1909). *Interpreter's Commentary on the New Testament Volume 1, The Epistle To The Corinthians and Galatians.* A. S. Barnes & Company, p. 40:

> "All these three acts – baptism, sanctification and justification – were effected in the name of the (or *our*) Lord Jesus Christ and in the spirit of our God. In particular, baptism is in the name of Jesus (the Trinitarian formula is not yet in use, Matt. xxvii.19)...."[185]

296. Paine, Levi L (1901). *The Ethnic Trinities And Their Relations To The Christian Trinity A Chapter in The Comparative History of Religion.* Boston and New York: Houghton, Mihlin and Company and Cambridge: The Riverside Press, p. 231:

---

[183]Note also that Professor Osborne Grant who has pointed out with respect to Matthew 28:19 that: *"Many scholars believe it resulted from a later Church tradition read back into the resurrection events."* And that: *"The major problem is that elsewhere the baptismal formula includes only one member ("in the name of Jesus")"* Grant, Osborne. *Redaction Criticism And The Great Commission: A Case Study Toward A Biblical Understanding Of Inerrancy.* Journal of the Evangelical Theological Society 19:2 (Spring 1976), p. 80.

[184]Dr. Carl Clemen, Professor in the University of Bonn.

[185]John Edgar McFadyen, Professor of Old Testament Literature and Exegesis, Know College, Toronto, Canada.

"When or how this formal originated is wholly unknown...and note historically that the form of baptism was 'into Christ' and not unto the Trinity. Paul knew nothing of this Trinitarian formula."[186]

297. Knowles, James (ed.) (1879?). *Baptism*. The Nineteenth Century A Monthly Review. Vol. VI. July – December 1879. London: C. Keegan Paul & Co., p. 692:[187]

"It was, if not always, yet whenever we hear of its use in the Acts of the Apostles, in the name of the 'Lord Jesus.' Doubtless the more comprehensive form in which Baptism is now everywhere administered in the threefold name of the Father, the Son and the Holy Spirit, soon superseded the simpler form of that in the name of the Lord Jesus only" a note also that in his footnote he comments that: "Acts ii. 38, viii.16, x.48. The form of the name of the Father, Son, and Holy Ghost, though found in early times, was not universal. Cyprian and Pope Nicholas I. acknowledge the validity of Baptism, 'In the name of the Lord Jesus.' See Dr. Smith's Dictionary of Christian Antiquities, vol. i., p. 162."

298. Dowley, Tim (2013). *Introduction To The History of Christianity*. (2nd ed). Minneapolis, Fortress Press, p. 73 and Dowley, Tim (2018). *A Short Introduction To The History of Christianity*. Minneapolis, Fortress Press, p. 40:

"Although at first people were often baptized in the name of Christ alone, it soon became standard to be baptized in the name of the Trinity."

299. Schröter, Jens (2013). *Trinitarian Belief, Binitarian Monotheism, And The One God: Reflections on The Origin of Christian Faith in Affiliation To Larry Hurtado's Christological Approach* in *Reflections on The Early Christian History of Religion*. Breytenbach, Cillies & Frey, Jörg (ed.). Boston & Leiden: Brill, pp. 171-172, 174-175:

---

[186] Levi Leonard Paine, Waldo Professor of Ecclesiastical History in Bangor Theological Seminary.

[187] Arthur Penrhyn Stanley, the very Reverent, Dean of Westminster Abbey, and an academic at heart being a former Regius Professor of Ecclesiastical History at the University of Oxford.

"At the outset, it has to be noted that the term "Trinity" itself does not occur in earliest Christian confessions nor is there any explicit reflection about a "Trinitarian God" in a conceptual or terminological way. At the earliest stages one finds instead individual formulae expressing the faith in God and Jesus Christ or Christological convictions about Jesus' pre-existence, his resurrection and exaltation, some of them in hymnic style, indicating that they were used in the worship of the early communities.3 These formulae as well as the writings of the New Testament have therefore to be distinguished from concepts about the relationship of God and Jesus Christ and the Trinitarian nature of God, developed by Christian theologians as e.g. Tertullian, Theophilus of Antioch or Origen from the middle of the second century onwards on the basis of biblical traditions and philosophical thoughts They have also to be differentiated from the elaborated creedal texts of the fourth and fifth century, as e.g. the Niceno-Constantinopolitan Creed or the Creed of Chalcedon in which the consubstantiality of God and Jesus Christ and the emanation of the Holy Spirit from the father (and the Son) are expressed…That in the beginning of Christianity converts were baptized "in the name of Jesus (Christ)" can be concluded from the formulations εἰς τὸ ὄνομα, ἐπὶ τὸ ὀνόματι or ἐν τῷ ὀνόματι Ἰησοῦ Χριστοῦ in the Pauline letters and the Acts of the Apostles… It is not surprising that an elaborated concept of the Trinitarian God does not occur in the New Testament since the authors of these writings came from a Jewish background and developed the faith in Jesus Christ on the basis of Jewish monotheism."[188]

300. Stampfer, Shaul (2013). *Did The Khazars Convert to Judaism?* Jewish Theological Studies, Volume 19, No. 3 (Spring/Summer), pp. 69-70:

"The mid-ninth-century correspondence between Khan Boris of the Bulgars and Pope Nicholas included the following: "You ask about what should be done concerning many people in your

---

[188] Jens Schröter is Professor of Exegesis and Theology of the New Testament and Early Christian Apocrypha at the Faculty of Theology at Humboldt University Berlin. Before 2009 he was a Professor of New Testament Studies at the universities of Erfurt, Hamburg and Leipzig.

country who you claim have been baptized by some Jew, though whether he is Christian or pagan you do not know. Of course, if these people have been baptized in the name of the holy Trinity or in the name of Christ alone, as we read in the Acts of the Apostles [Acts 19:5]—for as St. Ambrose explains, it is one and the same thing—it is agreed that they should not be baptized again."

301. Armstrong, Karen (1983). *The First Christian: Saint Paul's Impact on Christianity*. London and Sydney: Pan Books, p. 128 (here Karen is speaking about the Apostle Paul):[189]

"He had never heard of the Holy Trinity in our sense, even though he speaks of the Father, the Son and the Spirit."[190]

302. Roberts, Nancy (2011). *Trinity v. Monotheism A False Dichotomy*. The Muslim World, Volume 101, pp. 76, 82:

"Matthew 28:18–19. Doubts have been cast by some on the authenticity of Matthew 28:19 in its present form, one reason for which is that in Luke's Acts of the Apostles, believers are only said to have been baptized "in the name of Jesus Christ" (Acts 2:38, 10:48) or "in the name of the Lord Jesus" (Acts 8:16, 19:5)…As has been noted, the biblical evidence for the doctrine of the Trinity is ambiguous, whereas a clear and firm Biblical foundation can be cited for divine unity. God is explicitly declared to be "one" (cf. Deut. 6:4, "Hear, O Israel: The Lord our God is one Lord…"; Isaiah 44:6, "…I am the first and I am the last, besides me there is no God"; and I Cor. 8:4–6, "…there is no God but one"). Nowhere, however, is He declared to be three. This, together with the abstruse, confusing nature of the discussions that have surrounded the Trinity over the ages, the plethora of heresies which have arisen precisely in an attempt to make sense of the notion of God as three in one, and the tragic end met by individuals who, like Michael Servetus, were earnest

---

[189] Karen Armstrong OBE FRSL is a British author and commentator of Irish Catholic descent known for her books on comparative religion and is a former Roman Catholic Nun.

[190] This citation was found in the publication by Nancy Roberts on page 77 in *Trinity v. Monotheism*.

seekers of truth, would surely indicate the need to avoid dogmatic intransigence and literalism and, instead, to adopt a spirit of the utmost tolerance and caution when it comes to beliefs concerning what it means to speak of God as triune...trinitarian Christians can come to the realization that not all Christian believers are trinitarians, nor do they need to be in order to be faithful to the message Jesus brought."

303. _____ (1892). *Art. X–Summaries of Foreign Review.* The Scottish Review. January and April, Volume XIX. London: Alexander Gardner, p. 288:

"...Paul, it is argued from 1 Cor., chap. i., used no baptismal formula, certainly not the threefold formula of Matthew xxviii. The earliest formula was a simpler one...."

304. Robinson, J. A. T. (1953). *The One Baptism As A Category of New Testament Soteriology.* The Scottish Journal of Theology, Volume Six. Liechtenstein, Nendeln: Kraus, p. 266:

"The first act of the new era of the Church follows immediately and necessarily from it, when what has been given is transmitted by water in the name of Jesus (Acts 2:38)...The language of the washing, the mention of the name...all suggest the act of Christian initiation."[191]

305. Hurtado, Larry W. (2006). *The Earliest Christian Artifacts Manuscripts and Christian Origins.* Grand Rapids, Michigan: William B. Eerdmans Publishing Company, p. 118:

"Jesus' name clearly functioned with such divine significance, for example, in the early Christian ritual/devotional practice of appealing to/invoking him. Indeed, the biblical (OT) formula for worship given to God (to "call upon the name of the Lord") was appropriated to refer to this practice of invoking Jesus' name (e.g., Acts 2:21; Rom. 10:9-i3). To cite important settings for this practice, we have references indicating that Jesus' name was

---

[191]Rev. & Dr. J. A. T. Robinson was an Anglican Theologian, Bishop of Woolwich, Lecturer in Theology at Cambridge University, Fellow and Dean of Dhapel Trinity, and visiting Professor of McMaster University, Hamilton, Ontario, Canada.

invoked in the initiation ritual of baptism (e.g., Acts 2:38) and in exorcism."

306. Childs, Brevard S (1993). *Biblical Theology of The Old and New Testaments Theological Reflections on The Christian Bible*. Minneapolis: Fortress Press, pp. 364-365, 367, 376, 521:

"Although it is obvious that the New Testament has not developed a full-blown doctrine of the Trinity...it remains a difficult problem to trace the development within the early church from its initial focus on christology to its expanded triadic formulation...The New Testament witness which started with its experience of Christ as the unique manifestation of God sought to understand Christ's relationship to the Father. This theological reflection never evoked the need to correct the witness of the scriptures. The Old Testament remained the true Word of God also for the early church. Nor was there ever an antagonism or tension discovered within the Godhead, such as later Gnosticism suggested. Rather, different roles were assigned to the Father, the Son, and the Spirit...In sum, the early church's struggle to understand the relationship between Jesus Christ whom it confessed as Lord, and God who had revealed himself to Israel, lay at the heart of the development of Trinitarian theology...God's reality was thus experienced in its peculiar, distinctive activity which the church later struggled to articulate in Trinitarian language... The church's struggle with the Trinity was not a battle against the Old Testament, but rather a battle for the Old Testament, for the one eternal covenant of God in both unity and diversity. Historically, the doctrine of the Trinity developed from a christological centre (Cullmann, *Die ersten christlichen Glaubensbekenntnisse*)...First, it is incumbent on the interpreter, especially of the Old Testament, not to confuse the biblical witness with the reality itself. In order to hear the voice of each biblical witness in its own right, it is absolutely necessary to interpret each passage within its historical, literary, and canonical context. Even during the period of its greatest commitment to the allegorical method, the church never fully lost this insight. If one takes the Old Testament genre of the story seriously as one form of its witness, then to read back into the story the person of Jesus Christ, or to interpret the various theophanies as the manifestation of the second person of the Trinity, is to distort the witness and to drown out the Old Testament's own voice... Although the doctrine of the Trinity is not fully developed in either of the testaments..."[192]

307. Schreiner, Thomas R (2008). *New Testament Theology Magnifying God in Christ*. Grand Rapids, Michigan: Baker Academics, pp. 238-239, 259, 267, 460, 494, 506:

"Jesus' uniqueness as God's Son stands out in the baptismal formula (Matt. 28:19). Baptism is to be applied in the name of the Father, the Son, and the Spirit. There is one name, and yet three different entities that are to be invoked during baptism. Here we are on the brink of the full trinitarian formulas of later church history, although Matthew, of course does not work out his statement into the notion of three persons and one divine essence... There is no doubt, according to the Gospel of John, that Jesus is God. The Gospel climaxes with Thomas's declaration to Jesus: "My Lord and my God" (John 20:28).112 The disciples grasp who Jesus truly is when he is raised from the dead. The acclamation of Jesus' deity forms an inclusio with John 1:1, framing the entire Gospel. The same framing device exists in the prologue itself. The best textual reading of John 1:18 proclaims that Jesus is "the only God" (monogenēs theos)...Since Jesus as the Christ is the exalted Lord, Acts emphasizes the name of Jesus...It is quite striking, then, to see that believers are baptized in the name of Jesus Christ (Acts 2:38; 10:48)...The "trinitarian" references in Luke-Acts are not prominent, nor are they emphasized...Hebrews does not reflect on or develop a doctrine of the Trinity...no formal doctrine of the Trinity is worked out or explicated in the NT..."[193]

308. Marshall, I. Howard (2004). *New Testament Theology Many Witnesses, One Gospel*. Downers Grove, Illinois: InterVarsity Press, p. 634:

---

[192]Brevard Springs Childs was an American Old Testament scholar and Professor of Old Testament at Yale University from 1958 until 1999, who is considered one of the most influential biblical scholars of the 20th century.
[193]*Thomas R. Schreiner* is the James Buchanan Harrison Professor of New Testament Interpretation and a Professor of Biblical Theology at Southern Seminary.

"And, finally, when James mentions "the noble name of him to whom you belong" (Jas 2:7), this is surely a reference to baptism in the name of Jesus, again with all that this implies for the position of Jesus as Lord and Savior."[194]

309. Dunn, James D. G. (1998). *The Theology of Paul the Apostle*. Grand Rapids, Michigan: William B. Eerdmans Publishing Company, pp. 447, 540, 728:

"First, we should give due weight to what must have been the social significance of baptism from the beginning. Conversion, typically, was not some private spiritual transaction. It involved baptism. In his indisputable references to the rite of baptism, Paul takes it for granted that all his readers (including those unknown to him personally) had been baptized. The implication of 1 Cor. 1.13-15 is quite clearly that the Corinthians had all been baptized "in the name of Christ"...we do not hear of any believers who had not been baptized in the name of Jesus...the churches (of God) in Judea, in Galatia, in Asia, or in Macedonia. Each gathering of those baptized in the name of the Lord Jesus was "the assembly of God" in that place...Baptism was "in the name of" Christ."

310. Ladd, George Eldon (1974). *A Theology of The New Testament*. Grand Rapids, Michigan: William B. Eerdmans Publishing Company, pp. 244, 367, 383, 387:

"It is as believers are baptized in the name of Jesus that the Spirit is received (2:38; 10:43-48, etc.)...Peter told the Jews to be baptized in the name of Jesus the Christ (2:38; see also 3:6; 4:10; 8:12)... Now they were baptized not only in the name of the Lord Jesus but also with the Holy Spirit...Perhaps they were converts of Apollos who knew only the baptism of John until he met Priscilla and Aquila (18:25-26). When they were baptized in the name of the Lord Jesus, Paul laid his hands on them, and they too were baptized with the Spirit and spoke in tongues and prophesied (19:6)...baptism becomes the outward sign of admission to the Christian fellowship, and believers are baptized

---

[194] I. Howard Marshall, Emeritus Professor of New Testament Exegesis and Honorary Research Professor at the University of Aberdeen in Aberdeen, Scotland.

"in the name of Jesus Christ" (2:38)."[195]

311. Kaye, John (1888). *Works of John Kayne Bishop of Lincoln.* In Eight Volumes, Vol. IV. The Ecclesiastical History of Eusebius. London: Rivingtons, p. 4:

> "It is certain that previously to the commission here given, the disciples of Christ administered the rite of baptism by His authority. (See John iv. 1.) And we learn from Tertullian's Tract on Baptism, that the question "with what baptism they baptized?" "was agitated even in his day. He answers, with the baptism of John; because the baptism of Christ could not be ad ministered until the events from which it was to derive its efficacy, His passion and resurrection, had taken place. The jealousy, however, expressed by John's disciples (John iii. 26) implies that those of Christ baptized in their Master's name; and we should naturally expect that this would be the case. After the Apostles had been enjoined to baptize in the name of the Father, Son, and Holy Ghost, we find St. Peter exhorting his hearers to be baptized in the name of Jesus Christ (Acts ii. 38); and commanding Cornelius and his companions to be baptized in the name of the Lord. (Acts x. 48.) The converts, also, whom St. Paul found at Ephesus were baptized in the name of the Lord Jesus. (Acts xix. 5.) Baptism, therefore, in the name of Jesus Christ must have been equivalent to baptism in the name of the Holy Trinity."

312. Gardner, Percy (1899). *Exploratio Evangelica A Brief Examination of The Basis And Origin of Christian Belief.* New York: G. P. Putnam's Son & London: Adam and Charles Black, p. 444-445:[196]

> "What is certain is that, soon after that death, converts were baptized into the name of Jesus Christ...Thus the Christian element which was added to the Jewish and Pagan rite was the name into which disciples were baptized. In the Acts this name is that of "the Lord" or of "Jesus Christ." For example, St. Peter,

---

[195]*George Eldon Ladd* (1911–1982) was Professor of *New Testament* Exegesis and *Theology* at Fuller *Theological* Seminary, Pasadena, California.

[196]Percy Gardner was an English classical archaeologist and numismatist and Disney Professor of Archaeology University of Cambridge (1880-1887) and Professor of Classical Archaeology University of Oxford (1887-1925).

preaching on the day of Pentecost, is reported to have said, "Repent, and be baptized every one of you in the name of Jesus Christ, for the remission of sins. " And the same Apostle, on the occasion of his visit to Cornelius," "commanded them to be baptized in the name of the Lord." It has been maintained by some commentators that although the name of Christ only is here mentioned, we may suppose that the usual Trinitarian formula of baptism is intended. This explanation is indefensible, being quite inconsistent with the most authentic records of early Christianity, the Epistles of St. Paul to the Romans and the Corinthians. "So many of us," he says, "as were baptized into Jesus Christ, were baptized into his death," and again "Was Paul crucified for you, or were ye baptized into the name of Paul?" in which passage it is implied that the converts were baptized into the name of him who was crucified…Thus there can be no question that the earliest Christian baptism was into the name of Jesus Christ; and that the last verses of Matthew's Gospel, prescribing baptism into the name of Father, Son, and Holy Spirit, do not embody the teaching of the Master, or even of his Apostles, at the first… But it seems quite impossible that the custom of baptizing into the name of Christ only could have persisted among the early disciples, if the Master himself had, as a last solemn injunction, prescribed a different baptismal formula."

313. France, R. T. (1989). *Matthew Evangelist and Teacher*. Eugene, Oregon: Wipf & Stock, p. 316:

"…New Testament period, when baptism was, according to Acts, simply in the name of Jesus (Acts 2:38; 8:16; 10:48; 19:5)…Matthew 28:19…It is not necessarily true that Matthew intended this clause specifically for use as a set formula…."

314. MacEwen, Robert K. (2015). *Matthean Posteriority An Exploration of Matthew's Use of Mark and Luke as a Solution to The Synoptic Problem*. London & New York: Bloomsbury T&T Clark, p. 143:

"The fact that baptism performed in Acts are always in the name of Jesus…."[197]

---

[197] Robert K. MacEwen is a Lecturer of Biblical Studies and Director of The Chinese Theology Department at the East Asia School of Theology.

315. O'Neil, H. C. (1914). *Stokes' Complete One Volume Encyclopaedia*. New York: Frederick A. Stokes Company, p. 167:

> "The command to baptize all nations is in Matthew 28:19. The authenticity of the Trinitarian formula has been questioned as there is some reason for thinking that b. simply into the name of Christ was the primitive custom."

316. Leishman, Thomas (1871). *Thesis A Critical Account of The Various Theories on The Sacrament of Baptism*. Edinburgh: William Blackwood & Sons, p. 16:

> "It appears from words which follow the passage, and have probably an intended connection with it, that a baptismal rite, different from that of John, was being administered in the name of Christ and was recognized as the badge of discipleship."

317. White, James F. (1993). *A Brief History of Christian Worship*. Nashville, Tennessee: Abington Press:[198]

> "The earliest baptismal formula seems to be 'in the name of the Lord Jesus' (Acts 19:5). This is corroborated by passages such as Acts 2:38 'in the name of Jesus Christ,' 'in the name of the Lord Jesus' (Acts 8:16), 'calling on his name' (Acts 22:16)…In the first century, this formula was probably replaced by the familiar Trinitarian one found in Matthew 28:19, 'in the name of the Father and of the Son and of the Holy Spirit."

318. Davies, Horton (1961). *Worship and Theology in England From Watts and Wesley to Maurice*. Volume III. Princeton, New Jersey: Princeton University Press, pp. 87-88:[199]

> "The Order of Baptism has some interesting feature. Baptism

---

[198] James F. White holds the Bard Thompson Chair of Liturgical Studies at Drew University. He previously taught at the Perkins School of Theology for twenty-two years and was professor of liturgy at the University of Notre Dame until 1999. He has served as president of the North American Academy of Liturgy and received its Berakah Award. He also chaired the editorial committee of the Section on Worship of the Board of Discipleship of The United Methodist Church.

[199] Dr. Horton Davies is the Henry W. Putnam, Professor Emeritus of the History of Christianity at Princeton University.

may be administered...on the authority of Acts of the Apostle 2:38 and 19:5; by the formula 'I baptize thee into the name of Jesus Christ'...For you are baptized into the name of Jesus only...." - This reference to baptismal form and practice appears sometime in 1774(?) England [emphasis by the author].

319. Pathrapankal, J. (2003). *Mission of The Church in India Based on Acts 1:8* in *Bend Without Fear Hope and Possibilities for an Indian Church Essays in Honour of Professor Kurien Kunnumpuram SJ*. Jnana-Deepa: ISPCK, Indian Society for Promoting Christian Knowledge, p. 273:[200]

"But it is the opinion of many scholars that this mission command is a later addition to the Gospel and it is quite probable that in the mission command in Matthew also some additions have been introduced at a later time, especially with regard to the Trinitarian baptismal formula, because the early baptisms described in the Acts of the Apostles were all administered in the name of Jesus (Acts 8:16, 10:48, 19:5)."

320. Kuttiyanikkal, Ciril J. (2014). *Khrist Bhakta Movement: A Model for An Indian Church? In Culturation in Area of Community Building*. Tilburg Theological Studies. Munster, Germany: LIT Verlag, p. 276:

"However, the Christian baptism was distinguished from John's in its call for faith in Jesus, its being administered in Jesus' name...."

321. Konig, Andrea (2010). *Glaube and Denken Mission, Dialogue, and Peaceful Co-Existence*. Frankfurt, Germany: Peter Lang GmbH, p. 94:

"Second, different passages in the book of Acts of the Apostles show that in the early church baptism was given in the name of Jesus. If Jesus had asked his disciples to baptise in the name of the Father, Son, and Holy Spirit how could they baptise in Jesus' name? The Trinitarian formula is a later addition in Matthew and the words of the Great Commission were put into the mouth of Jesus."

---

[200]Dr. J. Pathrapankal, is an Indian New Testament scholar and Indian Jesuit Priest, a member of the academic staff of the faculty of Theology at Junana Deepa, Institute of Philosophy and Theology, Pune.

322. Loke, Andrew Ter Ern (2017). *The Origin of Divine Christology*. Society for New Testament Studies Monograph Series 169. New York: Cambridge University Press, p. 179:

> "As for the existence of other phrases in the early Christian documents that are associated with baptism, it is noted that all of them refer to Jesus…to the early Christians to summarize it using other forms such as 'into the name of the Lord', such that Jesus is still a central figure in the baptismal thinking…."[201]

323. Osborne, Grant (2010). *Matthew Exegetical Commentary on The New Testament*. Grand Rapids, Michigan: Zondervan, p. 1081:

> "The other issue whether the original formula was monadic, since other references to baptism in the NT use variations of 'in the name of Jesus Christ'…there is no reason to doubt the validity of this formula as authentic as both the monadic and Trinitarian forms may well have existed side by side…."

324. Kantzer, Kenneth S. and Gundr, Stanley N. (1979). *Perspectives on Evangelical Theology Papers from The Thirtieth Annual Meeting on Evangelical Theological Society*. Grand Rapids, Michigan: Baker Book House, p. 61:

> "…in the case of Matthew 28:19 it seems most likely that at some point the tradition or Matthew expanded on original monadic formula. Such redaction should not surprise us…."

325. Norris Jr., Richard A. (2006). *Confessional and Catechetical Formulas in First-and Early-second Century Christian Literature* in *One Lord, One Faith, One Baptism Studies in Christian Ecclesiality and Ecumenism in Honor of J. Robert Wright*. Grand Rapids, Michigan: William B. Eerdmans Publishing Company, p. 24:

> "Whatever interpretation is put on this text, there can be no question of its central importance for the history of creedal forms. By the middle of the second century at the latest,

---

[201] Andrew Ter Ern Loke is Research Assistant Professor at the Faith and Global Engagement Initiative, the University of Hong Kong. See also the University of Portland Review Volumes 29-31, p. 36 noting that *"on the other hand according to modern exegesis the trinitarian formula in Matthew 28:19 does not belong to the ipsissima verba of Jesus as Fr. Hagerty still suggests."*

baptismal formulas that conformed to the structure if not the exact language of the expression 'in the name of the Father and of the Son and of the Holy Spirit' seem to have been prevalent in the churches, and it is difficult not to suppose that these words of Matthew had some, even if not exclusive, responsibility for this development. On the other hand, if they are taken as prescribing the language–the precise words–of some baptismal formula, their presence in Matthew is difficult to account for in view of the fact that the practice they seem to inculcate is not obvious in any of the records of the first-century Christian movement. This difficulty, moreover, is not eased by the obvious step of discounting the truth-claim of Matthew's story. Even if one reads Matthew 28:19 not as *ipsiisma verba Domini* but as an allusion to later ecclesiastical practice attributed to Jesus by the tradition on which the author drew, the verse could be understood as enjoining a baptismal formula only if the use of such a triadic formula were a practice so settled and unquestioned that it could be given dominical authority without appearance of innovation. Yet there is no reason to suppose that this explanation is the case. The question of how to take Matthew 28:19 therefore still remains."[202]

326. McGiffert, Arthur. C. (1903). *A History of Christianity in the Apostolic Age* (Rev. Ed.). New York: Charles Scribner's, p.61:

"Of the trinitarian formula, into the name of the Father, the Son and Holy Spirit, which later became universal in the church, we have no trace in the New Testament, except in the single passage, Matt. Xxviii. 19. It is difficult to suppose that it was employed in the early days with which we are here concerned; for it involves a conception of the nature of the rite which was entirely foreign to the thought of these primitive Christians, and indeed no less foreign to the thought of Paul. When and how the formula arose, we do not know." [In the footnote (1) cited the following is also observed] "It is difficult in light of all we know of Jesus' principles and practice, and in light also of the fact that the early disciples, and Paul as well, baptized into the name of Christ alone, to

---

[202]Dr. Richard A. Norris, Jr., late Professor Emeritus of Church History, Union Theological Seminary, New York.

suppose that Jesus himself uttered the words: "Baptizing them into the name of the Father and of the Son and of the Holy Ghost," which are quoted in Matt. Xxviii.19. But it may be that he directed his apostles not simply to make disciples of all the nations but also to baptize them, as they had, perhaps, been in the habit already of baptizing those that joined their company. If, then, he simply gave the general direction to baptize (cf. the appendix of Mark xvi. 16), it would be very natural for a scribe to add the formula, "Into the name of the Father and of the Son and of they Holy Ghost," which was in common use in his day. On the hand, the fact must be recognized that Paul's indifference about performing the rite of baptism (see 1 Cor. i. 14 sq.) is hardly what we should expect if the eleven apostles received from Christ a direct command to baptize; and it is not impossible that the entire passage (Matt. Xxviii. 19b) is a later addition, as maintained by some scholars (cf. Teichmann's article, *Die Taufe bei Paulus*, in the *Zeitschrift fur Theologie und Kirche*, 1896, Heft 4, pp. 357 sq.)."[203]

327. Lester, Charles Stanley (1912). *The Historic Jesus A Study Of The Synoptic Gospels*. New York and London: The Knickerboxer Press, G.P. Putmam's Sons, pp. 399-400:

"There is no evidence of the use of this formula (Trinitarian form) in baptism before the year 130 A.D., nor did it become general until the late second century. Before at least the year 120 A.D., baptisms were in the name of Jesus Christ, to which custom Paul refers in the words (Gal. iii, 27)—"As many of you as were baptized unto Christ."[204]

328. Harrington, D. (2001). *The Church According to the New Testament What the Wisdom and Witness of Early Christianity Teaches us Today*. Rowman & Littlefield Publishers, Inc., p. 44:

"Early Christian baptism, however, was distinctive in several respects. First, Christian baptism was 'in the name of Jesus.' The association of baptism with the name of Jesus is assumed by Paul

---

[203] Arthur Cushman McGiffert was Washburn Professor of Church History in the Union Theological Seminary, New York.
[204] Dr. Charles Stanley Lester, Episcopal clergyman; rector of St. Paul's Episcopal Church, Milwaukee and a liberal Theologian.

(see Romans 6:3, 1 Corinthians 1:16; 15; Galatians 3:27) and mentioned also in Acts (see 2:38; 8:16; 10:48; 19:5). This formula seems to have been even more original than the Trinitarian formula in Matthew 28:19."[205]

329. Fortman, Edmund J. (1999) (reprint). *The Triune God A Historical Study of the Doctrine of the Trinity*. Eugene, Oregon: Wipf & Stock, pp. xv-xvi, 14-15, 21-23, 27, Part Two Introduction, 44-45, 151:

"...the New Testament writers...they call Jesus...Him God explicitly...We do not intend to seek in the Old Testament and in the New Testament what is not there, a formal statement of trinitarian doctrine...Obviously there is no trinitarian doctrine in the Synoptics or Acts...Paul has many triadic texts that present God (or the Father), Christ (or the Son or Lord), and the Spirit side by side in closely balanced formulas...These passages give no doctrine of the Trinity...but they offer material for the later development of trinitarian doctrine...Paul had any triadic texts and in some of them he seems to present Christ and the Spirit as distinct from one another and from the Father and on the same divine level with the Father. He has no formal trinitarian doctrine and no clear0cut realization of a trinitarian problem...In the Synoptic Gospels there is one passage that could imply that Jesus is God: Mt 1.23. In the Pauline writings there are three passages in which Jesus is probably God: Rom 9:5, Titus 2.13 and Heb 1.8. In the Johannine writings there are two passages in which Jesus is probably called God: Jn 1.18 and 1 Jn 5.20. And there are two passages in which He is clearly called God: Jn 1.1 and Jn 20.20. Thus John's Gospel not only ascribes to Jesus strictly divine functions that put Him on the same divine level as the Father, but it clearly calls him God. As this Gospel opens we meet a sublime song of a Word who is God, and as it ends we echo the words of Thomas, 'My Lord and my God'...The Biblical witness to God, as we have seen, did not contain any formal or formulated doctrine of the Trinity, any explicit teaching that in one God there are three co-equal divine persons...And it would take three centuries of gradual assimilation of the Biblical witness

---

[205]Dr. Daniel Harrington, S. J., Professor of New Testament at Weston Jesuit School of Theology.

to God before the formulation of the dogma of one God in three distinct persons would be achieved. To observe this gradual transition from an unformulated Biblical witness to a dogmatic formulation of a doctrine of the Triune God, it is first necessary to look to the Eastern Church where most of this development took place and study its witness to the Triune God in three phases: the pre-Nicene, the Nicene, and the post-Nicene…The Apostolic Fathers fall far short…in their doctrine of God…There is in them, of course, no trinitarian doctrine and no awareness of a trinitarian problem…At Rome the outstanding theologians of the 3rd century were Hippolytus and Novation. Hippolytus strongly opposed modalism and accused Popes Zephyrinus and Callistus of favoring it."[206]

330. Hastings, James (ed.) (1922). *Dictionary of the Apostolic Church*. Volume II Macedonia-Zion with Indexes. New York: Charles Scriber's Sons and Edinburgh: T&T Clark, pp. 73-74:

"That baptism in the Triune Name was universally current about A.D. 150 is scarcely in accordance with the evidence…But even if the passage be a genuine logion of Jesus, the knowledge of which may have been confined to only a few, preserved only in one Gospel which is dated c. A.D. 80 it cannot be used as evidence against what, so far as one knows, was an actual and universal custom. The slight variety in the words which record baptism in the name of Jesus–clearly of not significance–shows that there was indeed no stereotyped formula which must not be departed from but raises no doubt as to the fact that baptism was in the name not of three persons, but one."

331. Evans, Marian (1860). *The Life of Jesus Critically Examined by Dr. David Friedrich Strauss*. Volume II. New York: Calvin Blanchard, pp. 853-854:

"In Matthew (xxviii. 19 f.)…that such an allocation of Father, Son, and Spirit does not elsewhere appear, except as a form of salutation in apostolic epistles (2 Cor. xiii. 14: the grace of our Lord Jesus Christ, &c.); while as a more definite form of baptism

---

[206]Father & Rev. Edmund J. Fortman S.J., was a Jesuit teacher for more than 40 years and a renowned Catholic scholar.

it is not to be met with throughout the whole New Testament save in the above passage of the first gospel: for in the apostolic epistles and even in the Acts, baptism is designated as a…baptising in Christ Jesus, or in the name of the Lord Jesus, or their equivalent (Rom. vi. 3; Gal. iii. 27; Acts ii. 38; viii. 16; x. 48; xix. 5.), and the same threefold reference to God, Jesus, and the Holy Spirit is only found in ecclesiastical writers, as, for example, Justin. Indeed, the formula in Matthew sounds so exactly as if it had been borrowed from the ecclesiastical ritual, that there is no slight probability in the supposition that it was transferred from thence into the mouth of Jesus."[207]

332. _____ (1905). *Is the Doctrine of the Trinity a Part of Original Christianity*. Index of Current Literature Vol. XXXIX July-December 1905. New York: The Current Publishing Company, p. 407-408:

"Indeed, there are excellent reasons for believing that originally the command in the Matthew did not read as it does now. Up to the fourth century there are traces of a simpler form according to which Christians were baptized only in the name of Christ. This would be in perfect agreement with the Apostolic practice of baptizing in the name of Christ only…in the 'Shepherd of Hermes,' which dates about 100 A.D., mention is repeatedly made of baptism in the one name, but there is not a trace of any baptism in the name of the Trinity. And even a century later lively discussions were carried out on in the church as to whether baptism in the one name of Christ should be recognized by the church or not. At what time the enlarged formula of baptism in the name of the Father, Son and Holy Ghost, was introduced, it cannot be definitely determined, but probably it was about the period when the doctrine of the Trinity became the subject of debate in the churches. At any rate, it is more than probable that this Trinitarian formula is not part of original Christianity, but a later development."[208]

---

[207]Dr. David Friedrich Strauss was a German Liberal Protestant Theologian and writer.
[208]See also, Farnell, David F. and Andrews, Edward D. (2017). *Biblical Criticism What Are Some Outstanding Weaknesses of Modern Historical Criticism.* Cambridge, Ohio: Christian Publishing House, pp. 195-196, in which it was stated that at some stage *"Grant Osborne however, in his use of redaction critical*

333. Bauckham, Richard (2001). *James and Jesus* in *The Brother of Jesus James the Just and His Mission*. Chilton, Bruce and Neusner, Jacob (editors). Louisville, Kentucky: John Knox Press, P. 135:

> "Finally, he may notice that the 'beautiful name' invoked over Christians according to James 2:7 is most likely the name of Jesus invoked in baptism."[209]

334. Scorgie, Glen G. et. al. (2011). *Dictionary of Christian Spirituality*. Grand Rapid, Michigan: Zondervan:

> "The name of Jesus is invoked on the one baptized...."

335. Oropeza, B. J. (2000). *Paul and Apostasy Eschatology, Perseverance and Falling Away in The Corinthian Congregation*. Eugene, Oregon: Wipf & Stock, pp. 86-87:

> "Conversion–initiation also may have taken a form in which both the baptizer participated 'in the name of Jesus'...The baptizer may have invoked the name of Jesus...we may assume that such a background influenced Paul's understanding of baptism in the name of Jesus...'I baptise you in the name of Jesus' had to be pronounced over the baptizand to authenticate the baptism."[210]

336. McKnight, Scott (2011). *The Letter of James*. The New International Commentary on The New Testament. Grand Rapids, Michigan: William B. Eerdmans Publishing Company, pp. 201-202:

> "The 'name' Jesus is 'invoked' upon early Christians at their baptism...other texts indicate a baptism 'in the name of Jesus.'"

337. Witherington III, Ben (2007). *Letters and Homilies for Jewish Christians*

---

hermeneutics advocated that the Great Commission was not originally spoke by Jesus in the way that Matthew had recorded it, but that it seems most likely that at some point the tradition of Matthew expanded an original monadic formula." Citing: Osborne, Grant (1976). *Redaction Criticism and The Great Commission: A Case Study Toward a Biblical Understanding of Inerrancy*. Journal of The Evangelical Theological Society 19/2 (March) at 80.

[209]Dr. Richard Bauckham is Professor of New Testament Studies and Bishop Wardlaw Professor in the University of St. Andrews.

[210]B. J. Oropeza is Assistant Professor of Biblical Studies in the Division of Religion and Philosophy at Azusa Pacific University.

A Socio-Rhetorical Commentary on Hebrews, James and Jude. Downers Grove, Illinois: InterVarsity Press, p. 459:

> "James 2:7b may refer to the name of Jesus being called over believers as they are baptized...."[211]

338. Heil, John Paul (2012). *The Letter of James Worship to Live By*. Eugene, Oregon: Cascade Books, p. 70:

> "...The name of our Lord Jesus Christ of glory (2:1) which was ritually 'invoked' over them at their baptism (2:7)...." See also footnote 11 "The name of Jesus was called over the believer at baptism (Acts 8:16; 10:48)."[212]

339. Scaer, David P. (1994). *James the Apostle of Faith*. Eugene, Oregon: Wipf & Stock, p. 77:

> "The reference to 'the honorable name which was invoked over you' could very well be an allusion to Baptism. According to Acts, Baptism was carried out in the name of Jesus and the baptized Christians bore His name."[213]

340. Baker, William R. (2012). *The Community of Believers in James* in *The New Testament Church The Challenge of Developing Ecclesiologies*. Eugene, Oregon: Pickwick Publications, p. 222:

> "This phrasing probably refers to his name being formally pronounced over them when they were baptized. This corresponds to the fact that the New Testament converts as described as being baptized in the 'name of Jesus' or in the 'name of the Lord' (Acts 2:38; 8:16; 10:48; 19:5; note also Hermas, *Sim* 9.16.3)."[214]

---

[211] See also, Mongstad-Kvammen, Ingborg (2013). *Toward A Post-Colonial Reading of the Epistles of James, James 2:1-13 in its Roman Imperial Context*. Leiden, The Netherlands: Brill, p. 172.

[212] Dr. John Paul Heil, is a Priest of the Archdiocese of St. Louis, Professor of New Testament at The Catholic University of America.

[213] Dr. David P. Scaer, Professor of New Testament and Systematic Theology at Concordia Theological Seminary, Fort Wayne, Indiana and Editor of The Concordia Theological Quarterly.

[214] William R. Baker, Stone-Campbell Journal Editor, President Stone Campbell International and Professor of New Testament, Hope International University.

341. Boora, Kulwant Singh (2011). *The Roman Catholic Church And Its Recognition of The Validity of Baptism in The Name of Jesus (Acts 2:38) From 100 A.D. to 500 A.D*. Bloomington, Indiana: Authorhouse, p. 34:

"But very few doubt that baptism in the name of Jesus was practiced from the beginning of Christianity."[215]

342. Gowan, Donald E. (1994). *Theology in Exodus Biblical Theology in the Form of a Commentary*. Louisville, Kentucky: Westminster John Knox Press, p. 94:

"So, baptism was performed in the name of Jesus (Acts 2:38; 8:16...."[216]

343. Hartin, Patrick J. (2009). *James*. Sacra Pagina Series Volume 14. Collegeville, Minnesota: Liturgical Press, p. 268:

"...to the practice to which other traditions within early Christianity bear witness: e.g., in the Acts of the Apostles people are baptized 'in the name of Jesus Christ' (2:38; 8:16; 10:48)...."[217]

344. Mettinger, Tryggve N. D. (2005). *In Search of God The Meaning and Message of The Everlasting Names*. Philadelphia: Fortress Press, pp. 10-11:

"...I must refer to a specific New Testament passage...refers to the fact that Jesus' name was proclaimed over those who were baptized. Whoever was baptized in the name of Jesus...."[218]

345. McCartney, Dan G. (2009). *James*. Baker Exegetical Commentary on the New Testament. Grand Rapids, Michigan: Baker Academic, p. 143:

"That the name of Christ 'has been invoked upon' them...This could be a reference to baptism, therefore, as in Acts 2:38;

---

[215]Citing Professor James. D. G. Dunn.
[216]Donald E. Gowan is the Robert Cleveland Holland Professor Emeritus of Old Testament at Pittsburgh Theological Seminary.
[217]Patrick J. Hartin is an ordained Priest of the Diocese of Spokane, Washington and teaches courses in New Testament and Classical Civilization at Gonzaga University.
[218]Tryggve N. D. Mettinger is retired Professor of Hebrew Bible at Lund University, Sweden where he taught from 1978 to 2003.

10:48...."[219]

346. Strazicich, John R. (2007). *Joel's Use of Scripture and the Scripture's Use of Joel Appropriation and Resignification in Second Temple Judaism and Early Christianity.* Leiden, The Netherlands: Brill, p. 301:

> "In Acts, Ananias commands Paul to be baptized by calling on His name, refers to the act where the baptizand is to invoke Jesus' name during the rite of baptism..." see also footnote 50 "It would imply that the name of Jesus was invoked by the baptized in the act of his baptism or even...that the name of Jesus Christ was called over the candidate...."[220]

347. Block, Daniel I. (2011). *Bearing The Name of The Lord with Honor.* Bibliotheca Sacra 168 (January-March), p. 29:

> "James 2:7 is an equally striking reference, with even clearer echoes of Leviticus 24:11 and 16 on the one hand and Deuteronomy 28:10 and Daniel 9:18-19 on the other. "Are they not the ones who blaspheme the honorable name by which you were called [lit., 'the honorable name that is called/read on you']?" (author's translation). Some such custom may also underlie the expression "to be baptized in the name of Jesus Christ" (Acts 2:38; 10:48), because after baptism new believers were recognized as bearers of the Name."

348. Gunton, Colin E. (2003). *Father, Son & Holy Spirit Toward A Fully Trinitarian Theology.* London & New York: T&T Clark, p. 207:

> "The first is the commission recorded at the end of Matthew's Gospel. It is now widely believed that the dominical command to baptize in the name of the Father, Son and Holy Spirit is not a report of actual words of the risen Jesus, but the invention of the early Church."[221]

---

[219] Dan G. McCartney is Professor of New Testament Interpretation at Redeemer Seminary, Dallas, Texas.

[220] John R. Strazicich is Chair of Department of Biblical Studies at Kanana Fou Theological Seminary in American Samoa.

[221] Dr. Colin E. Gunton was Professor of Christian Doctrine, King's College, London and a Minster of the United Reformed Church.

349. Paroschi, Wilson (2009). *Acts 19:1-7 Reconsidered In Light of Paul's Theology of Baptism*. Andrews University Seminary Studies, Volume 47, No. 1, pp. 95-96:

> "By being performed in the name of Jesus, post-Pentecost Christian baptism dedicated the baptized person to Jesus Christ...As a post-Pentecost disciple who had been baptized in the name of Jesus (22:16)."[222]

350. Bromiley, Geoffrey W. (gen. ed.) (1986). *The International Standard Bible Encyclopedia Illustrated in Four Volumes. Volume One: A-D*. Grand Rapids, Michigan: William B. Eerdmans Publishing Company, p. 483:

> "The most common baptismal formulas in the NT 'in the name of Jesus Christ' (Acts 2:38; 10:48) and 'in the name of the Lord Jesus' (8:16; 19:5)...For in the baptism the name of Jesus is named over those who are baptized...."

351. Bowman Jr, Robert M. and Komoszewski, J. Ed. (2007). *Putting Jesus in His Place The Case for The Deity of Christ*. Grand Rapids, Michigan: Kregel Publications, p. 132:

> "Another activity that the early Christians performed in Jesus' name was baptism. The book of Acts states repeatedly that new believers were baptized in the name of Jesus Christ (Acts 2:38; 8:16; 10:48; 19:5, cf. 22:16)."[223]

352. Bauckham, Richard (1995). *James and The Jerusalem Church* in *The Book of Acts in its First Century Setting*. Volume 4 Palestinian Setting. Published jointly: Grand Rapids, Michigan: William B. Eerdmans Publishing Company and Carlisle, Cumbria: The Paternoster Press, p. 457:

> "Note also Ja 2:7...probably with specific reference to the invocation of the name of Jesus in baptism, as it also the case in

---

[222] Wilson Paroschi Latin American Adventist Theological Seminary Engenheiro Coelho, SP, Brazil.

[223] Robert M. Bowman is the Director of Research at the Institute for Religious Research and teaches Biblical Studies at Cornerstone University and J. Ed. Komoszewski is Pastor of Sojourners Church in Albert Lea, Minnesota and has taught Biblical and Theological Studies at Northeastern College.

Hermas, Sim. 8.6.4."

353. Green, Joel B. & Turner, Max (ed.) (1999). *Jesus of Nazareth Lord and Christ Essays on The Historical Jesus and New Testament Christology*. Eugene, Oregon: Wipf & Stock, p. 105:

> "...Matt 28:19, and that speaks of the future activity of the disciples, not the practice of Jesus himself. Moreover, as a result of its sophisticated trinitarian formula Matt. 28:19 is very generally assumed to be, it not a gloss of the text of Matthew, as least an anachronistic reading back of the later church's baptismal practice, at a relatively late stage in the Gospel tradition."

354. _____ (1865). *The General Baptist Magazine for 1865*. London: Marlborough & Co & Leicester: Winks & Son, p. 388:

> "Baptism In The Name of Jesus—This is one of the latest novelties brought out by the Plymouth Brethren, and is being very prominently put forth by them, especially in Ireland. Some of the leaders in connection with 'Merion Hall,' Dublin, who have for many years resisted all instruction as to believers' baptism, have at once been taken by this 'novelty,' and have submitted to immersion in the name of Jesus only. The Rev. W. Turpin, lately a minister of the Established Church in Dublin, and for a short time in Glasgow, has also been baptised after this fashion."[224]

355. Thompson, David M. (2006). *Baptism, Church and Society in Modern Britain from The Evangelical Revival to Baptism, Eucharist and Ministry*. Studies in Christian History and Thought. Eugene, Oregon: Wipf & Stock, p. 94:

> "Maurice's family background seems to have influenced his attitude to baptism, as did the rest of his theology. His father, Michael Maurice, was a Unitarian minister. In 1774 Theophilus Lindsay, himself a convert from the Church of England, published *The Book of Common Prayer reformed according to the plan of the later Dr. Samuel Clark*. The Exhortations in the baptismal

---

[224]Baptism in the name of Jesus only even in 1865 seems very prominent a practice in Ireland, England and presumably Scotland, since the Plymouth Brethren have been noted as baptizing in the name of Jesus only.

service in this book emphasized the universal character of the rite…The service also permitted the use of either the traditional trinitarian formula…or baptism 'into the name of Jesus Christ' (following Acts 2:38 and 19:5)…."

356. O'Collins SJ, Gerald (2018). *The Church in The General Epistles* in *The Oxford Handbook of Ecclesiology*. Oxford: Oxford University Press, p. 149:

"This 'excellent name' seems to be that of Jesus, the name invoked at the time of their baptism."

357. Bender, Kimlyn J. & Long, Stephen D. (2020). *T&T Clark Handbook of Ecclesiology*. London: Bloomsbury Publishing:

"Baptism in part of the basis of the Christian life at conversion…Those who came to be baptized must repent from dead works and turn to God in faith…The name of the Lord Jesus (cf. Acts 2:38; 8:16; 10:48; 19:5)…was invoked…."

358. White, R. E. O. (1994). *Christian Ethics*. Macon, Georgia: Mercer University Press, p. 208:

"…while 2:7 refers to the customary invocation of Christ' name at baptism…."

359. Adamson, James B. (1976). *The Epistle of James*. The New International Commentary on The New Testament. Grand Rapids, Michigan: William B. Eerdmans Publishing Company, p. 113:

"The innovation of the name…of Christ…The idea of a name being 'called upon' someone is common in the LXX…and here implies Christian professional…possibility with reference to a baptismal formula (Acts 8:16)."

360. Stuhlmacher, Peter (2018). *Biblical Theology of The New Testament*. Grand Rapids, Michigan: William B. Eerdmans Publishing Company, see Chapter 27:

"That such rich people blaspheme the 'excellent name' (of Christ) that was invoked over Christians at their baptism...."[225]

361. Levering, Matthew (2010). *Christ and The Catholic Priesthood Ecclesial Hierarchy and The Pattern of The Trinity*. Chicago, Illinois: Hillenbrand and Books, p. 50:[226]

> "The sign and seal of this, however, is baptism 'in the name of Jesus' at which this 'good name' was also invoked upon the baptized person...."[227]

362. Briggs, Charles Augustus (1913). *The Fundamental Christian Faith The Origin; History and Interpretation of The Apostles' and Nicene Creeds*. New York: Charles Scribner's Sons, p. 15:

> "The division by the names of the Trinity corresponds with the formula of baptism according to Mt. 28:19: baptizing them into the name of the Father, and of the Son, and of the Holy Spirit. This formula, it is true, is not in the exact words of Jesus to the Twelve; for the parallelism and measure of the logion and the usage of the Apostolic Church show that baptism was originally into my name: *into the name of Jesus Christ*, Acts 2:38, 10:48; *the name of the Lord Jesus*, Acts 8:16, 19:5; *into Christ Jesus*, Rom. 6:3; *into Christ*, Gal. 3:27 ; into the name of the Lord, Didache, ii , *Hermas, Vis., III, 7* ; the name of the Son of God, *Hermas, Sim ., IX, 13*."[228]

363. Bauckham, Richard (1996). *James and The Gentiles (Acts 15. 13–21)* in *History, Literature and Society in The Book of Acts*. Cambridge: Cambridge University Press, p. 169:

> "Most likely the invoking of the name over Christians was understood as a reference to baptism in the name of Jesus...."

364. McGiffert, Arthur C. (1902). *The Apostle's Creed Its Origin, Its Purpose, and Its Historical Interpretation*. Edinburgh: T&T Clark, pp. 179-180:

---

[225]Peter Stuhlmacher is a Protestant Theologian, Professor Emeritus of New Testament Studies at the University of Tubingen.
[226]This notation is found in footnote 102.
[227]Matthew Levering is a Professor of Theology at the University of Dayton.
[228]Dr. Charles Augustus Briggs, Butler Graduate Professor of Theological Encyclopedia and Symbols Union Theological Seminary, New York.

"And when we consider the baptismal formula enjoined by Christ, according to Matt. XXVIII. 19, the difficulty increases. The collocation "Father, Son, and Holy Spirit" sounds strange on Christ's lips, and suggests a conception of baptism entirely foreign to the thought of his immediate disciples, and equally foreign to the thought of Paul, whose idea of baptism seems in harmony only with the use of a single name, the name of Christ, in the formula. There is moreover no sign that the triune formula was ever employed in the apostolic age. So far as our sources enable us to judge, baptism in the earliest days was commonly into the name of Christ without mention of God and the Holy Spirit. Thus, we have "Into the name of Jesus Christ" in Acts II. 38, X. 48; "Into the name of the Lord Jesus" in Acts VIII. 16, XIX. 5; "Into Christ Jesus" in Rom. VI. 3; "Into Christ" in Gal. III. 27; "Into the name of the Lord" in Did. XI.; Hermas, Vis. III. 7, 3; "Into the death of the Lord" in the Apostolic Constitutions, VII. 25 (a passage based upon Did. XI.), and Apostolic Canons, 50; "Into the name of the Son of God" in Hermas, Sim. IX. 13, 16, 17. Compare also Col. II. 2; 1 Cor. I. 13, 15; X. 2; XII. 13; Barnabas 11. There is no reference to the triune formula in the literature of the apostolic or sub-apostolic age, except in Matt. XXVIII. 19 and in the Didache, chap. 7."[229]

365. Hardinge, Leslie (1972). *The Celtic Church in Britain.* London: SPCK, pp. 2-3, 18, 52, 102, 106:

"Written records of the presence of early Christians are extremely meagre. The earliest statements are merely passing illusions by a few church fathers. The first hint of a group of organized believers in Britain is in the story of the *Council of Aries* (314), convened by the Emperor Constantine. Three bishops, a presbyter, and a deacon are recorded as having come from Britain…Gildas lamented that British Christians were plagued by Arianism…The faith and works of a sixth-century Celtic saint evidently appeared "contrary to sound doctrine and the Catholic faith" to a pious writer of the twelfth century…In 601 Gregory sent Augustine the pallium and a letter in which he declared:

---

[229] Arthur Cushman McGiffert was Washburn Professor of Church History in the Union Theological Seminary, New York.

"You, my brother, are to exercise authority *in the name of our Lord and God Jesus Christ* both over those bishops whom you shall consecrate, and any who shall be consecrated by the Bishop of York, and also over all the British bishops"...Arianism was believed to have made inroads among early British Christians. Evidence for this has been drawn from the fact that mention of the names of the Father, Son, and Spirit were omitted from the baptismal formula...The question whether there should be one or three immersions was a subject of controversy in the Western Church even as late as the seventh century, particularly in Spain. Single immersion apparently was practised in Brittany even after the seventh century...F. E. Warren noted that the baptismal formula invoking the names of the Persons of the Trinity has been left out of the service found in the Stowe Missal. He pointed out the similarity between this and the Gelasian Sacramentary. F. C. Conybeare argued that it was this omission which rendered baptism by Celtic clerics invalid in the eyes of the Western Church...."[230]

366. Cheung, Luke L. (2003). *The Genre, Composition, and Hermeneutics of The Epistle of James*. Eugene, Oregon: Wipf & Stock, pp. 98-99:

"There is a long line of development...from the practice of baptism 'in/into the name of Jesus (Acts 2:38; 10:48) to the receiving of the (new) name in baptism (cf. Rev. 3:12; Hermas, *Sim*. 9.4.8; 13.7) and the use of the Lord's name invoked over the candidate in the rite (Hermas, *Sim*. 8.1.1; 6.4)...The messianically renewed people of God are regarded as those who have been baptised into Christ's name...."[231]

367. Law, Sophie (1980). *The Epistle of James*. Black's New Testament Commentaries. London: Adam & Charles Black, p. 105:

---

[230]Dr. Leslie Hardinge was former President of Adventist University of the Philippines (formerly Seventh-day Adventist Theological Seminary, Far East). Dr. Hardinge became a Bible teacher first at Union College, Lincoln Nebraska, and then in succeeding years Columbia Union College in Washington D.C. Newbold College in England and Pacific Union College, Angwin, California.

[231]Luke L. Cheung is Associate Professor of New Testament Studies at The China Graduate School of Theology in Hong Kong.

"The thought of themselves, however, as bearing the name of Jesus...Hermas, *Sim.* viii. 10.3, ix. 13.2f and 28.5). The point at which they took on this role was baptism, which is frequently defined as baptism in or into the name of Jesus: Acts ii. 38...."[232]

368. Boff, Lenoardo (1988). *Trinity and Society*. Translated from the Portuguese by Paul Burns. Eugene, Oregon: Wipf & Stock, pp. 35-36:

"There is still no doctrine of the Trinity in the New Testament...These cannot be lumped together to provide comprehensive proof...of the Trinity...Let us look at the main passages: *(a) Matthew 28:19* 'Go, therefore, make disciples of all the nations; baptize them in the name of the Father and of the Son and of the Holy Ghost." This baptismal formula is explicitly trinitarian, it is not found in any of the other Gospels and constitutes a peculiarity of Matthew. Scholars are virtually unanimous in declaring that the formula does not go back to the risen Christ. It represents the doctrinal crystallization of the community of the evangelist which had already reflected deeply on the meaning of the most important rite in the early church, baptism. At first, baptism was performed 'in the name of Jesus Christ' (see Acts 8:16; 19:5; 1 Cor. 13:15)."[233]

369. Blidstein, Moshe (2017). *Purity, Community, and Ritual in Early Christian Literature*. Oxford Studies in The Abrahamic Religions. Oxford: Oxford University Press, p. 109:

"The Pauline epistles are the earliest texts in which immersion is linked with the name of Jesus and with entrance to the Christian communities."[234]

---

[232]Sophie Law, lecturer in New Testament Studies, King's College, London, England.

[233]Leonardo Boff was born in Brazil in 1938 and received a doctorate from the University of Munich in Germany in 1970. For the following twenty years, he worked as Professor of Theology at the Franciscan School for Philosophy and Theology in Petropolis, Brazil. During the 1970s, he and Gustavo Gutierrez helped to define liberation theology. Since 1993 he has been a professor at the State University of Rio de Janeiro, where he is now Emeritus Professor of Ethics, Philosophy of Religion, and Ecology.

[234]Moshe Blidstein is Senior Lecturer, Department of General History, University of Haifa.

370. Morgan, Teresa (2020). *Being "in Christ" in the Letters of Paul Save Through Christ.* Tubingen: Mohr Siebeck, pp. 30, 120:

> "A number of scholars have suggested that *en Christo* derives from a baptismal formula which predates Paul: probably 'in the name of Jesus Christ', which is attested to both Paul and by Acts as used in baptism…In 1 Corinthians Paul…baptized none of you except Crispus and Gaius, so that no one of you can say you were baptized…rhetorical questions is that the Corinthians were not baptized in his name, but were baptized in the name of Christ. Since we have plenty of other relatively early evidence of people being baptized in the name of Jesus Christ, it is plausible that this is indeed how the Corinthians were baptized."[235]

371. Baird, William (2003). *History of New Testament Research From Jonathan Edwards to Rudolf Bultmann.* Volume Two. Minneapolis: Fortress Press, p. 250:

> "Bousset believes the *kyrios* cult continues to develop in the post apostolic age. The believer is baptized in the name of Jesus…."[236]

372. Zaugg, Elme Harry (1917). *A Generic Study of the Spirit Phenomena in The New Testament.* Chicago, Illinois: The University of Chicago Libraries:

> "Forgiveness of sins could be obtained by repentance, by being baptized in the name of Jesus and by receiving the gift of the Spirit."

373. Dahl, Nils Alstrup (2021). *The Apostle Paul Guides The Early Church.* Eugene, Oregon: Cascade Books, p. 104:[237]

> "Accordingly, the initiation and purification ceremonies did make the same kind of difference in the life of the members as baptism in the name of Jesus did for Christians. Christian baptism is important…so far we have dealt with…Jesus and to baptism in

---

[235]Teresa Morgan is Professor of Graeco-Roman History at the University of Oxford, England.
[236]Wilhelm Bousset (1865-1920) was Professor at Gissen.
[237]Nils Alstrup Dahl (1911-2001) was a native of Oslo, Norway and was a Professor of New Testament at Yale Divinity School.

his name."

374. Haight, Roger (2004). *Christian Community in History Historical Ecclesiology*. Volume 1. London & New York: Continuum, p. 97:

> "The two most important rites of early Christianity are baptism and the eucharist...The case of Paul provides evidence that baptism was practiced by the followers of Jesus soon after his death and resurrection, and an early formula of baptism in the name of Jesus is mentioned in Acts...(Acts 2:38)."[238]

375. Ludlow, Morwenna (2009). *The Early Church: The I. B. Tauris History of The Christian Church*. London: I. B. Tauris & Co Ltd:

> "A three-fold formula for baptism—'in the name of the Father, and of the Son and of the Holy Spirit'—seems to have become established very early, but baptism 'in the name of Jesus' was probably also very common."[239]

376. German, Martinez (2003). *Signs of Freedom Theology of The Christian Sacraments*. Mahwah, New Jersey: Paulist Press, pp. 102, 111:

> "Baptism is celebrated in the earliest communities 'in the name of Jesus'...The forgiveness of sins by one baptism is an essential tenet of Christian belief rooted as it is in the New Testament references to baptism: 'Repent, and be baptized everyone of you in the name of Jesus Christ so that your sins may be forgiven' (Acts 2:38)."[240]

377. Strecker, Georg (2000). *Theology of The New Testament*. Louisville, Kentucky: John Know Press & New York & Berlin: Walter de Gruyter, p. 308:

> "In addition, baptism results in (3) being placed within the community of the lordship of Jesus. This accords with the fact

---

[238]Roger Haight, S.J., has taught for over 30 years in Jesuits Schools of Theology and was past President of The Catholic Theological Society of American (1994-1995).
[239]Morwenna Ludlow is Lecturer in Patristics at the University of Exeter, England.
[240]Reverend German Martinez is Associate Professor of Systematic Theology and Sacraments at the Graduate School of Religion and Religious Education at Fordham University.

that baptism is administered 'in the name of the Lord Jesus' (Did 9.5; Acts 8:16). This is different from earliest Palestinian Christianity, in which baptism in the name of Jesus was primarily oriented to the coming of the Son of Man."[241]

378. Dunn, James D. G. (2009). *Beginning From Jerusalem Christianity in The Making*. Volume 2. Grand Rapids, Michigan: William B. Eerdmans Publishing Company, p. 185:

"According to Luke...baptized in the name of Jesus Christ...(2:38)...marks the formal inauguration of the new sect...Cornelius and his friends, who being baptized in the spirit nevertheless did no render baptism in the name of Jesus Christ unnecessary...In some ways the most striking feature of this new rite of baptism was that it was performed 'in the name of Jesus'...." See also footnote 73 "In (*epi*) the name of Jesus Christ (2:38)...The 1 Corinthians references again confirm that this formula had already become a standard rubric for Christian baptism."

379. Fuller, Reginald H. & Westberg, Daniel (2006). *Preaching The Lectionary The Word of God for The Church Today* (3rd ed.). Collegeville, Minnesota: Liturgical Press, p. 99:

"In the earliest community and for some time, baptism was administered in the name of Jesus. It is only in this passage of Matthew and in the Didache, a Christian writing probably dating back to the end of the first century, that we hear of the threefold formula. One may say, however, that the use of Jesus' name alone as a baptismal formula implies the threefold name...."[242]

380. Cwiekowski, Frederick J. (1988). *The Beginnings of The Church*. Mahwah, New Jersey: Paulist Press, p. 76:

"The first baptism were performed in the name of Jesus (Acts

---

[241]Georg Strecker was Professor of New Testament at the University of Gottingen.
[242]Reginald H. Fuller was an Anglo-American biblical scholar, ecumenist, and Anglican Priest and Daniel Westberg, a former Parish Priest who teaches Moral Theology and Christian Ethics at Nashotah House Episcopal Seminary in Wisconsin.

2:38; 8:16; 10:48; 19:5)…if…Jesus had given so explicit an instruction as we have it in Matthew, it would be very difficult to explain that baptism in Jesus' name so often referred to in Acts and Paul. In these early baptism in Jesus' name…."[243]

381. Coda, Piero (2020). *From The Trinity The Coming of God in Revelation and Theology*. Washington D.C.: The Catholic University of America Press, p. 249:

"The Acts of the Apostles tell of the practice in the earliest community of baptism 'in the name of Jesus' (see, e.g. Acts 1:5; 2:38). This formula means receiving baptism as Christ ordered and at the same time, taking part in this event of salvation, and their entering into the Church."[244]

382. Schweizer, Eduard (1975). *The Good News According to Matthew*. Translated by David E. Green. Atlanta, Georgia: John Know Press, p. 530:

"…baptism is spoken of as being in or through the name of Jesus (Acts 2:38; 8:16; 10:48; Rom 6:3; 1 Cor. 1:13; 15; 6:11; cf. 10:2). So that the addition of the threefold name represents a later development."[245]

383. Senn, Frank C. (1999). *A Stewardship of The Mysteries*. Mahwah, New Jersey: Paulist Press, p. 29:

"In the earliest community and for some time baptism was administer in the name of Jesus. It is only in this text, and in the church, manual known as the Didache (dating from the end of the first century), that we have the threefold Trinitarian formula. One may say, however, that the use of Jesus' name alone as a

---

[243]Frederick J. Cwiekowsi is a Priest of the Archdiocese of Hartford and a member of the Society of St. Sulpice. He is a Professor of Systemic Theology at St. Mary's Seminary and University in Baltimore and a visiting Professor of Christology and Ecclesiology in the Master of Religious Education program at the University of St. Thomas in Houston, Texas.
[244]Piero Coda is an Italian Theologian, President of Sophia University Institute, Italy and a member of The International Theological Commission.
[245]Dr. Eduard Schweizer was Professor of New Testament at The University of Zurich in Switzerland.

baptismal formula implies the threefold name."[246]

384. Garrettson (1825). *The Methodist Magazine, Designed as a Compend of Useful Knowledge, and of Religious and Missionary Intelligence, for the Year of Our Lord 1825.* Volume VIII, p. 11:

> "View of emphatic words, in the name of the Father, in the name of the Son and in the name of the Holy Ghost—Here are three distinct persons, and the baptism is in each name. When the first disciples went forth to minister among the Jews, they baptized in the name of Jesus Christ; this was doubtless to show them that Jesus Christ was very and indeed God.[247]

385. Monera, Arnold (2016). *"Baptism as Christian Initiation in the New Testament." Orientis Aura: Macau Perspectives in Religious Studies.* No. 1 (2 December), pp. 7, 23, 28, 29:

> "The formula 'in Jesus' name' probably represents an earlier stage than the Trinitarian formula of Matt 28:19…At the end Matthew's Gospel the risen Christ commands his remaining disciples to 'baptize in the name of the Father and of the Son and of the Holy Spirit' (28:19). According to Raymond Brown, 'The baptismal formula in the name of three divine agents was presumably in use in the Matthean church at this period, having replaced an earlier custom of baptizing in the name of Jesus (Acts 2:38; 8:16, etc.). Yet Luke portrays Peter, one of the Twelve, as calling his hearers on Pentecost, 'Be baptized into the name of Jesus Christ' (Acts 2:38), rather than into the triune name. Paul in his own letters speaks of his readers as 'baptized into Christ Jesus' (Rom 6:3) or simply 'baptized into Christ' (Gal 3:27). At one place Paul says that they are 'baptized into one body' (1 Cor 12:13). The Christological formula seems to be taken for granted by Paul…it is difficult to imagine that first-century Christian would dispense with a Trinitarian formula in favor of a purely Christological one. Consequently, the Christological formula must be considered earlier and more widespread. Only eventually the Trinitarian

---

[246]Frank C. Senn is the Pastor of Immanuel Lutheran Church, Evanston, Illinois.
[247]Published by N. Bangs and J. Emory, At the Methodist Printing Office, Crosby-Street (1825), p. 11, see No. 3 For March 1825, Vol. 8, "The Doctrine of the Trinity Scriptural" by Rev. Garrettson.

formula became prominent and then practically universal as it is well attested in second-century sources. The formula used in the community of Matthew towards the end of the first century can be considered an expansion of earlier, purely Christological one. Beyond that it is impossible to know how early or how widely the formula was used."[248]

386. Krentz, Edgar (1996). *Christianity's Boundary-Making Bath: The New Testament Meaning of Baptism, the Sacrament of Unity*. Institute of Liturgical Studies Occasional Papers (73), p. 113:

"Baptism is related to Jesus in a preeminent manner. Matthew 28:18-20 is the only passage in the New Testament using the trinitarian formula. Baptism in the name of Jesus (only) is the norm in the New Testament. Therefore, from a New Testament perspective, the insistence on the trinitarian formula is overpressing the evidence."

387. Boora, Kulwant Singh (2021). *The Acknowledgment, Recognition and Acceptance of The Apostolic Form of Baptism in The Name of Jesus Christ (Acts 2:38) From Biblical and Theological Scholars (Trinitarian & Non-Trinitarian), Including Ecumenical Councils & Committees and Various Religious Organizations and Groups*. A Reference Guide for Discussing Baptism in The Name of Jesus Christ (Acts 2:38). Published by Amazon Publishing, p. lix:

"Whichever way the baptism was performed, the surviving text of the *Didache* imposes the ritual formula attested in Matthew 28:19 of Father, Son, and Holy Spirit (Did 7.1 and 3). Bearing in mind, however, the slow progress of Trinitarian theology in the early church, the historicity of the *Didache*'s wording appears questionable for two reasons. At the earliest stage of the primitive church, according to both the Petrine and Pauline sections of the Acts of the Apostles (Chapter 1-12 and 13-28), baptism was administered not by invoking the Father, the Son, and the Holy

---

[248] Arnold T. Monera, Dean of Faculty of Religious Studies and Professor of Scripture, Theology and Biblical Greek at the University of St. Joseph, Macau. He is a member of the Catholic Biblical Association of the Philippines.

Spirit, but simply in the name of Jesus (Acts 2:38; 19:5)."[249]

388. Babu, Immanuel (2004). *Repent and Turn to God Recounting Acts*. Eugene, Oregon: Wipf & Stock, p. 38:

"Also, since in some conversion accounts baptism is administered 'in the name of Jesus' (Acts 2:38; 8:16; 10:48)...."[250]

389. Loader, William (2007). *The New Testament With Imagination A Fresh Approach To Its Writings and Themes*. Grand Rapids, Michigan: William B. Eerdmans Publishing Company, p. 61:

"But baptism also was a way of looking back to Jesus and a way of celebrating belonging together with him in the present. It became a moment of celebrating the coming of the Spirit, as it had been for Jesus. Baptism was now 'in the name of Jesus.' Which included a sense of belonging and also of acclaiming Jesus as 'Lord.'"[251]

390. Matkin, Michael J. (2008). *The Complete Idiot's Guide to Discovering The Origins of The Christian Religion Early Christianity*. New York: Penguin Group, p. 161:

"The early followers of Jesus, some of whom were previously followers of John, continued the practice of baptism...The one administering the baptism said something to the effect of, 'I baptize you in the name of Jesus....'"

391. Schnelle, Udo (2020). *The First One Hundred Years of Christianity An Introduction To Its History, Literature and Developments*. Translated by James W. Thompson. Grand Rapids, Michigan: Baker Academic, see Chapter 5, 5:5 Theological Institution and Discourse – Baptism:

"...Christian baptism was for the forgiveness of sins (cf. 1 Cor. 6:11; Acts 2:38)...At the same time the baptism of the Christ-

---

[249]These comments were made by Dr Géza Vermes, Dr. Vermes was a renowned Hungarian-British Biblical Scholar in his work published by Yale University Press. Dr Géza Vermes was best known for his translation of the Dead Sea Scrolls.
[250]Babu Immanuel, Associate Professor, Theological Centre for Asia College, Singapore.
[251]William Load is Professor Emeritus of New Testament at Murdoch University, Perth, Australia.

believers...in the name of the Lord Jesus/in the name of Jesus Christ. Several old formulaic expressions give evidence of a baptismal practice that attaches a central meaning to the 'name of Jesus'...in the name of the Lord Jesus, Acts 8:16; 19:5; cf. 1 Cor. 1:13, 15; Gal. 3:27; Rom. 6:3...in the name of Jesus Christ, Acts 10:48; cf. 1 Cor. 6:11...(in the name of Jesus Christ, Acts 2:38)."[252]

392. Brondos, David A. (2018). *Jesus' Death in New Testament Thought*. Volume 2 Texts. Mexico: Instituto Internaciondl de Estudios Superiores, p. 691:

"Among Jesus' first followers, baptism in Jesus' name seems clearly to have been understood in the same basic matter...Those who were baptized 'into' Christ; therefore, could also be said to have been baptized into this death."[253]

393. Galbreath, Paul (2011). *Leading Through The Water*. Herndon: Virginia: The Alban Institute, p. 79:

"The clarification that baptism was in the name of Jesus is amplified in the story of Paul's visit to Ephesus...This incident suggests that an ongoing process of clarifying language in the baptismal formula took place among early Christians."[254]

394. Bruce, F. F. (1983). *The Gospel of John Introduction, Exposition and Notes*. Grand Rapids, Michigan: William B. Eerdmans Publishing Company, p. 100:

"...in the new believing community...baptism was administered 'in the name of Jesus Christ' (Acts 2:38; cf. 10:48)...."

395. Berardino, Angelo Di (ed.) (2010). *We Believe in One Holy Catholic*

---

[252]Udo Schnelle, Professor of New Testament at the University of Halle, Wittenberg, Germany.
[253]David A. Brondos, is an Ordained Minister of The Evangelical Lutheran Church in America who has served as Professor of Theology and Biblical Studies at The Theological Community of Mexico since 1996.
[254]Paul Glabreath is Associate Professor of Preaching and Worship at Union Theological Seminary and Presbyterian School of Christian Education in Richmond, Virginia.

And Apostolic Church. Downers Grove, Illinois: InterVarsity Press, p. 88:

> "...in the name of the Father and of the Son and of the Holy Spirt...The text gives this formula that accompanied the rite. The formula is trinitarian, but we do not know the exact development of the rite...."[255]

396. Chiavenza, Nicola Ultrich, et. al. (2020). *The Power of Urban Water Studies in Premodern Urbanism*. Boston & Berlin: Walter De Gruyter GmbH, see Chapter 6:

> "Baptism therefore becomes crucial with respect to the divinity of Jesus...As the Acts of the Apostles tell us the Jesus followers Peter, Philppus, and Paul performed baptisms...During baptism, the name of Jesus was recited, and he was understood to be the now Lord of the believers...."

397. Hinlicky, Paul R. (2015). *Beloved Community Critical Dogmatics After Christendom*. Grand Rapids, Michigan: William B. Eerdmans Publishing Company, pp. 229-230:

> "One cannot underestimate the theological attention that the early church gave to the gospel tests regarding Jesus' baptism, for these, coupled with the actual practice of water baptism into Jesus' name from the earliest days (Acts 2:38)...."[256]

398. Jones, F. Stanley (2018). *From Jesus to Lord and Other Contributions of The Early Aramaic-Speaking Congregation in Jerusalem* in *Christian Origins and The Establishment of The Early Jesus Movement* edited by Porter, Stanley E. and Pitts, Andrew W. Leiden, The Netherlands: Brill, p. 1921:

> "The formula for early baptism into this group of believes has been carefully studied...namely, phrase 'into the name'...oldest phrasing was 'into the name of the Lord Jesus'...In recent times, it seems to have been forgotten that the Mandaens are also attested to have performed certain cultic actions 'into the name of'...." See also footnote 25 "...that 'Lord' belonged to the

---

[255] Angelo Di Berardino is President and Professor of Patrology at the Augustinian Patristic Institute (Augustinianum) in Rome, Italy.

[256] Paul R. Hinlicky is Tise Professor of Lutheran Studies at Roanoke College, Salem, Virginia.

earliest formula. The simple 'into the name of the Lord' is found in Did. 9:5 and Herm. Vis. 3.7.3; 'Jesus' is found additionally in Acts 8:36 and 19:5."[257]

399. Baker SJ, Kenneth (1983). *Fundamentals of Catholicism Grace The Church The Sacraments Eschatology*. Volume 3. San Francisco, California: Ignatius Press & New York: Homiletic Pastoral Review, p. 199:

"In Acts of the Apostles we find a number of statements to the effect that some of the first Christians were baptized 'in the name of Jesus Christ' (Acts 2:38) or 'in the name of the Lord Jesus' (Acts 8:16)...perhaps some baptisms were performed 'in the name of Jesus Christ...In any event, if the simple formula was used in the early stages, it soon was replaced with the trinitarian one....."[258]

400. Mitchell, Margaret A. (2021). *The Letter of James as a Document of Paulinism?* in *The Catholic Epistles Critical Readings Critical Readings in Biblical Studies* edited by Darian R. Lockett. London: T&T Clark, p. 313:

"...an apparent reference to baptism in the name of Jesus (Jas 2.7; I Cor. 6.11)...."[259]

401. Paine, William Henry (1917). *The Pauline Idea of Faith in its Relation to Jewish and Hellenistic Religion*. Harvard Theological Studies. Cambridge: Harvard University Press & London: Humphrey Milford, Oxford University Press, p. 84:

"The primitive Christians of Palestine, following the custom of John the Baptist, baptized converts from the beginning, and certainly from a very early date the rite was administered in the

---

[257] F. Stanley Jones is Professor of Religious Studies and Director of the Institute for the Study of Judeo-Christian Origins at California State University, Long Beach, California.
[258] Father Kenneth Baker SJ was for many years the editor of Homiletic and Pastoral Review, the premiere magazine for clergy and laity, and a Roman Catholic Priest in The Society of Jesus and a university professor and former President of Seattle University.
[259] Margaret M. Mitchell is Associate Professor of New Testament at the University of Chicago Divinity School and the Chair of the department of New Testament and Early Christian Literature.

name of Jesus Christ...."[260]

402. Wright, Nigel G. (2005). *Free Church, Free State The Positive Baptist Vision*. Eugene, Oregon: Wipf & Stock, p. 87:

> "Is baptism only in the name of Jesus valid? There are churches which practice 'Jesus' only baptism and follow the formula described in Acts of baptising 'in the name of the Lord Jesus.' It cannot be said that this is wrong or invalid since it is clearly set out in Acts as an effective form of baptism."[261]

403. Klein, William W. et al. (2004). *Introduction To Biblical Interpretation*. Nashville, Tennessee: Thomas Nelson, Inc., p. 152:

> "We embrace historical methods in our investigation of the meaning of Scripture. Sina faith is connected to what happened in history we commit ourselves to know biblical history, even where it conflicts with subsequent church tradition" See footnote 48 "...based on Acts 2:38, that baptism should be performed only in the name of Jesus Christ rather than the Trinity" "Thus, historical and literary methods become essential to understand and explain the biblical record."

404. Mencken, H. L. (1946). *Treatise on The God's* (2nd ed.). Baltimore: The John Hopkins University Press, p. 185:

> "Here is a square and unequivocal statement of Trinitarian doctrine—But Mark knows nothing of it and neither does Luke, and in the Acts of the Apostles baptism is invariably in the name of Jesus alone."[262]

405. Cremin, C. F. (1914). *How The Three Thousand Were Converted–II*. The Catholic University Bulletin. Volume XX, No. 6 (June), pp. 435-436:

> "A difficulty arises in regard to the form employed in the

---

[260] William Henry Paine, Hatch Professor of the Language and Literature of the New Testament in the General Theological Seminary, New York.
[261] Nigel G. Wright, Principal Emeritus of Spurgeon's College, London, and a former President of the Baptist Union of Great Britain, and an Ordained Minister.
[262] Henry Louis Mencken (c.1880-c.1956) was an American scholar and American journalist.

conferring of baptism. 'Be baptized...in the name of the Jesus Christ,' and not in the name of the Holy Trinity? There were theologians who held such a view, on the strength of the above and similar passages which occur in the Acts...The opinion of those theologians who held that baptism in the name of Jesus Christ was for a time valid...Thus alone can we account for the absence of evidence for a transition which must have been rather marked where baptism administered in the infant Church in the name of Jesus Christ, but later in the name of the Blessed Trinity."[263]

406. _____. (1829). *The London Encyclopaedia or Universal Dictionary et al in Twenty-Two Volumes.* Volume III. London: Thomas Tegg, p. 499:

"And so that baptising in the name of Jesus was for a season for the setting of the evidence of his Messias, and when that was thoroughly established, then it was used no more, but baptism was in the name of the Father, and of the Son, & c."

407. Bernard, Thomas Dehany (1904). *The Word and Sacraments and Other Papers Illustrative of Present Questions on Church Ministry and Worship.* London: Bemrose & Sons Ltd, p. 40:

"Hence the baptisms of the first period were all 'in the name of Jesus Christ,'...it may seem strange that the Apostles who had received the commission to baptize, did not apparently use the prescribed formula...."[264]

408. Torrey, Charles Cutler (1916). *The Composition and Date of Acts.* Harvard Theological Studies I. Cambridge: Harvard University Press, p. 84:

"...baptized converts from the beginning, and certainly from a very early date, the rite was administered in the name of Jesus Christ...."[265]

---

[263]C. F. Cremin, St. Paul Seminary, St. Paul, Minnesota was a Catholic scholar and theologian.
[264]Thomas Dehany Bernard (c.1815-c.1904), Prebendary and Chancellor of Wells, was a Church of England clergyman and former Vicar.
[265]Charles Cutler Torrey, Professor of The Semitic Languages in Yale University.

409. Klink III., Edward W. (2019). *Preaching and The Interpretation of Scripture A Call for Ecclesiastical Exegesis* in *Distinguishing The Church Explorations in Word, Sacrament, and Discipline.* Peters, Greg & Jenson, M. (ed.). Eugene, Oregon: Pickwick Publications, p. 14:

> "...for the same reason that baptism in the church is always done in the name of Jesus...Acts 10:48...."[266]

410. Ingham, R. (1871). *A Hand-Book on Christian Baptism* Part II. Subjects. London: Paternoster Row, p. 359:

> "In those times, when ecclesiastical organization was in many respects unsettled, baptism was...administered in the name of Jesus Christ...."

411. Anderson, John (1820). *Alexander and Rufus or a Series of Dialogues on Church Communion in Two Parts.* Pittsburgh: Cramer & Spear, p. 187:

> "That Christian baptism was invariably administered in the name of Jesus...."[267]

412. Kretzman, Paul E. (1921). *Popular Commentary of The Bible The New Testament Volume I. The Gospel According to Saint Matthew, Saint Mark, Saint Luke, Saint John, The Acts of The Apostles.* St. Louis, Missouri: Concordia Publishing House, p. 630:

> "...the disciples of the Lord were now baptizing in the name of Jesus...."[268]

413. Hunter, Sylvester Joseph (1900). *Outlines of Dogmatic Theology.* Volume III (2nd ed.). London: Longmans, Green & Co:

---

[266] Edward W. Klink, III. is senior pastor at Hope Evangelical Free Church in Roscoe, Illinois, formerly taught at Talbot School of Theology, Biola University in Southern California.

[267] John Anderson (c.1748-c.1830) born in England and brought up as a member of the Associate Presbyterian Church of Scotland, founder and professor of the first Presbyterian seminary in America (1794), which later became Pittsburgh Theological Seminary.

[268] Paul E. Kretzman, Professor of Theology, Concordia Seminary (1923-1946), Lutheran Pastor and past President Orthodox Lutheran Seminary Minneapolis and past President Orthodox Lutheran Conference.

"This view makes the form 'in the Name of Christ' to be still valid."[269]

414. Wijngaards, John (2012). *The Ordained Women Deacons of The Church's First Millennium*. Norwich: Canterbury Press, p. 63:

"The Trinitarian formula has been widespread. However, there is also ancient evidence for the use of 'I baptize you in the name of Jesus Christ' (Acts 2:38; 8:12, 16; 10:48; 19:5)."[270]

415. Osborne, Kenan B. (1987). *Christian Sacraments of Initiation Baptism, Confirmation, Eucharist*. Mahwah, New Jersey: Paulist Press, pp. 14-15:

"We also read in Acts that there might have been a baptism by Christians merely in the name of Jesus. Such a formula, documented by the New Testament...."[271]

416. Donovan, J. (1829). *The Catechism of The Council of Trent. Published by Command of Pope Pius the Fifth*. Dublin: Richard Coyne & Keating and Browne, p. 163:

"If at any time the Apostles baptized in the name of the Lord Jesus Christ only, (37) they did so, no doubt, by the inspiration of the Holy Ghost, in order, in the infancy of the Church, to render their preaching in the name of the Lord Jesus Christ more illustrious, and to proclaim more effectually his divine and infinite power."

417. Renan, Ernest (2018). *Origins of Christianity*. Volume II. Germany: Verlag GmbH, p. 79:

"The rite was the same in form as the baptism of John, but it was administered in the name of Jesus…in the name of the Father, and of the Son and of the Holy Ghost…But it is not probable that this formula at the early period which we are describing was

---

[269] Sylvester Joseph Hunter was an English Jesuit and of The Society of Jesus.
[270] John Wijngaards was a former Catholic missionary priest, scholar and one of the founding members of the Catholic Biblical Association of India.
[271] Kenan B. Osborne is a Professor Emeritus of the Graduate Theological Union, Berkeley, he was President of The Catholic Theological Society of America, he was cited earlier in this publication also referring to a different study.

yet employed."[272]

418. Stokes, G. T. (1891). *The Expositor's Bible: The Acts of The Apostles.* Volume 1. New York: A. C. Armstrong and Son, p. 84:

> "It is indeed admitted that while our Lord commanded the use of the historic baptismal formula in the concluding words of St. Matthew's Gospel, the formula itself is never expressly mentioned in the Acts of the Apostles. Not merely on the day of Pentecost, but on several other occasions, Christian baptism is described as if the Trinitarian formula was unknown."[273]

419. Knapp, George Christian (1850). *Lectures on Christian Theology.* (2nd ed.). New York: M. W. Dodd, p. 486:

> "II. On the Use of Formulas in Baptism…It has appeared strange to some that we find in the New Testament no passage from which it plainly appears that the words used in Matt. xxviii., in the name of the Father, & c., were used in the apostolical church…we might say with some, that although the formula in Matthew xxxviii., were not used in the apostolical church, but it was merely said in the name of Jesus."[274]

420. Jenks, William (ed.) (1834). *The Comprehensive Commentary on The Holy Bible Containing The Text According to The Authorised Version; Scott's Marginal References, Matthew Henry's Commentary, Condensed, etc., The Practical Observations of Rev. Thomas Scott, D. D.* Boston: Shattuck and Co & Brattleboro: Fessenden and Co, p. 631:

> "But Christian baptism, 'into the name of the Father, and of the Son, and of the Holy Ghost' was at this time not instituted…it appears to me…an intelligent manner, were baptized in the name of Jesus…been baptized in his name, were not re-baptized. Nor were they considered as unbaptized persons…."[275]

---

[272] Ernest Renan (c.1823-c.1892) was a French philosopher, historian and a scholar of religion, a leader in the school of critical philosophy in France.
[273] G. T. Stokes, Professor of Ecclesiastical History in the University of Dublin and Vicar of All Saints, Blackrock.
[274] George Christian Knapp was Professor of Theology in the University of Halle.
[275] Thomas Scott (c.1747-c.1821) was an influential preacher and writer of the Evangelical Revival Church of England.

421. Meschler, SJ., M (1950). *The Life of Our Lord Jesus Christ in Meditations.* Volume 1. St. Louis, Missouri: B. Herder Book Company, p. 207:

> "...baptism was probably administered in the name of Jesus...."[276]

422. Baird, Thomas Dickson (1816). *Science of Praise or an Illustration of The Nature and Design of Sacred Psalmody...A Series of Letters.* Zanesville, Ohio: Putnam Clark, p. 78:

> "This ordinance was commanded to be administered in his name: 'Repent and be baptized everyone of you in the name of Jesus Christ,' Acts ii.38. It is, perhaps too, worthy of remark, that while this ordinance in its institution, was directed to be administered in the name of the Father, and of the Son and of the Holy Ghost, the apostle, in his discourse, mentions only the name of Jesus Christ."

423. Gonzãlez, Justo L. (2001). *Acts The Gospel of The Spirit.* Maryknoll, New York: Orbis Books, see Chapter 4:

> "...originally baptism was only in the name of Jesus...Therefore, the mere fact that the baptism that the Samaritan received was 'in the name of Jesus' does not seem to have been the problem."[277]

424. B.C.R. (1917). *Theology.* The Living Church. Volume. LVIII (November 3). Milwaukee, Wisconsin, p. 802:

> "Holy baptism was administered in the name of Jesus: 'the Trinitarian formula...did not come into use till toward the end of the first century....'"

425. _____. (1981). *The Gospel According to Luke.* The Anchor Bible Volume 28, p. 240:

> "Matt 28:19...That so-called trinitarian form most likely

---

[276] M. Meschler SJ., was a German Jesuit.
[277] Dr. Justo L. Gonzãlez is Professor Emeritus of Church History, Columbia Theological Seminary, a United Methodist minister, he also served as Yale University Research Fellow (1968) and Professor of Historical Theological (1961-69) Evangelical Seminary, Puerto Rico and was a visiting Professor of Theology (1977-88) Interdenominational Theological Center.

represents a liturgical formula derived from some other, possibly later, Christian tradition. For in Acts it is often said that baptism was administered 'in the name of Jesus Christ' (Acts 2:38; 10:48) or 'in the name of the Lord Jesus' (8:16; 19:5; cf. 22:16)."

426. Ashmore, Harry S. (1961). *Encyclopedia Britannica A Survey of Universal Knowledge*. Volume 3 _____, p. 82:

"Everywhere in the oldest sources it is stated that baptism takes place 'in the name of Jesus.' For the first time in the relatively late final chapter of S. Matthew's Gospel the command to baptize with the trinitarian formula (in the name of the Father, and of the Son and of the Holy Spirit, Mt. xxvii.19) is out into the mouth of Jesus."

427. McDonald, Lee Martin (2004). *Introduction to Acts* in *The Bible Knowledge Background Commentary Acts–Philemon*. Evans, Graig A. (ed.). Colorado Springs, Colorado: Victar, p. 35:

"…it was a baptism administered in the name of Jesus. These are the typical words used in Acts to identify what kind of baptism was practiced (2:38; 8:16; 10:48; 19:5)…The Trinitarian formula of Matthew 28:19 is a later development in the practice of baptism in early Christianity."[278]

428. Sinclair, Scott Gambrill (2008). *An Introduction to Christianity for a New Millennium*. Lanham, Maryland: Lexington Books, pp. 55-56:

"Very quickly it became standard to baptize people in the name of the Father, and of the Son and of the Holy Spirit. It appears that in the earliest church, baptism was done in the name of Jesus, since the Acts of the Apostles repeatedly states this (e.g. Act 2:38). Soon, however, the church took literally Jesus' command at the end of Matthew's Gospel and began to baptize people in the name of the Three Persons of the Trinity."[279]

---

[278]Lee Martin McDonald, Principal and Professor of New Testament, Acadia Divinity College, Wolfville, Nova Scotia.
[279]Scott Gambrill Sinclair is an Episcopal Priest, he has taught at the University of California, Davis and Codrington College, Barbados, and is an Adjunct Professor at the Dominican University of California.

429. _____. (1872). *The Scottish Guardian January to June 1872*. Edinburgh: R Grant and Son & London, Oxford and Cambridge: Rivingtons, p. 67:

> "…baptism, in the name of Jesus the Christ…so baptism in His name represents true Christian baptism…."

430. Old, Hughes Oliphant (2002). *Worship Reformed According to Scripture*. Revised and Expanded Edition. Louisville, Kentucky: Westminster John Knox Press, p. 10:

> "The New Testament tell us very little about how baptism was administered. We are often told that baptism was given by someone in the name of Jesus to someone else…."[280]

431. Heine, Ronald E. (2013). *Classical Christian Doctrine Introducing The Essentials of the Ancient Faith*. Grand Rapids, Michigan: Baker Academic:

> "There is both continuity with and divergence from the practice of baptism in New Testament, in the Didache. The baptismal formula appears with that in Matthew 28:19, though some passages in the Acts of the Apostles suggest that baptism may have first been performed only in the name of Jesus (Acts 2:38; 19:5)."[281]

432. Schmaus, Michael (1975). *Dogma The Church as Sacrament*. Volume 5. Lanham, Maryland: Rowman & Littlefield Publishers Inc., p. 143:

> "Until for into the Middle Ages baptism was, wherever possible administered through immersion…This raises the question whether the words of baptism were or must be, christological or trinitarian. In the command by Jesus to baptize the trinitarian form is used, but Act always speaks of baptizing in the name, or on the name of Jesus…According to this view, baptism could be given in the early church and probably even later with the words 'in the name of Jesus'…This is all the more likely since we cannot regard the call to missionary work by Jesus Christ as reported in

---

[280]Hughes Oliphant Old is an American theologian, former pastor and a former member of the Center of Theological Inquiry in Princeton, New Jersey.

[281]Ronald E. Heine, Professor of Bible and Christian Ministry at Northwestern Christian University, Eugene, Oregon.

Matthew, who uses the trinitarian formula, as embodying the actual words of Jesus himself."[282]

433. Wells, George Albert (1971). *The Jesus of The Early Christians A Study in Christian Origins.* London: Pemberton Books, p. 135:

"In Mt. xxviii, 19 the risen Jesus bids the disciples 'go ye therefore and teach all nations, baptizing them in the name of the Father and of the Son and of the Holy Ghost. From Acts (ii, 38; viii, 16; x, 48; xix, 5) and from the epistles (Rom. vi, 3; Gal. iii, 27; I Cor. i, 12 and vi, 11) it is clear that in the earliest times baptism was administered not with this Trinitarian formula but simply 'in the name of Jesus Christ' or of 'the Lord Jesus'. Either Paul and the others deliberately defied Jesus, or the passage in Mt. could be a late interpolation written from a Trinitarian standpoint. This latter is the more likely hypothesis, especially since the passage has no parallel in Mk. or Lk. And if Jesus had enjoined the mission to all nations on his disciples as stated in Mt. it would be impossible to understand how they or their followers could have withstood Paul so hotly upon this very point...."[283]

434. Treier, Daniel J. & Sweeney, Douglas A. (editors) (2021). *Hearing and Doing The Word The Drama of Evangelical Hermeneutics in Honor of Kevin J. Vahoozer.* London& T&T Clark, p. 274:

"...Peter indeed directed new believers to be baptized with water in the name of Jesus Christ (Acts 10:48)...."

435. White, James F. (2000). *Introduction to Christian Worship.* (3rd ed.). Nashville, Tennessee: Abington:

"There are other texts that indicate that the earliest Christian baptisms were 'in the name of Jesus Christ' (Acts 2:38; and 8:12 and 16; 10:48; 19:5; 22:16)...."

436. Lake, Kirsopp (1920). *Landmarks in The History of Early Christianity.*

---

[282]Michael Schmaus was a German Roman Catholic theologian specializing in Dogmatics.
[283]Dr. George Albert Wells was Emeritus Professor of German at Birbeck, the University of London, England.

London: MacMillan and Co., Ltd, pp. 84-86:

> "The same is true of the other constituent element in primitive Christian baptism—the formula 'in the name of the Lord Jesus'...the Antiochean missionaries always practiced baptism 'in the name of the Lord Jesus.' The second is so obviously proved by Acts and the Pauline epistles that it requires no discussion...in the name of the Father, Son and Holy Spirit. That this verse is not historical but a late tradition, intended to support ecclesiastical practice, is shown by the absence of the triune formula of baptism in Acts and the Epistles...There can be little doubt that Acts ought to be trusted on this point."[284]

437. Stanley, Arthur Penrhyn (1884). *Christian Institutions Essays on Ecclesiastical Subjects.* (4th ed.). London: John Murray, p. 15:

> "And this was further impressed upon them by the name in which they were baptized. It was, if not always, yet wherever we hear of its use in the Acts of the Apostles, in the name of the Lord Jesus. Doubtless is the more comprehensive form in which baptism is now everywhere administered in the threefold name of the Father, the Son and the Holy Spirit, soon superseded the simpler form of that in the name of the Lord Jesus only."[285]

438. Spinks, Bryan D. (2006). *Reformation and Modern Rituals and Theologies of Baptism from Luther & Contemporary Practices.* Liturgy Worship and Society. Aldershot: Ashgate Publishing Limited, pp. 154-155:

> "Baptism Amongst Baptists...some smaller groups baptize in the

---

[284]Noted earlier, Dr. Kirsopp Lake, was an English New Testament scholar, church historian, he was ordained into the Church of England, he was the Curate of St. Mary the Virgin, Oxford from 1897-1904 and was Professor of Early Christian Literature at the University of Leyden, Holland and Winn Professor of Ecclesiastical History at Harvard Divinity School. Professor Lake was also cited earlier in this study.

[285]Arthur Penrhyn Stanley, late Dean of Westminster, Regius Professor of Ecclesiastical History at Oxford University, in 1851 he was made Canon of Canterbury Cathedral and later he became Canon of Christ Church, Oxford. In the southeastern chapel of Henry VII's chapel in Westminster Abbey is the grave and monument of Arthur P. Stanley, the great Victorian Dean of Westminster.

name of Jesus Christ rather than with the triune formula...."[286]

439. Gelpi, Donald L. (1993). *Committed Worship A. Sacramental Theology for Converting Christians*. Volume I. Adult Conversion and Initiation. Collegeville, Minnesota: The Liturgical Press, p. 212:

> "How, then, did the rites of initiation evolve in the course of the centuries? The New Testament, as we have seen...the apostolic Church the baptized were plunged into water or washed it as the minister invoked either the name of Jesus of the triune name (Acts 2:38; Matt 28:19)."[287]

440. Wien, Devon (1985). *The Biblical Significance of Baptism by Immersion*. Direction, Vol. 14, No. 1 (Spring), p. 11:

> "Jesus' actual water baptism and the interpretation of his whole ministry under the figure of baptism become a model in the early church of what happens as believers are baptized. In the Acts of the Apostles, baptism is administered "in the name of Jesus Christ" (2:38; 10:48) or "into the name of the Lord Jesus" (8:16; 19:5)."[288]

441. White, Thomas (2006). *What Makes Baptism Valid?* The Center for Theological Research (July). White Paper 7. Southwestern Baptist Theological Seminary, Fort Worth, Texas, p. 9:

> "A complete discussion of the formula throughout history would take more space than this brief article will allow. In brief, Scripture presents three possibilities concerning the formula for baptism. The most common formula can be found in Acts 2:38 where Peter states, "Repent, and each of you be baptized in the name of Jesus Christ." In Acts 19:5, Paul mentions baptism in name of the Lord Jesus. This is also mentioned in Acts 8:16, and 10:48. A second but related formula appears in Galatians 3:27, "As many of you as were baptized into Christ." The third and

---

[286]Bryan D. Spinks is Goddard Professor of Liturgical Studies and Pastoral Theology of Yale Institute of Sacred Music and Yale Divinity School.
[287]Donald L. Gelpi, S.J., teaches Historical and Systematic Theology at the Jesuit School of Theology in Berkeley.
[288]Devon Wiens heads the Department of Bible Theology at Fresno Pacific College, California.

most popular formula can only be found in Matt 28:19, "baptizing them in the name of the Father, and the Son, and the Holy Spirit"…The reason for this belief comes from the early evidence of the use of the triune formula found only once in Scripture. The Didache states, "Baptize in the name of the Father, and of the Son, and of the Holy Spirit." Justin Martyr wrote, "For, in the name of God, the Father and Lord of the universe, and of our Savior Jesus Christ, and of the Holy Spirit, they then receive the washing with water." Other early fathers could be quoted to demonstrate the use of the Trinitarian formula but for the purposes of this essay, the previously mentioned quotes should suffice. What is essential is that baptism occurs in the name of Jesus Christ, the second Person of the Trinity."

442. Shelton, James B. (2021). *"The Name of Jesus in Luke-Acts with Special Reference to the Gentile Missions," Spiritus.* Oral Roberts University Journal of Theology, Volume 6, No. 1, Article 6, p. 55:

"In Acts, the apostles baptize in the name of Jesus, Jesus Christ, or the Lord Jesus Christ (Acts 2:38; 8:16; 10:48; 19:5; see also Pauline practice, Rom 6:3; 1 Cor 1:13; Gal 3:27)…While there is some reason to consider baptism "in the name of Jesus," or similar variations, as the most ancient…."[289]

443. Duck, Ruth C. (1999). *The Trinity in Sunday Worship* in *Praising God The Trinity in Christian Worship*, Duck, Ruth C. & Wilson-Kastner, Patricia. Louisville, Kentucky: Westminster John Knox Press, p. 54:

"Since about the eight century, the words spoken with the administration of baptismal water are usually, 'I baptize you [or, you are baptized] in the name of the Father and of the Son and of the Holy Spirit.' These words provide a summary of Christian faith with its trinitarian structure. They echo words attributed to Jesus in Matthew 28:19: 'Go therefore and make disciples of all nations, baptizing them in the name of the Father and of the Son and of the Holy Spirit,' though it is likely that Jesus' original words may have been 'baptizing in my name.' Several passages in Acts and the early Christian document called the Didache ("The

---

[289]Dr. James B. Shelton is Senior Professor of New Testament, Oral Roberts University, Tulsa, Oklahoma.

Teaching of the Twelve Apostles") make it appear that baptisms were also done in the name of Jesus or in the name of Christ. It appears that for the first few centuries of the church, 'baptizing them in the name of the Father and of the Son and of the Holy Spirit' was more a summary of the theology of baptism than a formula always used in baptism."[290]

444. Kostenberger, Andreas J. & Alexander, T. Desmond (2020). *Salvation to The Ends of the Earth A Biblical Theology of Mission*. New Studies in Biblical Theology (2nd ed.). London: Apollos, p. 63:

"Baptism…the name…of the Father and the Son and the Holy Spirit…trinitarian formula in the entire New Testament. In the light of the fact that the early church is shown to have baptized in the name of Jesus Christ (Acts 2:38; 10:48) or 'the Lord Jesus' (Acts 8:16; 19:5) and Paul refers merely to baptism in the name of Christ (Gal. 3:27; Rom. 6:3)…It appears more likely that the early church felt no contradiction between Jesus' command to baptize in the name of the Father, the Son and the Holy Spirit, and its practice of baptizing in the name of Jesus, since the later implied the former."[291]

445. Thiselton, Anthony C. (2000). *The First Epistle to The Corinthians. The New International Greek Testament Commentary*. Grand Rapids, Michigan: William B. Eerdmans Publishing Company, pp. 138:

"The key point for Paul was not who performed the baptismal rite, but in whose name the convert was baptized…you were baptized in the name of Christ (and in the name of no other)…'in the name' implies the name of this name…."[292]

446. Thiselton, Anthony C. (2013). *The Holy Spirit – In Biblical Teaching,*

---

[290] Ruth C. Duck is Associate Professor of Worship at Garrett-Evangelical Theological Seminary in Evanston, Illinois.

[291] Andrew J. Kostenberger is Research Professor of New Testament and Biblical Theology, and Director of the Center for Biblical Studies at Midwest Baptist Theological Seminary in Kansas City, Missouri, and T. Desmond Alexander is Senior Lecturer and Director of post-graduate studies at Union Theological College in Belfast, Northern Ireland.

[292] Anthony C. Thiselton is Professor Emeritus of Christian Theology at the University of Nottingham, England.

Through the Centuries, and Today. Grand Rapids, Michigan: William B. Eerdmans Publishing Company, pp. 45-46:

> "(5) Postresurrection commands and promises: two postresurrection sayings. One saying is peculiar to Matthew, and the other is found only in Luke. The Great Commission of Matt. 28:19, 'Make disciples of all nations, baptizing them in the name of the Father, the Son, and the Holy Spirit...' is widely considered to be 'the expression of later reflection or revelation.' Some attribute it to Matthew's special interest in the community or church. But the Trinitarian formulation of the baptismal rite soon become established. It occurs, for example, in the Didache, which is either late first century or early second century (Didache 7.1 and 3). Christian baptism in Paul and in Acts is in the name of Christ alone."

447. Aus, Roger David (2017). *Two Puzzling Baptisms Studies in Judaism First Corinthians 10:1-5 and 15:29 Studies in Their Judaic Background*. Lanham, Maryland: Hamilton Books, p. xi, see Introduction paragraph 1:

> "The earliest Christians basically took over this rite, which was a 'baptism of repentance for the forgiveness of sins (v. 4). They modified it in part by performing it 'in the name of Christ.' Later to include the Father and the Holy Spirit (Matt. 28:19)." See also footnote 1 noting "cf. 'in the name of Jesus Christ' in Acts 2:38 and 10:48, and 'in the name of the Lord Jesus' in 8:16 and 19:5."[293]

448. Johnson, Luke Timothy (2001). *Reading Romans A Literary and Theological Commentary*. Macon, Georgia: Helwys Publishing, p. 102:

> "That baptism was the distinctive Christian ritual of initiation is clear enough...We know that it was carried out 'in the name of Jesus' (Acts 10:48)...."[294]

---

[293] Roger David Aus is Pastor Emeritus of the Evangelische Luther-Kirchengemeinde Alf-Reinichkendorf in Berlin, Germany.
[294] Luke Timothy Johnson is the Robert W. Woodruff Professor of New Testament and Christian Origins at Candler School of Theology and Senior Fellow at the Center for the study of Law and Religion, Emory University and noted and distinguished scholar in his field.

449. Barth, Markus & Blanke, Helmut (2000). *The Letter to Philemon – Critical Eerdmans Commentary*. Grand Rapids, Michigan: William B. Eerdmans Publishing Company, p. 235:

> "Especially the baptism stories o Acts 8:9-24 and 10:44-48 reveal that in the early church the human act of baptism with water...the (water) baptism in the name of the Lord Jesus...."[295]

450. Beasley-Murray, George R. (1999). *John*. World Biblical Commentary (rev. ed.) Volume 36. Grand Rapids, Michigan: Zondervan, see Part III:

> "The name of Christ was used in the baptismal initiation rites, first in the name Jesus or the Lord Jesus, but later in the name of the Father and of the Son and of the Holy Spirit (Matt. 28:19)."[296]

451. Beasley-Murray, George R. (1994). *Baptism in the New Testament*. Grand Rapids, Michigan: William B. Eerdmans Publishing Company, pp. 100, 163:

> "(i) As has been mentioned, baptism in Acts is always administered 'in the name of Jesus Christ' or 'in the name of the Lord Jesus (2:38, 8:16, 10:48, 19:5)...'in the name of the Lord Jesus Christ' reflects the use of the Name in the baptismal formula."[297]

452. Orr, James (General Editor) (1915). *The International Standard Bible Encyclopaedia*. Volume I. A–Clemency. Chicago: The Howard-Severance Company, pp. 392-393:

> "IV. The Formula of Baptism.–The Formula of Christian baptism...in Mt 28:19: 'I baptize thee in the name of the Father, of the Son, and of the Holy Ghost.' But it is curious that the

---

[295] Markus Barth (1915-1994) was Professor of New Testament Studies at the University of Basel, Switzerland, son of the renowned theologian, Karl Barth and Helmut Blanke student of Markus Barth now a Pastor in Germany.

[296] Dr. George R. Beasley-Murray is former Principal of Spurgeon's College, London and has served as James Buchanan Harrison Professor of New Testament Interpretation at Southern Baptist Theological Seminary in Louisville, Kentucky.

[297] For a comprehensive view of the discussion of baptism, including Matthew 28:19 in this publication refer to pages 77-125.

words are not give in any description of Christian baptism until the time of Justin Martyr: and there they are not repeated exactly but in a slightly extended and explanatory form...In every account of the performance of the rite in apostolic times a much shorter formula is in use. The 3,000 believers were baptized on the Day of Pentecost 'in the name of Jesus' (Acts 2:38); and the same formula was used at the baptism of Cornelius and those that were with him (Acts 10:48). Indeed, it would appear to have been the usual one, from St. Paul's question to the Corinthians: 'Were ye baptized into the name of Paul?' (I Cor 1:13)...Scholars have exercised a great deal of ingenuity in trying to explain how, with what appear to be the very words of Jesus given in the Gospel of Mt, another and much shorter formula seems to have been used throughout the apostolic church. Some have imagined that the shorter formula was that used in baptizing disciples during the lifetime of Our Lord (Jn 4:1-2), and that the apostles having become accustomed to it continued to use it during their lives...Others, again, insist that baptism in the name of one of the persons of the Trinity implies baptism in the name of the Three...but it is more than likely that the use of the shorter formula did not altogether die out, or, if it did, that it was revived. The historian Socrates informs us that some of the more extreme Arians 'corrupted' baptism by using the name of Christ only in the formula, while injunctions to use the longer formula and punishments, including deposition, threatened to those who presumed to employ the shorter which meet us in collections of ecclesiastical canons (*Apos. Canons, 43, 50*), prove that the practice of using the shorter formula existed in the 5th and 6th cents, at all events in the East."[298]

453. Hornik, Heidi J & Parsons, Mikeal C. (2017). *The Acts of the Apostles Through the Centuries Wiley Blackwell Bible Commentaries.* Chichester, West Sussex: John Wiley & Sons Ltd, pp. 134-135:

"Baptized in The Name of Jesus (Acts 10:48). British cleric Hanserd Knollys (1598-1691) perhaps reflecting some current

---

[298]Socrates of Constantinople, also known as Socrates Scholasticus was a 5th-century Christian church historian, a contemporary of Sozomen and Theodoret. He is the author of a *Historia Ecclesiastica* which covers the history of late ancient Christianity during the years 305 to 439.

debate about the use of the trinitarian baptismal formula, argues that Acts 10:48 ("he commanded them to be baptized in the name of Jesus Christ") is to be understood, not as an 'Exception,' but rather as the equivalent to in the Name of the Father, Son and Holy Spirit. For those three are one in Essence...There is not one baptism in the Name of the Father, Son, and Holy Spirit [Matt. 28:19] and another Baptism in the Name of the Lord Jesus Christ" (Knollys 1646.2). Katherine Sutton, a seventeenth-century prophetess and mystic, credited the 'Great Commission' of Matthew 28 and Acts 10:48 with convincing her to submit to believer's baptism: 'Now that which made me willing to obey the Lord, in this Ordinance was the Command of Jesus Christ in Mat. 28:19, and Act. 10:48, and the example of Christ and the practice of the Apostles, and primitive saints, together with the promise of the gift of the Holy Ghost, annexed thereunto' (Sutton 1663, 11-12)."

454. Robinson, Robert (1792). *Ecclesiastical Researches.* Cambridge: Francis Hodson. Robinson makes observations several times in his work of baptism in the name of Jesus Christ in Europe and by several groups etc. He especially noted that the Spanish Christians baptized in the name of Jesus Christ in addition to other groups, pp. 79, 80, 206-207, 213, 393-394, 602:[299]

"His majesty caused his converts to be baptized, that is, rebaptized, for the members of churches had been dipped once in the name of Christ...He convened an assembly at Toledo to try, if possible, to abate the zeal of the enthusiastical Catholic, and

---

[299]Robert Robinson was an English Dissenter, influential Baptist and scholar who made a lifelong study of the antiquity and history of Christian baptism. He simply reinforces to view of the world of biblical, historical, theological and ecclesiastical scholarship that evidences that baptism in the name of Jesus Christ was valid throughout the centuries from the Day of Pentecost to the present. See also, the article by Dr. Benjamin B. Warfield (1797), Article I. *The Archaeology of The Mode of Baptism*, The Bibliotheca Sacra in *Thoughts of The Christian Religion In A Letter to A Friend*. Boston: Printed and sold by Samuel Hall, Cornhill, pp. 615-617, noting that "...some Spanish Catholics to baptize with only one immersion." Not also, Socinianism is an anti-Trinitarian system named for Faustus Socinus (1539–1604) of Siena, Italy, who in turn was influenced by the teachings of Michael Servetus (1511– 1553), the Spanish physician and theologian who was burned at the stake as a heretic at Geneva.

to form a union between them and the Arians…The chief article of discussion was baptism, for all the arian Goths, the Priscillianifts, the followers of Bonofus, and others deemed heretics by the Catholics were literally anabaptists in regard to the Catholics(9). Themselves were baptized once only by dipping in the name of Christ; but when Catholics, who had been dipped in the name of the trinity, joined their churches, they rebaptized them…The Spanish Christians called heretics did not regulate their administration of baptism by any of the canons of the Catholic councils…some in the name of Christ…The practice of baptism at that time demands attention (5). The German nations in the empire were all Unitarians…Some of the Unitarians administered baptism in the name of Christ…This little piece was printed at Cracow, and as the preface says, is addressed 'by the little and afflicted flock in Poland, which was baptized in the name of Jesus of Nazareth, to all those, who thirst after eternal salvation.'"

455. French, Talmadge L. (1999). *Our God is One The Story of The Oneness Pentecostals*. Indianapolis, Indiana: Voice & Vision Publications, p. 210:

"The name of Jesus in Oneness theology is of utmost significance. The repeated use in the New Testament of the form 'in the name' signifies that it is the only distinguishing New Testament formula invoked over candidates in baptism."[300]

456. Dominguez, Eugene A. (2020). *Oneness Heroes In Spain and the Americas: Centuries IV-XXXI* Volume 1. Third Edition. Weldon Springs, Missouri, p. 41:

"Conti in his honorable work on Priscillian commented, "The trinitarian concept of Priscillian seems to be unquestionable and constant monarchian… [and] continues to describe with dense and poetic language the nature of the Father, who appears to be, according to the Monarchian position of Priscillian, a single person assuming the aspects and roles of the Son and the Holy Spirit."72 González reported that Pricilian, among scholars it is argued that he maintained a theology similar to Sabellianism

---

[300]Dr. Talmadge L. French is a prominent apostolic scholar and theologian in the apostolic oneness movement.

among other accusations. In addition, he believed in the gifts of the Spirit, that the name of God is Jesus, that repentance precedes baptism in water, and according to Robert Robinson many of the Spanish Priscillianists for many years baptized in the name of Jesus Christ."

457. Hawthorne, Gerald F., et. al. (1993). *Dictionary of Paul and His Letters. A Compendium of Contemporary Biblical Scholarship.* Downers Grove, Illinois: InterVarsity Press, in which Senior Professor G. R. Beasley-Murray comments speaking on Baptism:[301]

"1.1. Baptism 'in the name of Jesus.' In Paul's letters, as in the book of Acts, baptism is typically represented as baptism 'in the name' of Jesus. This is reflected in a significant manner in Paul's handling of the divisions in the Corinthian* church. He cites its members as saying, 'I belong to Paul,' 'I belong to Apollos,' 'I belong to Cephas (=Peter*),' I belong to Christ' (1 Cor. 1:12). Paul, with some indignation, asks, 'Has Christ been apportioned to any single group among you? Was Paul crucified for you? Or were you baptized in the name of Paul?' This final question echoes the language of baptism in the name of Jesus; its use in the context suggests that its normal usage is to make a person a follower of Jesus, even to belong to him, and somehow to be involved in his crucifixion* and enjoy a special relation to him...The baptizer invokes the name of Jesus over the baptized, and the baptized calls on the name of the Lord* as he or she is baptized (for the former cf. Jas 2:7; for the latter cf. Acts 22:16)."

458. _____ (1835). *The Penny Cyclopaedia of The Society for The Diffusion of Useful Knowledge* Volume III. Athanaric-Bassano. London: Charles Knight, p. 413:

"Baptizing them in the name of the Father, and of the Son, and of the Holy Ghost. These words have been adopted as the formula...yet it is remarkable that we do not find these words to have been used as a baptismal formula in any of the baptisms of which we have an account in the book of Acts: and in the account of some of them it is expressly said that the parties were baptized in the name of Jesus (see Acts ii.38; xix.5)."

---

[301] See section B Baptism in the *Dictionary of Paul and His Letters.*

459. Wood, Susan K. (2009). *One Baptism Ecumenical Dimensions of The Doctrine of Baptism*. Collegeville, Minnesota: Liturgical Press, p. 79:

> "This act of public confession includes the public celebration of baptism, whereby the believer by immersion is baptized in the name of the Father, and the Son and the Holy Spirit (or in the name of Jesus)."[302]

460. Wainwright, Arthur C. (2001). *The Trinity in The New Testament*. Eugene, Oregon: Wipf & Stock, p. vii:

> "...there is no formal statement of the doctrine of the Trinity in the New Testament."

461. Sanders, Fred (2005). *The Image of The Immanent Trinity Rahner's Rule and the Theological Interpretation of Scripture Issues in Systematic Theology & 12*. New York: Peter Lang, p. 19:

> "The triadic formulas of the New Testament are usually of liturgical or confessional provenance and indicate the Christian community's attempts to make sense of earlier layers of tradition. To cite the only most famous of the triads, the risen Lord's charge at the end of Matthew's gospel to 'baptize in the name of the Father and of the Son and of the Holy Spirit' has long been regarded as a passage so theologically dense that it stands out oddly from its Matthean (indeed its New Testament) context."

462. Schaff, Phillip (1910). *History of The Christian Church*. Volume II Ante-Nicene Christianity A.D. 100-325. New York: Charles Scribner's Sons, p. 529:

> "...the baptismal formula (Matt. 28:19) furnished the trinitarian frame-work of the earliest creeds or baptismal confessions of Christendom."

---

[302]Susan K. Wood makes reference to the comments of Dr. Thorwald Lorenzen who offers a summary of the generally accepted Baptist practice of baptism. Susan K. Wood, SCL, is chair of the department of theology at Marquette University. Active in ecumenical work, she serves on the U.S. Lutheran–Roman Catholic Dialogue, the U.S. Roman Catholic–Orthodox Theological Consultation, the conversation between the Roman Catholic Church and the Baptist World Alliance, and the International Lutheran–Roman Catholic Dialogue.

463. Gillis, Chester (1989). *A Question of Final Belief John Hick's Pluralistic Theory of Salvation*. London: The MacMillan Press Ltd, p. 11:

> "As recently as 1970, in speaking of the non-Christian world, the Frankfurt Declaration stated: 'We therefore challenge all non-Christians, who belong to God on the basis of creation, to believe in him [Jesus Christ] and to be baptized in his name, for in him alone is eternal salvation promised to them."

464. Morden, Peter J. (2010). *C. H. Spurgeon and Baptism The Importance of Baptism*. Baptist Quarterly, 43:7, pp. 404-405:

> "Perhaps most of all, Spurgeon's focus was on baptism as the 'badge' of full-blooded, radical discipleship. Such discipleship would undoubtedly be costly. In 'Baptism Essential To Obedience' he declared,–He that 'believeth and is baptized' into the adorable name of Jesus swears…to follow Christ, and Christ alone, believing in him though ever man be a liar, and resolving for him to live, for him to die, and in him to find hope here and eternal felicity hereafter."[303]

465. Moss, Claude B. (1949) (reprint). *The Christian Faith An Introduction To Dogmatic Theology*. Eugene, Oregon: Wipf & Stock, p. 341:

> "Pope Nicholas I appears to have recognized baptism 'in the name of Jesus Christ' as valid…."[304]

466. _____ (2016). *Saint Thomas Aquinas Collection [22 Books]*. Aeterna Press:

> "Whether Baptism Can be Conferred in The Name of Christ?..It seems that baptism can be conferred in the name of Christ. For just as there is 'one Faith,' so there is 'one Baptism' (Eph. 4:5). But it is related (Acts 8:12) that 'in the name of Jesus Christ they

---

[303] See also the comments of John Wesley "Was not he alone crucified for you all; and were ye not all baptized in his name?... testified your faith by being baptized in the name of Christ…", see John Wesley, *Wesley Note's Romans–Revelation*, Wesley Heritage Library Commentaries, Wesleyan Heritage Publications (1998).

[304] Dr. Claude B. Moss was an Anglican Theologian who served as Vice-Principal of Boniface College, Warminster who work was renowned during his time in the Church of England.

were baptized, both men and women.' Therefore, now also can baptism be conferred in the name of Christ...Furthermore, Ambrose says (De Spir. Sanct. i.): 'If you mention Christ, you designate both the Father by Whom He was anointed, and the Son Himself, Who was anointed, and the Holy Ghost Whom He was anointed.' But baptism can be conferred in the name of the Trinity: therefore also in the name of Christ...Further, Pope Nicholas I, answering questions put to him by the Bulgars said: 'Those who have been baptized in the name of the Trinity, or only in the name of Christ, as we read in the Acts of the Apostles (it is all the same, as Blessed Ambrose saith), must not be rebaptized...Therefore, Baptism can be celebrated in the name of Christ by....'"

467. Selwyn. Edward Gordon (ed.) (1926). Essays Catholic & Critical. New York and Toronto: The MacMillan Co, London: Society for Promoting Christian Knowledge (2nd ed.), pp. 410 and footnote 1 on page 414:[305]

"Secondly, we gather that, on the external side, the differentia of Christian Baptism is found in the employment of the "name of Jesus" part of a spoken formula...The early and universal substitution of the Name of the Father, Son, and Holy Ghost for the "Name of the Lord Jesus" was presumably due to the influence of Matt. xxviii. 19. In view of the eighteen centuries of prescription which the use of the Three-fold Name can now claim, the modern Church is doubtless justified in making its employment an absolute condition of the technical "validity" of the rite as administered at the present day; but the Roman Catholic scholar, W. Koch (*Die Taufe im* N.T., 1921, p. 7) quotes Pope Nicholas I (*Respons. ad consult. Bulgar., ap. Denzinger - Bannwart, Encheiridion Symb. et Def., 335*), Cajetan, and Hadrian of Utrecht (later Pope Hadrian VI) as asserting the standing validity of baptism "in the name of Jesus" or of Christ."[306]

---

[305]In this publication the work on the Sacraments is produced by Norman Powell Williams, Fellow and Precentor of Exeter College, Oxford, lecturer in Theology at Exeter and Pembroke Colleges, Oxford and Examining Chaplain to the Bishop of New Castle. See also Collins, Berkeley G. (1915). *The Sacrament of Baptism in The New Testament*. The Expository Times. Volume 27, Issue 3.

[306]For more regarding Pope Hadrian VI, see Boora, Kulwant Singh (2021) (revised

468. Reyroux, Frederick (MDCCCXXXIV). *Christian Theology: Translated from The Latin of Benedict Pictet.* London: R. B. Seeley and W. Burnside, p. 490:

> "…baptism is valid, which is administered by a heathen or Jewish adventurer, merely baptizing in the name of Christ, as was the opinion of Pope Nicholas I., and of the council of Florence."[307]

469. Langford-James, R. LL. (1924). *The Doctrine of Intention.* New York and Toronto: The MacMillan Co., & London: Society for Promoting Christian Knowledge, p. 54:

> "8. If the intention of the minister is of the essence of the Sacrament, how, then, can Jews, etc., baptize? He quotes on this point the decision of Pope Nicholas I on the subject. The question as to whether those baptized by a Jew, or a Pagan were to be re-baptized had been referred to him. His reply was: "Those who were baptized in the Name of the Sacred Trinity, or even in the Name of Jesus, as is read in the Acts of the Apostles, ought not to be re-baptized, because the Baptism is not theirs but His (quia *non illorum sed ejus est*)."[308]

470. Hergenrother, Joseph Adam Gustav (1870). *Anti-Janus: An Historical-Theological Criticism of The Work, entitled 'The Pope and the Council,' by Janus.* Dublin: W. B. Kelly & London: Burn, Oates & Company and Simpkin, Marshall & Co; New York: The Catholic Publishing Society, p. 83:

> "8. Nicholas I., we are told, declared baptism given in the name of Jesus to be valid."[309]

---

edition). *The Three Roman Catholic Popes on The Validity of Baptism in The Name of Jesus (Acts 2:38) and The Two Catholic Popes on the Oneness Christological view of God.* Published by Amazon Publishing (Book 8).

[307] Benedict Pictet was Pastor and Professor of Divinity in The Church and University of Geneva.

[308] R. Ll. Langford-James, D. D., sometime scholar of Keble College, Oxford, Vicar of St. James', Edgbaston.

[309] Dr. Joseph A. G. Hergenrother, Cardinal of the Catholic Church and German Theologian and scholar, Professor of Cannon Law and of Ecclesiastical History at the University of Wurzburg.

471. Bullinger, Ethelbert William (2007). *How to Enjoy The Bible; Or, 'The Word,' and 'The Words,' How To Study Them.* New York: Cosimo Publications (originally published in 1921), p. 136:

> "On the other hand, we have evidence of the baptism in the one name in the days of Cyprian, for he condemns those who held that it was sufficient to say 'in the name of Jesus Christ.' But it was declared to be valid by the Council of Frejus, A.D. 792, and also by Pope Nicholas I, as late as (858-867)."[310]

472. Bromiley, G. W. (ed.) (1953). *Zwingli and Bullinger.* The Library of Christian Classics Ichthus Edition. Philadelphia, Pennsylvania: The Westminster Press, p. 145:

> "For that reason the disciples baptized in the name of Jesus Christ. Hence our name Christians, that is, we are initiated into Christ and dedicated to him. Nowhere do we read that the disciples baptized in the name of the Father, the Son and the Holy Ghost. Therefore it is evident that the words of Matthew 28 were not instituted as a form and the theologians have made the biggest mistake of their lives in their exposition of this text."[311]

473. Uyl, Anthony (ed.) (2017). *Ambrose: Selected Works and Letters by Saint Ambrose.* Originally edited by Phillip Schaff (1819-1893). Woodstock, Ontario, Canada: Devoted Publishing, p. 128:

> "…St. Ambrose taught, as some others certainly did (probably on his authority), that baptism in the Name of Christ alone, without mention of the other Persons, is valid."

474. Boersma, Hans & Matthew Levering (ed.) (2015). *The Oxford Handbook of Sacramental Theology.* Oxford: Oxford University Press:

> "To be baptized in his name was to become part of his body, the church. The apostles of Jesus quickly put into practice his

---

[310] Ethelbert William Bullinger (1837-1913) was Vicar of the Church of England, Biblical Scholar and dispensationalist Theologian. He was born in Canterbury, England, his family is traced its lineage back to the noted Swiss Reformer, Heinrich Bullinger (1504-1557).

[311] Ulrich Zwingli (1484-1531), Pastor and Theologian, was the most important reformer in the Swiss Protestant Reformation.

command. On the day of Pentecost Peter urged those in Jerusalem, "Repent, and be baptized every one of you in the name of Jesus Christ so that your sins may be forgiven" (Acts 2:38)."

475. _____ (1857). *The Intellectual Repository and New Jerusalem Magazine*. Vol. IV – Enlarged Series. London: The General Conference of The New Church, p. 27:

> "How far the historical data supplied in the Acts of the Apostles are adequate to decide the question, I will not pretend to say; I may, however, venture to affirm that the evidence appears to preponderate in favour of the strict grammatical meaning of the statement — that the Apostles did literally baptize in the name of Jesus only."

476. MacArthur, John (1994). *The MacArthur New Testament Commentary Acts 1-12*. Chicago, Illinois: Moody Publishers:

> "By calling on each of them to be baptized in the name of Jesus Christ Peter does not allow for any "secret disciples" (cf. Matt. 10:32–33). Baptism would mark a public break with Judaism and identification with Jesus Christ…Baptism was always in the name of Jesus Christ."

477. Turley, Stephen Richard (2015). *The Ritualized Revelation of The Messianic Age Washings and Meals in Galatians and 1 Corinthians*. London: Bloomsbury Publishing PLC, p. 31:

> "…since baptism was 'in the name of Jesus Christ' (Acts 2:38; 1 Cor. 6:11)."[312]

478. Thomassen, Einar (2006). *The Spiritual Seed The Church of The Valentinians*. Nag Hammadi & Manichaean Studies. Leiden: Brill, p. 403:

> "The study of the various liturgies above has shown the importance of the 'Name' both in the invocations over the candidate and in other contexts…In the Shepherd of Hermas we

---

[312]Stephen Richard Turley is a theologian, social theorist, Christian educator. He is a faculty member at Delaware Valley Classical School in New Castle, DE where he teaches theology, Greek and rhetoric, he is also a Professor of Fine Arts at Eastern University.

find the following...the Name is conferred on the candidate on his immersion in the water...The background for this association of the Name with the baptismal water is evidently the notion that baptism takes place 'in the Name of' the redeeming divine agent. NT text's contain allusions to a baptism in the Name of Jesus (frequent in the book of Acts)...."[313]

479. Sandnes, Karl Olav (2011). *Seal and Baptism in Early Christianity* in *Ablution, Initiation, and Baptism Late Antiquity, Early Judaism and Early Christianity*. Hellholm, David (ed.). Berlin & Boston: Walter de Gruyter GmbH & Co. Kg, p. 1451:

"There are the ones who have heard the word...and wanted to be baptized in the name of the Lord (herm. 15.3 [= Vis. 3.7.3.]). This is the only occurrence of...found in the Shepherd of Hermas. Baptism happens 'in the name of the Lord,' a traditional formula associated with the initiation water rite." See footnote 38 "I find the arguments that baptism in the name of Jesus is envisioned here convincing; see e.g. *Brox, Der Hirt des Hermas*, 138; Osiek, *Shepherd of Hermas*, 75; L. Hartman, 'Into the Name of the Lord,' 37-50. Cf. Acts 2:38; 10:48; 19:5."[314]

480. Hagerland, Tobias (2011). *Jesus and The Forgiveness of Sins An Aspect of His Prophetic Mission*. New York: Cambridge University Press, pp. 100, 118, 119:

"Baptism in the name of Jesus...Paul seems to refer to the invocation of the name of Jesus over the person who is baptized...Christian texts to associate baptism in the name of Jesus with forgiveness...It was show in this chapter that, while baptism is said to be performed 'in the name of Jesus' it is God who grants forgiveness."[315]

481. Hill, William J. (1982). *The Three-Personed God: The Trinity As a Mystery of Salvation*. Washington D. C.: Catholic University of America

---

[313] Einar Thomassen, Professor Emeritus, Study of Religion, Department of Archaeology, History, Cultural Studies and Religion at the University of Bergen.
[314] Karl Olav Sandnes is Professor of New Testament Studies at MF Norwegian School of Theology.
[315] Tobias Hagerland is Senior Lecturer in Religious Studies and Theology, specializing in Biblical Studies at the University of Gothenburg.

Press, pp. 27, 196:

> "Go, therefore, make disciples of all the nations; baptize them in the name of the Father and of the Son and of the Holy Spirit (28:19). This text, however, does not occur in the other Gospels, and Peter in Acts mentions Baptism only 'in the name of Jesus Christ' (2:38)...the Holy Spirit, while personal, is not a distinct person within divinity...."

482. Jarrell, W. A. (1894). *Baptist Church Perpetuity or The Continuous Existence of Baptist Churches From The Apostolic To The Present Day Demonstrated By The Bible And By History*. Dallas, Texas: Jarrell, p. 175:

> "The Baptists 'appear supported by history in considering themselves the descendants of the Waldenses'...In an old Waldensian tract we read: "Those that believed they baptized in the name of Jesus Christ."

483. Wood, J. H. (1847). *A Condensed History of The General Baptists of The New Connexion Preceded by Historical Sketches of The Early Baptists*. London: Simpkin, Marshall and Co., Leciester: J. F. Winks, p. 37:

> "1170 A.D. - A tract called "The noble Lesson" was published, probably about the year 1170. Dr. Henderson calls it 'one of the most venerable of the ancient Vaudois productions.' This document, like the preceding, has no reference to infant-baptism: of the apostles it is observed - They spoke, without fear, of the doctrine of Christ; they preached to Jews and Greeks, working miracles; and those that believed they baptized in the name of Jesus."[316]

484. Lawson, John (1961). *A Theological and Historical Introduction to The Apostolic Fathers*. Eugene, Oregon: Wipf & Stock, p. 80:

> "...scholar have argued that originally in the New Testament period Baptism was in the Name of Jesus Christ alone, and that this primitive usage is called to mind by the wording of such passages as Acts ii:38; viii:37, x:48."

---

[316] See also A History of the Baptist Volume I and II, John T. Christian (2014) in which is also notes that "The Noble Lessons say: "*Baptize* those who believe in the *name of Jesus* Christ" (Moreland, Churches of Piedmont, 112)."

485. Newman, Barry C. (2015). *The Gospel, Freedom, and The Sacraments Did The Reformers Go Far Enough?* Eugene, Oregon: Resource Publishers, p. 121:

> "Is there any evidence that some people baptized in the name of Jesus or the Lord Jesus or Jesus Christ?...An interesting questions. In fact, in the story of Paul baptizing the lion, just referred to, Paul baptizes the lion three times in the name of Jesus Christ. In that same work, a woman, Thecla, is supposed to have baptized herself, just before her death in an arena with the cry, 'In the name of Jesus Christ, I baptize myself on the last day (of my life).' In The *Shepherd of Hermas*, a work written, perhaps early in the second century, there is a reference to a person in baptism, bearing the name of the Son of God. Even in the *Didache* there is a reference to those baptized in the Lord's name."

486. Bruskewitz, Fabian (1997). *A Shepherd Speaks.* San Francisco, California: Ignatius Press, 131:[317]

> "The document called the 'Shepherd of Hermas' speaks about the name of Jesus and how the candidate for Baptism were instructed, presumably by a creed, in the meaning of the name into which they were to be baptized (Acts 8:16)."

487. Thianto, Yudha (2012). *The Formula of Baptism and the Equality of the Godhead Joseph Bingham (1668-1723) and the Trinitarian Controversy in Late-Stuart England* in *The New Evangelical Subordinationism? Perspectives on The Equality of God and Th Father and God the Son.* Eugene, Oregon: Pickwick Publications, p. 200:

> "Bingham noted the some of his contemporaries held that non-Trinitarian formulae for baptism were acceptable…He pointed out that sometimes some sects baptized only in the name of Christ. He believed that in the early church baptism in the name of Christ only was an exception…However, he realized that Vossius and Petavius thought that Basil allowed the use of this formula. Bingham explicitly referred to Vossius' *De Bapismo disputation* II, thesis 5, and Petavius' *De Theologicis dogmatibus,*

---

[317]Bishop Fabian Bruskewitz, was a prelate of the Roman Catholic Church, he was the eight Bishop of Lincoln, Nebraska and retired in 2012.

Volume II, Book II, chapter XIV, section VI."[318]

488. Mosheim, John L. V. (1852). *Historical Commentaries on The State of Christianity During The First Three Hundred and Twenty-Five Years From The Christian Era.* Volume II. New York: Converse, pp. 7, 90:

> "The Romans, whom the other Europeans followed, seem to have always held, that reclaimed heretics, who had been already baptized in the name of Jesus Christ, did not need a second baptism...But others for the most part, to whom the reputation of the ancient Roman Pontiffs does not appear of very great importance, thin that Stephen believed all persons baptized in the name of Christ, might be received into the fellowship of the better church, without another baptism."

489. Wright, J. Robert (ed.) (2005). *Ancient Christian Commentary on Scripture Old Testament IX, Proverbs, Ecclesiastes, Songs of Solomon.* Downers Grove, Illinois: InterVarsity Press, p. 402:

> "Treatise on Rebaptism (third century). An anonymous treatise arguing, possibly against Cyprian that those receiving baptism by heretics in the name of Jesus out not to be rebaptized."

490. Felder, Cain Hope ((2021). *Race, Racism and The Biblical Narratives* in *Stony The Road We Trod.* African American Biblical Interpretation. Thirtieth Anniversary Expanded Edition. Minneapolis: Minnesota: Fortress Press, p. 161:

> "...suggest that the principal significance of verse 37 is that it is 'perhaps the earliest form of the baptismal Creed. It is also remarkable that it is an expansion of the baptismal formula 'in the name of Jesus Christ,' not of the trinitarian formula."

491. Ludemann, Gerd (2005). *Acts of The Apostles What Really Happened In The Earliest Days of The Church.* Amherst, New York: Prometheus

---

[318]For additional information regarding Gerardus Joannes Vossius (c.1577-c.1649) and Dionysius Petavius (c.1583-c.1652) see pages 69-70 of Boora (2011), *The Roman Catholic Church and Its Recognition of the Validity of Baptism in the Name of Jesus.*

Books, 195:[319]

> "The addition, which was known to Irenaeus, may give a second-century formula of interrogation before baptism…which was still performed simply in the name of Jesus and not in the threefold name of the Trinity. Matt. xxvii.19 (C.S.C. Williams A Commentary on The Acts of the Apostles [New York: Harper & Brothers Publishers, 1957], p. 120)."

492. Turner, John D. (2008). *The Place of the Gospel of Judas in Sethian Tradition* in *The Gospel of Judas in Context* Proceedings of the First International Conference on the Gospel of Judas, Paris, Sorbonne, October 27-28, 2006, edited by Madeleine Scopello. Leiden: Brill, p. 228:

> "As the Gospel of Judas now stands, it constitutes a vicious polemic against the sacrificial theology of the so-called apostolic churches at the turn of the third century; they have been defiled by perishable wisdom (43, 26-44,5.). Markedly singled out are their ritual practices such as baptism in the name of Jesus by which one participates in his death and resurrection…."[320]

493. Ehrman, Bart D. (1993). *The Orthodox Corruption of Scripture The Effect of Early Christological Controversies on The Text of The New Testament.* New York: Oxford University Press, p. 162:

> "In Acs 2:38; when Peter speaks of being baptized 'in the name of Jesus Christ.'"[321]

494. Slee, Michelle (2003). *The Church in Antioch in The First Century CE Communion and Conflict.* Journal for the Study of The New Testament Supplement Series 266. London: Sheffield Academic Press, p. 62:

> "…and this only need baptism in the name of Jesus…Note there

---

[319]Gerd Ludemann is Professor of the History and Literature of the early Christianity at the University of Gottingen and form Associate Professor of New Testament at Vanderbilt Divinity School.

[320]John D. Turner is Cotner Professor of Religious Studies, Charles J. Mach University Professor of Classics and History, University of Nebraska-Lincoln.

[321]Bart D. Ehrman is a New Testament scholar and is a James A. Gray Distinguished Professor at the University of North Carolina, Chapel Hill.

is a similar change in terminology in evidence in the writings of Justin Martyr: when he addresses himself to Jews, he speaks of baptism in the name of Jesus only (see Dial. 39.2.)...Thus the presence of the Trinitarian formula in the Didache does not indicate that the text in its final form should be given a second century C.E. date."

495. White, Thomas et. al. (ed.) (2008). *Restoring Integrity in Baptist Churches*. Grand Rapids, Michigan: Kregel Publications, p. 116:

"The Formula for Baptism...What is essential is that baptism occurs in the name of Jesus Christ, the second person of the Trinity...."

496. Beard, Jennifer L. (2007). *The Political Economy of Desire*. New York, New York: Routledge (speaking about Christopher Columbus), p. 60:

"Like Jesus Christ's apostle, Peter, Columbus calls the New World to be baptized in the name of Jesus Christ...."[322]

497. Boora, Kulwant Singh (2011). *The Roman Catholic Church And Its Recognition of The Validity of Baptism in The Name of Jesus (Acts 2:38) From 100 A.D. to 500 A.D.* Bloomington, Indiana: Authorhouse, 62-63:

"Nevertheless, we are told that some who were commanded to be baptized in the name of Jesus...the mention of one person of the Trinity must imply the presence, name, and authority of Them all; as the passage is understood by Irenaeus – *in Christi*

---

[322]It has been noted that in the early history of America that in Columbia, North during the earlier part of the 1800s a religious group and sect was called out for baptizing in the name of Jesus and adhering to a New Testament Christology that assumed only one distinct person in the absolute Godhead, thus, discrediting any distinction within the Godhead, see *A Dictionary of All Religions and Religious Denominations, Antient and Modern, Jewish, Pagan, Mohametan, or Christian: Also of Ecclesiastical History*. (3rd London Edition). I. Westley; W. Simpkin and R. Marshall; and W. Baynes and Son, London (1824), p. 127. Also note the leading Mexican Apostolic Historian, Dr. Manuel Gaxiola has explained that individuals in Latin America (namely Mexico) of Russian descents had ancestors who were baptized in the name of Jesus long before 1900 A.D., see page 80-81 of Boora, Kulwant Singh. *The Roman Catholic Church And Its Recognition of The Validity of Baptism In The Name of Jesus (Acts 2:38) From 100 A.D. to 500 A.D.* Authorhouse, Bloomington, Indiana (2011).

nomine subauditur qui unxit, et qui unetus est, et ipsa unction in qua unctus est. (Lib. Iii. Cap. 20.)."[323]

498. Vorgrimler, Herbert (1992). *Sacramental Theology.* Collegeville, Minnesota: The Liturgical Press, p. 110:

"In 866, Nicholas I sent an answer to Bulgaria, where such cases were supposed to have occurred, that whenever someone had been baptized…in the name of Christ, the person was not to be rebaptized…."[324]

499. Chung-Kim, Esther & Hains, Todd R. (2014). *Reformation Commentary on Scripture New Testament VI ACTS.* Downers Grove, Illinois: InterVarsity Press, p. 30:

"Christian Baptism is One. Cardinal Cajetan: From this is appears that it is the same thing to be baptized in the name of Christ and to be baptized in the name of the Father and of the Son and of the Holy Spirit. If in fact the apostles had a command from Christ to baptize in the name of the Father and of the Son and of the Holy Spirit, it would not have changed the substantial form of baptism (so that they would teach something else and do something else), if this form and that form had been different. For it is permitted that there be diversity with respect to the words (by which it is done), but nevertheless the words are the same with respect to the signification. Commentary on Acts 2:38" See in footnote 3 citing "Cajetan, In *Acta Apostolorum,* 216r."

500. Turner, Paul (2020). *The Sacraments Bulleting Inserts For The Liturgical Life of The Parish.* Chicago, Illinois: Liturgy Training Publications, p. 15:

"Baptismal Formula…The formula can be traced back to the conclusion of the Gospel of Matthew, where Jesus commands the disciples to go out to all the world, baptizing in the name of the Father, the Son, and the Holy Spirit (28:19). Although, there

---

[323]Citing the work of William Jones published London, Oxford and Cambridge, see also *The Catholic Study Bible* (2nd ed.), New American Bible Revised Edition, New York: Oxford University Press, p. 429 state that *"Christians are baptized in the name of Jesus."*
[324]Herbert Vorgrimler, Catholic Theologian, Professor and Dean in Munster, Germany.

is some evidence in the Acts of the Apostles for Baptism in the name of Jesus."[325]

501. Reid, Alchin (ed.) (2016). *T&T Clark Companion to Liturgy*. London & New York: Bloomsbury T&T Clark, p. 178:

> "The baptismal bath given in the name of Jesus develops in the third and four the centuries into a complex of solemn rites...."

502. _____ (1836). *Religious Intelligence - Jamaica*. The Baptist Missionary Magazine of Nova Scotia and New Brunswick Published under the Direction of The Missionary Boards of The Province. Vol. III. Halifax, Novia Scotia: The Nova Scotia Office, p. 151:

> "Twenty-four were baptized in the name of Jesus...."[326]

503. Boora, Kulwant Singh (2011). *Baptism in the Name of Jesus (Acts 2:38) From Jerusalem to Great Britain*. Indiana: Authorhouse, p. 18:[327]

> "On 4 November 1980 Marley, a member of the twelve tribes of Israel since the mid-1970's was baptized into the Ethiopian Orthodox Church by Laike Mariam Mandefro, now known as Abuna Yesehag...After all, the Ethiopian Orthodox Church baptized in the name of Jesus Christ and not in the name of Haile Selassie."[328]

---

[325]Paul Turner was cited earlier in this publication also, Dr. Paul Turner is Pastor of Cathedral of The Immaculate Conception in Kansas City, Missouri, and Director of the Office of Divine Worship for the Catholic Diocese of Kansas City-St. Joseph.

[326]With regards to Jamaica, it was noted in one publication that *"Oneness Pentecostalism had a significant presence in Britain from the 1960's, with a number of Apostolic Pentecostal denominations arriving with immigrants from the West Indies."* Bobbington, David & Jones, Ceri Jones (2013). *Evangelism & Fundamentalism in the United Kingdom During The Twentieth Century*. Oxford: Oxford University Press

[327]This citation provides additional information on the comments following from Dijk.

[328]This particular quote is from Frank Jan Van Dijk (1993). *Jahmaica: Rastafari and Jamaican Society 1930-1990*, p. 282.

504. Roswith I. H. Gerloff (2010). *A Plea for British Theologies, Volume 1. The Black Church Movement in Britain in Its Transatlantic Cultural and Theological Interaction with Special Reference to The Pentecostal Oneness (Apostolic) and Sabbatarian Movements.* Eugene, Oregon: Wipf & Stock, this publication provides further insight into the comments of Frank Jan Van Dijk with regards to Bob Marley's mother, p. 156:

> "The second reference we find in E. Cashmore's book on Ras Tafari in England, saying that Bob Marley's mother was 'a devout member of an Apostolic church' in St. Ann. Though it is said that she could not interest her son in 'religious pursuits,' we are sure that his 'prophetic' spirit and also his musical 'vibrations' must have been influenced by this heritage which, however, certainly also sparked off his rebellion against an a-political heaven: *'We're sick and tired of your easing kissing game to die and go to heave in Jesus name we know and understand almighty God is a living man'* (533)."

505. McDowell, Bruce A. (2017). *Christian Baptism The Sign and Seal of God's Covenant Promise.* God's Word Publishing, p. 77:

> "Alexander Cambell (1788-1866), founder of the movement, believed that after initial mental assent to belief in Christ, salvation is a process completed by baptism. He wrote, 'We have the most explicit proof that God forgives sins for the name's sake of his Son, or when the name of Jesus Christ is named upon in immersion…(Cited in Fred Mortiz, 'The Landmark controversy: A Study in Baptist History and Polity,' Maranatha Baptist Seminary (May 22, 2012)."

506. Thayer, Thos B. (ed.) (1864). *Article VII. Formula of Baptism.* The Universalist Quarterly and General Review. New Series-Volume I. Boston: Tompkins & Co., pp. 98-99:

> "From the several authorities now exhibited, it would seem that we are justified in saying: 1. That either men were never baptized in the name of the Father, and of the Son, and of the Holy Ghost, or through an unaccountable carelessness no record was made of it in the writings of the New Testament. 2. That all Christians are baptized in the name of Christ alone…Christians were sometimes baptized in the name of Jesus Christ; sometimes in the name of the Lord Jesus, and sometimes simply in the name of the

Lord."

507. Cooke, R. J. (1903). *The Baptismal Formula of The Apostolic Age. The Methodist Review. (Bimonthly) Volume LXXXV.-Fifth Series, Volume XIX.* Kelley, William V. (ed.). New York: Eaton & Mains & Cincinnati: Jennings & Pye, p. 38-39, 41, 43:

"Thus, "after the third century," writes Professor Allen 'the formula of baptism was in the name of the Trinity, and baptism otherwise performed was declared invalid; but in the early Church, as also in the apostolic age, there is evidence that the baptismal formula of the name of Jesus only was not unusual.' This is a conservative statement, but Professor McGiffertt goes beyond this and says of this Trinitarian formula: "It is difficult to suppose that it was employed in the early days with which we are concerned; for it involves a conception of the nature of the rite which was entirely foreign to the thought of these primitive Christians, and, indeed, no less foreign to the thought of Paul. When and how the formula arose, we do not know. In a note he adds that it is difficult to suppose that Jesus uttered the words, " Baptizing them in the name of the Father, and of the Son, and of the Holy Ghost," which are quoted in Matt. xxviii, 19...It must be ad mitted that in the New Testament the formula, "In the name of the Father, and of the Son, and of the Holy Ghost," occurs nowhere except in the single passage Matt. xxviii, 19...The difficulty, however, of accepting the authenticity of the formula -text in Matthew from the supposed fact that " the early disciples, and Paul as well, baptized into the name of Christ alone, " which they would not have done had Christ given the commandment quoted in Matthew, is of another character. Nowhere in the New Testament is the formula repeated. On the contrary, everywhere in the Acts where baptism is mentioned, we find that it was administered only εἰς, or ἐπί τo ὄνομα, εν τῷ ὀνόματι Ιησού, or Χριστού...Definite, decisive patristic evidence for or against the use of the Trinitarian formula in the subapostolic Church...is wanting... We can only say Cyprian does not object to receiving the followers of Marcion because they were baptized in the name of Christ only."

508. McGiffert, Arthur Cushman (1924). *The God of The Early Christians*. New York: Charles Scribner's Sons, pp. 52-54, 60-61, 76:

"Conceivably there may have been many in the early generations whose God was Jesus Christ and who knew no other God...forming strong evidence of a form of primitive Gentile Christianity whose God was Jesus Christ alone...For one thing it is quite certain and beyond dispute that Christ was widely recognized as divine among the early Christians...lecture reference was made to the attitude of Paul and John, both of whom thought of Christ as divine. Certain ancient manuscripts of the book of Acts put into Paul's mouth, in a We-passage, the words: "The Church of God...which he purchased with his own blood." The Epistle to Titus refers to the "appearing of the glory of our great God and Saviour Christ Jesus"? and in the Epistle to the Hebrews (1:8) the words of the Psalm, "Thy throne, O God...is forever and ever," are represented as addressed to the Son. From the second century we have many more documents than from the first, and in them Christ is called God even more frequently. As remarked in the previous lecture, Ignatius, in the early part of the century, spoke of him as God...over and over again, and Polycarp, writing shortly afterward, referred to him — at least according to certain manuscripts — as "our Lord and God, Jesus Christ." In 2 Peter, dating from the middle of the century, he is spoken of as "our God and Saviour Jesus Christ," and the author of 2 Clement, writing perhaps about the same time, calls him God...more than once and even refers to him as a father. In 2 Clement, indeed, it is said explicitly: "We must think of Jesus Christ as of God (περί Ιησού Χριστού ὰs trepà Deoú), as of the judge of living and dead" (1:1); and throughout the epistle the same functions are ascribed indifferently to God and to Christ, and they are spoken of as if they were for all practical purposes identical. The second-century apologist, Justin Martyr, defends the worship of Christ and refers to him more than once as another God"...Thus, in the Pastoral Epistles, though Christ is called God only in Titus 2:13, Lord is used both of God and Christ, and while God and Christ are frequently distinguished, it is sometimes impossible to tell whether Lord refers to the former or the latter.2 Similarly, in the book of Acts Lord is used both of God and of Christ...In the Acts of John, which date from about the same time, prayers to Christ as God are very numerous. "Now the time of refreshing and confidence is with thee, O Christ; now for us weary ones the time of help from thee, physician who healest without cost. Keep my entrance here from being made sport of. I beseech thee, Jesus, help such a great multitude to come to thee, thou Master of the universe " (22). Glory be to thee, my Jesus, the only God of truth" (43). "God of the ages, Jesus Christ, God of truth" (82) .2 In the Acts of Peters and the Acts of Thomas, both of which belong to the early third century, but whose sources go back to the second century, the situation is similar. Thus, in the Acts of Peter the apostle prays: "Thou most good and alone holy, in thy name have I spoken, for thou didst appear unto us, O God Jesus Christ" (5); and again: "Thou alone art the Lord God. For praising thee how many lips we need, that we may be able to give thanks unto thee for thy mercy" (21). And in the Acts of Thomas, Thomas says: "I give thanks to thee, Lord Jesus, that thou hast revealed thy truth in these men. For thou alone art the God of truth and not another…Christians in the primitive church whose God was Jesus Christ and Jesus Christ alone, attention may be called to the continued use of the original formula of baptism in his name. That this formula preceded the triune formula of Matt. 28:19 may be taken for granted.…"

509. Adger, John B. (1899). *My Life And Times 1810-1899*. Richmond, Virginia: The Presbyterian Committee of Publication, p. 302:

"Hence it is not strange if the apostles are reported to have baptized in the name of Christ, though they were commanded to baptize in the name of the Father, Son and Holy Ghost (Acts viii. 16; xix. 5; Matthew xxviii. 19); for all the divine gifts held forth in baptism are found in Christ alone. And yet it cannot but be that he who baptizes in the name of Christ has also in ked the name of the Father and the Spirit."

510. Gonzãlez, Justo L. (2019). *A History of Early Christian Literature*. Louisville, Kentucky: Westminster John Knox Press, p. 156:

"Such is the case, for instance, of that administered by the Marcionites, who baptize only in the name of Jesus.…"

511. Keener, Craig S. (2012). *Acts An Exegetical Commentary Introduction And 1:1-2:47*. Volume I. Grand Rapids, Michigan: Baker Academic:

> "...Paul's ironic response to Corinthian misunderstanding in 1 Cor 1:13-15, which may well presuppose baptism in Jesus' name...The supposed conflict with the trinitarian formula in Matt. 28:19 (thought to represent a later stage or different geographic region)...Although there is little direct historical support outside Matthew for that formula's being earlier...."[329]

512. Vanhoozer, Kevin J. (2005). *Dictionary for Theological Interpretation of The Bible*. Grand Rapids, Michigan: Baker Academics, p. 29:

> "...and the fact that Paul baptizes the Ephesian dozen in water in the name of Jesus (19:5)...."

513. Green, Gene L. (2020). *Vox Petri A Theology of Peter*. Eugene, Oregon: Cascade Books, p. 280:

> "...it is made clear that baptism in the name of Jesus leads to the reception of the Spirit (Acts 2:38)."

514. Cupitt, Don (1979). *The Debate About Christ*. London: SCM Press, p. 28:

> "Nobody thinks Matthew's formula goes back to Jesus himself because the earliest baptism seems to have been in the name of Jesus only...."[330]

515. Fitzmyer, Joseph A. (1997). *The Anchor Bible The Acts of The Apostles*. Volume 31. New York, New York: Doubleday, p. 266:

> "Commentators debate, however, about the sense of the phrase. Some believe that Luke knew of baptism being administered in the early church "in the name of Jesus Christ" (as in 8: 16; 10:48; 19: 5; 22: 16) and not with the trinitarian formula derived from Matt 28: 19... 'The name of Jesus/Christ/the Lord' or 'his name'

---

[329]Craig S. Keener is F. M. and Ada Thompson Professor of Biblical Studies at Ashbury Theological Seminary.

[330]Don Cupitt, Philosopher, Theologian, Anglican Priest and was the Dean of Emmanuel College, Cambridge.

or simply 'the name' becomes a Lucan refrain in Acts (3:6, 16; 4:10, 17, 18, 30; 5:40; 8:12, 16; 9:14-16, 21, 27, 28; 10:48; 15:26; 16:18; 19:5, 13, 17; 21:13; 22:16; 26:9). Luke's use of it echoes the OT use of…'name,' which makes a person present to another: "For as is his name, so is he" (1 Sam 25:25). For Luke the 'name of Jesus' connotes the real and effective representation of Jesus himself. One puts faith in it, is baptized into it; miracles are worked through it and salvation is found in it; disciples preach the name and suffer for it."

516. Keith, Chris & Roth, T. Deiter (2015). *Mark, Manuscripts And Monotheism Essays in Honor of Larry W. Hurtado.* Library of New Testament Studies. London & New York: Bloomsbury T&T Clark, p. 180:

"(3) use of the name of Jesus, as in baptism in the name of Jesus and other practices, including 'calling on the name of Jesus.'"

517. Moorhead, John (2015). *The Popes and The Church of Rome in Late Antiquity.* New York: Routledge:

"…for whereas Christ had mandated baptism in the name of the Trinity (Matt. 28:19), Peter had told people to be baptised in the name of Jesus Christ (Acts 2:38)…in the ninth century Pope Nicholas was prepared to accept baptism in the name of Christ."[331]

518. Pallikunnil, Jamerson K (2018). *Mission and Liturgy Content and Convergence and Congruence with Special Reference to the Malankara Mar Thoma Syrian Church.* Bloomington, Indiana: AuthorHouse:

"The decisive distinction of early Christian baptism from its roots in John's baptism was that it was carried out in the name of Jesus Christ (Acts 2:38; 8:16; 10:48; 19:5)."[332]

---

[331] John Moorhead is Professor Emeritus at the University of Queensland, Australia.
[332] Dr. Jameson K. Pallikunnil, Rev. Dr., is an ordained minister of the Malankara Mar Thoma Syrian Church, who holds two post graduate degrees in Sociology and Liturgical Theology and was bestowed with Ph.D from St. Patrick's College, Maynooth, Ireland. He is now serving as the vicar of the Switzerland and Belfast Mar Thoma Congregations.

519. Whilhite, Shawn J. (2019). *The Didache A Commentary.* Apostolic Fathers Commentary Series 1. Eugene, Oregon: Cascade Books, p. 62:[333]

> "Baptism occurs in the name of Jesus in Acts (2:38; 8:12; 8:16; 12:48; 19:5)."

520. Chupungco, Anscar J. (2000). *Handbook for Liturgical Studies IV Sacraments and Sacramentals.* The Pontifical Liturgical Institute. Collegeville, Minnesota: The Liturgical Press, p. 8:

> "In the apostolic community baptism of water is conferred 'in the name of Jesus' (Acts 2:38; 10:48; 19:5; 22:16; see also 1 Cor. 1:13-16; 6:11: Gal. 3:27; Rom. 6:3)."[334]

521. Deiss, Lucien (1979). *Springtime of The Liturgy, Liturgical Texts of The First Four Centuries.* Collegeville, Minnesota: The Liturgical Press, p. 46:

> "The simplest were doubtless limited to an assertion of the lordship of the risen Christ: 'Jesus is Lord!' (1. Cor. 12:3). By these words, the neophyte was ratifying the baptismal formula that had been pronounced over him and that contained an 'invocation' of the name of Jesus."[335]

522. Dalton, William Joseph (1989). *Christ's Proclamation To the Spirits of 1 Peter 3:18-4:6.* Analecta Biblica 23. Roma: Editrice Pontificio Instituto Biblico, p. 209:

> "It has even been urged that baptism 'in the name of Jesus' involved the invoking of his name in faith...."[336]

523. Nolloth, Charles Frederick (1917). *The Rise of The Christian Religion.* London: MacMillan and Co., Limited, pp. 471-472:

---

[333]Shawn J. Whilhite, Assistant Professor of Christian Studies, California Baptist University and Pastor at Redeemer Baptist Church.

[334]In this publication the cited is of Adrien Nocent, OSB, *Christian Initiation During the First Four Centuries.*

[335]Father Lucien Deiss was widely known in Europe and the United States as a Roman Catholic scholar in the fields of sacred scripture and patristics.

[336]William Joseph Dalton, SJ. (Jesuit), Catholic Theological College, Melbourne, Australia.

"...plea against the genuineness of Matt. xxviii. 19 is that, had the command been given, the contention of the Apostle Paul about the right of the mission to the Gentiles would be historically inexplicable.' 'For this solemn command of Jesus to baptize would have removed all hesitation which arose in Jerusalem against the mission of Paul.' *Feine, Theologie des* N.T. p. 221. As Wendt points out, 'In the disputes between Paul and the primitive community, the question was not as to whether the Messianic salvation was accessible to non - Israelite people, but as to the conditions under which Gentiles might be received into the Messianic community.' *Die Lehre Jesu*, p. 584. Feine...says that ' the formal authenticity of the passage (Matt. xxviii. 19) is to be challenged and that it is to be admitted that the later community recognized its experience of the effect of Christian Baptism as being in accordance with the will of the Lord and referred it to a direct saying of Jesus.' p. 222. Kirsopp Lake (Encycl. of Religion and Ethics, art. 'Baptism (Early Christian') holds that the fact of the passage standing in every version of Matt. xxviii. does not prove that it was an original saying of Christ, as it might be due to an editorial insertion...Weizsäcker, after speaking of allusions in the Acts to Baptism in the Name of Jesus..Heitmüller rejects Matt. xxviii. 19 as a saying of our Lord on the ground that Baptism in the Apostolic and sub -Apostolic ages, and indeed up to the third century, was only practised in the Name of Jesus Christ, and he quotes (after citing passages from St. Paul and the Acts), *Ep. Barn. xvi.* 6; *Hermas*, Vis. iii. 7. 3; and *Simil. viii.* 6. 4; ix. 12. 5... ' In early times, the formula Te baptizo in Nomine Domini Jesu Christi was usually admitted with the proviso that a baptism in the Name of Jesus was to be regarded as having been also in the Name of the Father and of the Holy Spirit' G. L. Hahn, D. Lehre von den Sakramenten, 1864, p. 147."

524. Nolloth, Frederick Charles (1908). *The Person of Our Lord And Recent Thought*. London: MacMillan And Co., Limited, pp. 219, 260:

"All that can be said against the formula in v. 19 is that it possibly belongs to a later stratum of theological thought, and that the fact of its having a theological tinge excludes it from the sayings of Christ...disciples who were initiated by Baptism, which as we know was soon administered in the Threefold Name, are to be enlisted in His own Name. Thus, the formula of Eusebius would, as Loisy observes (*Autour d'un petit Livre*, p. 232), accord with those passages in the Pauline Epistles and in the Acts which speak of Baptism administered in the Name of Jesus Christ."[337]

525. Wall, W. (1889). *The History of Infant Baptism In Two Parts*. London: Griffith, Farran, Browne & Co., Ltd, pp. 175-176:

"But a more material thing, in which some of them do deviate both from the express command of our Saviour, and the received practice of the Church, is in the form of baptism. One sort of them do count it indifferent whether they baptise with these words: "In the Name of the Father, and of the Son, and of the Holy Spirit" or with these: "In the Name of the Lord Jesus. "And do in their public confession allow either of the forms. And I have heard that some of them do affectedly choose the latter." Citing in footnote 49 *"Confes. of Anabapt. Reprinted Lond., 1691."*

526. McClymond, Michael J. (2018). *The Devil's Redemption A New History and Interpretation of Christian Universalism*. Grand Rapids, Michigan: Baker Academics:[338]

"From Shenoute's reassurances about the legitimacy of "Jesus only" baptism, it seems that some people in the fourth-century Egypt must have been baptized only in Jesus' name, and not in the name of the Trinity."

527. Jenott, Lance (2011). *The Gospel of Judas Coptic, Texts, Translation and Historical Interpretation of the 'Betrayer's Gospel.'* Tubingen, Germany: Mohr Siebeck, p. 36:

"In…Gospel of Judas…Judas assumes that those who receive baptism in the name of Jesus can also participate in this liberating

---

[337] Charles Frederick Nolloth, Oriel College, Oxford and formerly Rector of All Saints, Lewes. See also, Mason, T. W. (1947). *Entry into Membership of The Early Church*. The Journal of Theological Studies. Volume os-XLVIII, Issue 189-190 (January-April), pp. 25-33.
[338] Michael J. McClymond is Professor of Modern Christianity at Saint Louis University, St. Louis.

victory."[339]

528. Norgren, William A. & Rusch, William G. (ed.) (2001). *Toward Full Communion and Concordat of Agreement.* Lutheran-Episcopal Dialogues Series III. Eugene, Oregon: Wipf & Stock Publishers, p. 37:

> "We know little about details of practice in the first century, but there may well have been some variations of formula (baptism in the name of Jesus or that of the Trinity)."

529. Barrier, Jeremy (2009). *The Acts of Paul and Thecla.* Tubingen, Germany: Mohr Siebeck, pp. 161-16.:

> "And she cast herself into the water, saying 'in the name of Jesus Christ I baptize myself for the last day…Thecla therefore cast herself into water in the name of Jesus Christ…'in the name of Jesus Christ' also found in *Herm, Vis 3.7.3; Origen, Comm. Rom. 5.8*…First, those who are being initiated into Christ will devote themselves to prayer. Then they will step into the water, naked, and the presbyter will baptize them in the name of Jesus Christ (*Tertullian, Bpt. 17* and *Hippolytus, Trad. Ap. 21*)…"[340]

530. Byars, Ronald P. (2011). *The Sacraments in Biblical Perspective Interpretation: Resources for The Use of Scripture in the Church.* Louisville, Kentucky: Westminster John Knox Press:

> "The so-called Great Commission includes instruction that Jesus gave to his eleven remaining disciples after the resurrection: 'Go therefore and make disciples of all nations, baptizing them in the name of the Father and of the Son and of the Holy Spirit' (Matt. 28:19)…verses that conclude the Gospel of Matthew were not present in the original…The baptismal formula in the name of the three divine agents was presumably in use in the Matthean church at this period, having replaced an earlier custom of baptizing in the name of Jesus…the doctrine of the Trinity was not officially formulated and adopted by councils of the church

---

[339]Lance Jenott, Lecturer Washington University in St. Louis, Department of Classics and program in Religious Studies.
[340]Jeremy Barrier, Assistant Professor of Biblical Literature at Heritage Christian University, Florence, Alabama.

until the fourth century."[341]

531. Kung, Hans, et. al. (ed.) (1982). *Right to Dissent*. Edinburgh: T&T Clark, p. 36:

> "Stephen held that baptism in the name of Jesus Christ was valid baptism, whether performed inside or outside of the Church (73:16; 74:5; 75:7, 9, 11)."

532. Curteis, George Herbert (1897). *Dissent, In Its Relation To The Church of England, Eight Lectures Preached Before the University of Oxford in The Year 1871 on the Foundation of the Late Rev. John Bampton, M.A., Canon of Salisbury*. London: MacMillan and Co., Ltd., New York: The MacMillan Co., p. 310:

> "The Prayer-book for the use of the Unitarian Congregation in Little Portland Street…At Baptism, there are four alternative forms:…(2) 'I baptize thee in the name of Jesus Christ.'"[342]

533. Neal, J. M. (1869). *Catechetical Notes and Class Questions, Literal and Mystical, Chiefly on The Earlier Books of Holy Scripture*. London, Oxford and Cambridge: Rivingtons, p. 125:

> "…Presbyterians and Socinians, who sometimes baptize in the name of Jesus of Nazareth."

534. Hawkins, Edward (1841). *An Inquiry Into The Connected Uses of The Principal Means of Attaining Christian Truth in Eight Sermons Preached Before The University of Oxford at the Bampton Lecture for The Year MDCCCXL*. Oxford: John Henry Parker, p. 358:

> "Unitarians who are Baptists, who when they baptize at all, do it, as I have heard, simply 'in the name of Jesus.'"[343]

535. Templin, J. Alton (2006). *Pre-Reformation Religious Dissent in The Netherlands, 1518-1530*. Lanham, Maryland: University Press of

---

[341]Ronald P. Byars is Professor Emeritus of Preaching and Worship at Union Presbyterian Seminary, Richmond, Virginia.
[342]George Herbert Curteis, late Fellow of Sub-Rector of Exeter College, Principal of the Lichfield Theological College, and Prebendary of Lichfield Cathedral.
[343]Dr. Edward Hawkins, Provost of Oriel College, and Canon of Rochester.

American, Inc., p. 181:

> "There is little mention of baptism. Pistorious, however, was accused of baptizing in the name of Jesus only, and not the three persons of the Trinity."

536. Peirce, James (1717). *A Vindication of The Dissenters In Answer to Dr. William Nichol's Defence of The Doctrine and Discipline of The Church of England in Three Parts.* London: John Clark, p. 179:

> "Or if they attribute the effect of the Baptism to the majesty of the name, that whoever are anywhere, or any how baptiz'd in the name of Jesus Christ, must be reckon'd renew'd and sanctify'd."

537. Smallfield, George (ed.) (1822). *The Christian Reformer, or New Evangelical Miscellany. By The Editor of The Monthly Repository of Theology And General Literature.* January to December, Inclusive 1822. Vol. VIII. Hackney: Sherwood, Neely and Jones, Paternoster-Row, p. 64:

> "Trinitarian Baptism. A Correspondent has sent us an account of the administration of baptism, by immersion, to certain adults, on Christmas-day, in a country town. He bears witness to the order and decorum of the ceremony, and to the useful instructions that were delivered upon the occasion. But as the administrator used the baptismal form, Matt. xxvii, 19, evidently in a Trinitarian sense, which the other Scriptures shew, that neither our Lord nor the Evangelists put upon the words, our correspondent observes: "Though the Baptists and Conformists use three names in baptizing, *the apostles used the name of Jesus Christ only*, Acts ii. 38; and in his name alone worked miracles, chap. iii. 6. What is the reason that those who call Jesus "the God-man" and the "God incarnate," are yet afraid to confide in his name, and *to follow the example of the Apostles?*"

538. Tanquerey, Adolphe (1959). *A Manual of Dogmatic Theology.* New York: Desolee Company, p. 220:

> "In the Acts of the Apostles, it is stated that some were baptized in the name of Jesus Christ: in consequence, some, among them St. Bede, Peter Lombard, Cajetan, thought that Baptism

conferred in the name of Jesus was valid."[344]

539. Smedley, Edward et al. (1845). *Encyclopaedia Metropolitana; or Universal Dictionary of Knowledge on an Original Plan: Comprising of Twofold Advantage of a Philosophical and An Alphabetical Arrangement, with Appropriate Engravings.* Volume II. London: B. Fellowes, et al., p. 889:

> "The ecclesiastical courts of this country have laid it down that the baptism of dissenters is sufficient for the purpose of entitling a person to burial (Kemp. v. Wickes, and more recently Escott v. Mastin); but they suppose the baptism administered in the name of the Holy Trinity. The decision is one much controverted. The case has not yet been tried of an Unitarian baptism in the name of Jesus Christ only."

540. _____. *The Encyclopaedia Britannica* (1910) (11th ed.) Volume VI. Chatelet to Constantine. New York: The Encyclopaedia Britannica Company, p. 328:

> "The references in the New Testament to baptism "in the name of Jesus" (or the Lord Jesus) (Acts ii. 38, viii. 16, X. 48, xix. xix. 5; Rom. vi. 3; Gal. iii. 27), which are, by some critics taken to refer to a primitive Christological baptismal formula."

541. Heath, Gordon L. & Dvorak, James D. (2011). *Baptism. Historical, Theological and Pastoral Perspective.* McMaster Theological Studies Series. Eugene, Oregon: Pickwick Publications, p. 235:

> "Usually, baptism in the name of Jesus is required to be recognized by the Church...."

542. Breen, J. D. (1885). *Anglican Orders: Are they Valid? A Letter to A Friend.* Revised and Enlarged Edition. London: Burns and Oates; New York: Catholic Publication Society Company, pp. 28-29:

> "A friend of my own (the son of a Presbyterian clergyman, but for some time a member of the Church of England) bears me out in this experience. He was present in 1868 at St. Paul's Established Church, Glasgow, when a certain Mr. McAuslane (baptizing on behalf of the regular minister, Dr. Jamieson) used

---

[344] Adolphie Tanquerey was a Theologian and Sulpician Priest.

the…formula, 'I baptize you in the name of the Lord Jesus.'"

543. Hilton III, John & Johnson, Jana (2018). *The Word Baptize in The Book of Mormon* in *Interpreter* A Journal of Mormon Scripture. Volume 29. Orem, Utah: The Interpretation Foundation, pp. 78-79:

"However, a shift takes place after Christ's extensive emphasis on being baptized in his name. As discussed previously, Christ clearly emphasized the connection between his name and baptism. Prior to 3 Nephi 26, Mormon never speaks of being baptized in the name of Christ. However, after Mormon provides an account of Christ's ministry, we see several examples where he might previously have employed the phrase "baptized unto repentance" but now substitutes it with a reference to being baptized in the name of Christ. For example, we read, "as many as were baptized in the name of Jesus were filled with the Holy Ghost" (3 Nephi 26:17), "And they who were baptized in the name of Jesus were called the church of Christ" (3 Nephi. 26:21), and "And as many as did come unto them, and did truly repent of their sins, were baptized in the name of Jesus" (4 Nephi 1:1). Table 7 illustrates situations in which Mormon might have employed the phrase baptized unto repentance but instead speaks of being baptized in the name of Jesus. Table 7. Mormon's descriptions of baptism before and after Christ's ministry to the Lehites…Mormon writing after 3 Nephi 25. "And they who were baptized in the name of Jesus were called the church of Christ" (3 Nephi 26:21). "The disciples of Jesus were journeying and were…baptizing in the name of Jesus (3 Nephi 27:1) "And as many as did come unto them, and did truly repent of sins, were baptized in the name of Jesus" (4 Nephi 1:1). Mormon does not only speak of being baptized in the name of Jesus in his narrative descriptions. In a sermon to his people, Mormon says, "repent, and be baptized in the name of Jesus" (Mormon 7:8) a statement that mimics Christ's statements in his personal ministry to the Nephites and is repentance" different from Alma statement "Come and be baptized unto repentance" (Alma from 5:62, Alma 7:14)."[345]

---

[345] John Hilton III is an Associate Professor at Brigham Young University and is the author of over 60 peer-reviewed articles. Jana Johnson graduated from Brigham

544. _____. (1759). *A Dictionary of The Holy Bible: Containing A Historical Account of the Persons, etc.* In Three Volumes. Vol I. London: J. Beecroft, et. al., p. 191:

> "Many of the fathers and some councils believed, that the apostles sometimes had baptized in the name of Jesus Christ only…Several others of the fathers, many councils, and eminent school-men, believe that the apostles sometimes baptized in the name of Jesus Christ alone, and that this baptism was good and lawful."

545. Engel, Carte Katherine (2009). *The Evolution of The Bethlehem Pilgergemeine* in *Pietism in Germany and North American 1680-1820*, edited by Strom, Jonathan, et. al. Farnham, Surrey: Ashgate Publishing Limited:[346]

> "When Count Nikolaus Ludwig Von Zinzendorf took leave of his Pennsylvania followers in January 1743, he left them with some advice that typified his approach to religious matters…then the next person to be baptized should be done in the name of Jesus…."

546. Wood, Irving F. (1905). *New Light on Some Familiar New Testament Problems* in *The American Journal of Theology* edited by The Divinity Faculty of the University of Chicago, Volume IX. Chicago, Illinois: The Chicago Press, pp. 338-339:

> "In 1903 Bousset and Gunkel began the publication of a series entitled "Forschungen zur Religion und Literatur des Alten und Neuen Testa ments." The first volume was Gunkel's *Zum religionsgeschichtlichen Verständnis des Neuen* Testaments. The second volume is Heitmüller's *Im Namen Jesu*.' According to the sub-title, the book is especially concerned with the use of the term in the baptismal formula of the early church. The preface raises the question: "What meaning has baptism 'in the name of Jesus ' in the oldest Christianity?" The first part of the book is devoted to a linguistic investigation of the *formulæ, év, éné tṵ óvópatí tuvos,* and

---

Young University in 2013 with a BA in linguistics and minors in editing and geography.
[346]See Chapter 11.

eis tò ovomá alvos in the New Testament and other early Christian literature, in the LXX, and in profane Greek. For the last, the recently edited ostraka and papyri from Egypt furnish especially rich material. His conclusion (p. 127) is that the reduction of these terms in the modern translations to the dead level of a single term, " to baptize in the name of Christ," is a loss of an important original distinction. The phrases " to baptize *év* and *énè tự óvóuatı* " serve as a description of the act of baptism. They affirm that the baptism was performed under the naming of the name of Jesus."

547. _____. (1845). The Christian Messenger and Family Magazine; Devoted to the Dissemination of Primitive Christianity Enlarged Series. Vol. I. London: Simpkins, Marshall and Co., p. 232:

"Believers were to obtain remission in the name of Jesus by being baptized in his name."

548. Finch, Geo Wm. (1895). *Baptism, Ancient and Modern* in *The Tablet A Weekly Newspaper and Review* – New Series, Vol. LIII (Vol. LXXXV). January to June. London: Tablet Office, p. 1015:

"Now the question of baptism involves a curious biblical difficulty…I cannot escape from the inference that St. Peter baptized and commanded baptism in the name of the Second Person of the Blessed Trinity…in the name of Jesus Christ of the remission of sins…Only they were baptized in the name of the Lord Jesus…they were baptized in the name of the Lord Jesus…Will Father Breen be kind enough to explain, whether baptism in the name of Christ only would be valid at the present time?"

549. Votaw, Clyde W. (1898). *The Primitive Era of Christianity As Recorded In The Acts of The Apostles 30-63 A.D.* A Series in Inductive Studies in The English Bible. Chicago, Illinois: The University Chicago Press, p. 58:[347]

"Why were they not baptized into the Father, Son, and Holy

---

[347] Dr. Clyde W. Votaw, instructor in New Testament Literature in the University of Chicago.

Ghost (vs. 48, cf. Matt. 28:19)?...3. Institutions.–The observance of the Jewish ceremonial law was a feature of the life of most of the Christians, though it may be inferred that the followers of Stephen were free from it.—The new Gentile converts were baptized in the name of Jesus Christ."

550. Meyers, Ruth A. (1997). *Continuing The Reformation Re-Visioning Baptism in The Episcopal Church*. New York, New York: Church Publishing, Inc., p. 1:

"From these descriptions and from other New Testament reference to baptism, we can conclude that baptism followed conversion and was administered with water in the name of Jesus...."[348]

551. Davis, John Jefferson (2015). *Theological Reflections on Ministry and The Christian Life Practicing Ministry in The Presence of God*. Eugene, Oregon: Cascade Books:

"The scholastic theologians of the Middles Ages discussed Matthew 28:19 in regard to the particular questions raised by the difference between Matthew and the book of Acts as to the proper words of baptism. The first Gospel uses the trinitarian formula; the book of Acts speaks of 'baptism in the name of the Lord Jesus' alone (Acts 2:38; 10:48; 19:5). Alexander of Hales, Albertus Magnus, Bonaventure, Aquinas, and Duns Scotus held that the apostles baptized in the name of Jesus alone in view of a special dispensation. In the period following the Council of Trent (1545-63), however, the prevailing Roman Catholic view became that the apostles in fact made use of the triune formula, but the language of the book of Acts was intended to emphasize the distinction between the baptism of John and the Baptist and the proper Christian baptism commanded by Christ."[349]

552. Deferrari, Roy J. (1951). *Hugh of Saint Victor on The Sacraments of The*

---

[348] Ruth A. Meyers is Dean of Academic Affairs and Hodges-Haynes Professor of Liturgics at Church Divinity School of the Pacific and currently an assisting Priest at All Souls Episcopal parish in Berkeley.

[349] John Jefferson Davis is Professor of Systematic Theology and Chair of the division of Christian thought at Gordon-Conwell Theological Seminary.

Christian Faith (De Sacraments). Cambridge, Massachusetts: The Mediaeval Society of America, p. 287:

> "And so they have been baptized in the name of Jesus Christ, and baptism was not repeated in these but renewed. For there is one baptism."

553. Herrmann, Erick H. (2016). *The Babylonian Captivity of The Church, 1520*. The Annotated Luther Volume 3 Church and Sacraments. Minneapolis, Minnesota: Fortress Press, p. 66:

> "'I baptize you in the name of Jesus Christ' although it is certain the apostles used this formula in baptizing...."[350]

554. Harrison, Wes (2001). *The Renewal of The Practice of Adult Baptism by Immersion During The Reformation Era, 1525-1700*. Restoration Quarterly Special Issue on Baptism. Volume 43, Number 2, Second Quarter, p. 106:

> "The most significant early catechism of the Polish Brethren (1574) also described baptism as both an immersion in water and an emersion into a new spiritual life in Christ: Baptism [is] the immersion into water and the emersion of a person who believes in the gospel and exercises repentance in the name of the Father and Son and Holy Spirit, or in the name of Jesus Christ, whereby he publicly professes that by the grace of God the Father he has been washed from all his sins in the blood of Christ by the aid of the Holy Spirit; so that having been ingrafted into the body of Christ he may mortify the old Adam and be transformed into the heavenly Adam, in the firm assurance of eternal life after the resurrection."[351]

555. Goodwin, K, Shane (2019). *The History of the Name of the Savior's Church*. BYU Studies Quarterly: Vol. 58, Issue 3, Article 2, p. 6:

> "The Book of Mormon tells of a challenge faced by those living during the time of Christ's visit to the Americas. Although "they

---

[350]Dr. Erik Herrmann is professor of Historical Theology, Dean of Theological Research and Publications and director of the Center for Reformation Research at Concordia Seminary, St. Louis.
[351]Dr. Wes Harrison, Ohio Valley College.

who were baptized in the name of Jesus were called the church of Christ" (3 Ne. 26:21)...."

556. Schmidt, Nathaniel (1911). *The New Jesus Myth And Its Ethical Value.* The International Journal of Ethics, Volume 22, Number 1, p. 28:

> "It certainly cannot be looked upon as incredible that Apollos should have heard some of the things concerning the historic Jesus, and himself taught, without knowing any other baptism than that of John. The synoptic Jesus himself knows no other baptism, the present form of Matt. 28: 19f. being of very late origin; and Apollos may have heard in Alexandria very much concerning Jesus of Nazareth without any word reaching him as regards a distinct water-baptism in the name of Jesus, or a spirit-baptism giving special powers."[352]

557. Tanner, John S. (2001). *Of Men and Mantles: Kierkegaard on the Difference between a Genius and an Apostle.* BYU Studies Quarterly: Vol. 40, Issue 2, Article 7, pp. 150-151:

> "On Friday, July 19, 1850, Erastus snow (fig. 1), an Apostle newly arrived in Denmark, went to the Vor Frue Kirke to watch Bishop J. P. Mynster ordain a priest. There, surrounded by Bertel Thorvaldsen's famous statutes of the Christus and the Twelve Apostles (fig. 2), Elder Snow reflected on the apostate condition of the State Church of Denmark. His journal entry reads as follows: '19th July 1 attended an ordination of a priest in Frue kirke (Ladys church) which was attended with much pomp and show. This 'Frue kirke'...is truly an elegant & costly building. At the head of the main saloon before the alter sic stands Jesus in statuary in the act of preaching & on either side of the room are the full size statues of the 12 apostles which were carved in marble in Rome and while viewing this scene & the curious ceremonies of the day...had such feelings as...never before had how long thought...if these were...figures teaching & acting as they did 1800 years ago would they be permitted to grace this temple of the 'Great Whore' or even suffered to exist among this people but a short time ago these very priests who with their long robes are now officiating were the chief instruments in imprison

---

[352] Professor Nathaniel Schmidt, Cornell University.

[*sic*] P. C. Monster a Baptist minister for teaching the people *to repent & be baptised in the name of Jesus*....being then the only baptism in Denmark.'"

558. Wallace, Ronald S. (1998). *The Ten Commandments A Study of Ethical Freedom*. Eugene, Oregon: Wipf & Stock, p. 61:

"It is quite clear for instance that in New Testament times Baptism in the name of Jesus was a source of strength to the early Christians in the struggle they had in living the Christian life."[353]

559. Rice, Howard L. & Huffstutler, James C. (2001). *Reformed Worship*. Louisville, Kentucky: Geneva Press, p. 55:

"...the Trinitarian formula, 'I baptize you in the name of the Father and of the Son and of the Holy Spirit,' became normative rather than the more primitive formula that baptized in the name of Jesus alone (Acts 8:15-16)."

560. Hodge, Charles W. (1878). *Apostolic History and Literature Prepared by the Senior Class For The Use of Students in Princeton Theological Seminary*. Princeton: Press Printing Establishment, p. 125:

"Notice that this, the first mention of the baptismal formula made in Acts, is in the name of Jesus Christ, instead of the Trinity, as commanded in Matt. 28: 19-20."[354]

561. Reventlow, Henning Graf (2010). *History of Biblical Interpretation From The Enlightenment To The Twentieth Century*. Volume 4. Atlanta, Georgia: The Society of Biblical Literature, p. 163:[355]

"One may see the Trinity only in the baptismal *formula* at the end of the Gospel of Matthew (28:19). The ancient church had known only *baptism* in the *name of Jesus* (Acts 2:38; 22:16; Apologie 2:86–

---

[353]Ronald S. Wallace held pastorates throughout Scotland before becoming Professor of Biblical Theology at Columbia Theological Seminary.

[354]Charles W. Hodge was a Presbyterian Theologian and Principal of Princeton Theological Seminary between 1851-1878.

[355]Henning Graf Reventlow, German Protestant Theologian and was Professor Emeritus of Old Testament Exegesis and Theology, Faculty of Protestant Theology, University of the Ruhr, Bochum, Germany.

90). This trinitarian formula could only have been inserted into Matt 28 at a later time."

562. Conybeare, Fred. C. (1910). *Myth, Magic, and Morals A Study of Christian Origins*. London: Watts & Co., p. 327:

"The Roman Church in the second century, as against the Eastern communions, made the question doubly acute by deciding that the baptism of heretics was valid so long as it was administered even with the shorter formula "in the name of Jesus Christ.""

563. Clarke, Howard (2003). *The Gospel of Matthew and its readers: a historical introduction to the First Gospel*. Bloomington, Indiana: Indiana University Press, p. 248:

"The Great Commission of 16-20 offers a summary of Matthew's theology. Jesus' final appearance, recalling Daniel 7:14 ("dominion" over "all people, nations and languages"), is a kind of minor Parousia, anticipating the second coming; but it also looks back to Moses, since it takes place on a mountain, perhaps the "mountain" of the Sermon and the transfiguration. Like Moses with Joshua, Jesus can look into the future as he delegates authority for his disciples' worldwide mission—though he says nothing here of their passing on this power to others. "Teach," because converts must be taught how to live new lives; "baptizing," because their repentance of sin must be ritualistically demonstrated (and this initiation rite became distinctive of Christianity); and "observe," because they must follow the new laws of Christ (and this last injunction became a Reformation proof text against Roman "additions")...In the "Hebrew Matthew" it is simply "Go and teach (them) to carry out all the things which I have commanded you forever." This is the "short form" of the Great Commission, thought by some to have been the original conclusion to which Matthew added the Trinitarian baptism formula. The invocation "in the name of the Father, and of the Son, and of the Holy Ghost," called the "Baptismal Affirmation," is unique in the New Testament, where baptisms are usually in the name of Jesus (Acts 8:16, 10:48, 19:5), and may reflect a baptismal formula from the early church."[356]

564. _____ (1847). *The Church of England Quarterly Review.* Volume XX. London: William Edward Painter, Strand, p. 24:

> "Those who were baptized in the name of Christ alone, or of the Lord alone, would have pledged themselves to all this, because these were the doctrines of the Church concerning baptism from the beginning, as we learn from the passages in Scripture to which reference has already been made...."

565. Lambert, John C. (1903). *The Sacraments in The New Testament.* Edinburgh: T&T Clark, p. 236:

> "...Ambrose, more than a century later, justifying baptism into the name of Christ alone, on the ground that in naming Christ we are really naming the other two Persons of the Trinity...it is difficult to resist the conclusion that from the first there must have existed in the Early Church the tradition of a baptism by the use of the simpler formula...accordingly in the light of subsequent history, it seems reasonable to regard constant references in Acts to baptism into the name of Christ as pointing to a corresponding formula that was actually employed."[357]

566. _____. (1856). *The Primitive Church Magazine, Advocating The Constitution, Faith, and Practice of The Apostolic Churches "One Lord One Faith One Baptism" Ephesians IV.* Volume XIII.-New Series. London: Paternoster Row, p. 251:

> "Kingston-On-Thames.—On Monday evening, August 10, our brother T. W. Medhurst baptized two persons in the name of Jesus, after a discourse from Acts ii. 47–last clause;–and on Monday evening, August 31st, he administered the solemn ordinance again to four others, in the same holy name."

567. Gonzàlez, Justo L. (2005). *Essential Theological Terms.* Louisville, Kentucky: Westminster John Know Press, p. 26:

---

[356]Robert Clarke is Professor Emeritus of Classics at The University of California at Santa Barbara.
[357]John C. Lambert was a Scottish Minister who was famous for his missionary adventure stories.

"From New Testament accounts, it is clear that baptism was practiced in the early church from its very beginning–according to Acts, immediately after Pentecost. It is mentioned, discussed, or alluded to in almost every book of the New Testament–although little is said about how it is to be administered, and sometimes administered 'in the name of Jesus'...."

568. Coleman, Christopher B. (1908). *The Indiana Quarterly Magazine of History*. Volume IV. Indianapolis, Indiana: The Indiana Historical Society, pp. 20-22, 27:

"Beverly Vawter was born in Virginia in 1789, moved to Kentucky in 1792, where his father united with the Baptist church. At the age of ten he was baptized into the Baptist church. He remained in the Baptist church until his twenty- second year, when he was excluded. (Pioneer Preachers, p. 105.) He thought no more about religion for five or six years. Vawter was, however, a firm believer in the doctrine of eternal election, and in the direct gift of God through the secret operation of the Holy Spirit. He felt his need of a greater faith, and, in search of " light," applied to a New Light preacher, then to his Baptist uncle, and finally to a Presbyterian preacher. None of these men was able to satisfy him. Vawter became interested in the study of Matthew, Mark, and the Acts of the Apostles, and in 1817 be gan comparing the teachings of these books with the teachings of the Baptist church. He chanced to read B. W. Stone's "Essay on Faith." Among the quotations were Romans 10:17, and John 20:30. These helped him in matters of faith. He became more dissatisfied with the Baptist doctrine. He was still on his quest for pardon when he happened upon these texts: "He that believeth and is baptized shall be saved"; " Repent and be baptized, every one of you , in the name of Jesus Christ , for the remission of sins, and you shall receive the gift of the Holy Spirit"...Joseph Hostetler, leader of the Dunkards in the Edinburg Con ference of 1828, came into the reformation in the following way: In 1816, after reading and finding what a believer " must do to be saved," he was baptized at his own request. He was then nine teen years of age. His newly discovered doctrines were, that a believer must repent, confess and be baptized in His name for the remission of sins...He held the views of Campbell a long time before he preached them, fearing the attitude of the people toward these opinions. But finally, after being urged by his friends, who knew his views, to preach them, he preached that "Men are required to repent and be baptized in the name of Jesus Christ for the remission of sins," for the first time at a protracted meeting at Edgar, Illinois, in 1833."

569. Lewis, W. G. (1865). *De Pressense on Baptism.* The Baptist Magazine for 1865. Volume LVII. (Series V.–Vol. IX.). London: Paternoster Row, p. 431:

"In these times, when ecclesiastical organization was in many respects unsettled, baptism was equivalent to a profession of faith. Administered in the name of Jesus Christ...."

570. _____. (1890). *The Doctrine of The Trinity Attacked. Education.* The Saints Herald. Volume 37–Whole No. 867, No. I.. Lamoni, Iowa, p. 530:

"Quite a large number of Methodist ministers assembled yesterday morning in weekly session in the parlors of Central M. E. Church. Rev. D. read a paper on 'The Methodist Doctrine of the Trinity.' He attacked the doctrine with much determination. He said that…Christian baptism is in the name of Jesus Christ alone. The use of the three names would be polytheism. Some clergymen make applications of water-which is not Christian baptism. The great reformation of the age is in the theology. There is a special demand for preaching the one God, Jesus Christ. Some people pray to the Father in the name of Jesus Christ, but Jesus is 'the name high over all, in hell, or earth, or sky'–the one object of worship in heaven, and should be on earth. To speak of three persons creates confusion."

571. _____. (1700). The History of the Works of the Learned, &c. Volume II. London: R. Hodes, p. 327:

"As to baptism, which is administered only in the name of Jesus Christ, divines are not of the same opinion about it. Father Martene quotes several Authorities to prove that the Apostles and Ancient Church did frequently baptize so."

572. Rashdall, Hastings. (1907). *The Motive of Modern Missionary Work.* The American Journal of Theology edited by The Divinity Faculty of The University of Chicago. Volume XI. Chicago, Illinois: The University of Chicago Press, p. 372:

> "Even if they form part of the true text of the present Gospel of Matthew, their historical character is open to grave suspicion. Wherever baptism is alluded to in the Epistles and Acts, it is always baptism in the name of the Lord; in the earlier part of the Didache we find the same phrase. Even in the ninth century we find a pope recognizing that the formula, "I baptize thee in the name of Jesus Christ," might be valid. Such a state of things would be hardly conceivable, had our Lord ever commanded baptism with the trinitarian formula. To say that baptism in the name of the Lord means simply "Christian baptism"-i.e., baptism in the name of the Trinity–is a palpable subterfuge, which will convince no one whose critical sense is not hopelessly distorted by the desire to bolster up traditional views. And now Mr. Conybeare has shown that the passage is frequently quoted by Eusebius in another form: "Go ye and make disciples of all nations in my name, teaching them to observe all things whatsoever I commanded you." This points either to an earlier state of the text or to the existence of some gospel -perhaps the "Logia"—earlier than the present Matthew."[358]

573. Pope, Hugh (ed.) (1934). *The Layman's New Testament.* London: Sheed & Ward, p. 429:

> "In fact, nowhere in the New Testament do we find the full form of Mt. xxviii, 19 explicitly used, the truth being that 'in the Name of Jesus Christ' implied all that He stood for, and He was the second Person of the Trinity. Those baptized, then, in His Name were–explicitly or implicitly–baptized in the Name of the Trinity."

574. _____. (1853). *The History of The Life of Our Lord Jesus Christ, from His Incarnation Until His Ascension, Denoting and Incorporating The Words of the Scared Text from the Vulgate, Also, The History of The Acts*

---

[358] Dr. Randall Hastings, New College, Oxford University, was a Philosopher, Historian, Theologian and Anglican Priest.

of The Apostles, Connected, Explained, And Blended With Reflections. New York: D&J Sadlier, p. 583:

> "Some ancient writers of respectability were of opinion that the apostles had commenced baptizing with this formula: I baptize thee in the name of Jesus Christ."

575. Moody, Dale (1981). *The Word of Truth A Summary of Christian Doctrine Based on Biblical Revelation*. Grand Rapids, Michigan: William B. Eerdmans Publishing Company, p. 8:

> "...the emphasis on the Trinity led to the longer form and three immersions rather than the original one immersion in the name of Jesus Christ or the Lord Jesus, as in the Acts of the Apostles."

576. Hitchcock, James. (2012). *History of The Catholic Church From The Apostolic Age To The Third Millennium*. San Francisco: Ignatius Press:

> "Athanasius noted that the Church baptized in the name of Jesus and offered prayers to Him and that, if Jesus were not God, He could not have redeemed the human race."[359]

577. Rees, T. (1915). *The Holy Spirit In Thought And Experience*. New York: Charles Scribner's Sons, p. 110:

> "...threefold formula of Father, Son, and Holy Spirit (2 Cor. xiii. 14), and the simple formula of baptism in the name of Jesus (Acts ii. 38, viii. 16, x. 48, xix. 5) had given way to the threefold baptismal formula in New Testament times (Mr. xxviii. 19)."[360]

578. Hall, Francis J. (1920). *The Church And The Sacramental System*. New York: Longmans, Green and Co., London: Paternoster Row, p. 325:

> "Even if it be a fact that in New Testament days the form 'in the name of Jesus Christ' was occasionally used, this is not the form which has been instituted and transmitted to the post-apostolic Church."[361]

---

[359]Dr. James Hitchcock is a longtime Professor of History at St. Louis University.
[360]T. Rees, Principal of The Independent College, Bangor, North Wales.
[361]Francis J. Hall, Professor of Dogmatic Theology in The General Theological Seminary, New York City.

579. _____. (1880). *The Church of England Pulpit and Ecclesiastical Review.* January to June 1880. Vol. IX. London: Church of England Pulpit Office, pp. 57-58:

> "The Brethren practise adult Baptism, and Baptize only in the name of Jesus...Plymouth Brethren not only practise adult baptism, but they Baptize only in the name of Jesus."[362]

580. Cross, F. L. & Livingston, E. A. (ed.) (2005). *The Oxford Dictionary of The Christian Church.* (3rd ed.). New York: Oxford University Press, p. 1137:

> "Name of Jesus...the Name of Jesus is used in the New Testament as a synonym for Jesus Himself...The disciples...regularly baptize in it (Acts 2:38, 8:16, etc...."

581. Holden, George (1855). *The Anglican Catechist; or A Manual of Instruction Preparatory to Confirmation.* London: Joseph Masters, p. 142:

> "We sometimes read of the Apostles baptizing, in the Name of Jesus alone, Acts ii.38; viii.16; x.48; xix.5;...."

582. Thomas, Owen C. & Wondra, Ellen K. (2002). *Introduction To Theology.* (3rd ed.). New York: Moorehouse Publishing, p. 269:

> "In the New Testament, the condition of membership in the Church was fairly clear; baptism in the name of Jesus (Acts 2:38; 8:16; 10:48;...."

583. Colenso, John William (1866). *Natal Sermons A Series of Discourses Preached in The Cathedral Church of St. Peters, Maritzburg.* London: Paternoster Row, p. 145-146:

> "He admitted his followers into his flock by baptism though 'Jesus himself baptized not, but his disciples': and the command in Matt.xxviii.19, 'Go ye therefore , and teach all nations,

---

[362]It is interesting to note that with respect to Jehovah Witnesses as stated by one Roman Catholic scholar that they baptize in the name of Jesus, "The baptism of the Jehovah is considered invalid since it is not administered with the Trinitarian formula but in the name of Jesus for the remission of sins." See, Pospishill, Victor J. (1993), *Eastern Catholic Church Law According to The Code of Cannons of the Eastern Churches*, Saint Maron Publications, p. 421.

baptizing them in the Name of the Father and of the Son and of the Holy Ghost,' would be conclusive as to the fact of his having directly enjoined the practice, were it not that this formula, with its full expression of the Name of the Trinity, betrays the later age in which the passage in which it occurs was most probably written. For in the Acts of the Apostles, we read repeatedly of per sons being baptized in the name of Jesus Christ, ii.38, in the name of the Lord Jesus, viii.16, 'in the name of the Lord,' x.48, 'into the name of the Lord Jesus, 'xix. 9; and so we find, 'Arise, and be baptized, and wash away thy sins, calling upon the name of the Lord,' xxii.16. In the Epistles, again, we read of being baptized 'into Christ Jesus,' being baptized into Christ's death,' Rom.vi. 3, being baptized into Christ, ' Gal.iii.27. But we never find any reference whatever to the formula, "in the Name of the Father, and of the Son, and of the Holy Ghost,' which would be strange, if these words had been expressly laid down by Christ himself, as the form to be always used in Baptism. And in fact, this clear enunciation of the doc trine of the Trinity in Unity belongs, as is well known, to a later age than that of the Apostles. But the above passages are sufficient to show that baptism was practised from the first, by Christ's direction, as the initiatory rite, by which believers were to be admitted into the company of his disciples. They were baptized 'into him' or 'into his name,' as their Master and Lord."[363]

584. Evans, Craig A. (ed.) (2004). *The Bible Knowledge Background Commentary Acts-Philemon*. Colorado Springs, Colorado: Victor, p. 514:

"…it was a baptism administered in the name of Jesus. These are the typical words used in Acts to identify what kind of baptism was practiced (2:38; 8:16; 10:48; 19:5)…The Trinitarian formula of Matt. 28:19 was not regularly used in the early church until the second century and later."

585. Hase, Charles (1855). *History of The Christian Church*. New York: D. Appleton and Company, p. 41:

"Baptism as an initiatory rite was performed simply in the name

---

[363]Dr. & Rev. John William Colenso, Bishop of Natal.

of Jesus."[364]

586. Garett, Jr., James Leo (1990). *Systematic Theology Biblical, Historical, and Evangelical.* Eugene, Oregon: Wipf & Stock, p. 565:

"As already noted, baptism, as recorded in Acts, unlike the baptismal formula in Matt. 28:19, was always either 'in the name of Jesus Christ' (2:38; 10:48) or 'in the name of the Lord' (8:16; 19:5)...on the basis of Acts 22:16 that in the apostolic era the baptizand actually invoked or confessed the name of Jesus and has concluded that it is probable that the name of Jesus was also called by the baptizer."[365]

587. Ludemann, Gerd (1995). *What Really Happened to Jesus A Historical Approach to The Resurrection.* Louisville, Kentucky: Westminster John Knox Press, p. 59:

"The triadic formulation of baptism 'in the name of the Father and of the Son and of the Holy Spirit' is striking, since in the early period baptism was simply in Christ (Gal. 3.27) or in the name of Jesus (I Cor. I.13; Acts 8.16; 19.5; cf. Did. 9.5)."

588. Ralph, Margaret Nutting (2006). *Breaking Open The Lectionary Cycle B Lectionary Readings in Their Biblical Context for RCIA, Faith Sharing Groups, and Lectors.* Mahwah, New Jersey: Paulist Press, p. 141:

"...the trinitarian formula that the disciples are told to use when baptizing: '...baptizing them in the name of the Father, and of the Son, and of the Holy Spirit.' This formula does not appear in the descriptions of early baptisms in Acts. In Acts, during Peter's speech at Pentecost, he tells the people to 'repent and be baptized, every one of you, in the name of Jesus Christ for the forgiveness of your sins; and you shall receive the gift of the holy Spirit' (Acts 2:38). At the baptism of Cornelius Peter orders that Cornelius and his family 'be baptized in the name of Jesus Christ' (Acts 10:48)."

---

[364]Dr. Charles was a German Protestant Theologian, Church Historian, Professor of Theology in the University of Jena.

[365]James Leo Garrett, Jr., is distinguished Professor of Theology, Emeritus, at Southwestern Baptist Theological Seminary and was a noted as a renowned Baptist Theologian.

589. Broadus, John A. (1886). *Commentary on The Gospel of Matthew.* Philadelphia, Pennsylvania: American Baptist Publication Society, p. 596:

> "The design of Christian baptism...performed upon ourselves in the name of Jesus, or in the name of the Father, and of the Son and of the Holy Spirit...."

590. Meier, John P. (1980). *Matthew.* Collegeville, Minnesota: Liturgical Press, p. 372:

> "To be sure, this formula was not the original one used by the early church, which rather baptized 'in the name of Jesus' (Acts 2:38; 10:48). The trinitarian formula arose at some point in the liturgy of Mt's church...."[366]

591. Ginther, James R. (2009). *The Westminster Handbook To Medieval Theology.* The Westminster Handbooks To Christian Theology. Louisville, Kentucky: John Knox Press, p. 21:

> "...did a recipient need to be baptized in the name of the Trinity, or was the name of Christ sufficient? Most solutions tried to establish baptism in the name of the Trinity as the absolute norm without necessarily invalidating baptisms done in the name of Christ. The latter had scriptural support and had been approved by Pope Nicholas I (r.858-867), whose letter was later incorporated into cannon law."[367]

592. Dummelow, J. R. (1925). *A Commentary on The Holy Bible by Various Writers Complete in One Volume with General Articles and Maps.* New York: MacMillan Company, p. 721:

> "...that all the baptisms described in the NT are into the name of Jesus, not into the name of the Trinity (Acts 2:38; 8:16; 10:48; 19:5) and that so definite and as it were, stereotyped, a

---

[366]Father John P. Meier, S.T.D., cited earlier in this publication in a different study, namely, the *Two Disputed Questions*, was W. K. Warren IV Professor of Theology at The University of Notre Dame, is a Roman Catholic Priest and a noted Roman Catholic scholar.

[367]James R. Ginther is Associate Professor of Medieval Theology at St. Louis University in Missouri.

formulation of Trinitarian doctrine, must be later than the apostolic age. These arguments are not without weight...."

593. Caragounis, Chrys C. & Fornberg, Tord (ed.) (2011). *The Tripartite Formula in Matt. 28:19 and Baptism in the Three Names (1922)*. Anton Fridrichsen Exegetical Writings A Selection. Eugene, Oregon: Wipf & Stock:

"We know, however, that the earliest Christian baptism took place in the name of Jesus alone (1 Cor. 1:13, 6:11, Acts 2:38; 8:16; 10:48; 19:5; cf. Jas 2:7 and the passages from Hermas, mentioned below)...In the West, however, the validity of baptism in Jesus' name alone was asserted time and time again...Luther and Zwingli declared baptism in Jesus' name fully valid...Matt. 28.19 is not a baptismal formula in the strict sense, that is to say no word for word report of what was said over the baptismal candidate, but characterizes the act of baptism...that the one who administered the baptism, at some occasion pronounced Jesus' name...over the one who was baptized...We do not know for certain when and where they began to use Matt. 28.19...it must have taken place during the second century...how baptism in the three names suppressed baptism in the name of Jesus...."[368]

594. Elowsky, Joel C. (ed.) (2009). *We Believe in The Holy Spirit Ancient Christian Doctrine 4*. Downers Grove, Illinois: InterVarsity Press, p. 246:

"...to baptize in the name of the Father, Son and Holy Spirit. This formula for baptism, while not the only formula used in the New Testament period, became the most common" citing footnote 1 "There was also baptism for, in or on the name of Jesus; cf. 1 Cor. 1:13, 15; Gal. 3:27; Rom 6:3; Acts 2:38; 10:48)."

595. Wright SJ, John H. (2013). *Divine Providence in The Bible Meeting the Living And True God*. Volume II New Testament. Mahwah, New Jersey: Paulist Press, p. 77:

"This was baptism with water (Acts 8:38; 10:47) the name of the Lord Jesus (Acts 8:16; 10:48; 19:5)...It seems that the one being

---

[368] Anton Fridrichsen was a Norwegian-born Swiss Theologian and scholar.

baptised called upon the name of Jesus Christ (Acts 22:16)."[369]

596. Coutts, Joshua J. F. (2017). *The Divine Name in The Gospel of John*. Tubingen, Germany: Mohr Siebeck, pp. 143-144:

"...it is clear from the context of Acts that the concept of God's name has been fully absorbed by Jesus' name, such that the 'name of the Lord' is 'the name of Jesus.' Similarly, in the earlies traditions, believers are baptized into Jesus's name. It is only in the (arguably) later Matthean formula, known also to the Didachist and Odish, that we encounter baptism 'in the name of the Father and of the Son and of the Holy Spirit' (Matt 28:19; Did. 7.1; Odes Sol. 23.22)."[370]

597. Abreu, Savio (2020). *Heaven's Gates and Hell's Flames A Sociological Study of New Christian Movements in Contemporary Goa*. New Delhi: Oxford University Press:

"Christian baptism was initially administered in the early Church in the 'name of Jesus'...Biblical evidence strongly suggests that Matthew 28L19 was a later expansion of the simpler and earlier baptismal formula 'in the name of Jesus'...."[371]

598. Sell, Alan P. F. (2008). *Hinterland Theology A Stimulus to Theological Construction*. Studies in Christian History and Thought. Eugene, Oregon: Wipf & Stock, p. 37:

"...Ridgley, made some general remarks concerning the proper recipients of baptism...if he thinks that we need not to be tied to a particular form of words, so that on occasion baptism in the name of Jesus alone is in order, the sacrament is not invalid...."[372]

599. Screech, M. A. (1994). *Clement Marot: a Renaissance poet discovers the*

---

[369] John H. Wright, SJ was past President of The Catholic Theological Society of America.

[370] Joshua J. F. Coutts, Lecturer in New Testament at Regent College, Vancouver, Canada.

[371] Savio Abreu, Assistant Professor of Sociology & Anthropology at St. Xavier's College and is a Catholic Priest.

[372] Thomas Ridgley (c.1667-c.1734), while very little is known about Thomas Ridgley he was born in London, England and was an English dissenter.

gospel: Lutheranism, Fabrism and Calvanism in the Royal Courts of France and of Navarre and in the Ducal Court. Leiden, The Netherlands: Brill, p. 20:

> "Luther is well aware, of course, that in Scripture sufficient baptism is in the name of Christ. He prefers the longer version but refuses to condemn the short one:...the formula I baptise thee in the name of Jesus Christ, by which rite it is certain that the Apostles baptised, as we can read in the Acts of the Apostles [10:48], and would allow no formula to be valid..."[373]

600. Bauerschmidt, Frederick C. & Buckley, James L. (2017). *Catholic Theology An Introduction*. Chichester, West Sussex: Wiley Blackwell, p. 308:

> "Acts 8:12 speaks of Baptism performed 'in the name of Jesus.' If this is understood to refer to a verbal formula...this has been seen as an early practice that 'virtually' incorporated the name of the Trinity (see e.g., Thomas Aquinas, St. 3 q. 66. A. 6)...."

601. Drummond, T. (1809). *To the Editor of The Monthly Repository*, Ipswich, December 14, 1808 in the *Monthly Repository of Theology and General Literature January-December 1808*. Volume III. London: C Stower, Paternoster Row, pp. 715-716:

> "Many thousands have been baptized into the name of Jesus Christ only...."

602. Hawkins, John (1785?). *An Appeal to Scripture, Reason & Tradition in Support of the Doctrines Contained in A Letter To The Roman Catholics of The City of Worcester From The Late Chaplain of That Society etc*. Worcester: J. Tymbs; London: H. Gardner, Birmingham, and most other booksellers in the Kingdom, p. 349:

> "Many of the ancients, as well as moderns, maintain that baptism was sometimes conferred by the apostles in the name of Christ alone. This was the opinion of Irenaeus, Basil, Ambrose, Hilary, Pope Nicholas, Ven. Bede, S. Bernard, Hugues of S. Victor, the Mater of Sentences, Alexander Hales, Thomas Aquinas, Pope Adrian IV, Cardinal Cajetan."

---

[373] M. A. Screech is a Senior Research Fellow of All Souls College and an Extraordinary Fellow Elect of Wolfson College, Oxford.

603. Wordsworth, C H R (1857). *The New Testament of Our Lord and Saviour Jesus Christ in The Original Greek with Notes. Part-II.–The Acts of The Apostles.* London: Rivingtons, p. 14:

> "Since Jesus commanded His Apostles to baptize in the Name of the Father, and of the Son, and of the Holy Ghost, therefore the Baptism administered by them in Christ's Name was Baptism in the Name of the Holy Trinity. He that is baptized in the Name of Christ, is baptized in the Name of the *Holy Trinity*; for the Father and the Holy Spirt are inseparable from the son...One Person of the Holy Trinity does not exclude another, but includes it...Hence also we may prove the *Divinity of Christ.* To be baptized in the Name of Jesus, is to be baptized in the Name of the Triune God, which could not be, *unless Jesus Christ were God.*"[374]

603. Jarvis, Cynthia A. & Johnson, E. Elizabeth (Gen. ed.) (2013). *Feasting on the Gospel Matthew, Volume 2 Chapters 14–28.* A Feasting on The Word's Commentary. Louisville, Kentucky: Westminster John Knox Press, p. 370:

> "Jesus commands his disciples to baptize 'in the name of the Father and of the Son and of the Holy Spirit' (v. 19b)...Of course, there were various baptismal formulas among early Christian communities, and only later did this triune name become the standard language for Christian baptism....early baptismal formula practiced by some Christian communities...baptized 'in the name of Jesus' (cf. Acts 2:38; 10:48)."

604. Keck, Leander E. (2003). *Jesus in The Gospels.* Study Manual Disciple Second Generation Studies. Nashville, Tennessee: Abington Press:

> "Matthew 28:19...Earlier baptism had been 'in the name of Jesus Christ' alone, as Acts 2:38; 8:16; 10:48; 19:5; 1 Corinthians 1:13-15 show...."[375]

---

[374]Dr. C H R Wordsworth was canon of Westminster from 1844-1869 and was also vicar of Stanford-in-the-Vale-cum-Goosey, Berkshire and became Bishop of Lincoln in 1869.
[375]Leander E. Keck, Winkley Professor of Biblical Theology Emeritus, and former Dean of Yale University Divinity School.

605. Sondy, Amanullah De, et. al. (2020). *Judaism, Christianity and Islam An Introduction to Monotheism*. London: Bloomsbury Publishing, p. 71:

> "...Christians argue the three persons of the Trinity are present, will become the found of the Trinitarian baptismal formula recited by the earliest Christians. The book of Acts has the apostle Peter claims, 'Repent and be baptized, everyone of you, in the name of Jesus Christ for the forgiveness of your sins. And you will receive the gift of the Holy Spirit' (Acts 2:38). Other moments in Acts show clearly Christians being baptized in the name of Jesus Christ."

606. Howard, George (1995). *Hebrew Gospel of Matthew*. Macon, Georgia: Mercer University Press, p. 193:

> "In 1965, Hans Kosmala argued in favor of the originality of the short form of the ending of Matthew, suggesting that Matthew's susceptibility to liturgical modification allowed the trinitarian baptismal formula to be added to the text. By the time this formula was added, no other baptismal formula, such as, 'in the name of Jesus' was any longer in use."[376]

607. Scirghl, Thomas J. (2000). *An Examination of The Problems of Inclusive Language in The Trinitarian Formula of Baptism*. Studies in Religion and Society Volume 42. New York: The Edwin Mellen Press, p. 162:

> "...since clearly the original baptismal formula describes baptism into the name of Jesus."[377]

608. Elser, Phillip F. (ed.) (2000). *The Early Christian World Volume I-II*. New York: Routledge, p. 645:

> "The pattern attaching to water baptism appears ordinarily to have entailed 'faith', the particular manifestation of this faith is an

---

[376] George Howard, Professor of Religion University of Georgia.

[377] Thomas J. Scirghl, is a Priest of The Society of Jesus, is an Assistant Professor of Systematic Theology at Fordham University in the Bronx, New York City. What is interesting is the Professor Sirghl notes that "According to Karl Barth, the account of baptism in the Greek New Testament employ three different words for 'in' *epi* (through, by means) *en* (under the authority of), *eis* (going into). Matthew 28:19 uses eis, a more active form of the preposition, suggesting that the baptized person is going into the Trinity or participating in it" pp. 162-163.

attitude of repentance, and the use of 'the name' of Jesus. It is likely that the most common form of liturgical use of this name had a Christological focus...common for the one baptizing to pounce it.

609. Barnes, Charles Randall (1924). *The People's Bible Encyclopedia – Biographical, Geographical, Historical, and Doctrinal Illustrated By Nearly Four Hundred Engravings, Maps, Charts, Etc.* Chicago: The People's Publication Society, p. 1204:

"Baptism, Believers'. From the beginning the Christian Churches practiced baptism and practiced it in the name of Jesus (Acts 2:38; 16:38; 10:48; 19:5; Gal. 3:24; Rom. 6:3; 1 Cor. 1:13-15; 12:13: Eph. 4:5; John 3:5). The clearly did so under the conviction that they were acting according to the will of Christ, and, therefore, under the highest authority...the New Testament, which knows only baptism in the name of Jesus...."

610. Smith, Henry B. & Schaff, Philip (1874). *Theological and Philosophical Library: A Series of Text-Books, Original and Translated for Colleges and Theological Seminaries.* New York: Scribner, Armstrong & Co.

"Therefore no one need be surprised that even in the Apostolic age persons were baptized solely in the name of Jesus...."

611. Lampe, Geoffrey W. H. (2004). *The Seal of The Spirit A Study in The Doctrine of Baptism and Confirmation in The New Testament and The Fathers.* Eugene, Oregon: Wipf & Stock, p. 52:

"...those who accept Him as the Christ are baptized in the name of Jesus the Anointed for the remission of sins."

612. Godet, Frederic (1899). *Introduction to The New Testament The Collection of The Four Gospels And The Gospel of St. Matthew.* Edinburgh: T&T Clark, p. 164:

"...the primitive form had been simply baptism in the name of Jesus...."[378]

---

[378]Frederic Goet, Swiss Protestant Theologian, Professor in the faculty of The Independent Church of Neuchatel.

613. Delitzsch, Franz (2005). *Commentary on The Epistle of The Hebrews. Volume I.* Eugene, Oregon: Wipf & Stock, pp. 274-275:

"The Christian Catechumen coming out of Judaism had to be instructed how New Testament baptism in the name or Jesus...."

614. Shelley, Bruce L. (2008). *Church History in Plain Language.* (3rd ed.). Nashville, Tennessee: Thomas Nelson

"During the apostolic period, church members encountered the central truths of the faith in a number of ways. Although at first converts were often baptized in the name of Jesus alone, baptism in the name of the Trinity soon became standard practice."[379]

615. Cadoux, Cecil John (1928). *Catholicism and Christianity A Vindication of Progressive Protestantism.* U.K.: Allen & Unwin, p. 344:

"Early Christian baptism was always in the name of Jesus, not in the name of the Trinity...."[380]

616. Canney, Maurice A. (1921). *An Encyclopaedia of Religions.* New York: E. P. Dutton & Co., London: George Routledge & Sons Ltd, p. 53:

"Persons were baptized at first 'in the name of Jesus Christ' (Acts ii. 38, x. 48) or 'in the name of the Lord Jesus' (Acts viii.16, xix. 5). Afterwards with the development of the doctrine of the Trinity they were baptized 'in the name of the Father, and of the Son and of the Holy Ghost'...."

617. IIunga, Bakole wa (2015). *Paths of Liberation A Third World Spirituality.* Eugene, Oregon: Wipf & Stock, p. 185:

"This is why after the resurrection his disciples in their turn would urge everyone to be baptized in the name of Jesus as a sign of conversion to Jesus...Acts 2:38...."[381]

618. Filtvedt, Ole Jakob (2015). *The Identity of God's People and the Paradox*

---

[379] Bruce L. Shelley was a long time Professor of Church History and Historical Theology at Denver Seminary.
[380] Cecil John Cadoux, Mackennal Professor of Church History and Vice-Principal, Mansfield College, Oxford University.
[381] Bakole wa IIunga, Archbishop of Kananga.

of Hebrews. Tubingen, Germany: Mohr Siebeck, p. 171:

> "The statement that the those who enter have had their bodies washed in pure water…in my view, the best and simplest explanation is that the baptism he refers to in 10.22 was performed in the name of Jesus…."[382]

619. Gagarin, Michael (ed.) (2010). *The Oxford Encyclopedia of Ancient Greece & Rome.* Volume 1. Academy-Bible. New York: Oxford University Press, p. 119:

> "…the first believers, and baptism 'in the name of Jesus' became a key distinguishing mark of the new sect…."

620. Rampton, Martha (2021). *Trafficking with Demons Magic, and Gender from Late Antiquity to 1000.* New York: Cornell University Press, p. 93:

> "The Acts of the Apostles (19:5) and Just Martyr speak of baptism in the name of Jesus or the Holy Spirit and not according to a Trinitarian formula. Paul insisted that the converts of Ephesus be baptized 'in the name of the Lord Jesus' and receive the 'Holy Spirit.'"[383]

621. Ferguson, Paul (2011). *Great is The Mystery of Faith Exploring Faith Through The Words of Worship.* Norwich: Canterbury Press, pp. 97-98:

> "Obviously, then, Christian baptism goes back to the time of the Apostles…baptism 'in the name of Jesus'…became recognized as the distinctive and once-for-all mark of initiation, that is, becoming a member of the Church, the body of Christ."[384]

622. Elwell, Walter A. & Treier, Daniel J. (2017). *Evangelical Dictionary of Theology.* (3rd ed.). Grand Rapids, Michigan: Baker Academics:

---

[382] Ole Jakob Filtvedt, MF Norwegian School of Theology.

[383] Martha Rampton is Professor of History at Pacific University. See also Bruce Bawer which notes that *"In four centuries the simple and easily understandable formula in Matthew ['I baptize you in the name of Jesus'] had become a highly complex trinitarian speculation."* Stealing Jesus How Fundamentalism Betrays Christianity. New York: Three Rivers Press (1997), p. 57.

[384] Paul Ferguson is the Archdeacon of Cleveland and Warden Reader in the Dioceses of York.

"From the Greek baptisma 'baptism' denotes washing or plunging in water, which from earliest days (Acts 2:41) has been the rite of Christian initiation...It consists of going in or under baptismal water in the name of Jesus Christ (Acts 19:5)...."

623. Walton, Steve, et al. (2011). *Reading Acts Today Essays in Honour of Loveday C. A. Alexander.* New York: T&T Clark International, p. 194:

"Thus people are baptised into the name of Jesus (2:38; 8:12; 16, 10:48; 19:5; 22:16), a characteristic which may suggest the invocation of the name of Jesus over them leading to the people becoming the possession of Jesus."

624. The author leaves with you the comments of Thomas Jefferson born in Albemarle County, Virginia in 1743, the third President of the United States of America from (1801-1809), the principal author of the Declaration of Independence (1776) at the age of 33, who succeeded Benjamin Franklin as Minister to France in 1785, who also wrote a bill establishing religious freedom, enacted in 1786, and died on the notable day of independence on the 4th of July in the year 1826, he commented about the doctrine of the trinity:

"...an unintelligible proposition of Platonic mysticisms that three are one and one is three; and yet one is not three and three are not one...I never had sense enough to comprehend the Trinity, and it appeared to me that comprehension must precede assent."[385]

****

"To this day the surest criterion of an apostolic church is its adherence to the apostolic teaching"

Late world renowned British New Testament scholar, Professor F.F. Bruce (1964). *The Church of Jerusalem.* Christian Brethren Research Fellowship Journal 4 (April), p.6.

---

[385] See Sanford, Charles B. (1984). *The Religious Life of Thomas Jefferson.* Charlottesville, University of Press Virginia, pp. 88-89.

"Thus the Lord, Jesus Christ, has for Paul now assumed a role that belonged exclusively to Yahweh in the Jewish tradition of which Paul had been—and still considers himself to be—a part."

> Fee, Gordon D. (2018). *Jesus The Lord According to Paul the Apostle A Concise Introduction*. Grand Rapids, Michigan: Baker Academic.

"In the early second century...the new church was...to work out its dual commitments to monotheism (inherited from Judaism) and its worship of Jesus as truly God (and truly human)...."

> Hindson, Ed. & Mitchell, Dan (2013). *The Popular Encyclopedia of Church History*. Eugene, Oregon: Harvest House Publishers, p. 23.[386]

---

[386] This publication also notes a point of interest with respect to the Apostolic Fathers that they are not a point of authority on doctrine "Like the writers of the canonical New Testament documents, the Apostolic Fathers wrote epistles, or letters, written to assuage the concerns or needs of particular individuals or local assemblies. They had a fairly wide appeal in the second century and later, as reported by Eusebius (Hist. Eccl. III. 16; IV.23) and attested by their inclusion in some of the earliest collections of the canonical writings, including the Codex Alexandrinus and the Codex Sinaiticus. The letters of the Apostolic Fathers were never intended to be scholarly treatises on matters of doctrine or philosophy...."

CONCLUSION

Baptism in the name of Jesus Christ is all too evident in the pericope, genre, and narratives of the New Testament with its apostolic practice and continuation since the Day of Pentest to the present. The evidence is overwhelmingly strong, biblically correct, theologically sound and convincingly apparent as documented throughout the centuries and history that is notably noted by the world of historical, biblical, and theological scholarship worldwide.

Theologians, biblical experts, scholars, and historians are in total agreement that baptism in the New Testament was clearly done in the name of Jesus Christ (Acts 2:38) and are also in harmony and agreement that it continued since the Day of Pentecost for the evidence undoubtedly supports it. The baptismal form in Matthew 28:19 as stated at from the outset, can only be put into prospective upon a proper and somewhat thorough investigation into its introduction and development.

These components will pave the way for a better conceptual understanding of how Matthew 28:19 evolved into a baptismal formula, ritual, and practice. Thus, sliding away from the practice as outlined in the Book of Acts and New Testament Epistles, even though baptism in the name of Jesus Christ is the only water baptism that can forgive sins and not Matthew 28:19. However, from what has been presented it would seem quite sufficient and adequate to provide the reader with information about the evidence verifying baptism in the name of Jesus from a wide variety of sources, scholars, and literature both past and present.

Since much of what you had read is self-explanatory and largely speaks for itself, your opinion should lead you to a wholesome view that testifies to the practice in the Book of Acts and the later development of the triune form. By now, you should come to some conclusion or put another way, reasonable minds would come to but one conclusion, and that is, that baptism in the name of Jesus Christ was practiced by the New Testament church that continued throughout the centuries.

The development of the trinitarian form of baptism from its christological, binitarian and trinitarian development provide great impetus to the story behind the triune form and its triadic tone that was eventually shaped into trinitarian theology. But in the words of Professor Jane Schaberg, it was aptly stated that "*I conclude further that there is not sufficient evidence to indicate that the triadic phrase, either at the midrashic or at the Matthean redactional stage, is trinitarian.*"[387] The renowned trinitarian scholar, Edmund J. Fortman speaking of the New Testament notes that "Obviously there is no trinitarian doctrine in the Synoptics or Acts."[388]

The noted work of J.N.D Kelly notes that "The repeated description of baptism as 'in the name of the Lord Jesus' (cf., e.g., Acts 8, 16; 19, 5; I Cor. 6, 11) certainly seems to imply that the formula "Jesus is Lord" had a place in the rite."[389] Similarly, on their work on Catholicism, Professors Gerald O'Collins and Mario Farrugia speaking on the subject of baptism note that "At some point in the first century Christian communities stopped baptizing simply 'in the name of Jesus' (e.g. Acts 2: 38; 10: 48) and began baptizing 'in the name [singular] of the Father and of the Son and of the Holy Spirit' (Matt. 28: 19)."

With that said, there can be no doubt that Matthew 28:19, baptism in the name of the Father, Son and Holy Ghost developed post-New Testament, which was not practiced by the apostles or New Testament church or saints. Only upon a closer examination of this subject will one properly see the evidence that notably shows that baptism in the New Testament was always in the name of Jesus. It would be safer to follow the practice of the apostles as established in the Book of Acts, as opposed to following a practice that has no biblical practical application.

---

[387]Schaberg, Jane (1982). *The Father, The Son And The Holy Spirit The Triadic Phrase in Matthew 28:19b*. SBL Dis. Series 61. CA: Published by Scholar Press, p. 336. Kelly, J. N. D. (1972).

[388]Fortman, Edmund J. (1999) (reprint). *The Triune God A Historical Study of the Doctrine of the Trinity*. Eugene, Oregon: Wipf & Stock, p. 14.

[389]Kelly, J. N. D. (1972). *Early Christian Creeds*. (3rd ed.). New York: Longman, Inc., p. 15.

"...Jesus Christ is God in the same sense as the Father is, and no more or less, since 'there never was a time when he was not'... whatever a Christian thinks or says of God, he or she should think and say of Jesus Christ as well. For Nicaea to understand God was to understand Jesus Christ and not vice versa because Jesus is the revelation of God and in him the Godhead fully dwells...the validity of Jesus Christ the real man and real God as the ultimate reality and meaning is challenged. Jesus Christ is the ultimate reality and meaning of both heaven and earth. It is precisely because Jesus Christ as real God and real man is the ultimate reality and meaning of both the divine and the human that every conceivable system in its positive aspect is not only open to God, but Christ the true God and true man is both its foundation and its meaning."

Jesus Christ as Ultimate Reality and Meaning. A Contribution to the Hermeneutics of Counciliar Theology Tibor Horvath, Regis College, Toronto, Ontario, Canada, University of Toronto Press Journal (1994), pp. 265, 269.

"Baptism is described as into Jesus' name (e.g. Acts 2:38)...So dominant was the use of the name "Jesus" in the religious life of the apostolic church that the whole mission can be described as proclamation "in his name" (Luke 24:47)...."

> McGrath, Alister E. (editor) (2017). *The Christian Theology Reader*. Chichester: West Sussex, Wiley Blackwell, p. 198.

"Spanish Tract on Baptism. I had written in Spanish a tract on baptism last winter. I shall now publish it. In the tract, I insert the notes of the official Catholic Bible here (Scio's) to prove immersion to have been apostolic baptism. It has great weight here. The people here are anxious to go back to primitive Christianity."

_____. (1870). *The Missionary Magazine Published by The American Baptist Missionary Union.* Volume L. Boston: Missionary Rooms, pp. 385-386.

Bibliography

Books

Abreu, Savio (2020). *Heaven's Gates and Hell's Flames A Sociological Study of New Christian Movements in Contemporary Goa*. New Delhi: Oxford University Press

_____. (1759). *A Dictionary of The Holy Bible: Containing A Historical Account of the Persons, etc*. In Three Volumes. Vol I. London: J. Beecroft, et. al.

Adamson, James B. (1976). *The Epistle of James*. The New International Commentary on The New Testament. Grand Rapids, Michigan: William B. Eerdmans Publishing Company

Adger, John B. (1899). *My Life And Times 1810-1899*. Richmond, Virginia: The Presbyterian Committee of Publication

Allen, Alexander V. G. (1898). *International Theological Library Christian Institutions*. Edinburgh: T&T Clark

Allen, Ronald J. (2013). *Acts of the Apostles*. Minneapolis: Fortress Press

Amanze, James N. (2006). *Ecumenism in Botswana The Story of the Botswana Christian Council 1964-2004*. Gaborne: Paulist Press

Anderson, John (1820). *Alexander and Rufus or a Series of Dialogues on Church Communion in Two Parts*. Pittsburgh: Cramer & Spear

Archer, Kenneth J. (2009). *A Pentecostal Hermeneutic Spirit, Scripture and Community*. Cleveland, Tennessee: CPT Press

Armitage, Thomas (1890). *A History of The Baptists; Traced by Their Vital Principles and Practices From The Time of Our Lord and Saviour Jesus Christ to The Year 1889.* New York: Bryan, Taylor, & Co. & Cincinnati: Jones Brothers Publishing Co.

Armstrong, John H. (ed) (2007). *Understanding Four Views on Baptism.* Grand Rapids, Michigan: Zondervan

Armstrong, Karen (1983). *The First Christian: Saint Paul's Impact on Christianity.* London and Sydney: Pan Books

Ashmore, Harry S. (1961). *Encyclopedia Britannica A Survey of Universal Knowledge.* Volume 3

Aus, Roger David (2017). *Two Puzzling Baptisms Studies in Judaism First Corinthians 10:1-5 and 15:29 Studies in Their Judaic Background.* Lanham, Maryland: Hamilton Books

Babu, Immanuel (2004). *Repent and Turn to God Recounting Acts.* Eugene, Oregon: Wipf & Stock

Baird, Thomas Dickson (1816). *Science of Praise or an Illustration of The Nature and Design of Sacred Psalmody, A Series of Letters.* Zanesville, Ohio: Putnam Clark

Baird, William (2003). *History of New Testament Research From Jonathan Edwards to Rudolf Bultmann.* Volume Two. Minneapolis, Fortress Press

Baker SJ, Kenneth (1983). *Fundamentals of Catholicism Grace The Church The Sacraments Eschatology.* Volume 3. San Francisco, California: Ignatius Press & New York: Homiletic Pastoral Review

Baker, William R. (2012). *The Community of Believers in James* in *The New Testament Church The Challenge of Developing Ecclesiologies.* Eugene, Oregon: Pickwick Publications

Barnes, Charles Randall (1924). *The People's Bible Encyclopedia – Biographical, Geographical, Historical, and Doctrinal Illustrated By Nearly Four Hundred Engravings, Maps, Charts, Etc.* Chicago: The People's Publication Society

Barrett, C. K. (1994). *A Critical and Exegetical Commentary on The Acts of the Apostles Preliminary Introduction and Commentary on Acts I-XIV* Volume I. Edinburgh: T&T Clark

Barrier, Jeremy (2009). *The Acts of Paul and Thecla.* Tubingen, Germany: Mohr Siebeck

Barth, Markus & Blanke, Helmut (2000). *The Letter to Philemon – Critical Eerdmans Commentary.* Grand Rapids, Michigan: William B. Eerdmans Publishing Company

Barton, John (2002). *The Biblical World.* Volume II. London: Routledge

Basil Studer edited by Andrew Louth (1993). *Trinity and Incarnation The Faith of the Early Church.* London & New York: T&T Clark

Bauckham, Richard (1995). *James and The Jerusalem Church* in *The Book of Acts in its First Century Setting.* Volume 4 Palestinian Setting. Published jointly: Grand Rapids, Michigan: William B. Eerdmans Publishing Company and Carlisle, Cumbria: The Paternoster Press

Bauckham, Richard (1996). *James and The Gentiles (Acts 15. 13–21)* in *History, Literature and Society in The Book of Acts.* Cambridge: Cambridge University Press

Bauckham, Richard (2001). *James and Jesus* in *The Brother of Jesus James the Just and His Mission.* Chilton, Bruce and Neusner, Jacob (editors). Louisville, Kentucky: John Knox Press

Bauerschmidt, Frederick C. & Buckley, James L. (2017). *Catholic Theology An Introduction.* Chichester, West Sussex: Wiley Blackwell

Bavinck, Herman (2008). *Reformed Dogmatics Holy Spirit, Church, And New Creation* Volume Four. Grand Rapids, Michigan: Baker Academics

Beard, Jennifer L. (2007). *The Political Economy of Desire.* New York, New York: Routledge

Beard, John R. (1860) *Reason's Why I Am A Unitarian In A Series of Letters To A Friend* (2nd ed.). London: Simpkin, Marshall & Co

Beasley-Murray, George R (reprint) (1994). *Baptism in the New Testament*. Grand Rapids, Michigan: William B. Eerdmans Publishing Company

Beasley-Murray, George R. (1999). *John.* World Biblical Commentary (rev. ed.) Volume 36. Grand Rapids, Michigan: Zondervan

Bender, Kimlyn J. & Long, Stephen D. (2020). *T&T Clark Handbook of Ecclesiology*. London: Bloomsbury Publishing

Bender, Ross T. & Sell, Alan P. I. (ed.) (1991). *Baptism, Peace and the State in the Reformed and Mennonite Traditions*. Waterloo, Ontario: Wilfrid Laurier University Press

Bennett, W. H. and Adeney, Walter F. (4th ed.) (1907). *A Biblical Introduction With A Concise Bibliography*. New York: Thomas Whittaker

Berardino, Angelo Di (ed.) (2010). *We Believe in One Holy Catholic And Apostolic Church*. Downers Grove, Illinois: InterVarsity Press

Barnard, Leslie William (1966). *Studies in The Apostolic Fathers and Their Background*. Schocken Books

Bernard, Thomas Dehany (1904). *The Word and Sacraments and Other Papers Illustrative of Present Questions on Church Ministry and Worship*. London: Bemrose & Sons Ltd

Beyschlag, Willibald (1895). *New Testament Theology or Historical Account of the Teaching of Jesus And Primitive Christianity According to the New Testament Sources*. In Two Volumes. Edinburgh: T & T Clark

Bicknell, E. J. & Carpenter, H. J. (ed.) (2007). *A Theological Introduction to The Thirty-Nine Articles of The Church of England* (Third Edition). Oregon: Eugene, Wipf & Stock

Blidstein, Moshe (2017). *Purity, Community, and Ritual in Early*

Christian Literature. Oxford Studies in The Abrahamic Religions. Oxford: Oxford University Press

Bobbington, David & Jones, Ceri Jones (2013). *Evangelism & Fundamentalism in the United Kingdom During The Twentieth Century*. Oxford: Oxford University Press

Bock, Darrell L. (2011). *A Theology of Luke's Gospel And Acts Biblical Theology of The New Testament*. Grand Rapids, Michigan: Zondervan.

Boff, Lenoardo (1988). *Trinity and Society*. Translated from the Portuguese by Paul Burns. Eugene, Oregon: Wipf & Stock

Bonhoeffer, Dietrich (1963). *The Cost of Discipleship*. New York: MacMillan Publishing Co., Inc.

Boora, Kulwant Singh (2011). *The Roman Catholic Church And Its Recognition of The Validity of Baptism in The Name of Jesus (Acts 2:38) From 100 A.D. to 500 A.D.* Bloomington, Indiana: Authorhouse

Boora, Kulwant Singh (2021) (revised edition). *The Three Roman Catholic Popes on The Validity of Baptism in The Name of Jesus (Acts 2:38) and The Two Catholic Popes on the Oneness Christological view of God*. Published by Amazon Publishing

Boora, Kulwant Singh (2021). *The Acknowledgment, Recognition and Acceptance of The Apostolic Form of Baptism in The Name of Jesus Christ (Acts 2:38) From Biblical and Theological Scholars (Trinitarian & Non-Trinitarian), Including Ecumenical Councils & Committees and Various Religious Organizations and Groups*. A Reference Guide for Discussing Baptism in The Name of Jesus Christ (Acts 2:38). Published by Amazon Publishing KDP

Boersma, Hans & Matthew Levering (ed.) (2015). *The Oxford Handbook of Sacramental Theology*. Oxford: Oxford University Press

Bosch, David J. (1983). *The Structure of Mission: An Exposition of Matthew 28:16-20. The Great Commission in Matthew* in *Exploring*

Church Growth edited by Wilbert R. Shenk. Eugene, Oregon: Wipf & Stock

Bowman Jr, Robert M. and Komoszewski, J. Ed. (2007). *Putting Jesus in His Place The Case for The Deity of Christ*. Grand Rapids, Michigan: Kregel Publications

Bradshaw, Paul F. (2009). *Reconstructing Early Christian Worship*. Minnesota: Liturgical Press

Bradshaw, Paul (2010). *Early Christian Worship A basic Introduction to Ideas and Practice*. (2nd ed.). London: SPCK

Brasher, Brenda E. (editor) (2001). *Encyclopedia of Fundamentalism*. Volume 3 of Religion & Society. New York: Routledge

Brandt, Edward J. (1989). *The Book of Mormon: Second Nephi, The Doctrinal Structure*

Briggs, Charles Augustus (1913). *The Fundamental Christian Faith The Origin; History and Interpretation of The Apostles' and Nicene Creeds*. New York: Charles Scribner's Sons

Breen, J. D. (1885). *Anglican Orders: Are they Valid? A Letter to A Friend*. Revised and Enlarged Edition. London: Burns and Oates; New York: Catholic Publication Society Company

Britton, Thomas Hopkins (MDCCCLI). *The Sacramental Articles of The Church of England Vindicated From Recent Misrepresentations and Illustrated by The Writings of Their Compliers and Last Editor And by Other Documents Published Under The Sanction of The Church Between The Years 1536 and 1571*. London: Joseph Masters, Aldersgate Street and New Bond Street

Broadus, John A. (1886). *Commentary on The Gospel of Matthew*. Philadelphia, Pennsylvania: American Baptist Publication Society

Brondos, David A. (2018). *Jesus' Death in New Testament Thought*. Volume 2 Texts. Mexico: Instituto Internaciondl de Estudios Superiores

Bromiley, Geoffrey W. (gen. ed.) (1986). *The International Standard Bible Encyclopedia Illustrated in Four Volumes. Volume One: A-D.* Grand Rapids, Michigan: William B. Eerdmans Publishing Company

Bromiley, G. W. (ed.) (1953). *Zwingli and Bullinger.* The Library of Christian Classics Ichthus Edition. Philadelphia, Pennsylvania: The Westminster Press

Brown, Raymond E. (2008). *Christ in the Gospels of the Liturgical Year.* Expanded Edition. Liturgical Press

Brownson, James V. (2007). *An Introduction To Baptism in Scripture and The Reformed Tradition.* Michigan: William B. Eerdmans Publishing Company

Bruce, F. F. (1963). *The Books and the Parchments Some Chapters on The Transmission of The Bible* (revised edition). Westwood, New Jersey: Fleming H. Revel Company

Bruce, F. F. (1983). *The Gospel of John Introduction, Exposition and Notes.* Grand Rapids, Michigan: William B. Eerdmans Publishing Company

Bruskewitz, Fabian (1997). *A Shepherd Speaks.* San Francisco, California: Ignatius Press

Bullinger, Ethelbert William (2007). *How to Enjoy The Bible; Or, 'The Word,' and 'The Words,' How To Study Them.* New York: Cosimo Publications (originally published in 1921)

Bultmann, Rudolf K (2007). *Theology of The New Testament. Trans.* Kendrick Grobel. First Published (1951), 2 volumes. Waco, Texas: Baylor University Press

Burn, A. E (1899). *An Introduction To The Creeds And To The Te Deum.* London: Methuen & Co.

Byars, Ronald P. (2011). *The Sacraments in Biblical Perspective Interpretation: Resources for The Use of Scripture in the Church.* Louisville, Kentucky: Westminster John Knox Press

Cadoux, Cecil John (1928). *Catholicism and Christianity A*

Vindication of Progressive Protestantism. U.K.: Allen & Unwin

Canney, Maurice A. (1921). *An Encyclopaedia of Religions.* New York: E. P. Dutton & Co., London: George Routledge & Sons Ltd

Caragounis, Chrys C. & Fornberg, Tord (ed.) (2011). *The Tripartite Formula in Matt. 28:19 and Baptism in the Three Names (1922).* Anton Fridrichsen Exegetical Writings A Selection. Eugene, Oregon: Wipf & Stock

Carson, Thomas, et. al. (editors) (2003). *New Catholic Encyclopedia* by The Catholic University of America. Michigan: Gale

Cheung, Luke L. (2003). *The Genre, Composition, and Hermeneutics of The Epistle of James.* Eugene, Oregon: Wipf & Stock

Chiavenza, Nicola Ultrich, et. al. (2020). *The Power of Urban Water Studies in Premodern Urbanism.* Boston & Berlin: Walter De Gruyter GmbH

Childs, Brevard S (1993). *Biblical Theology of The Old and New Testaments Theological Reflections on The Christian Bible.* Minneapolis: Fortress Press

Chung-Kim, Esther & Hains, Todd R. (2014). *Reformation Commentary on Scripture New Testament VI ACTS.* Downers Grove, Illinois: InterVarsity Press

Chupungco, Anscar J. (2000). *Handbook for Liturgical Studies IV Sacraments and Sacramentals.* The Pontifical Liturgical Institute. Collegeville, Minnesota: The Liturgical Press

Clarke, Howard (2003). *The Gospel of Matthew and its readers: a historical introduction to the First Gospel.* Bloomington, Indiana: Indiana University Press

Clemen, Carl (1912). *Primitive Christianity And Its Non-Jewish Sources.* Edinburgh: T&T Clark

Coakley, Sarah (1993). *Why Three? Some Further Reflections on The Origin of The Doctrine of The Trinity* in *The Making and Remaking of Christian Doctrine Essays in Honour of Maurice Wiles.* Oxford:

Clarendon Press

Coda, Piero (2020). *From The Trinity The Coming of God in Revelation and Theology*. Washington D.C.: The Catholic University of America Press

Colenso, John William (1866). *Natal Sermons A Series of Discourses Preached in The Cathedral Church of St. Peters, Maritzburg*. London: Paternoster Row

Collins, Raymond F. & Harrington, Daniel J. (editors) (1999). *First Corinthians*. Minnesota: Liturgical Press

Comfort, Phillip W. (general. editor) (2009). *1 and 2 Corinthians*. Tyndale Cornerstone Bible Commentary Volume 15. Carol Stream, Illinois: Tyndale House Publishers, Inc.

Cooke, R. J. (1900). *History of The Ritual of The Methodist Episcopal Church With A Commentary on Its Offices*. Cincinnati: Jennings & Pye & New York: Eaton & Mains

Conybeare, Fred C. (1898). *The Character of The Heresy of The Early British Church*. In: *The Transactions of the Honourable Society of Cymmrodorion Session 1896-97*. London: Issued By The Society

Conybeare, Fred. C. (1910). *Myth, Magic, and Morals A Study of Christian Origins*. London: Watts & Co.

Coutts, Joshua J. F. (2017). *The Divine Name in The Gospel of John*. Tubingen, Germany: Mohr Siebeck

Cross, F. L. & Livingston, E. A. (ed.) (2005). *The Oxford Dictionary of The Christian Church*. (3rd ed.). New York: Oxford University Press

Cupitt, Don (1979). *The Debate About Christ*. London: SCM Press

Curteis, George Herbert (1897). *Dissent, In Its Relation To The Church of England, Eight Lectures Preached Before the University of Oxford in The Year 1871 on the Foundation of the Late Rev. John Bampton, M.A., Canon of Salisbury*. London: MacMillan and Co.,

Ltd., New York: The MacMillan Co.

Cunningham O.P, James J. (2006). St. *Thomas Aquinas Summa Theologiae Baptism and Confirmation* Volume 57 (3a. 66-72). New York: Cambridge University Press

Cwiekowski, Frederick J. (1988). *The Beginnings of The Church*. Mahwah, New Jersey: Paulist Press

Dahl, Nils Alstrup (2021). *The Apostle Paul Guides The Early Church*. Eugene, Oregon: Cascade Books

Dale, James W. (1874). *An Inquiry into the Usage of Baptize and the nature of Christic and Patristic Baptism as Exhibited in the Holy Scriptures and Patristic Writings* by James W. Dale, D.D. (Pastor of Wayne Presbyterian Church, Delaware County, PA) Pennsylvania: WM. Rutter & Co

Dalton, William Joseph (1989). *Christ's Proclamation To the Spirits of 1 Peter 3:18-4:6*. Analecta Biblica 23. Roma: Editrice Pontificio Instituto Biblico

Davis, John Jefferson (2015). *Theological Reflections on Ministry and The Christian Life Practicing Ministry in The Presence of God*. Eugene, Oregon: Cascade Books

Davison, Andrew (2013). *Why Sacraments?* London: SPCK

Davies, Horton (1961). *Worship and Theology in England From Watts and Wesley to Maurice*. Volume III. Princeton, New Jersey: Princeton University Press

Deferrari, Roy J. (1951). *Hugh of Saint Victor on The Sacraments of The Christian Faith (De Sacraments)*. Cambridge, Massachusetts: The Mediaeval Society of America

Deiss, Lucien (1979). *Springtime of The Liturgy, Liturgical Texts of The First Four Centuries*. Collegeville, Minnesota: The Liturgical Press

Delitzsch, Franz (2005). *Commentary on The Epistle of The Hebrews*. Volume I. Eugene, Oregon: Wipf & Stock

Dix, Dom Gregory (2005). *The Shape of The Liturgy*. London & New York: Bloomsburg T&T Clark

Dods, Marcus, et. al. (ed.) (1907). *An Exposition of the Bible A Series of Expositions Covering All The Books of The Old And New Testament. Vol. V. St. Luke-Galatians*. Hartford, Connecticut: The. S. S. Scranton Co.

Dominguez, Eugene A. (2020). *Oneness Heroes In Spain and the Americas: Centuries IV-XXXI* Volume 1. Third Edition. Weldon Springs, Missouri

Donovan, J. (1829). *The Catechism of The Council of Trent. Published by Command of Pope Pius the Fifth*. Dublin: Richard Coyne & Keating and Browne

Douglas, J. D., et. al. (1989). *The Concise Dictionary of The Christian Tradition, Doctrine Liturgy History*. Grand Rapids, Michigan: Zondervan

Dowley, Tim (2018). *A Short Introduction To The History of Christianity*. Minneapolis, Fortress Press

Dowley, Tim (2013). *Introduction To The History of Christianity*. (2nd ed). Minneapolis, Fortress Press

Draper, Jonathan A. (2010). *The Didache* in *The Apostolic Fathers An Introduction*. Waco, Texas: Baylor University Press

Drown, Edward S (1917). *The Apostles Creed To-Day*. New York: The MacMillan Company

Due, William J. La (2006). *The Trinity Guide to The Christian Church*. London & New York: Continuum

Drummond, T. (1809). *To the Editor of The Monthly Repository*, Ipswich, December 14, 1808 in the *Monthly Repository of Theology and General Literature January-December 1808*. Volume III. London: C Stower, Paternoster Row

Duck, Ruth C. (1999). *The Trinity in Sunday Worship* in *Praising God The Trinity in Christian Worship*, Duck, Ruth C. & Wilson-

Kastner, Patricia. Louisville, Kentucky: Westminster John Knox Press

Dummelow, J. R. (1925). *A Commentary on The Holy Bible by Various Writers Complete in One Volume with General Articles and Maps*. New York: MacMillan Company

Dunn, James D. G. (1970). *Baptism in the Holy Spirit A Re-examination of the New Testament Teaching on the Gift of The Spirit in Relation to Pentecostalism today*. Philadelphia, Pennsylvania: The Westminster Press

Dunn, James D. G. (1993). *The Theology of Paul's Letter to The Galatians New Testament Theology*. Cambridge: Cambridge University Press

Dunn, James D. G. (1998). *The Theology of Paul the Apostle*. Grand Rapids, Michigan: William B. Eerdmans Publishing Company

Dunn, James D. G. (1996). *The Acts of the Apostles*. Peterborough: Epworth Press

Dunn, James D. G. (1996). *The Acts of the Apostles*. Grand Rapids, Michigan: William B. Eerdman Publishing Company

Dunn, James D. G. (2009). *Beginning From Jerusalem Christianity in The Making*. Volume 2. Grand Rapids, Michigan: William B. Eerdmans Publishing Company

Draper, Jonathan A. & Jefford, Clayton N. (2015). *The Didache A Missing Piece of The Puzzle in Early Christianity*. Atlanta: Society of Biblical Literature

Edmunds, Albert J. (1917). *Studies In The Christian Religion*. Philadelphia: Innes & Sons

Edwards, Mark (2018). *Early Ecclesiology in The West* in *The Oxford Handbook of Ecclesiology* edited by Paul Avis. Oxford: Oxford University Press

Ehrman, Bart D. (1993). *The Orthodox Corruption of Scripture The Effect of Early Christological Controversies on The Text of The New*

Testament. New York: Oxford University Press

Elowsky, Joel C. (ed.) (2009). *We Believe in The Holy Spirit Ancient Christian Doctrine 4*. Downers Grove, Illinois: InterVarsity Press

Elser, Phillip F. (ed.) (2000). *The Early Christian World Volume I-II*. New York: Routledge

Elwell, Walter A. & Treier, Daniel J. (2017). *Evangelical Dictionary of Theology*. (3rd ed.). Grand Rapids, Michigan: Baker Academics

Emery, Giles and Matthew Levering (ed.) (2011). *The Oxford Handbook of The Trinity*. Oxford: Oxford University Press

Engel, Carte Katherine (2009). *The Evolution of The Bethlehem Pilgergemeine* in *Pietism in Germany and North American 1680-1820*, edited by Strom, Jonathan, et. al. Farnham, Surrey: Ashgate Publishing Limited

Erickson, Millard J. (2000). *Making Sense of the Trinity: Three Crucial Questions*. Grand Rapids, Michigan: Baker Academics

Evans, Craig A. (ed.) (2004). *The Bible Knowledge Background Commentary Acts-Philemon*. Colorado Springs, Colorado: Victor

Evans, Ernest (2016). *Tertullian's Homily on Baptism The Text Edited with an Introduction Translation, and Commentary*. Eugene, Oregon: Wipf & Stock

Evans, Marian (1860). *The Life of Jesus Critically Examined by Dr. David Friedrich Strauss*. Volume II. New York: Calvin Blanchard

Fahey, Michael Andrew (1971). *Cyprian and the Bible A Study in Third-Century Exegesis*. Mohr

Farnell, David F. and Andrews, Edward D. (2017). *Biblical Criticism What Are Some Outstanding Weaknesses of Modern Historical Criticism*. Cambridge, Ohio: Christian Publishing House

Farrelly O.S.B., M. John (2005). *The Trinity Rediscovering the Central Christian Mystery*. New York: Sheed & Ward

Faulkner, John Alfred (1912). *Crises in The Early Church.* New York & Cincinnati: The Methodist Book Concern

Fee. Gordon, D. (1987). *The New International Commentary On The New Testament, The First Epistle To The Corinthians.* Grand Rapids, Michigan: Wm.B.Eerdsmans

Fee, Gordon D. (1996). *Paul, the Spirit And The People of God.* Grand Rapids, Michigan: Baker Academic

Fee, Gordon D. (2018). *Jesus The Lord According to Paul the Apostle A Concise Introduction.* Grand Rapids, Michigan: Baker Academic

Feingold, Lawrence (2021). *Touched by Christ The Sacramental Economy.* Steubenville, Ohio: Emmaus Academic

Felder, Cain Hope ((2021). *Race, Racism and The Biblical Narratives* in *Stony The Road We Trod.* African American Biblical Interpretation. Thirtieth Anniversary Expanded Edition. Minneapolis: Minnesota: Fortress Press

Ferguson, Everett (2009). *Baptism in The Early Church History, Theology and Liturgy in The First Five Centuries.* William B. Eerdmans Publishing Company, Grand Rapids, Michigan

Ferguson, Paul (2011). *Great is The Mystery of Faith Exploring Faith Through The Words of Worship.* Norwich: Canterbury Press

Filtvedt, Ole Jakob (2015). *The Identity of God's People and the Paradox of Hebrews.* Tubingen, Germany: Mohr Siebeck

Finn, Thomas M. (1997). *From Death to Rebirth Ritual and Conversion in Antiquity.* Mahwah, New Jersey: Paulist Press

Fitzmyer, Joseph A. (1997). *The Anchor Bible The Acts of The Apostles.* Volume 31. New York, New York: Doubleday

Forney, C. H. (1883). *The Christian Ordinances Being A Historical Inquiry Into The Practice of Trine Immersion, The Washing of The Saints' Feet And The Love-Feast.* Harrisburg, Pennsylvania: Board of Publication of The General Eldership of The Church of God

Fortman, Edmund J. (1999) (reprint). *The Triune God A Historical Study of the Doctrine of the Trinity*. Eugene, Oregon: Wipf & Stock

France, R. T. (2007). *The Gospel of Matthew The New International Commentary on The New Testament*. Grand Rapids, Michigan: William B. Eerdmans Publishing Company

France, R. T. (1989). *Matthew Evangelist and Teacher*. Eugene, Oregon: Wipf & Stock

Freed, Edwin D. (2005). *The Apostle Paul and His Letters*. London & Connecticut: Equinox Publishing Ltd

French, Talmadge L. (1999). *Our God is One The Story of The Oneness Pentecostals*. Indianapolis, Indiana: Voice & Vision Publications

Fuller, Reginald H. & Westberg, Daniel (2006). *Preaching The Lectionary The Word of God for The Church Today* (3rd ed.). Collegeville, Minnesota: Liturgical Press

Gagarin, Michael (ed.) (2010). *The Oxford Encyclopedia of Ancient Greece & Rome*. Volume 1. Academy-Bible. New York: Oxford University Press

Galbreath, Paul (2011). *Leading Through The Water*. Herndon: Virginia: The Alban Institute

Gardner, Percy (1899). *Exploratio Evangelica A Brief Examination of The Basis And Origin of Christian Belief*. New York: G. P. Putnam's Son & London: Adam and Charles Black

Garrett, Jr., James Leo (1990). *Systematic Theology Biblical, Historical, and Evangelical*. Eugene, Oregon: Wipf & Stock

Gelpi, Donald L. (1993). *Committed Worship A. Sacramental Theology for Converting Christians*. Volume I. Adult Conversion and Initiation. Collegeville, Minnesota: The Liturgical Press

Gerfen, Ernst (1897). *Baptizein The Voice of the Scriptures and Church History Concerning Baptism*. Columbus, Ohio: Press of Lutheran Book Concern

German, Martinez (2003). *Signs of Freedom Theology of The Christian Sacraments*. Mahwah, New Jersey: Paulist Press

Gilbert, George Holley (1912). *Jesus*. New York: The Macmillan Company

Gillis, Chester (1989). *A Question of Final Belief John Hick's Pluralistic Theory of Salvation*. London: The MacMillan Press Ltd

Ginther, James R. (2009). *The Westminster Handbook To Medieval Theology*. The Westminster Handbooks To Christian Theology. Louisville, Kentucky: John Knox Press

Godet, Frederic (1899). *Introduction to The New Testament The Collection of The Four Gospels And The Gospel of St. Matthew*. Edinburgh: T&T Clark

Goll, James W. (2011). *A Radical Faith Essentials For Spirit-Filled Believers*. Bloomington, Minnesota: Chosen Books

Gonzãlez, Justo L. (2001). *Acts The Gospel of The Spirit*. Maryknoll, New York: Orbis Books

Gonzãlez, Justo L. (2005). *Essential Theological Terms*. Louisville, Kentucky: Westminster John Know Press

Gonzãlez, Justo L. (2019). *A History of Early Christian Literature*. Louisville, Kentucky: Westminster John Knox Press

Gowan, Donald E. (1994). *Theology in Exodus Biblical Theology in the Form of a Commentary*. Louisville, Kentucky: Westminster John Knox Press

Grant, Sharon J. (2019). *Rebaptism Calmly Considered: Christian Initiation and Resistance in The Early A.M.E. Church of Jamaica*. Pickwick Publications: Eugene, Oregon

Green, Joel B. & Turner, Max (ed.) (1999). *Jesus of Nazareth Lord and Christ Essays on The Historical Jesus and New Testament Christology*. Eugene, Oregon: Wipf & Stock

Green, Gene L. (2020). *Vox Petri A Theology of Peter*. Eugene,

Oregon: Cascade Books

Grundeken, Mark (1984). *Community Building in the Shepherd of Hermas A Critical Study of Some Key Aspects*. Leiden: Brill

Guericke, H. E. F. (M.DCCC.LL). *Manual of The Antiquities of The Church*. London: John W. Parker and Son

Gunton, Colin E. (2003). *Father, Son & Holy Spirit Toward A Fully Trinitarian Theology*. London & New York: T&T Clark

Haenchen, Ernst (1971). *The Acts of The Apostles A Commentary*. Philadelphia, Pennsylvania: The Westminster Press

Hagerland, Tobias (2011). *Jesus and The Forgiveness of Sins An Aspect of His Prophetic Mission*. New York: Cambridge University Press

Haight, Roger (2004). *Christian Community in History Historical Ecclesiology*. Volume 1. London & New York: Continuum

Hall, Francis J. (1920). *The Church And The Sacramental System*. New York: Longmans, Green and Co., London: Paternoster Row

Hanson, Anthony T. (1982). *The Image of the Invisible God*. London: SCM Press

Hare, Douglas R. A. (1967). *The Theme of Jewish Persecutions of Christians in The Gospel According to St. Matthew* Society for New Testament Studies Monograph Series 6. Cambridge: At The University Press

Hardinge, Leslie (1972). *The Celtic Church in Britain*. London: SPCK

Harnack, Adolf Von (1894). *History of Dogma*. Volume 1. Boston: Little, Brown and Company

Harrington, D. (2001). *The Church According to the New Testament What the Wisdom and Witness of Early Christianity Teaches us Today*. Rowman & Littlefield Publishers, Inc.

Harris, Charles (1905). *Pro Fide A Defence of Natural And Revealed Religion*. London: John Murray

Hartin, Patrick J. (2009). *James*. Sacra Pagina Series Volume 14. Collegeville, Minnesota: Liturgical Press

Hartman, Lars (1997). *'Into The Name of The Lord Jesus'* Studies of the New Testament and Its World. Edinburgh: T&T Clark

Hase, Charles (1855). *History of The Christian Church*. New York: D. Appleton and Company

Hastings, James et. al. (1908). *A Dictionary of Christ and the Gospels. Volume II Labour-Zion with Appendix and Indexes*. New York: Charles Scribner's Sons & Edinburgh: T&T Clark

Hastings, James (ed.) (1922). *Dictionary of the Apostolic Church. Volume II Macedonia-Zion with Indexes*. New York: Charles Scriber's Sons and Edinburgh: T&T Clark

Hawkins, Edward (1841). *An Inquiry Into The Connected Uses of The Principal Means of Attaining Christian Truth in Eight Sermons Preached Before The University of Oxford at the Bampton Lecture for The Year MDCCCXL*. Oxford: John Henry Parker

Hawkins, John (1785?). *An Appeal to Scripture, Reason & Tradition in Support of the Doctrines Contained in A Letter To The Roman Catholics of The City of Worcester From The Late Chaplain of That Society etc*. Worcester: J. Tymbs; London: H. Gardner, Birmingham, and most other booksellers in the Kingdom

Hawthorne, Gerald F., et. al. (1993). *Dictionary of Paul and His Letters. A Compendium of Contemporary Biblical Scholarship*. Downers Grove, Illinois: InterVarsity Press

Heath, Gordon L. & Dvorak, James D. (2011). *Baptism Historical, Theological and Pastoral Perspectives*. Eugene, Oregon: Wipf & Stock

Heath, Gordon L. & Dvorak, James D. (2011). *Baptism. Historical, Theological and Pastoral Perspective*. McMaster Theological

Studies Series. Eugene, Oregon: Pickwick Publications

Hefele, Charles Joseph (1894). *A History of The Christian Councils From The Original Documents, of The Close of The Council of Nicaea A.D. 325* (2nd ed.). Edinburgh: T & T Clark

Heil, John Paul (2012). *The Letter of James Worship to Live By*. Eugene, Oregon: Cascade Books

Heine, Ronald E. (2013). *Classical Christian Doctrine Introducing The Essentials of the Ancient Faith*. Grand Rapids, Michigan: Baker Academic

Hergenrother, Jospeh Adam Gustav (1870). *Anti-Janus: An Historical-Theological Criticism of The Work, entitled 'The Pope and the Council,' by Janus*. Dublin: W. B. Kelly & London: Burn, Oates & Company and Simpkin, Marshall & Co; New York: The Catholic Publishing Society

Herrmann, Erick H. (2016). *The Babylonian Captivity of The Church, 1520*. The Annotated Luther Volume 3 Church and Sacraments. Minneapolis, Minnesota: Fortress Press

Hey, John (1822). *Lectures in Divinity Delivered in The University of Cambridge by John Hey, D.D, As Norrisian Professor, From 1780 to 1795* (2nd ed.). Cambridge: J. Smith

Hill, William J. (1982). *The Three-Personed God: The Trinity As a Mystery of Salvation*. Washington D. C.: Catholic University of America Press

Hindson, Ed. & Mitchell, Dan (2013). *The Popular Encyclopedia of Church History*. Eugene, Oregon: Harvest House Publishers

Hinlicky, Paul R. (2015). *Beloved Community Critical Dogmatics After Christendom*. Grand Rapids, Michigan: William B. Eerdmans Publishing Company

Hitchcock, James. (2012). *History of The Catholic Church From The Apostolic Age To The Third Millennium*. San Francisco: Ignatius Press

Hodge, Charles W. (1878). *Apostolic History and Literature Prepared by the Senior Class For The Use of Students in Princeton Theological Seminary*. Princeton: Press Printing Establishment

Holden, George (1855). *The Anglican Catechist; or A Manual of Instruction Preparatory to Confirmation*. London: Joseph Masters

Holmen, Tom and Porter, Stanley E. (ed.) (2011). *Handbook for the Study of the Historical Jesus* Volume I. Leiden, The Netherlands: Brill

Holmes, Stephen R. (2012). *The Quest for The Trinity The Doctrine of God in Scripture, History and Modernity*. Downers Grove, Illinois: InterVarsity Press

Holmes, Stephen R. (2012). *The Holy Trinity Understanding God's Life*. Crownhill, Milton Keynes: Paternoster

Hornik, Heidi J & Parsons, Mikeal C. (2017). *The Acts of the Apostles Through the Centuries Wiley Blackwell Bible Commentaries*. Chichester, West Sussex: John Wiley & Sons Ltd

Howard, George (1995). *Hebrew Gospel of Matthew*. Macon, Georgia: Mercer University Press

Hunter, Sylvester Joseph (1900). *Outlines of Dogmatic Theology*. Volume III (2nd ed.). London: Longmans, Green & Co

Hurtado, Larry W. (2016). *Destroyer of gods Early Christian Distinctiveness in The Roman World*. Waco, Texas: Baylor University Press

Hurtado, Larry W. (2000). *At the Origins of Christian Worship The Context and Character of Earliest Christian Devotion*. Grand Rapids, Michigan: William B. Eerdmans Publishing Company

Hurtado, Larry W. (2005). *Lord Jesus Christ*. Grand Rapids, Michigan: William. B. Eerdmans Publishing Company

Hurtado, Larry W. (2006). *The Earliest Christian Artifacts Manuscripts and Christian Origins*. Grand Rapids, Michigan: William B. Eerdmans Publishing Company

Ingham, R. (1871). *A Hand-Book on Christian Baptism* Part II. Subjects. London: Paternoster Row

Ilunga, Bakole wa (2015). *Paths of Liberation A Third World Spirituality*. Eugene, Oregon: Wipf & Stock

Jackson, Samuel Macauley, et. al. (1908). *The New Schaff-Herzog Encyclopedia of Religious Knowledge Embracing Biblical, Historical, Doctrinal, and Practical Theology and Biblical, Theological, and Ecclesiastical Biography From The Earliest Times To The Present Day*. Volume I Aachen-Basilians. London and New York: Funk and Wagnalls Company

Jarrell, W. A. (1894). *Baptist Church Perpetuity or The Continuous Existence of Baptist Churches From The Apostolic To The Present Day Demonstrated By The Bible And By History*. Dallas, Texas: Jarrell

Jarvis, Cynthia A. & Johnson, E. Elizabeth (Gen. ed.) (2013). *Feasting on the Gospel Matthew, Volume 2 Chapters 14–28*. A Feasting on The Word's Commentary. Louisville, Kentucky: Westminster John Knox Press

Jenks, William (ed.) (1834). *The Comprehensive Commentary on The Holy Bible Containing The Text According to The Authorised Version; Scott's Marginal References, Matthew Henry's Commentary, Condensed, etc., The Practical Observations of Rev. Thomas Scott, D. D*. Boston: Shattuck and Co & Brattleboro: Fessenden and Co

Jenott, Lance (2011). *The Gospel of Judas Coptic, Texts, Translation and Historical Interpretation of the 'Betrayer's Gospel.'* Tubingen, Germany: Mohr Siebeck

Jenson, Robert W. (2002). *The Triune Identity God According to The Gospel*. Eugene, Oregon: Wipf & Stock

Johnson, Luke Timothy (2001). *Reading Romans A Literary and Theological Commentary*. Macon, Georgia: Helwys Publishing

Johnson, Marshall D. (2002). *Making Sense of the Bible Literary*

Type as an Approach to Understanding. Grand Rapids, Michigan: William B. Eerdmans Publishing Company

Johnson, Maxwell E. (2007). *The Rites of Christian Initiation Their Evolution and Interpretation Revised and Expanded Edition.* Minnesota: Liturgical Press

Jones, F. Stanley (2018). *From Jesus to Lord and Other Contributions of The Early Aramaic-Speaking Congregation in Jerusalem* in *Christian Origins and The Establishment of The Early Jesus Movement* edited by Porter, Stanley E. and Pitts, Andrew W. Leiden, The Netherlands: Brill

Jonge, Marinus de (1988). *Christology in Context: The Earliest Christian Response to Jesus.* Pennsylvania: The Westminster Press

Jowitt, Robert (1837?). Thoughts on Water-Baptism. Darton and Harvey: London

Jung, C. G. (1969). *A Psychological Approach to The Dogma of The Trinity II* in Collected Works of C. G. Jung, Volume II. Psychology and Religion: West and East. Princeton, New Jersey: Princeton University Press

Kantzer, Kenneth S. and Gundr, Stanley N. (1979). *Perspectives on Evangelical Theology Papers from The Thirtieth Annual Meeting on Evangelical Theological Society.* Grand Rapids, Michigan: Baker Book House

Kaye, John (1888). *Works of John Kayne Bishop of Lincoln.* In Eight Volumes, Vol. IV. The Ecclesiastical History of Eusebius. London: Rivingtons

Keck, Leander E. (2003). *Jesus in The Gospels.* Study Manual Disciple Second Generation Studies. Nashville, Tennessee: Abington Press

Keener, Craig S. (2012). *Acts An Exegetical Commentary Introduction And 1:1-2:47.* Volume I. Grand Rapids, Michigan: Baker Academic

Keith, Chris & Roth, T. Deiter (2015). *Mark, Manuscripts And Monotheism Essays in Honor of Larry W. Hurtado*. Library of New Testament Studies. London & New York: Bloomsbury T&T Clark

Kelly, J. N. D. (1972). *Early Christian Creeds*. (3rd ed.). New York: Longman, Inc.

Kesich, Veselin (2007). *Formation and Struggles The Birth of the Church AD 33-200*. The Church in History Volume I, Part 1. Crestwood, New York: St. Vladimir's Seminary Press

Kim, Ig-Jin Kim (2003). *History and theology of Korean pentecostalism: Sunbogeum (pure gospel) Pentecostalism*. Zoetermeer, Netherlands: Uitgeverij Boekencentrum

Klein, William W. et al. (2004). *Introduction To Biblical Interpretation*. Nashville, Tennessee: Thomas Nelson, Inc.

Klink III., Edward W. (2019). *Preaching and The Interpretation of Scripture A Call for Ecclesiastical Exegesis* in *Distinguishing The Church Explorations in Word, Sacrament, and Discipline*. Peters, Greg & Jenson, M. (ed.). Eugene, Oregon: Pickwick Publications

Knapp, George Christian (1850). *Lectures on Christian Theology*. (2nd ed.). New York: M. W. Dodd

Koester, Helmut (2000). *Introduction to the New Testament: History and Literature of Early Christianity*. Volume 2. Berlin: Walter de Gruyter & Co.

Konig, Andrea (2010). *Glaube and Denken Mission, Dialogue, and Peaceful Co-Existence*. Frankfurt, Germany: Peter Lang GmbH

Kostenberger, Andreas J. & Alexander, T. Desmond (2020). *Salvation to The Ends of the Earth A Biblical Theology of Mission*. New Studies in Biblical Theology (2nd ed.). London: Apollos

Kresge, Elijah Everett (1922). *The Church and the Ever-Coming Kingdom of God (A discussion on the evolution of a righteous social order with special reference to the mission of the church in the process)*. New York: The Macmillan Company

Kretzman, Paul E. (1921). *Popular Commentary of The Bible The New Testament Volume I. The Gospel According to Saint Matthew, Saint Mark, Saint Luke, Saint John, The Acts of The Apostles*. St. Louis, Missouri: Concordia Publishing House

Kung, Hans, et. al. (ed.) (1982). *Right to Dissent*. Edinburgh: T&T Clark

Kung, Hans (2007). *Islam Past, Present & Future*. Oxford: Oneworld Publication

Kupp, David D. (1996). *Matthew's Emmanuel Divine Presence and God's People in The First Gospel*. Society for New Testament Studies Monograph Series 90. Cambridge: Cambridge University Press

Kuttiyanikkal, Ciril J. (2014). *Khrist Bhakta Movement: A Model for An Indian Church? In Culturation in Area of Community Building*. Tilburg Theological Studies. Munster, Germany: LIT Verlag

Ladd, George Eldon (1974). *A Theology of The New Testament*. Grand Rapids, Michigan: William B. Eerdmans Publishing Company

Lake, Kirsopp (1920). *Landmarks in The History of Early Christianity*. London: MacMillan and Co., Ltd.

Lambert, John C. (1903). *The Sacraments in The New Testament*. Edinburgh: T&T Clark

Lampe, Geoffrey W. H. (2004). *The Seal of The Spirit A Study in The Doctrine of Baptism and Confirmation in The New Testament and The Fathers*. Eugene, Oregon: Wipf & Stock

Langford-James, R. LL. (1924). *The Doctrine of Intention*. New York and Toronto: The MacMillan Co., & London: Society for Promoting Christian Knowledge

Law, Sophie (1980). *The Epistle of James*. Black's New Testament Commentaries. London: Adam & Charles Black

Lawson, John (1961). *A Theological and Historical Introduction to The Apostolic Fathers*. Eugene, Oregon: Wipf & Stock

Leishman, Thomas (1871). *Thesis A Critical Account of The Various Theories on The Sacrament of Baptism*. Edinburgh: William Blackwood & Sons

Lemcio, Eugene E. (1991). *The Past of Jesus in The Gospels*. Society for New Testament Studies Monograph Series. New York: Cambridge University Press

Lester, Charles Stanley (1912). *The Historic Jesus A Study Of The Synoptic Gospels*. New York and London: The Knickerboxer Press, G.P. Putmam's Sons

Levering, Matthew (2010). *Christ and The Catholic Priesthood Ecclesial Hierarchy and The Pattern of The Trinity*. Chicago, Illinois: Hillenbrand and Books

Levering, Matthew (2012). *Jesus and The Demise of Death Resurrection, Afterlife and the Fate of the Christian*. Waco, Texas: Baylor University Press

Lloyd-Jones, D. Martyn (1994). *The Baptism and Gifts of The Spirit*. Grand Rapids, Michigan: Baker Book House

Loader, William (2007). *The New Testament With Imagination A Fresh Approach To Its Writings and Themes*. Grand Rapids, Michigan: William B. Eerdmans Publishing Company

Lockett, H. D. (1905). *Inaugural Lectures Delivered by Members of the Faculty During if First Session, 1904-05*. Publication of the University of Manchester Theological Series No.1. London & Manchester: Sheratt & Hughes Publishers

Loke, Andrew Ter Ern (2017). *The Origin of Divine Christology*. Society for New Testament Studies Monograph Series 169. New York: Cambridge University Press

Ludemann, Gerd (1995). *What Really Happened to Jesus A Historical Approach to The Resurrection*. Louisville, Kentucky: Westminster John Knox Press

Ludemann, Gerd (2005). *Acts of The Apostles What Really Happened*

In The Earliest Days of The Church. Amherst, New York: Prometheus Books

Ludlow, Morwenna (2009). *The Early Church: The I. B. Tauris History of The Christian Church*. London: I. B. Tauris & Co Ltd

MacArthur, John (1994). *The MacArthur New Testament Commentary Acts 1-12*. Chicago, Illinois: Moody Publishers

Macbridge, John David (1853). *Lectures on The Articles of The United Church of England and Ireland*. Oxford: John Henry Press & London: Strand

MacEwen, Robert K. (2015). *Matthean Posteriority An Exploration of Matthew's Use of Mark and Luke as a Solution to The Synoptic Problem*. London & New York: Bloomsbury T&T Clark

Marmion, Declan & Nieuivenhove (2011). *An Introduction to The Trinity*. New York: Cambridge University Press

Marsh, Herbert G. (1941). *The Origin and Significance of The New Testament Baptism*. Manchester: Manchester University Press

Marshall, I. Howard (2004). *New Testament Theology Many Witnesses, One Gospel*. Downers Grove, Illinois: InterVarsity Press

Martos, Joseph (2015). *Deconstructing Sacramental Theology and Reconstructing Catholic Ritual*. Eugene, Oregon: Resource Publication an imprint of Wipf & Stock

Matkin, Michael J. (2008). *The Complete Idiot's Guide to Discovering The Origins of The Christian Religion Early Christianity*. New York: Penguin Group

Mays, James L. (ed.) (1998). *Acts Interpretation A Biblical Commentary for Teaching and Preaching*, Atlanta: John Know Press

McCartney, Dan G. (2009). *James*. Baker Exegetical Commentary on the New Testament. Grand Rapids, Michigan: Baker Academic

McClymond, Michael J. (2018). *The Devil's Redemption A New History and Interpretation of Christian Universalism*. Grand Rapids,

Michigan: Baker Academics

McDonald, Lee Martin (2004). *Introduction to Acts* in *The Bible Knowledge Background Commentary Acts–Philemon*. Evans, Graig A. (ed.). Colorado Springs, Colorado: Victar

McDonnell & Montague, George T. (1994). *Christian Initiation and Baptism in The Holy Spirit Evidence from The First Eight Centuries.* Minnesota: Liturgical Press

McDonnell, Kilian (2003). *The Other Hand of God The Holy Spirit as the Universal Touch and Goal*. Collegeville, Minnesota: Liturgical Press

McDonnell, Kilian (1996). *The Baptism of Jesus in The Jordan: the Trinitarian and Cosmic Order of Salvation*. Collegeville, Minnesota: The Liturgical Press

McDowell, Bruce A. (2017). *Christian Baptism The Sign and Seal of God's Covenant Promise.* God's Word Publishing

McFayden, John. E (1909). *Interpreter's Commentary on the New Testament Volume 1, The Epistle To The Corinthians and Galatians.* A. S. Barnes & Company

McGiffert, Arthur C. (1902). *The Apostle's Creed Its Origin, Its Purpose, and Its Historical Interpretation.* Edinburgh: T&T Clark

McGiffert, Arthur. C. (1903). *A History of Christianity in the Apostolic Age* (Rev. Ed.). New York: Charles Scribner's

McGiffert, Arthur Cushman (1924). *The God of The Early Christians*. New York: Charles Scribner's Sons

McGrath, Alister E. (1997). *Studies in Doctrine.* Grand Rapids, Michigan: Zondervan Publishing House

McKnight, Scot (2018). *It Takes A Church to Baptize What The Bible Says About Infant Baptism.* Grand Rapids, Michigan: Brazos Press

McKnight, Scott (2011). *The Letter of James.* The New International Commentary on The New Testament. Grand Rapids, Michigan:

William B. Eerdmans Publishing Company

Meeks, Wayne A. (2002). *In Search of The Early Christians*. New Haven and London: Yale University Press

Meier, John P. (1980). *Matthew*. Collegeville, Minnesota: Liturgical Press

Mencken, H. L. (1946). *Treatise on The God's* (2nd ed.). Baltimore: The John Hopkins University Press

Meschler, SJ., M (1950). *The Life of Our Lord Jesus Christ in Meditations*. Volume 1. St. Louis, Missouri: B. Herder Book Company

Mettinger, Tryggve N. D. (2005). *In Search of God The Meaning and Message of The Everlasting Names*. Philadelphia: Fortress Press

Mildert, William Van (MDCCC.LVL). *The Works of The Rev. Daniel Waterland, D.D.* Oxford: At The University Press

Milburn, Gordon (1901). *A Study of Modern Anglicanism*. London: Swan Sonnenschen & Co

Milavec, Aaron (2003). *The Didache Faith, Hope, & Life of The Earliest Christian Communities, 50-70 C.E.* New Jersey: The Newman Press

Mitchell, Margaret A. (2021). *The Letter of James as a Document of Paulinism?* in *The Catholic Epistles Critical Readings Critical Readings in Biblical Studies* edited by Darian R. Lockett. London: T&T Clark

Moberly, R.W.L (2000). *The Bible, Theology, and Faith*. Cambridge: Cambridge University Press

Moeller, Wilhelm (1892). *History of The Christian Church A.D. 1-600* – translated from The German by Andrew Rutherfurd. London: Swan Sonnenschein & Co; New York: MacMillan & Co

Mongstad-Kvammen, Ingborg (2013). *Toward A Post-Colonial Reading of the Epistles of James, James 2:1-13 in its Roman Imperial*

Context. Leiden, The Netherlands: Brill

Montague, George T. (2011). *First Corinthians Catholic Commentary on Sacred Scripture*. Grand Rapids, Michigan: Baker Academics

Moody, Dale (1981). *The Word of Truth A Summary of Christian Doctrine Based on Biblical Revelation*. Grand Rapids, Michigan: William B. Eerdmans Publishing Company

Moorhead, John (2015). *The Popes and The Church of Rome in Late Antiquity*. New York: Routledge.

Moore, Charles E. (ed.) (2016). *Called to Community The Life Jesus Wants for His People*. Walden, New York: Plough Publishing House

Morgan, Teresa (2020). *Being "in Christ" in the Letters of Paul Save Through Christ*. Tubingen: Mohr Siebeck

Morris, Leon L. (1992). *The Gospel According to Matthew*. Michigan: Grand Rapids. Wm. B. Eerdmans Publishing Company

Mosheim, John L. V (1832). *Institutes of Ecclesiastical History; Ancient And Modern in Four Books, Much Corrected, Enlarged and Improved from the Primary Authorities. Vol. III*. Hew Haven

Mosheim, John L. V. (1852). *Historical Commentaries on The State of Christianity During The First Three Hundred and Twenty-Five Years From The Christian Era*. Volume II. New York: Converse

Moss, Claude B. (reprint) (1949). *The Christian Faith An Introduction To Dogmatic Theology*. Eugene, Oregon: Wipf & Stock

Moule, C. F. D. (3rd ed.) (2000). *The Holy Spirit*. London and New York: Continuum

Mulder, John M. (1991). *Sealed In Christ The Symbolism of The Seal of The Presbyterian Church (U.S.A.)*. Louisville, Kentucky: Geneva Press

Meyers, Ruth A. (1997). *Continuing The Reformation Re-Visioning Baptism in The Episcopal Church*. New York, New York: Church

Publishing, Inc.

Neal, J. M. (1869). *Catechetical Notes and Class Questions, Literal and Mystical, Chiefly on The Earlier Books of Holy Scripture.* London, Oxford and Cambridge: Rivingtons

Newman, Barry C. (2015). *The Gospel, Freedom, and The Sacraments Did The Reformers Go Far Enough?* Eugene, Oregon: Resource Publishers

Newman. Carey, C. et. al. (ed.) (1999). *The Jewish Roots of Christological Monotheism Papers from the St. Andrews Conference on the Historical Origins of the Worship of Jesus.* Leiden: Brill

Nolloth, Frederick Charles (1908). *The Person of Our Lord And Recent Thought.* London: MacMillan And Co., Limited

Nolloth, Charles Frederick (1917). *The Rise of The Christian Religion.* London: MacMillan and Co., Limited

Norgren, William A. & Rusch, William G. (ed.) (2001). *Toward Full Communion and Concordat of Agreement.* Lutheran-Episcopal Dialogues Series III. Eugene, Oregon: Wipf & Stock Publishers

Norris, Frederick (2002). *Christianity A Short Global History.* Oxford: One World Publications

Norris Jr., Richard A. (2006). *Confessional and Catechetical Formulas in First-and Early-second Century Christian Literature* in *One Lord, One Faith, One Baptism Studies in Christian Ecclesiality and Ecumenism in Honor of J. Robert Wright.* Grand Rapids, Michigan: William B. Eerdmans Publishing Company

O'Collins, Gerald (2008). *Catholicism A Very Short Introduction.* New York: Oxford University Press

O'Collins SJ, Gerald (2014). *The Tripersonal God Understanding and Interpreting The Trinity.* (2nd ed.). Mahwah, New Jersey: Paulist Press

O'Collins SJ, Gerald & Farrugia, Mario (2015). *Catholicism The Story of Catholic Christianity.* New York: Oxford University Press

O'Collins SJ, Gerald (2018). *The Church in The General Epistles* in *The Oxford Handbook of Ecclesiology*. Oxford: Oxford University Press

Old, Hughes Oliphant (2002). *Worship Reformed According to Scripture*. Revised and Expanded Edition. Louisville, Kentucky: Westminster John Knox Press

Olson, Roger E. & Hall, Christopher A. (2002). *The Trinity*. Michigan: William B. Eerdmans Publishing Company

O'Neil, H. C. (1914). *Stokes' Complete One Volume Encyclopaedia*. New York: Frederick A. Stokes Company

Oropeza, B. J. (2000). *Paul and Apostasy Eschatology, Perseverance and Falling Away in The Corinthian Congregation*. Eugene, Oregon: Wipf & Stock

Orr, James (General Editor) (1915). *The International Standard Bible Encyclopaedia*.Volume I - A–Clemency. Chicago: The Howard-Severance Company

Osborne, Grant (2010). *Matthew Exegetical Commentary on The New Testament*. Grand Rapids, Michigan: Zondervan

Osborne, Kenan B. (1987). *Christian Sacraments of Initiation Baptism, Confirmation, Eucharist*. Mahwah, New Jersey: Paulist Press

Osborne, Kenan B. (1997). *The Resurrection of Jesus New Considerations for Its Theological Interpretation*. Oregon: Eugene, Wipf & Stock

Otten, Bernard J. (1922). *A Manual of The History of Dogmas Volume I The Development of Dogmas During The Patristic Age 100-869*. (3rd edition). Missouri: B. Herder

Otten, Bernard J. (1918). *A Manual of The History of Dogmas*. Volume II The Development of Dogmas During The Middles Ages and After 869-1907. London & Missouri: B. Herder Book Co.

Paine, Levi L (1901). *The Ethnic Trinities And Their Relations To*

The Christian Trinity A Chapter in The Comparative History of Religion. Boston and New York: Houghton, Mihlin and Company and Cambridge: The Riverside Press

Paine, William Henry (1917). *The Pauline Idea of Faith in its Relation to Jewish and Hellenistic Religion*. Harvard Theological Studies. Cambridge: Harvard University Press & London: Humphrey Milford, Oxford University Press

Pallikunnil, Jamerson K (2018). *Mission and Liturgy Content and Convergence and Congruence with Special Reference to the Malankara Mar Thoma Syrian Church*. Bloomington, Indiana: AuthorHouse

Parsons, Michael C. (ed.) (2008). *Acts Commentaries on The New Testament*. Grand Rapids, Michigan: Baker Academics

Pathrapankal, J. (2003). *Mission of The Church in India Based on Acts 1:8* in *Bend Without Fear Hope and Possibilities for an Indian Church Essays in Honour of Professor Kurien Kunnumpuram SJ*. Jnana-Deepa: ISPCK, Indian Society for Promoting Christian Knowledge

Peoples, William (1904). *Roman Claims in The Light of History*. London: Paternoster Row, New York: E. S. Gorham

Peterson, David G. (2012). *Transformed by God New Covenant Life and Ministry*. Downers Grove, Illinois: InterVarsity Press

Peterson, David G. (2013). *Encountering God Together Biblical Patterns for Ministry and Worship*. Nottingham, England: Inter-Varsity Press

Peirce, James (1717). *A Vindication of The Dissenters In Answer to Dr. William Nichol's Defence of The Doctrine and Discipline of The Church of England in Three Parts*. London: John Clark

Pohle, Joseph (1917). *The Sacraments A Dogmatic Treatise*. Volume I. St. Louis & London: B Herder (2nd revised ed.)

Pokorny, Petr (2013). *From Gospel to The Gospels History,*

Theology and Impact of The Biblical Term 'Euangelion' Boston & Berlin: Walter de Gruyter

Pope, Hugh (ed.) (1934). *The Layman's New Testament.* London: Sheed & Ward

Purves, George T. (1908). *Christianity In The Apostolic Age.* New York: Charles Scribner Sons

Qualben, Lars P. (2009). *The Lutheran Church In Colonial America.* Eugene, Oregon: Wipf & Stock

Rackham, Richard Belward (1901). *The Acts of The Apostles An Exposition.* London: Methuen & Co

Ralph, Margaret Nutting (2006). *Breaking Open The Lectionary Cycle B Lectionary Readings in Their Biblical Context for RCIA, Faith Sharing Groups, and Lectors.* Mahwah, New Jersey: Paulist Press

Rampton, Martha (2021). *Trafficking with Demons Magic, and Gender from Late Antiquity to 1000.* New York: Cornell University Press

Rees, T. (1915). *The Holy Spirit In Thought And Experience.* New York: Charles Scribner's Sons

Reid, Alchin (ed.) (2016). *T&T Clark Companion to Liturgy.* London & New York: Bloomsbury T&T Clark

Renan, Ernest (2018). *Origins of Christianity.* Volume II. Germany: Verlag GmbH

Reventlow, Henning Graf (2010). *History of Biblical Interpretation From The Enlightenment To The Twentieth Century.* Volume 4. Atlanta, Georgia: The Society of Biblical Literature

Reyroux, Frederick (MDCCCXXXIV). *Christian Theology: Translated from The Latin of Benedict Pictet.* London: R. B. Seeley and W. Burnside

Rice, Howard L. & Huffstutler, James C. (2001). *Reformed Worship.*

Louisville, Kentucky: Geneva Press

Riddle, J. E. (M.DCCC.XXXIX). *A Manual of Christian Antiquities: or, An Account of The Constitution, Ministers, Worship, Discipline, and Customs of The Ancient Church Particularly During The Third, Fourth and Fifth Centuries to Which is Prefixed An Analysis of The Writings of The Ante-Nicene Fathers.* London: John W. Parker

Robinson, Robert (1792). *Ecclesiastical Researches.* Cambridge: Francis Hodson

Robson, John (1908). *The Resurrection Gospel A Study of Christ's Great Commission.* Edinburgh and London: Oliphant, Anderson & Ferrier

Rogers, Elizabeth Frances (1917). *Peter Lombard And The Sacramental System.* New York.

Rosa, Peter de (1988). *Vicars of Christ Darkside of The Papacy* _____.

Rosemann, Phillip W. (2004). *Peter Lombard Great Medieval Thinkers.* London & New York: Oxford University Press

Roswith I. H. Gerloff (2010). *A Plea for British Theologies, Volume 1. The Black Church Movement in Britain in Its Transatlantic Cultural and Theological Interaction with Special Reference to The Pentecostal Oneness (Apostolic) and Sabbatarian Movements.* Eugene, Oregon: Wipf & Stock

Sabatier, Auguste (1904). *The Religions of Authority And The Religion of The Spirit.* London: Williams & Norgate and New York: McClure, Phillips & Co.

Sandnes, Karl Olav (2011). *Seal and Baptism in Early Christianity* in *Ablution, Initiation, and Baptism Late Antiquity, Early Judaism and Early Christianity.* Hellholm, David (ed.). Berlin & Boston: Walter de Gruyter GmbH & Co. Kg

_____ (2016). *Saint Thomas Aquinas Collection [22 Books].* Aeterna Press

Sanders, Fred (2005). *The Image of The Immanent Trinity Rahner's Rule and the Theological Interpretation of Scripture Issues in Systematic Theology & 12*. New York: Peter Lang

Sandnes, Karl Olav (2011). *Seal and Baptism in Early Christianity in Ablution, Initiation, and Baptism, Late Antiquity, Early Judaism, and Early Christianity*. Berlin and New York: Walter de Gruyter

Sandt, Huub Van De & Flusser, David (2002). *The Didache Its Jewish Sources and Its Place in Early Judaism and Christianity*. Minneapolis, Fortress Press

Sanford, Charles B. (1984). *The Religious Life of Thomas Jefferson*. Charlottesville, University of Press Virginia

Scaer, David P. (1994). *James the Apostle of Faith*. Eugene, Oregon: Wipf & Stock

Schaberg, Jane (1982). *The Father, The Son And The Holy Spirit The Triadic Phrase in Matthew 28:19b*. SBL Dis. Series 61. CA: Published by Scholar Press

Schaff, Phillip (1854). *History of The Apostolic Church With A General Introduction To Church History*. New York: Charles Scribner

Schaff, Phillip (1910). *History of The Christian Church*. Volume II Ante-Nicene Christianity A.D. 100-325. New York: Charles Scribner's Sons

Schmauk, Theodore & Benze, C. Thedore (1911?). *The Confessional Principle And The Confessions of The Lutheran Church As Embodying The Evangelical Confession of The Christian Church*. Philadelphia: General Council Publication Board MCMXI

Schmaus, Michael (1975). *Dogma The Church as Sacrament*. Volume 5. Lanham, Maryland: Rowman & Littlefield Publishers Inc.

Schnackenburg, Rudolf (2002). *The Gospel of Matthew*. Michigan: William B. Eerdmans Publishing Company

Schnelle, Udo (2020). *The First One Hundred Years of Christianity*

An Introduction To Its History, Literature and Developments. Translated by James W. Thompson. Grand Rapids, Michigan: Baker Academic

Schreiner, Thomas R (2008). *New Testament Theology Magnifying God in Christ.* Grand Rapids, Michigan: Baker Academics

Schröter, Jens (2013). *Trinitarian Belief, Binitarian Monotheism, And The One God: Reflections on The Origin of Christian Faith in Affiliation To Larry Hurtado's Christological Approach* in *Reflections on The Early Christian History of Religion.* Breytenbach, Cillies & Frey, Jörg (ed.). Boston & Leiden: Brill

Schreiner, Thomas R. and Wright, Shawn (2000). *Believer's Baptism, Sign of the New Testament Covenant in Christ.* B&H Publishing

Schwarz, Hans (2017). *The Trinity The Central Mystery of Christianity.* Minneapolis: Fortress Press

Schweitzer, Albert (2005). *The Quest of The Historical Jesus.* Mineola, New York: Dover Publications, Inc.

Schweizer, Eduard (1975). *The Good News According to Matthew.* Translated by David E. Green. Atlanta, Georgia: John Know Press

Scirghl, Thomas J. (2000). *An Examination of The Problems of Inclusive Language in The Trinitarian Formula of Baptism.* Studies in Religion and Society Volume 42. New York: The Edwin Mellen Press

Scott, Thomas (1879). *The Church of England Catechism.* London: Thomas Scott

Scorgie, Glen G. et. al. (2011). *Dictionary of Christian Spirituality.* Grand Rapid, Michigan: Zondervan

Screech, M. A. (1994). *Clement Marot: a Renaissance poet discovers the gospel: Lutheranism, Fabrism and Calvanism in the Royal Courts of France and of Navarre and in the Ducal Court.* Leiden, The Netherlands: Brill

Selwyn. Edward Gordon (ed.) (1926). *Essays Catholic & Critical.* New York and Toronto: The MacMillan Co, London: Society for Promoting Christian Knowledge (2nd ed.)

Sell, Alan P. F. (2008). *Hinterland Theology A Stimulus to Theological Construction.* Studies in Christian History and Thought. Eugene, Oregon: Wipf & Stock

Senn, Frank C. (1999). *A Stewardship of The Mysteries.* Mahwah, New Jersey: Paulist Press

Shelley, Bruce L. (2008). *Church History in Plain Language.* (3rd ed.). Nashville, Tennessee: Thomas Nelson

Silvoso, Ed (2017). *Ekklesia Rediscovering God's Instrument for Global Transformation.* Bloomington, Minnesota: Chosen Books

Simpson, W. J. Sparrow (1915). *The Resurrection And Modern Thought.* London: Longman's, Green and Co.

Sinclair, Scott Gambrill (2008). *An Introduction to Christianity for a New Millennium.* Lanham, Maryland: Lexington Books

Slee, Michelle (2003). *The Church in Antioch in The First Century CE Communion and Conflict.* Journal for the Study of The New Testament Supplement Series 266. London: Sheffield Academic Press

Smallfield, George (ed.) (1822). *The Christian Reformer, or New Evangelical Miscellany. By The Editor of The Monthly Repository of Theology And General Literature.* January to December, Inclusive 1822. Vol. VIII. Hackney: Sherwood, Neely and Jones, Paternoster-Row

Smedley, Edward et al. (1845). *Encyclopaedia Metropolitana; or Universal Dictionary of Knowledge on an Original Plan: Comprising of Twofold Advantage of a Philosophical and An Alphabetical Arrangement, with Appropriate Engravings.* Volume XV. London: B. Fellowes, et al.

Smedley, Edward et al. (1845). *Encyclopaedia Metropolitana; or*

Universal Dictionary of Knowledge on an Original Plan: Comprising of Twofold Advantage of a Philosophical and An Alphabetical Arrangement, with Appropriate Engravings. Volume II. London: B. Fellowes, et al.

Smith, Henry B. & Schaff, Philip (1874). *Theological and Philosophical Library: A Series of Text-Books, Original and Translated for Colleges and Theological Seminaries*. New York: Scribner, Armstrong & Co.

Smith, William & Cheetham, Samuel (ed.) (1875). *A Dictionary of Christian Antiquities Being A Continuation of The Dictionary of The Bible* In Two Volumes—Vol. I. Boston: Little, Brown And Company

Smithson, John Henry (1864). [2nd ed] [No. 26] *On Baptism, and Its Divine Uses In Promoting The Salvation of Man* in Tracts, Theological, Practical, Controversial and Psychological, etc, Volume 5. London: Alven; Hodson & Manchester: Bottomley, Son and Tolley

Smyth, Egbert, et. al., (1889). *The Andover Review A Religious And Theological Monthly. Vol. XI.–January-June.–1889.* Boston: Houghton, Mifflin And Company; Cambridge: The Riverside Press

Sondy, Amanullah De, et. al. (2020). *Judaism, Christianity and Islam An Introduction to Monotheism*. London: Bloomsbury Publishing

Soyars, Jonathan E. (2019). *The Shepherd of Hermas and the Pauline Legacy*. Supplement to Novum Testamentum Volume 176. Leiden: Brill

Spinks, Bryan D. (2006). *Reformation and Modern Rituals and Theologies of Baptism from Luther & Contemporary Practices*. Liturgy Worship and Society. Aldershot: Ashgate Publishing Limited

Stanley, Arthur Penrhyn (1884). *Christian Institutions Essays on Ecclesiastical Subjects*. (4th ed.). London: John Murray

Stevens, George Barker (1905). *The Teachings of Jesus*. New York: The Macmillan Company

Stier, Rudolf (MDCCCLI). *The Words of The Lord Jesus* by Pope, William B. Volume Seventh. Philadelphia: Smith, English, And Co; New York: Sheldon & Co; Boston: Gould & Lincoln

Stokes, G. T. (1891). *The Expositor's Bible: The Acts of The Apostles*. Volume 1. New York: A. C. Armstrong and Son

Stone, Darwell (1905). *Holy Baptism* (4th ed.). London: Longmans, Green and Co.

Stookey, Laurence Hull (1982). *Baptism Christ's Act in The Church*. Nashville, Tennessee: Abington Press

Strange, James Riley (2010). *The Moral World of James Setting the Epistle in its Greco-Roman and Judaic Environments*. Studies in Biblical Literature 136

Strecker, Georg (2000). *Theology of The New Testament*. Louisville, Kentucky: John Know Press & New York & Berlin: Walter de Gruyter

Streett, R. Alan (2018). *Caesar and the Sacrament Baptism: A Rite of Resistance*. Eugene, Oregon: Cascade Books

Strazicich, John R. (2007). *Joel's Use of Scripture and the Scripture's Use of Joel Appropriation and Resignification in Second Temple Judaism and Early Christianity*. Leiden, The Netherlands: Brill

Strelan, Rick (1996). *Paul, Artemis, and the Jews in Ephesus* in ll Section Town: Paul in Ephesus, Berlin and New York: Walter de Gruyter

Stuhlmacher, Peter (2018). *Biblical Theology of The New Testament*. Grand Rapids, Michigan: William B. Eerdmans Publishing Company

Sullivan, William L. (1919). *From The Gospel To The Creeds Studies in the Early History of the Christian Church*. Boston, Massachusetts: The Beacon Press

Swete, Henry Barclay (1912). *The Holy Spirit in The Ancient Church A Study of Christian Teachings in the Ancient Fathers*. London:

Macmillan & Co

Symonds, Herbert (1916). *Catholicity*: in *The Constructive Quarterly A Journal of The Faith, Work And Thought of Christendom*. Volume IV March To December 1916. London: Oxford University Press & New York: George H. Doran Company

Tanquerey, Adolphe (1959). *A Manual of Dogmatic Theology*. New York: Desolee Company

Taylor, Adam (1818). *The History of The English General Baptists In Two Parts Part First: The English General Baptists of The Seventeeth Century*. T. Bore Row, Turnpike: London

Tabor, James D. (2006). *The Hidden History of Jesus, His Royal Family, and the Birth of Christianity The Jesus Dynasty with a New Epilogue*. New York: Simon & Schuster Paperbacks

_____. *The Encyclopaedia Britannica* (1910). (11th ed.). Volume III. Cambridge: At The University Press

Thomas, Owen C. & Wondra, Ellen K. (2002). *Introduction To Theology*. (3rd ed.). New York: Moorehouse Publishing

_____. *The Encyclopaedia Britannica* (1910). (11th ed.). Volume VI. Chatelet to Constantine. New York: The Encyclopaedia Britannica Company

_____ (1835). *The Penny Cyclopaedia of The Society for The Diffusion of Useful Knowledge* Volume III. Athanaric-Bassano. London: Charles Knight

_____. (1909). *Twenty-Seventh Annual Session of The Baptist Congress Held in The Madison Avenue Baptist Church New York City. November 9, 10, and 11*. Chicago and New York: The University Press of Chicago Press

Templin, J. Alton (2006). *Pre-Reformation Religious Dissent in The Netherlands, 1518-1530*. Lanham, Maryland: University Press of American, Inc.

Temple, S.T.L., Patrick Joseph (1922). *The Boyhood Consciousness of Christ A Critical Examination of Luke ii. 49*. New York: The Macmillan Company

Thayer, Thos B. (ed.) (1864). *Article VII. Formula of Baptism*. The Universalist Quarterly and General Review. New Series-Volume I. Boston: Tompkins & Co

Thianto, Yudha (2012). *The Formula of Baptism and the Equality of the Godhead Joseph Bingham (1668-1723) and the Trinitarian Controversy in Late-Stuart England* in *The New Evangelical Subordinationism? Perspectives on The Equality of God and Th Father and God the Son*. Eugene, Oregon: Pickwick Publications

Thiselton, Anthony C. (2000). *The First Epistle to The Corinthians. The New International Greek Testament Commentary*. Grand Rapids, Michigan: William B. Eerdmans Publishing Company

Thiselton, Anthony C. (2013). *The Holy Spirit – In Biblical Teaching, Through the Centuries, and Today*. Grand Rapids, Michigan: William B. Eerdmans Publishing Company

Thompson, David M. (2006). *Baptism, Church and Society in Modern Britain from The Evangelical Revival to Baptism, Eucharist and Ministry*. Studies in Christian History and Thought. Eugene, Oregon: Wipf & Stock

Thompson, James W. (2020). *Apostle of Persuasion Theology and Rhetoric in the Pauline Letters*. Grand Rapid, Michigan: Baker Academic

Thompson, John (1994). *Modern Trinitarian Prospective*. New York: Oxford University Press

Thompson, Nicholas (2005). *Eucharistic Sacrifice and Patristic Tradition in the Theology of Martin Baucer 1534-1546*. Leiden: Brill

Thomassen, Einar (2006). *The Spiritual Seed The Church of The Valentinians*. Nag Hammadi & Manichaean Studies. Leiden: Brill

Tixeront, J. (1923). *History of Dogmas*. Translated from the Fifth French Edition by H. L.B. Vol. II. From St. Athanasius to St.

Augustine (318-430) (2n ed.). Missouri: St. Louis & London: B. Herder Book Co.

Treier, Daniel J. & Sweeney, Douglas A. (2021). *Hearing and Doing The Word The Drama of Evangelical Hermeneutics in Honor of Kevin J. Vahoozer*. London& T&T Clark

Tuner, S.T.D., Paul (2008). *Catholic Initiation or Christian Initiation of Adults* in Deep Down Things Essays on Catholic Culture. Cirincione, Joseph A. (ed.) Lanham, Maryland: Lexington Books

Turley, Stephen Richard (2015). *The Ritualized Revelation of The Messianic Age Washings and Meals in Galatians and 1 Corinthians*. London: Bloomsbury Publishing PLC

Turner, John D. (2008). *The Place of the Gospel of Judas in Sethian Tradition* in *The Gospel of Judas in Context* Proceedings of the First International Conference on the Gospel of Judas, Paris, Sorbonne, October 27-28, 2006, edited by Madeleine Scopello. Leiden: Brill

Turner, Paul (2020). *The Sacraments Bulleting Inserts For The Liturgical Life of The Parish.* Chicago, Illinois: Liturgy Training Publications

Uyl, Anthony (ed.) (2017). *Ambrose: Selected Works and Letters by Saint Ambrose.* Originally edited by Phillip Schaff (1819-1893). Woodstock, Ontario, Canada: Devoted Publishing

Vanhoozer, Kevin J. (2005). *Dictionary for Theological Interpretation of The Bible.* Grand Rapids, Michigan: Baker Academics

Vaughan, Robert editor for The Wycliffe Society, *Tracts and Treatises of John De Wycliffe, D.D., with Selections and Translations from His Manuscript, and Latin Works*. London: Blackburn and Pardon, MDCCCXLV

Voorst, Robert E. Van (1989). *The Ascents of James History and Theology of a Jewish-Christian Community.* SBL Dissertation Series 112. Atlanta, Georgia: Scholar Press

Vorgrimler, Herbert (1992). Sacramental Theology. Collegeville, Minnesota: The Liturgical Press

Vos, Geerhardus (2016). *Reformed Dogmatics. Volume 5: Ecclesiology The Means of Grace, Eschatology.* Bellingham, WA: Lexham Press

Votaw, Clyde W. (1898). *The Primitive Era of Christianity As Recorded In The Acts of The Apostles 30-63 A.D. A Series in Inductive Studies in The English Bible.* Chicago, Illinois: The University Chicago Press

Wace, Henry & Buchheim, C. A. (1883). *First Principles of The Reformation of The Ninety-Five Theses and The Three Primary Works of Dr. Martin Luther Translated into English.* London: John Murray

Wall, W. (1889). *The History of Infant Baptism In Two Parts.* London: Griffith, Farran, Browne & Co., Ltd

Wallace, Ronald S. (1998). *The Ten Commandments A Study of Ethical Freedom.* Eugene, Oregon: Wipf & Stock

Walker, Williston (1921). *A History of The Christian Church.* New York: Charles Scribner's Sons

Walton, Steve, et al. (2011). *Reading Acts Today Essays in Honour of Loveday C. A. Alexander.* New York: T&T Clark International

Wainwright, Arthur C. (2001). *The Trinity in The New Testament.* Eugene, Oregon: Wipf & Stock

Wedderburn, Alexander J. M. (2005) (reprint). *A History of The First Christians.* New York & London: T&T Clark International A Continuum Imprint

Wells, George Albert (1971). *The Jesus of The Early Christians A Study in Christian Origins.* London: Pemberton Books

Wernle, Paul (1904). *The Beginnings of Christianity.* Volume II. The Development of The Church. London: Williams & Norgate, New York: G. P. Putnam's Sons

Whilhite, Shawn J. (2019). *The Didache A Commentary*. Apostolic Fathers Commentary Series 1. Eugene, Oregon: Cascade Books

White, James F. (1993). *A Brief History of Christian Worship*. Nashville, Tennessee: Abington Press

White, James F. (2000). *Introduction to Christian Worship*. (3rd ed.). Nashville, Tennessee: Abington

White, R. E. O. (1994). *Christian Ethics*. Macon, Georgia: Mercer University Press

White, Thomas et. al. (ed.) (2008). *Restoring Integrity in Baptist Churches*. Grand Rapids, Michigan: Kregel Publications

W. M. Weber (1920). *Manifestation of The Risen Jesus: In The Open Court A Monthly Magazine Volume XXXIV*. Chicago: The Open Court Publishing Company

Wielenga, Bastiaan (2016). *The Reformed Baptism Form A Commentary*. Jenison, Michigan: Reformed Free Publishing Association

Wickham, J. A. (1850). *A Synopsis of The Doctrine of Baptism, Regeneration, Conversion, &*. London: George Bell

Wijngaards, John (2012). *The Ordained Women Deacons of The Church's First Millennium*. Norwich: Canterbury Press

Williams, Rodman, J (1996). *Renewal Theology: Systematic Theology from a Charismatic Perspective (Three Volumes in one)*. Grand Rapids, Michigan: Zondervan Publishing House

Witherington III, Ben (2019). *Biblical Theology The Convergence of the Canon*. Cambridge: Cambridge University Press

Witherington III, Ben (2007). *Troubled Waters The Real New Testament Theology of Baptism*. Waco, Texas: Baylor University Press

Witherington III, Ben (2007). *Letters and Homilies for Jewish Christians A Socio-Rhetorical Commentary on Hebrews, James and*

Jude. Downers Grove, Illinois: InterVarsity Press

Wood, J. H. (1847). *A Condensed History of The General Baptists of The New Connexion Preceded by Historical Sketches of The Early Baptists*. London: Simpkin, Marshall and Co., Leciester: J. F. Winks

Wood, Susan K. (2009). *One Baptism Ecumenical Dimensions of The Doctrine of Baptism*. Collegeville, Minnesota: Liturgical Press

Wordsworth, C H R (1857). *The New Testament of Our Lord and Saviour Jesus Christ in The Original Greek with Notes. Part-II.–The Acts of The Apostles*. London: Rivingtons

Wright SJ, John H. (2013). *Divine Providence in The Bible Meeting the Living And True God*. Volume II New Testament. Mahwah, New Jersey: Paulist Press

Wright, Nigel G. (2005). *Free Church, Free State The Positive Baptist Vision*. Eugene, Oregon: Wipf & Stock

Wright, J. Robert (ed.) (2005). *Ancient Christian Commentary on Scripture Old Testament IX, Proverbs, Ecclesiastes, Songs of Solomon*. Downers Grove, Illinois: InterVarsity Press

Wright, N.T. (1992). *The New Testament And The People of God Christian Origins and The Question of God*. Minneapolis, MN: Fortress Press

Zaugg, Elme Harry (1917). *A Generic Study of the Spirit Phenomena in The New Testament*. Chicago, Illinois: The University of Chicago Libraries

Zetterholm, Magnus & Byrskog, Samuel (2012). *The Making of Christianity Conflicts, Contacts, and Construction: Essays in Honor of Bengt Holmberg*. Coniectanea Biblica New Testament Series 47. Winona Lake, Indiana: Eisenbrauns

Zimmer, Heinrich (1902). translated by Meyer A. *The Celtic Church in Britain and Ireland*. London: David Nutt

Articles and Journals

_____ (1892). *Art. X–Summaries of Foreign Review.* The Scottish Review. January and April, Volume XIX. London: Alexander Gardner

Alexander, Kimberly Ervin (2008). *Matters of Conscience, Matters of Unity, Matters of Orthodoxy: Trinity and Water Baptism in Early Pentecostal Theology and Practice.* Journal of Pentecostal Theology, Volume 17, Issue 1, Leiden: Brill

Anderson, K. C. (1915). *Christianity Old and New.* The Monist, Volume 25, Issue 4

Ascough, Richard S. (1994). *An Analysis of the Baptismal Ritual of the Didache.* Studia Liturgica 24

Astley, Jeff (2015). *Forming Disciples: Some Educational and Biblical Reflections.* Rural Theology, Volume 13, No. 1 (May)

B.C.R. (1917). *Theology.* The Living Church. Volume. LVIII (November 3). Milwaukee, Wisconsin

Bacon, Benjamin Wisner (1913). *Two Forgotten Creeds.* The Harvard Theological Review. Volume 6, No. 3 (July)

Bacon, Benjamin Wisner. (1929). *New and Old in Jesus's Relation to John.* Journal of Biblical Literature, Volume 48, No. 1/2, Primitive Christianity and Judaism: A Symposium

Baker, Josiah (2020). *'One Lord, One Faith, One Baptism'? Between Trinitarian Ecumenism and Oneness Pentecostals.* Journal of Pentecostal Theology 29. Leiden: Brill

Bampton, T. A. (1944). *The Sacramental Significance of Christian Baptism* Baptist Quarterly 11

Barnard, L. W. (1961). *The Epistle of Barnabas: A Paschal Homily?* Vigiliae Christianae, Volume 15, Issue 1 (March)

Bevenot SJ, Maurice (1978). *Cyprian's Platform in The Rebaptism Controversy.* The Heythrop Journal. Volume 19, Issue 2 (April)

Beveridge, J. (1901). *Recent Foreign Theology.* The Expository

Times, Volume 12, Issue 8 (January)

Blevins, William L. (1974). *The Early Church: Acts 1-5*. Review and Expositor, Volume 71, Issue 4 (December)

Block, Daniel I. (2011). *Bearing The Name of The Lord with Honor*. Bibliotheca Sacra 168 (January-March)

Bock, Darrell L. (2003). *Jewish Expressions in Mark 14. 61-62 And The Authenticity of The Jewish Examination of Jesus*. Journal for the Study of the Historical Jesus, Volume 1. Issue 2.

Bond, Albert R (1918). *Baptism Into Or Unto*. Review & Expositor 15.2

Bratcher, Robert G. (1957). *The Church of Scotland's Report on Baptism*. Review & Expositor 54

Bratcher, Robert G. (1963). "*'The Name' in Prepositional Phrases in the New Testament*," The Bible Translator 14

Brink, Gijsbert Van Den & Erp, Stephan Van (2009). *Ignoring God Triune? The Doctrine of the Trinity in Dutch Theology*. International Journal of Systematic Theology Volume 11 Number 1 January

Bruce, F. F (1940). "*The End of the First Gospel*" The Evangelical Quarterly 12

Bruce, F. F. (1964). *The Church of Jerusalem* Christian Brethren Research Fellowship Journal 4 (April)

Burrows, E. W. (1977). *Understanding of Baptism in Baptist Traditions with Special Reference to Modern Trends*. Indian Journal of Theology 26

Campbell, R. A (1996). *Jesus and His Baptism*. Tyndale Bulletin 47.2 (November)

Carl, Harold F (1999). "*Relational Language in John 14-16: Implications for the Doctrine of the Trinity*" Global Journal of Classic Theology Issue Volume 2., No. 1 (12/99)

Case, Shirley Jackson (1910). *The Missionary Idea in Early Christianity*. The Biblical World, Volume 36, No. 2 (August)

Chase, F. H. (1905). *The Lord's Command to Baptise (St. Matthew XXVIII 19)*. Journal of Theological Studies 6, No. 24

Chester, Andrew (2011). *High Christology – Whence, When and Why?* Early Christianity Volume 2, Issue 1

Christie, Francis A. (1909). *The Composition of Matthews Gospel*. The Biblical World, Volume 34, No. 6 (December). The University of Chicago Press

Coleman, Christopher B. (1908). *The Indiana Quarterly Magazine of History*. Volume IV. Indianapolis, Indiana: The Indiana Historical Society

Collins, Berkeley G. (1915). *The Sacrament of Baptism in The New Testament*. The Expository Times. Volume 27, Issue 3.

Conybeare, F. C. (1897). *Christian Demonology. IV*. Jewish Quarterly Review, Volume 9, Issue 4 (July)

Conybeare, F. C. (1901). The Eusebian form of the Text Matt. 28, 19. Zeitschrift für die Neutestamentliche Wissenschaft, Volume 2, Issue 1

Cooke, R. J. (1903). The Baptismal Formula of The Apostolic Age. The Methodist Review. (Bimonthly) Volume LXXXV.-Fifth Series, Volume XIX. Kelley, William V. (ed.). New York: Eaton & Mains & Cincinnati: Jennings & Pye.

Cremin, C. F. (1914). *How The Three Thousand Were Converted–II*. The Catholic University Bulletin. Volume XX, No. 6 (June)

Cross, Anthony R. (2008). The Evangelical Sacrament: *baptisma semper rejormandum*. The Evangelical Quarterly 80.3

Cross, Terry L. (1993). *Toward A Theology of The Word And The Spirit: A Review of J. Rodman William's Renewal Theology*. Journal of Pentecostal Theology, Volume 1, Issue 3

Dearman, Marion (1974). *A Study of Pentecostal Values*. Journal for The Scientific Study of Religion. Volume 13, No. 4. (December 1974)

De Long, Kindalee Pfremmer (2014). *"Look, Here is Water: Baptism in the Book of Acts"* Leaven: Vol. 22: Issue 4, Article 7

Dix O.S.B., Gregory (1948). *"The Seal" in the Second Century*. Theology, Volume 51, Issue 331

Douglas, Finkbeiner (1991). *An Examination of "Make Disciples of AU Nations" in Matthew 28:18-20*. Calvary Baptist Theological Journal 12

Draper, Jonathan A. (2006). *The Apostolic Fathers: The Didache*. The Expository Times, Volume 117, No. 5

Duffield, Ian K. (2017). *Difficult texts: Matthew 28:19-20*. Theology Vol. 120(2)

Dunn, G. D. (2004). *Heresy and Schism According to Cyprian of Carthage*. The Journal of Theological Studies, Volume 55, Issue 2

Elazar-DeMota, Yehonatan (2021). *A Comparative Analysis of Berith and the Sacrament of Baptism and How They Contributed to the Inquisition*. Religions 12: 346

Fanning, Don (2014). *"The Great Commission."* Eruditio Ardescens: Vol. 1: Iss. 2, Article 2, in The Journal of Liberty Baptist Theological Seminary

Felton, Gayle Carlton (reprint) (2006). *By Water and the Spirit Making Connections for Identity and Ministry*. This study guide includes the full text of By Water and the Spirit: A United Methodist *Understanding of Baptism*, adopted by the 1996 General Conference of The United Methodist Church. Nashville, Tennessee: Discipleship Resources

Finch, Geo Wm. (1895). *Baptism, Ancient and Modern* in *The Tablet A Weekly Newspaper and Review* – New Series, Vol. LIII (Vol. LXXXV). January to June. London: Tablet Office

Garrettson (1825). *The Methodist Magazine, Designed as a Compend of Useful Knowledge, and of Religious and Missionary Intelligence, for the Year of Our Lord 1825.* Volume VIII

Goodwin, K, Shane (2019). *The History of the Name of the Savior's Church.* BYU Studies Quarterly: Vol. 58, Issue 3, Article 2

Harrison, Wes (2001). *The Renewal of The Practice of Adult Baptism by Immersion During The Reformation Era, 1525-1700.* Restoration Quarterly Special Issue on Baptism. Volume 43, Number 2, Second Quarter

Hilton III, John & Johnson, Jana (2018). *The Word Baptize in The Book of Mormon* in *Interpreter* A Journal of Mormon Scripture. Volume 29. Orem, Utah: The Interpretation Foundation

Holladay, Carl R. (2012). *Baptism in the New Testament and Its Cultural Milieu: A Response to Everett Ferguson, Baptism in the Early Church.* Journal of Early Christian Studies, Volume 20, Number 3, Fall 2012

Hoff, Marvin D. (1964). *Baptism As A Means of Grace.* Reformed Review

Hogsten, James Doug (2008). *The Monadic Formula of Water Baptism: A Quest for Primitivism via a Christocentric and Restoration Impulse.* Journal of Pentecostal Theology 17

Howard, George (1988). *A Note on The Short Ending of Matthew.* The Harvard Theological Review, Volume 81, No. 1 (January)

Hultgren, Arland J. (1994). *Baptism in the New Testament: Origins, Formulas and Metaphors.* Word & World 14/1

Hurtado, Larry W. (1998). *The Origin of The Nomina Sacra: A Proposal.* Journal of Biblical Literature, Volume 117, No. 4 (Winter)

Imbelli, Robert P (1992). Book Review: *Christian Initiation and Baptism in the Holy Spirit: Evidence from the First Eight Centuries.* Theological Studies, Volume 53, Issue 2

_____ (1905). *Is the Doctrine of the Trinity a Part of*

Original Christianity. Index of Current Literature Vol. XXXIX July-December 1905. New York: The Current Publishing Company

Kaiser, Christopher B. (1991). *Biblical Theology and the Patristic Doctrine of the Trinity: In What Ways Can Their Relationship Be Established?* Reformed Review 45(2)

Kay, James F. (1993). *Critic's Corner In Whose Name? Feminism and the Trinitarian Baptismal Formula*. ThTo 49

Kreitzer, Larry (1991). *Baptism In The Pauline Epistles With Special Reference To The Corinthian Letters*. The Baptist Quarterly 34.2

Krentz, Edgar (1996). *Christianity's Boundary-Making Bath: The New Testament Meaning of Baptism, the Sacrament of Unity. Institute of Liturgical Studies Occasional Papers*. 73

Knowles, James (ed.) (1879?). *Baptism*. The Nineteenth Century A Monthly Review. Vol. VI. July – December 1879. London: C. Keegan Paul & Co.

Lake, Kirsopp (1924). *The Apostle's Creed*. Harvard Theological Review, Volume 17, Issue 2 (April)

Lampe, Geoffrey W. H. (1952). *The Holy Spirt and Baptism*. The Churchman 66.4

Lewis, W. G. (1865). *De Pressense on Baptism*. The Baptist Magazine for 1865. Volume LVII. (Series V.–Vol. IX.). London: Paternoster Row

Longenecker, Richard N. (1968). *Some Distinctive Early Christological Motifs*. New Testament Studies, Volume 14, Issue 4 (July)

Lupi, Joseph (2000). *God and the Trinity in the Fathers The First Two Centuries*. Melita Theologica, 51(2)

Machen, J. Gresham (1924). *The God of The Early Christians*. The Princeton Theological Review. Volume XXII. Princeton: Princeton University Press & London: Humphrey Milford, Oxford University Press

Macrae, S.J., George W. (1973). *"Whom Heaven "Must Receive Until The Time"* Reflections on the Christology of Acts. Interpretation 27, No. 2

Macy, Howard R. (2011). *"Baptism and Quakers"* Faculty Publications - College of Christian Studies. Paper 16

Mahoney SJ, John (1974). *The Church of The Holy Spirit in Aquinas.* The Heythrop Journal, Volume 15, Issue 1

Mason, T. W. (1947). *Entry into Membership of The Early Church.* The Journal of Theological Studies. Volume os-XLVIII, Issue 189-190 (January-April)

Meier, John P. (1977). *Two Disputed Questions.* Journal of Biblical Literature, Volume 96, No. 3 (September)

Miller, Leo F. (1925). *The Formula of Baptism in the Early Church.* The Catholic Historical Review, Volume 10, No. 4 (January).

Moehlman, Conrad Henry (1933). *The Origin of The Apostles' Creed.* The Journal of Religion, Volume 13, No. 3 (July)

Monera, Arnold (2016). *"Baptism as Christian Initiation in the New Testament." Orientis Aura: Macau Perspectives in Religious Studies.* No. 1 (2 December)

Moule, C. F. D. (1976). *The New Testament and the Doctrine of the Trinity: a short report on an old theme.* The Expository Times, Volume 88, Issue 1

Morden, Peter J. (2010). *C. H. Spurgeon and Baptism The Importance of Baptism.* Baptist Quarterly, 43:7.

Mueller, Wayne (1975). *The Development of the Baptismal Rite in the Christian Church.* [PT 464 – Liturgical and Musical Studies Through the Church Year 1975 WLS Summer Sessions]

Müller, M. (1999). *The Theological Interpretation of the Figure of Jesus in the Gospel of Matthew.* New Testament Studies, Volume 45, Issue 2

Neatby, Rev. G. W. (1932). *The Meaning of Baptism And Its Relation To Infant*. The Churchman, The Evangelical Quarterly, Vol 046/1

O'Dea, Paul (1950). *Early Christian Baptism and the Creed by Joseph H. Crehan* Review by: Paul O'Dea. The Irish Monthly, Vol. 78, No. 924 (Jun. 1950)

Osborne, Grant (1976). *Redaction Criticism And The Great Commission: A Case Study Toward A Biblical Understanding Of Inerrancy*. Journal of the Evangelical Theological Society 19:2 (Spring)

Paroschi, Wilson (2009). *Acts 19:1-7 Reconsidered In Light of Paul's Theology of Baptism*. Andrews University Seminary Studies, Volume 47

Parsons, Martin (1958). *The Theology of Baptism*. The Churchman 72.2

Peerbolte, L.J. Lietaert (2003). *Paul the Missionary, Contributions to Biblical Exegesis & Theology 34*. Peeters Publishing

Prescott, W. W. (1914). *Why We Are Protestants*. The Protestant Magazine Volume VI, No. 2 (February)

Ramshaw, Gail (2002). *In The Name Towards Alternative Baptismal Idioms*. The Ecumenical Review, Volume 54, Issue 3

Rashdall, Hastings. (1907). *The Motive of Modern Missionary Work*. The American Journal of Theology edited by The Divinity Faculty of The University of Chicago. Volume XI. Chicago, Illinois: The University of Chicago Press

Regev, Eyal (2004). *Moral Impurity and the Temple in Early Christianity in Light of Ancient Greek Practice and Qumranic Ideology*. The Harvard Theological Review, Vol. 97, No. 4 (Oct., 2004)

_____ (1836). *Religious Intelligence - Jamaica*. The Baptist Missionary Magazine of Nova Scotia and New Brunswick Published under the Direction of The Missionary Boards of The

Province. Vol. III. Halifax, Novia Scotia: The Nova Scotia Office

Richardson, Canon R. D. (1943). *The Doctrine of the Trinity: Its Development, Difficulties and Value*. Harvard Theological Review, Volume 36, Issue 02

Roberts, Nancy (2011). *Trinity v. Monotheism A False Dichotomy*. The Muslim World, Volume 101

Robinson, J. A. T. (1953). *The One Baptism As A Category of New Testament Soteriology*. The Scottish Journal of Theology, Volume Six. Liechtenstein, Nendeln: Kraus

Schmidt, Nathaniel (1911). *The New Jesus Myth And Its Ethical Value*. The International Journal of Ethics, Volume 22, Number 1

Schwöbel, Christoph (2009). *The Trinity between Athens and Jerusalem*. Journal of Reformed Theology 3. Leiden: Brill

Shelton, James B. (2021). "The Name of Jesus in Luke-Acts with Special Reference to the Gentile Missions," Spiritus. Oral Roberts University Journal of Theology, Volume 6, No. 1, Article 6

Sibley, Thomas (2015). *"In Jesus' Name" Is More Than a Closing Phrase of a Christian's Prayer*. Evangelical Journal of Theology, Vol. IX No. 1

Sim, David C. (2014). *Is Matthew 28:16-20 The Summary of The Gospel*. HTS Theological Studies, 70 (1)

Smith, D. Moody (1974). *Glossolalia and Other Spiritual Gifts in a New Testament Perspective*. Interpretation A Journal of Bible and Theology, Volume 28, Issue 3

Stampfer, Shaul (2013). *Did The Khazars Convert to Judaism?* Jewish Theological Studies, Volume 19, No. 3 (Spring/Summer)

Stewart, Alistair C. (2011). *The Christological Form of the Earliest Syntaxis: The Evidence of Pliny*. Studia Liturgica 41

Smyth, Newman, et. al. (1883). *The Revision of Creeds I*. The North American Review (January). Volume 136, No. 314, published by the

University of Northern Iowa

Tanner, John S. (2001). *Of Men and Mantles: Kierkegaard on the Difference between a Genius and an Apostle.* BYU Studies Quarterly: Vol. 40, Issue 2, Article 7

_____. (1917). *The American Journal of Theology* edited by The Divinity Faculty of the University of Chicago and Colleagues in Allied Department, The University of Chicago Press, Chicago, Illinois, Volume XXI

_____. (1847). The Church of England Quarterly Review. Volume XX. London: William Edward Painter, Strand

_____. (1865). *The General Baptist Magazine for 1865.* London: Marlborough & Co & Leicester: Winks & Son

_____. (1857). *The Intellectual Repository and New Jerusalem Magazine.* Vol. IV – Enlarged Series. London: The General Conference of The New Church

_____. (1829). *The London Encyclopaedia or Universal Dictionary et al in Twenty-Two Volumes.* Volume III. London: Thomas Tegg

_____. (1856). *The Primitive Church Magazine, Advocating The Constitution, Faith, and Practice of The Apostolic Churches "One Lord One Faith One Baptism" Ephesians IV.* Volume XIII.- New Series. London: Paternoster Row

_____. (1890). *The Doctrine of The Trinity Attacked. Education.* The Saints Herald. Volume 37–Whole No. 867. Lamoni, Iowa

_____. (1872). *The Scottish Guardian January to June 1872.* Edinburgh: R Grant and Son & London, Oxford and Cambridge: Rivingtons

_____. (1892). *The Scottish Review January and April (1892)* Vol. XIX. In: Theologisch Tijdschrift. London: Alexander Gardner

Thistlethwaite, Susan Brooks (1991). *On the Trinity*. Interpretation A Journal on Bible and Theology 45

Tilborg, Sjef Van (2001). *Acts 17:27—"that they might feel after him and find..."* HTS Theological Studies, Volume 57, Issue 1/2

Torrey, Charles Cutler (1916). *The Composition and Date of Acts*. Harvard Theological Studies I. Cambridge: Harvard University Press

Viviano, Benedict Thomas (2010). *God in The Gospel According to Matthew*. Interpretation A Journal of Bible and Theology (October)

Vorster, Hans (1999). *We Confess One Baptism for the Forgiveness of Sins New Impulses for the Ecumenical Discussion of Baptism*. The Ecumenical Review, Volume 51, Issue 3, The Quarterly of the World Council of Churches

Wainwright, Geoffrey (1974). *The Rites and Ceremonies of Christian initiation: Developments in the Past*. Studia Liturgica Vol. 10

Wallace, Daniel B. (2003). *Greek Grammar and the Personality of the Holy Spirit*. Bulletin for Biblical Research 13.1

Watson, Jonathan D. (2018). *The Ongoing 'Use' of Baptism: A Hole in the Baptist (Systematic) Baptistery?* Southwestern Journal of Theology, Volume 61, Number 1 (Fall)

Welch, John W. (1996). *From Presence to Practice: Jesus, the Sacrament Prayers, the Priesthood, and Church Discipline in 3 Nephi 18 and Moroni 2-6*. Journal of Book of Mormon Studies: Vol. 5: No. 1, Article 4

Wenham, D (1973). *The Resurrection Narratives In Matthew's Gospel*. Tyndale Bulletin 24

Wheeler, Edward J. (editor) (1905). *Is the Doctrine of the Trinity a Part of Original Christianity?* Index of Current Literature Vol. XXXIX July-December. New York: The Current Literature Publishing Company

Whitaker, E. C. (1965). *The History of The Baptismal Formula*. The

Journal of Ecclesiastical History. Volume 16, Issue 1

White, Thomas (2006). *What Makes Baptism Valid?* The Center for Theological Research (July). White Paper 7. Southwestern Baptist Theological Seminary, Fort Worth, Texas

Wien, Devon (1985). *The Biblical Significance of Baptism by Immersion.* Direction, Vol. 14, No. 1 (Spring)

Wightman, J. Clover (1874). *Papal Infallibility.* The Baptist Quarterly Volume VIII. Philadelphia: American Baptist Publication Society

Wilburn, Ralph G. (1965). *The One Baptism and The Many Baptisms.* Theology Today, Volume 22, Issue 1 (April)

Wilks, John G. F. (1995). *The Trinitarian Ontology of John Zizioulas.* Vox Evangelica 25

Wood, Irving F. (1905). *New Light on Some Familiar New Testament Problems* in *The American Journal of Theology* edited by The Divinity Faculty of the University of Chicago, Volume IX. Chicago, Illinois: The Chicago Press

Zeitlin, Solomon (1924). *The Halaka in The Gospels and Its Relation to The Jewish Law at The Time of Jesus.* Hebrew Union College Annual, Vol. 1

Ziesler, J. A. (1979). *The Name of Jesus in the Acts of the Apostles. Journal for the Study of the New Testament.* Volume 2, Issue 4

ABOUT THE AUTHOR

Kulwant Singh Boora is an American-British Indian who was born in Birmingham, England, United Kingdom, and grew up in a Sikh family of Indian Punjabi descent. He holds a Bachelor of Arts with Honor (B.A. Hons) from Staffordshire University, and studied law at Sutton Coldfield College, Sutton Coldfield, England in association with the Institute of Legal Executives College of Law where he completed his Professional Diploma in Law and High Professional Diploma in Law. He went onto complete his Graduate Diploma in Law/CPE (Law Society of England and Wales Common Professional Examinations) with Hertfordshire University School of Law, England.

He also graduated with his LL.M (Master of Laws degree) from an American ABA law school, Western Michigan University Thomas M. Cooley Law School. and graduated with his second LL.M (Master of Laws) from Staffordshire University School of Law, England. He studied Theology and Biblical Interpretation graduating with a Diploma in Theology (Biblical Interpretation) with Single Honors from the University of Wales and undertook study with the Oxford University Department of Continuing Education, Oxford, England.

Mr. Boora is also an Attorney and Counselor-at-Law, a member of the State Bar of Michigan, and the founder of The Boora Law Group P.L.C., a Michigan law firm where he engages in the practice of law as a trial lawyer. He is admitted to practice in Michigan State Courts, Michigan Court of Appeals, and Michigan Supreme Court. He is admitted to practice before various United States federal courts, United States Court of Appeals for the Sixth Circuit, United States Tax Court, United States Court of Appeals for the Federal Circuit, and United States Court of International Trade and Federal District trial courts. Attorney Boora is also admitted to practice before a Native American Indian Tribal Court in the State of Michigan, namely the Nattawaseppi Band of the Potawatomi Tribal Court.

Attorney Boora served as a Federal Judicial Intern to a United States District Court Federal Judge in the Northern District of Ohio. He is also admitted to practice law as a Fellow and Chartered Legal Executive lawyer in the United Kingdom. Mr. Boora was awarded the peer selected nomination by Thomson Reuters, Super Lawyers as a Rising Star for 2019, 2020, 2021 and 2022 and is a featured lawyer and attorney in Who's Who in America. He continues to pursue his research interests in the field of biblical, theological, and historical studies regarding baptism in the name of Jesus. His research on baptism in the name of Jesus and the oneness of God is also housed in Yale University.